10-
KB

Yakitate!! Japan

TAKASHI HASHIGUCHI

10

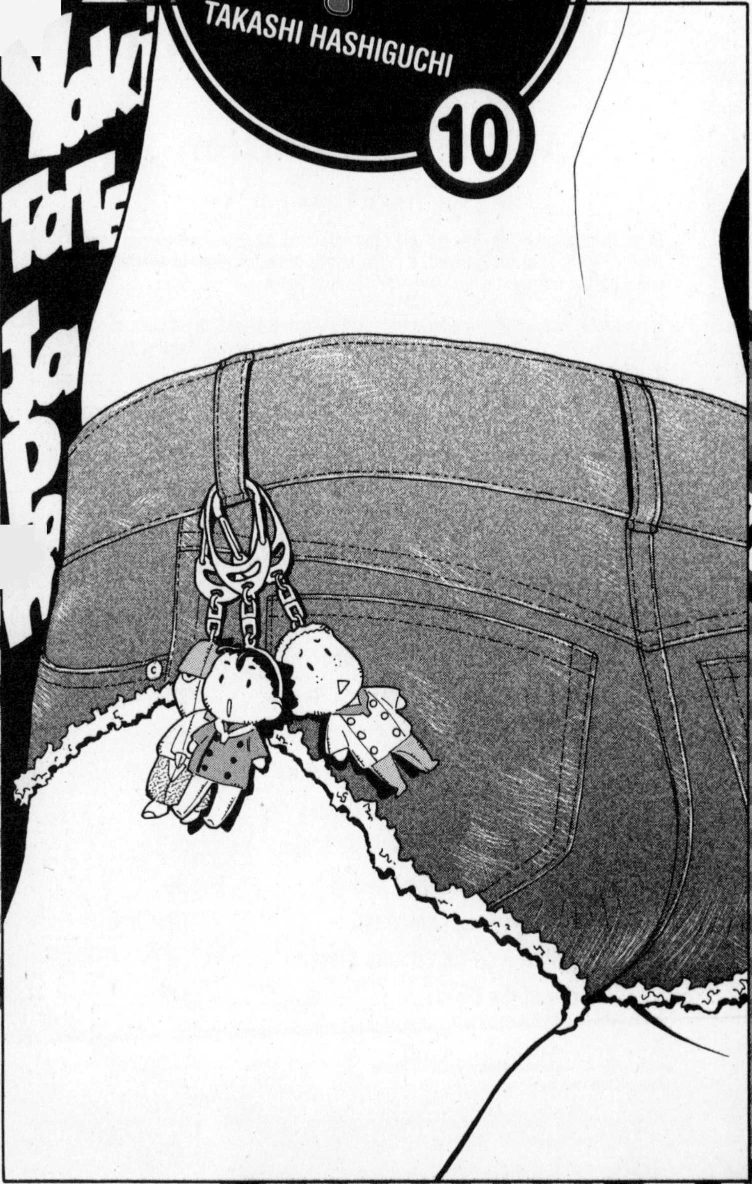

YAKITATE!! JAPAN
10
VIZ Media Edition

★The Story Thus Far★

In the first round of the Monaco Cup final selection, Azuma and his team barely scrape by the first assignment, a super speed bake-off, and successfully become part of the eight teams that will advance further.

However, a sinister plot rears its ugly head when Kirisaki, the owner of rival bakery St. Pierre, puts pressure on the tournament steering committee in an effort to crush the Japanese team.

The guidelines for the second round are quickly altered and the venue for the competition is switched to a deserted island. There, Team Pantasia must forage for ingredients to make a sweet confectionery bread while at the same time surviving on the treacherous tropical island.

A host of traps await them on the island with Azuma and his friends literally putting their lives on the line from the word "go." Despite these hardships, they still manage to make paste from potatoes and sap from palm trees to complete a taiyaki bread, but…

CONTENTS

Research Assistance/Bakery Consultant:
Koichi Uchimura.

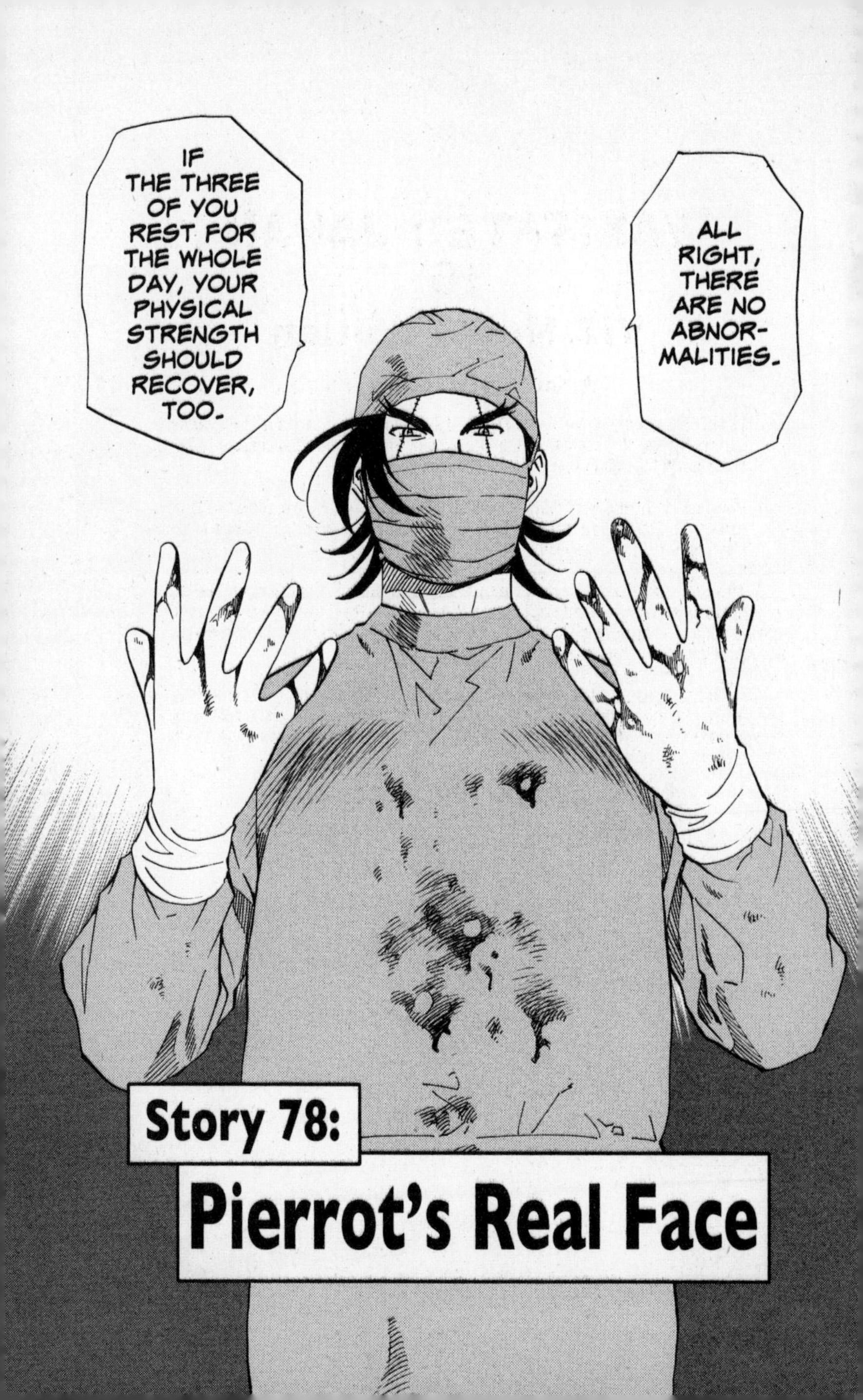
ALL RIGHT, THERE ARE NO ABNOR-MALITIES.
IF THE THREE OF YOU REST FOR THE WHOLE DAY, YOUR PHYSICAL STRENGTH SHOULD RECOVER, TOO.

Story 78: Pierrot's Real Face

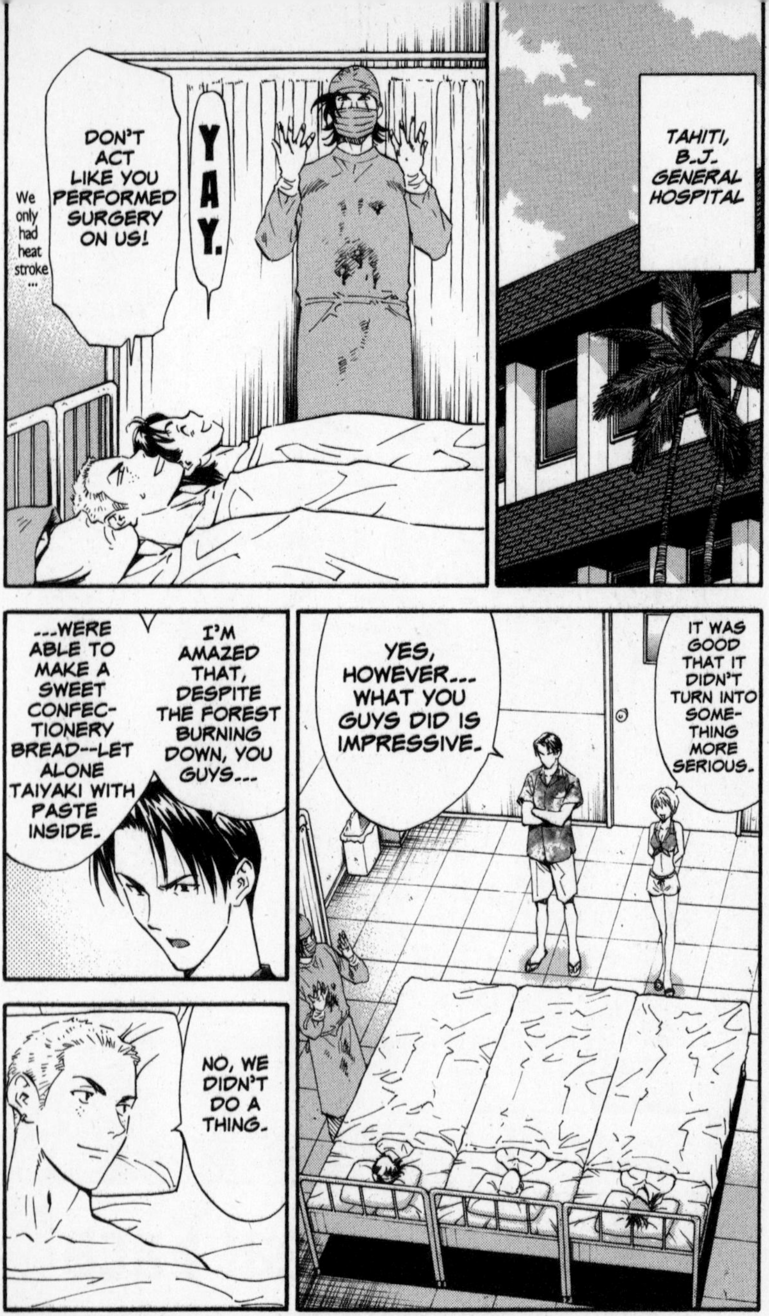
TAHITI, B.J. GENERAL HOSPITAL
YAY.
DON'T ACT LIKE YOU PERFORMED SURGERY ON US!
We only had heat stroke...
IT WAS GOOD THAT IT DIDN'T TURN INTO SOME-THING MORE SERIOUS.
YES, HOWEVER... WHAT YOU GUYS DID IS IMPRESSIVE.
I'M AMAZED THAT, DESPITE THE FOREST BURNING DOWN, YOU GUYS...
...WERE ABLE TO MAKE A SWEET CONFEC-TIONERY BREAD--LET ALONE TAIYAKI WITH PASTE INSIDE.
NO, WE DIDN'T DO A THING.

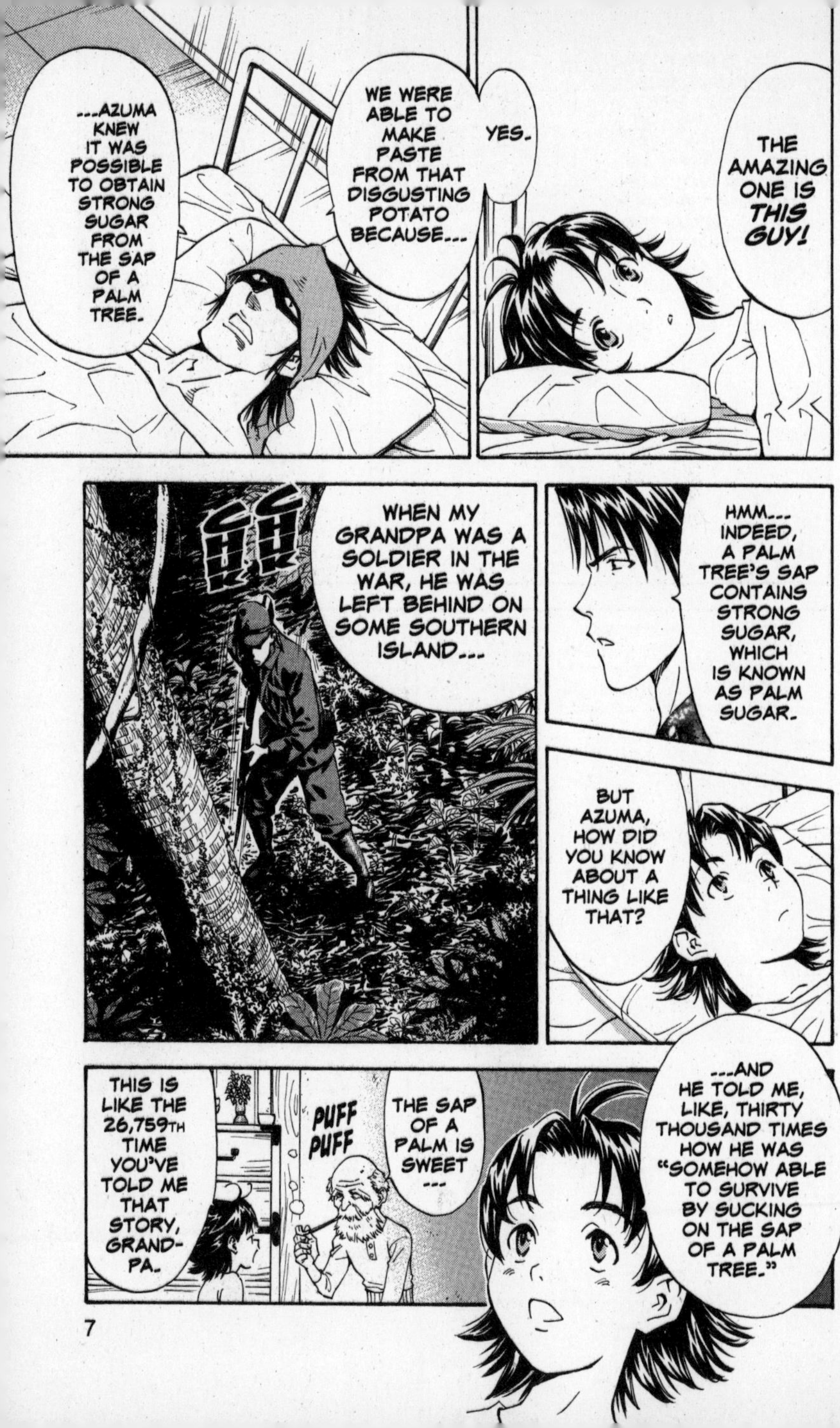
THE AMAZING ONE IS THIS GUY!
YES.
WE WERE ABLE TO MAKE PASTE FROM THAT DISGUSTING POTATO BECAUSE...
...AZUMA KNEW IT WAS POSSIBLE TO OBTAIN STRONG SUGAR FROM THE SAP OF A PALM TREE.
HMM... INDEED, A PALM TREE'S SAP CONTAINS STRONG SUGAR, WHICH IS KNOWN AS PALM SUGAR.
BUT AZUMA, HOW DID YOU KNOW ABOUT A THING LIKE THAT?
WHEN MY GRANDPA WAS A SOLDIER IN THE WAR, HE WAS LEFT BEHIND ON SOME SOUTHERN ISLAND...
CHK CHK
...AND HE TOLD ME, LIKE, THIRTY THOUSAND TIMES HOW HE WAS "SOMEHOW ABLE TO SURVIVE BY SUCKING ON THE SAP OF A PALM TREE."
PUFF PUFF
THE SAP OF A PALM IS SWEET...
THIS IS LIKE THE 26,759TH TIME YOU'VE TOLD ME THAT STORY, GRAND-PA.

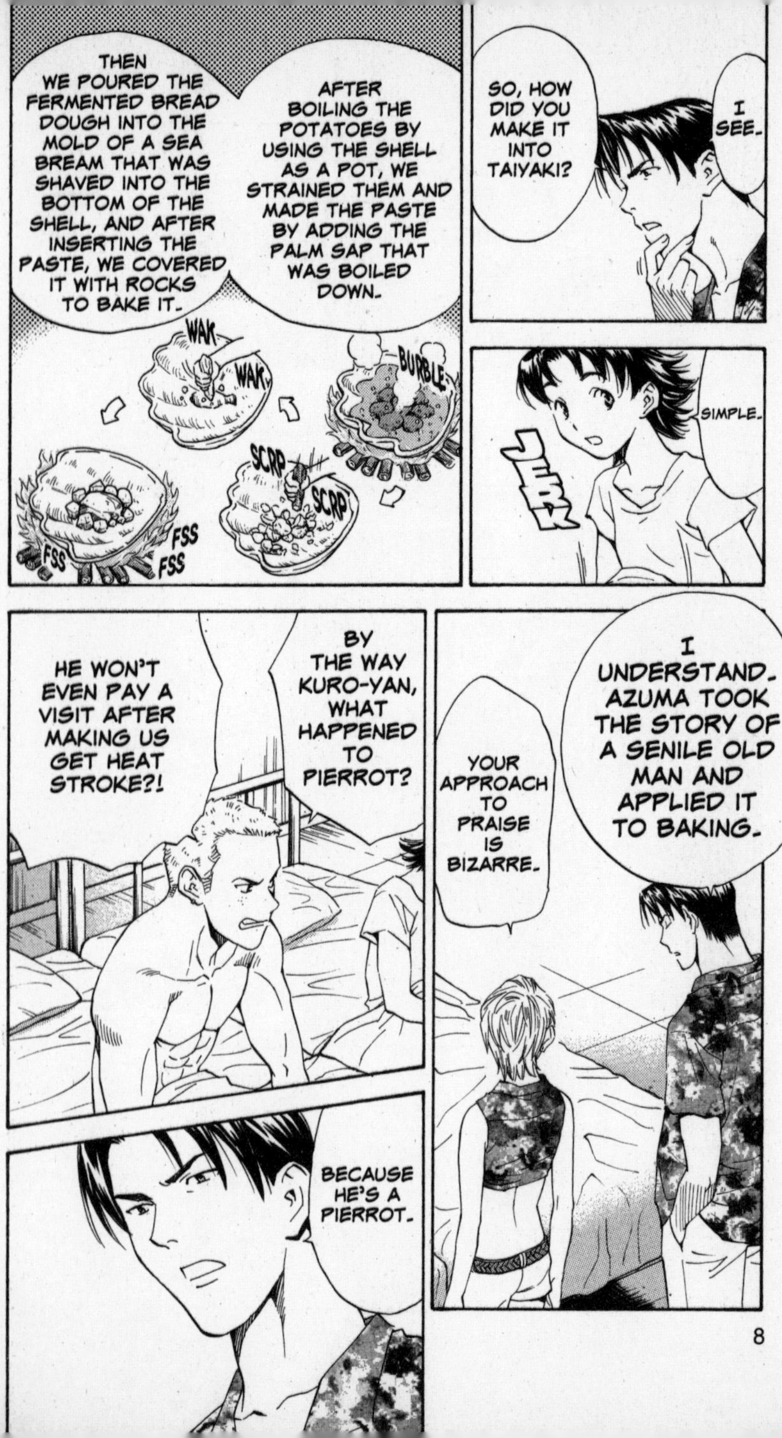
I SEE.
SO, HOW DID YOU MAKE IT INTO TAIYAKI?
SIMPLE.
JERK
AFTER BOILING THE POTATOES BY USING THE SHELL AS A POT, WE STRAINED THEM AND MADE THE PASTE BY ADDING THE PALM SAP THAT WAS BOILED DOWN.
THEN WE POURED THE FERMENTED BREAD DOUGH INTO THE MOLD OF A SEA BREAM THAT WAS SHAVED INTO THE BOTTOM OF THE SHELL, AND AFTER INSERTING THE PASTE, WE COVERED IT WITH ROCKS TO BAKE IT.
BURBLE
WAK
WAK
SCRP
SCRP
FSS
FSS
FSS
I UNDERSTAND. AZUMA TOOK THE STORY OF A SENILE OLD MAN AND APPLIED IT TO BAKING.
YOUR APPROACH TO PRAISE IS BIZARRE.
BY THE WAY KURO-YAN, WHAT HAPPENED TO PIERROT?
HE WON'T EVEN PAY A VISIT AFTER MAKING US GET HEAT STROKE?!
BECAUSE HE'S A PIERROT.

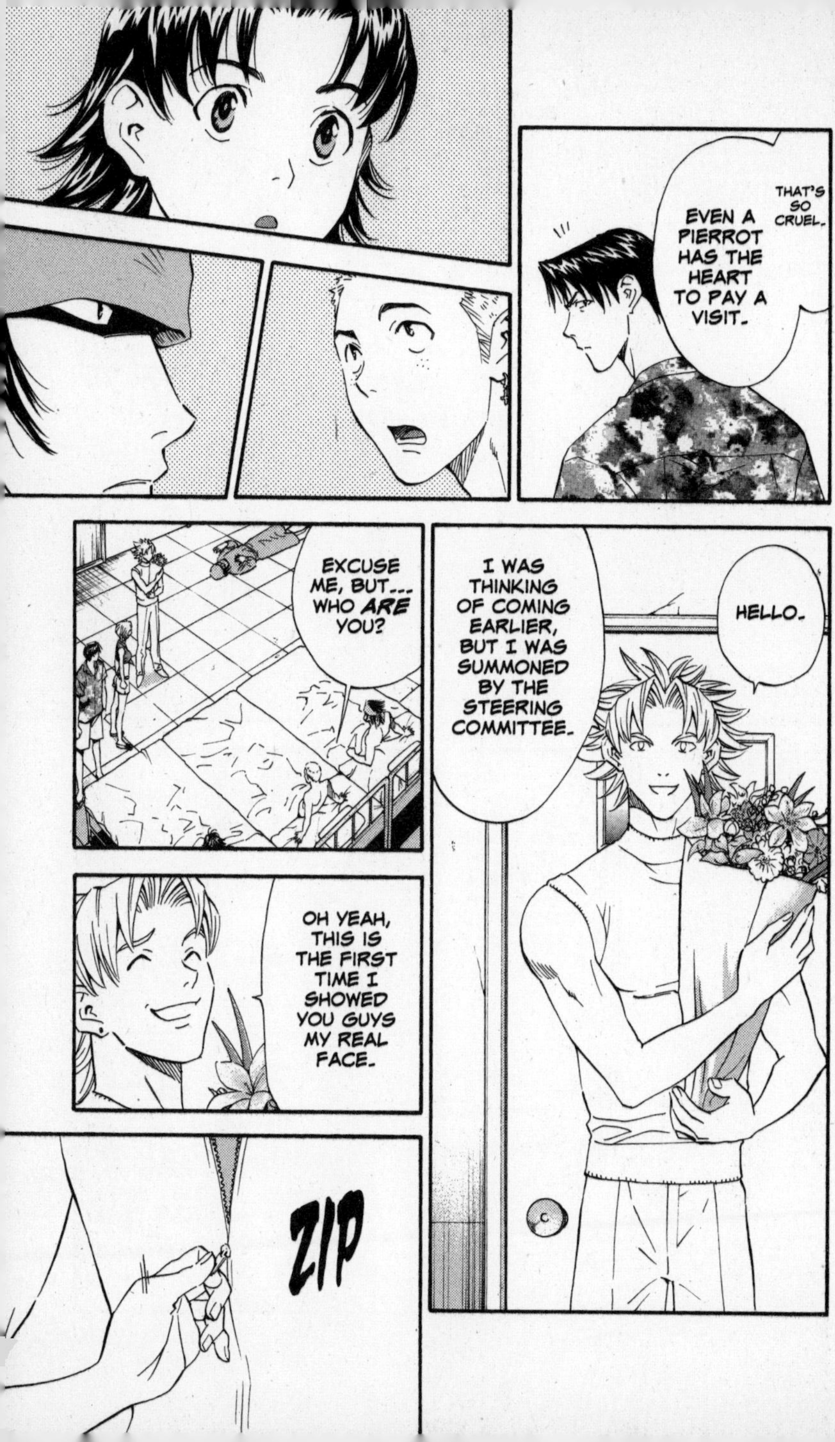
THAT'S SO CRUEL.
EVEN A PIERROT HAS THE HEART TO PAY A VISIT.
HELLO.
I WAS THINKING OF COMING EARLIER, BUT I WAS SUMMONED BY THE STEERING COMMITTEE.
EXCUSE ME, BUT... WHO *ARE* YOU?
OH YEAH, THIS IS THE FIRST TIME I SHOWED YOU GUYS MY REAL FACE.
ZIP

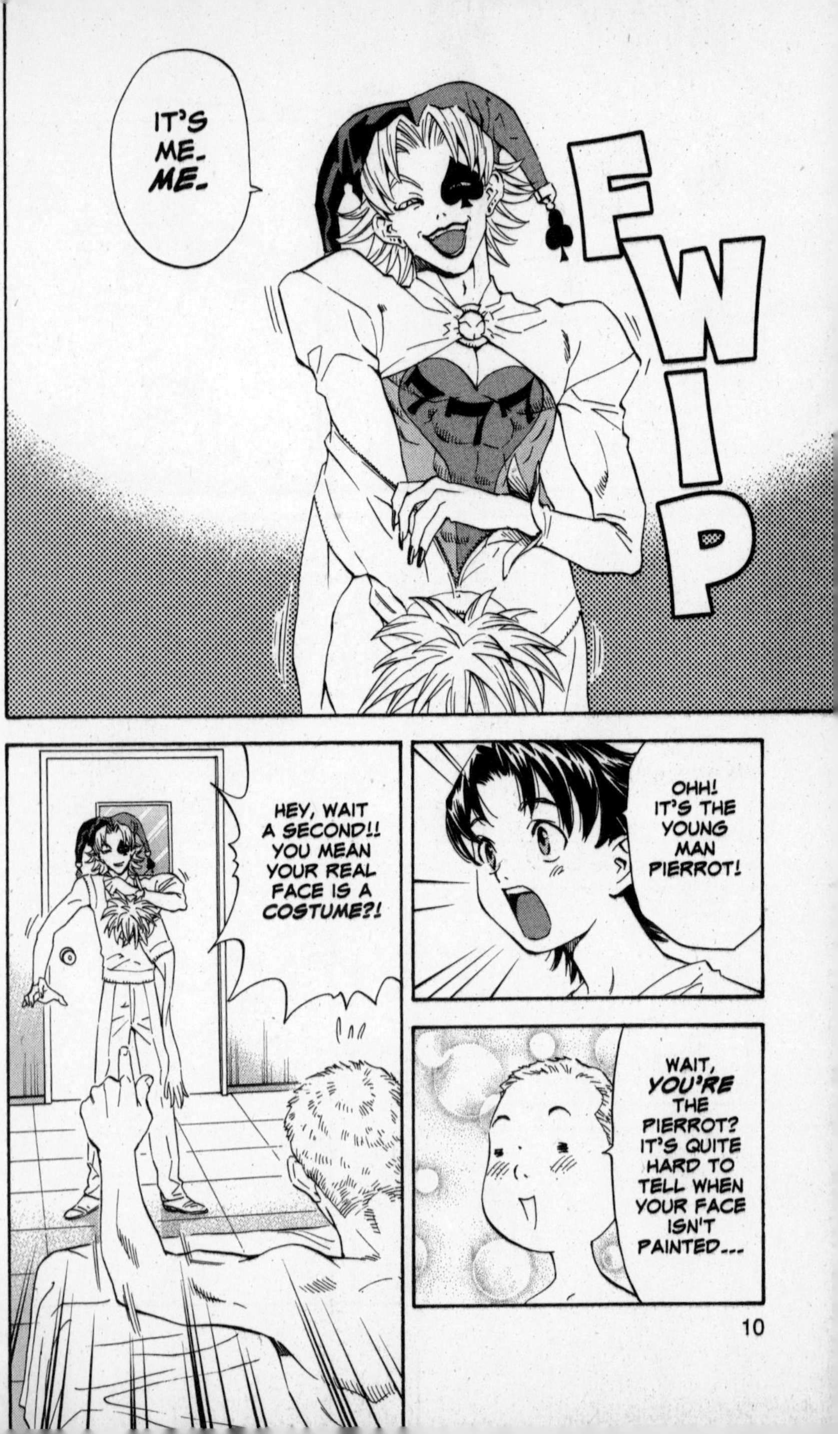
IT'S ME_ ME_
FWIP
OHH! IT'S THE YOUNG MAN PIERROT!
WAIT, YOU'RE THE PIERROT? IT'S QUITE HARD TO TELL WHEN YOUR FACE ISN'T PAINTED...
HEY, WAIT A SECOND!! YOU MEAN YOUR REAL FACE IS A COSTUME?!

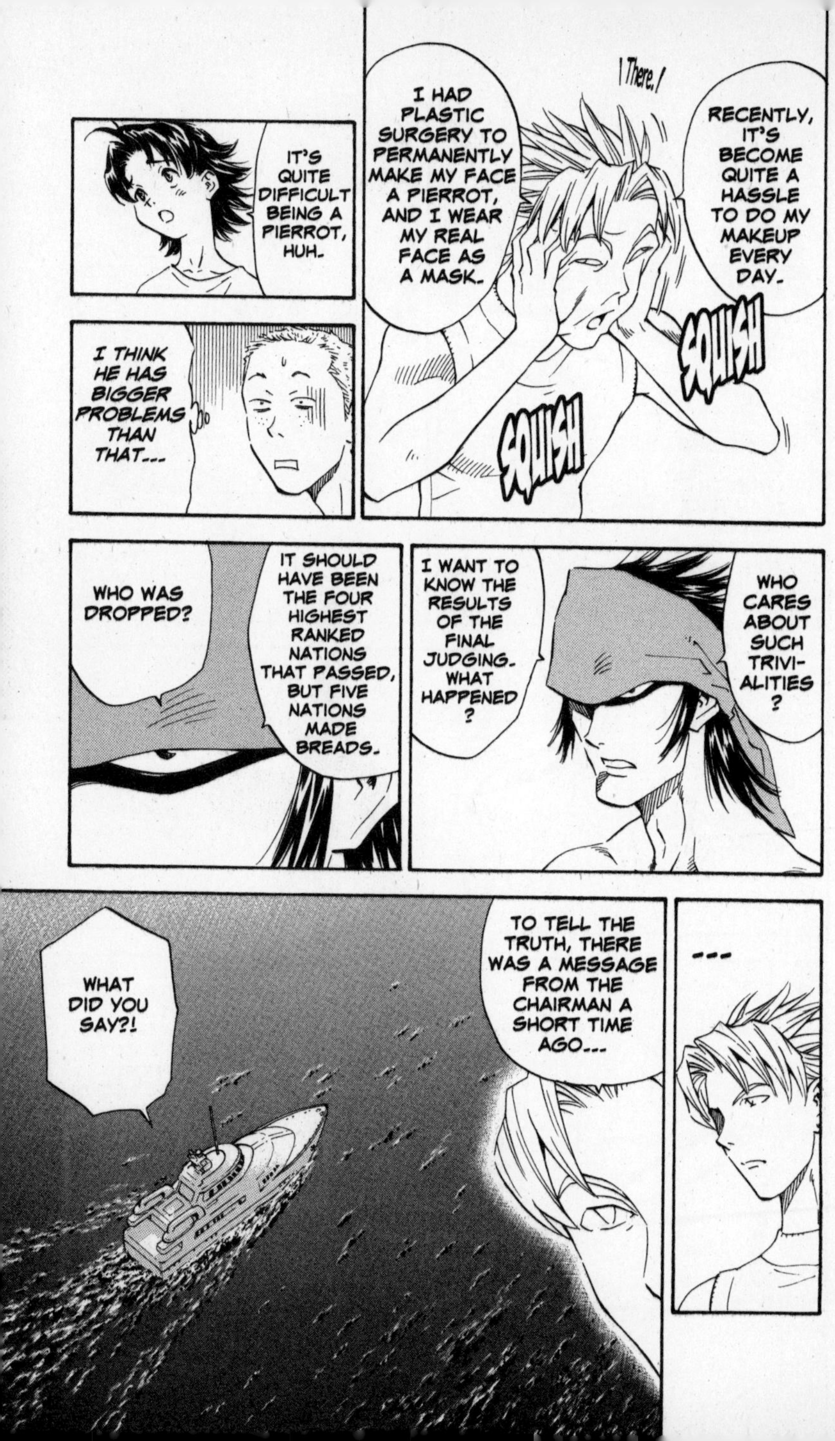
There.
RECENTLY, IT'S BECOME QUITE A HASSLE TO DO MY MAKEUP EVERY DAY.
I HAD PLASTIC SURGERY TO PERMANENTLY MAKE MY FACE A PIERROT, AND I WEAR MY REAL FACE AS A MASK.
SQUISH
SQUISH
IT'S QUITE DIFFICULT BEING A PIERROT, HUH.
I THINK HE HAS BIGGER PROBLEMS THAN THAT...
WHO CARES ABOUT SUCH TRIVI-ALITIES?
I WANT TO KNOW THE RESULTS OF THE FINAL JUDGING. WHAT HAPPENED?
IT SHOULD HAVE BEEN THE FOUR HIGHEST RANKED NATIONS THAT PASSED, BUT FIVE NATIONS MADE BREADS.
WHO WAS DROPPED?
...
TO TELL THE TRUTH, THERE WAS A MESSAGE FROM THE CHAIRMAN A SHORT TIME AGO...
WHAT DID YOU SAY?!

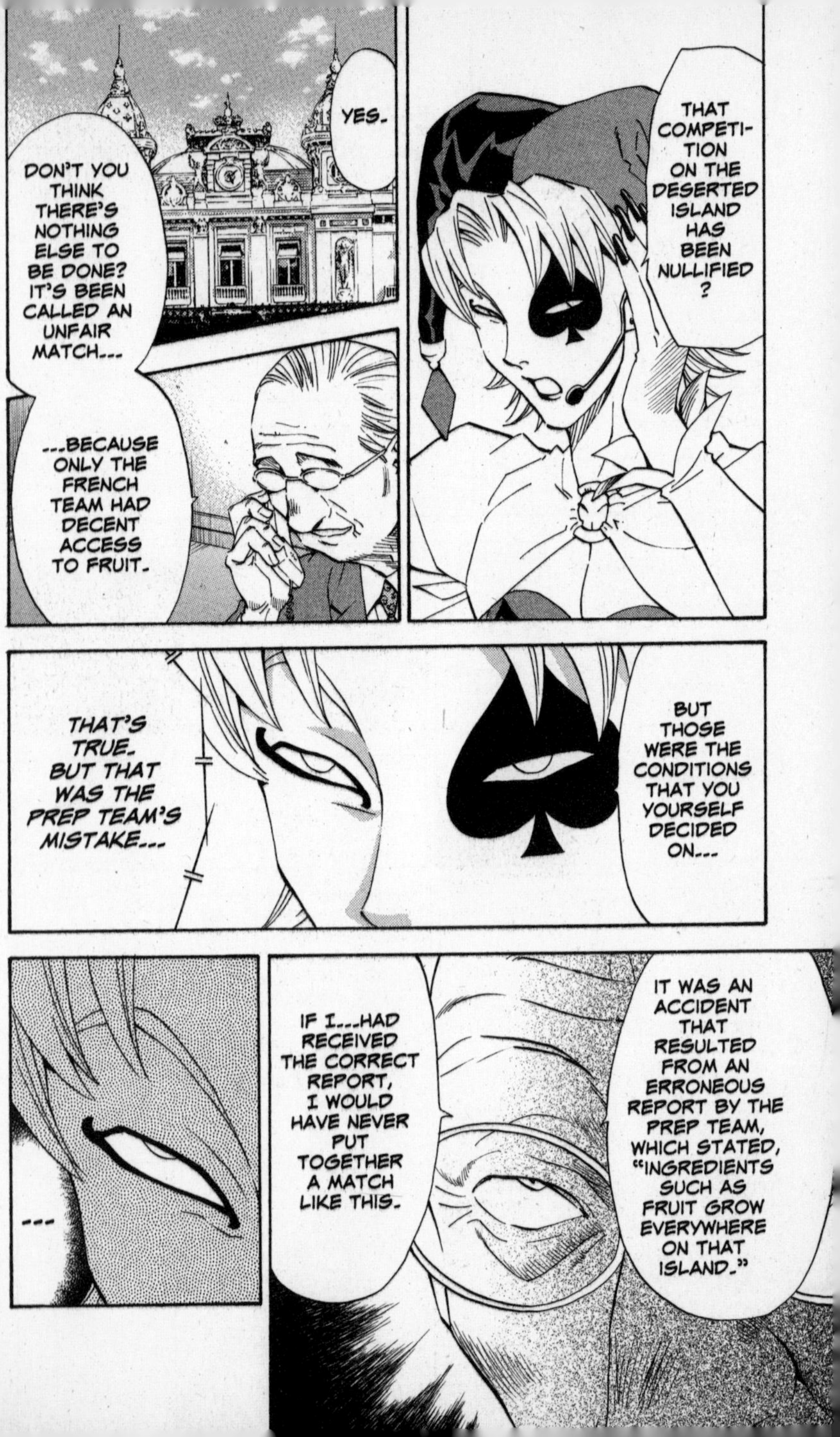
THAT COMPETITION ON THE DESERTED ISLAND HAS BEEN NULLIFIED?
YES.
DON'T YOU THINK THERE'S NOTHING ELSE TO BE DONE? IT'S BEEN CALLED AN UNFAIR MATCH...
...BECAUSE ONLY THE FRENCH TEAM HAD DECENT ACCESS TO FRUIT.
BUT THOSE WERE THE CONDITIONS THAT YOU YOURSELF DECIDED ON...
THAT'S TRUE. BUT THAT WAS THE PREP TEAM'S MISTAKE...
IT WAS AN ACCIDENT THAT RESULTED FROM AN ERRONEOUS REPORT BY THE PREP TEAM, WHICH STATED, "INGREDIENTS SUCH AS FRUIT GROW EVERYWHERE ON THAT ISLAND."
IF I...HAD RECEIVED THE CORRECT REPORT, I WOULD HAVE NEVER PUT TOGETHER A MATCH LIKE THIS.
...

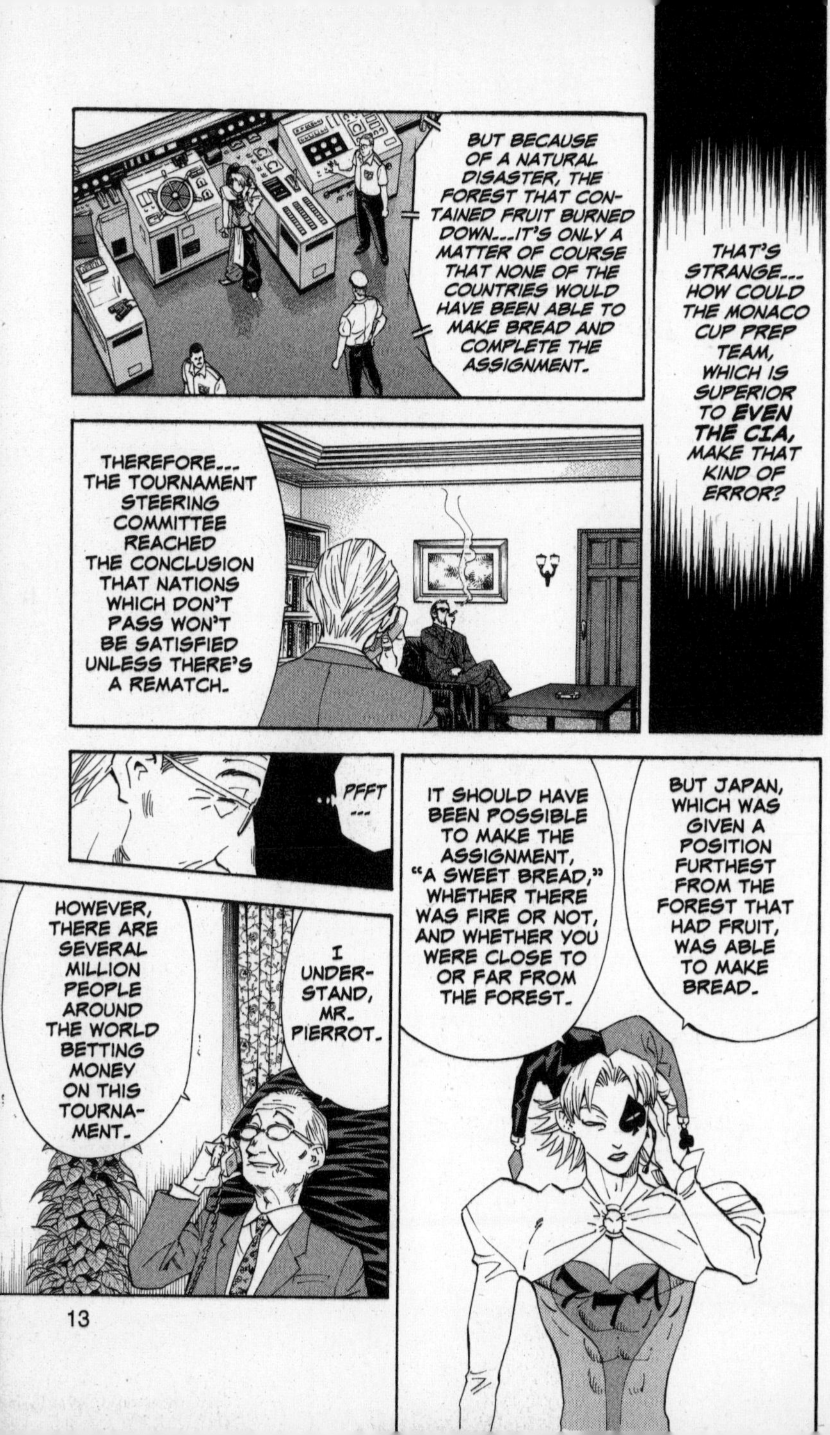
THAT'S STRANGE... HOW COULD THE MONACO CUP PREP TEAM, WHICH IS SUPERIOR TO EVEN THE CIA, MAKE THAT KIND OF ERROR?
BUT BECAUSE OF A NATURAL DISASTER, THE FOREST THAT CONTAINED FRUIT BURNED DOWN... IT'S ONLY A MATTER OF COURSE THAT NONE OF THE COUNTRIES WOULD HAVE BEEN ABLE TO MAKE BREAD AND COMPLETE THE ASSIGNMENT.
THEREFORE... THE TOURNAMENT STEERING COMMITTEE REACHED THE CONCLUSION THAT NATIONS WHICH DON'T PASS WON'T BE SATISFIED UNLESS THERE'S A REMATCH.
BUT JAPAN, WHICH WAS GIVEN A POSITION FURTHEST FROM THE FOREST THAT HAD FRUIT, WAS ABLE TO MAKE BREAD.
IT SHOULD HAVE BEEN POSSIBLE TO MAKE THE ASSIGNMENT, "A SWEET BREAD," WHETHER THERE WAS FIRE OR NOT, AND WHETHER YOU WERE CLOSE TO OR FAR FROM THE FOREST.
PFFT...
I UNDERSTAND, MR. PIERROT.
HOWEVER, THERE ARE SEVERAL MILLION PEOPLE AROUND THE WORLD BETTING MONEY ON THIS TOURNAMENT.

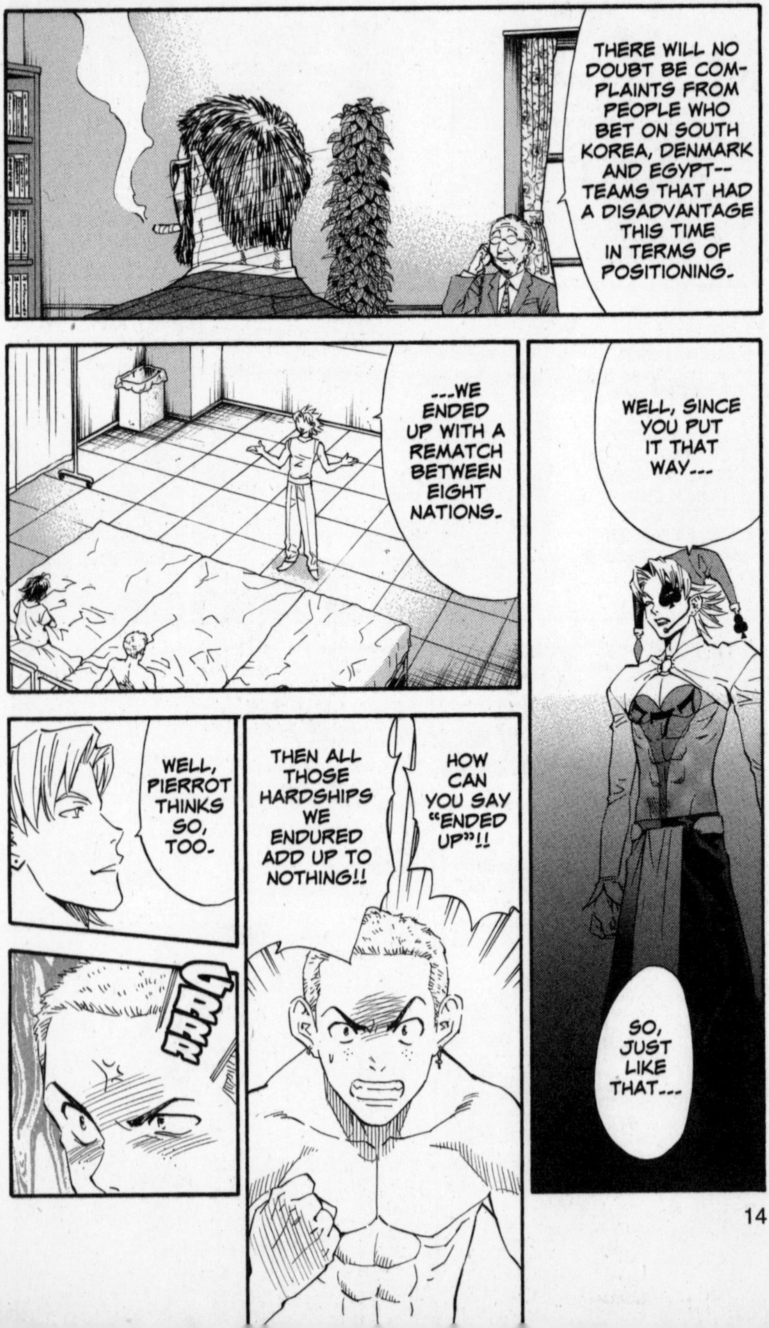
THERE WILL NO DOUBT BE COM-PLAINTS FROM PEOPLE WHO BET ON SOUTH KOREA, DENMARK AND EGYPT--TEAMS THAT HAD A DISADVANTAGE THIS TIME IN TERMS OF POSITIONING.
WELL, SINCE YOU PUT IT THAT WAY...
SO, JUST LIKE THAT...
...WE ENDED UP WITH A REMATCH BETWEEN EIGHT NATIONS.
HOW CAN YOU SAY "ENDED UP"!!
THEN ALL THOSE HARDSHIPS WE ENDURED ADD UP TO NOTHING!!
WELL, PIERROT THINKS SO, TOO.
GRRR

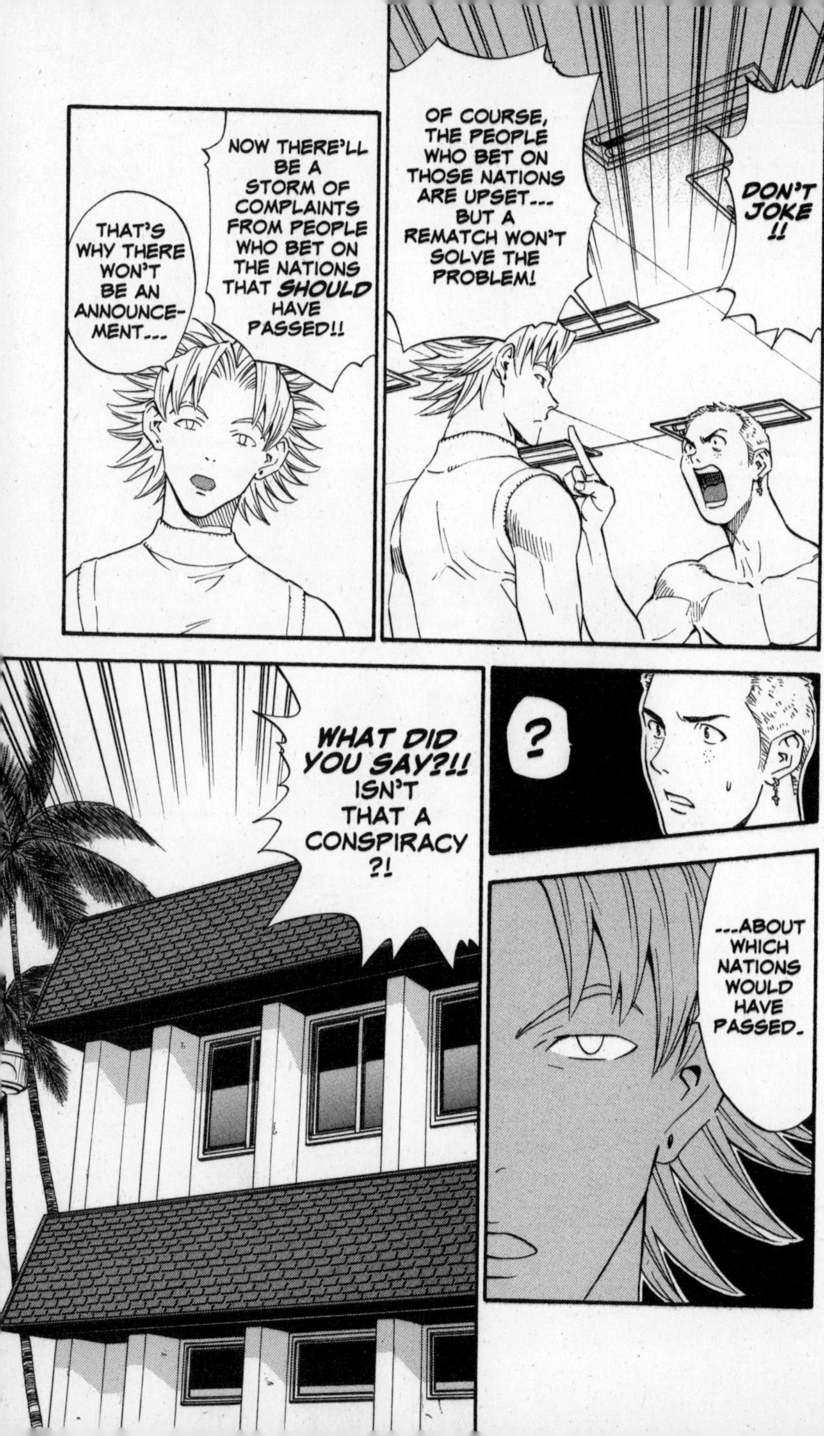
DON'T JOKE!!
OF COURSE, THE PEOPLE WHO BET ON THOSE NATIONS ARE UPSET... BUT A REMATCH WON'T SOLVE THE PROBLEM!
NOW THERE'LL BE A STORM OF COMPLAINTS FROM PEOPLE WHO BET ON THE NATIONS THAT SHOULD HAVE PASSED!!
THAT'S WHY THERE WON'T BE AN ANNOUNCEMENT...
?
...ABOUT WHICH NATIONS WOULD HAVE PASSED.
WHAT DID YOU SAY?!! ISN'T THAT A CONSPIRACY?!

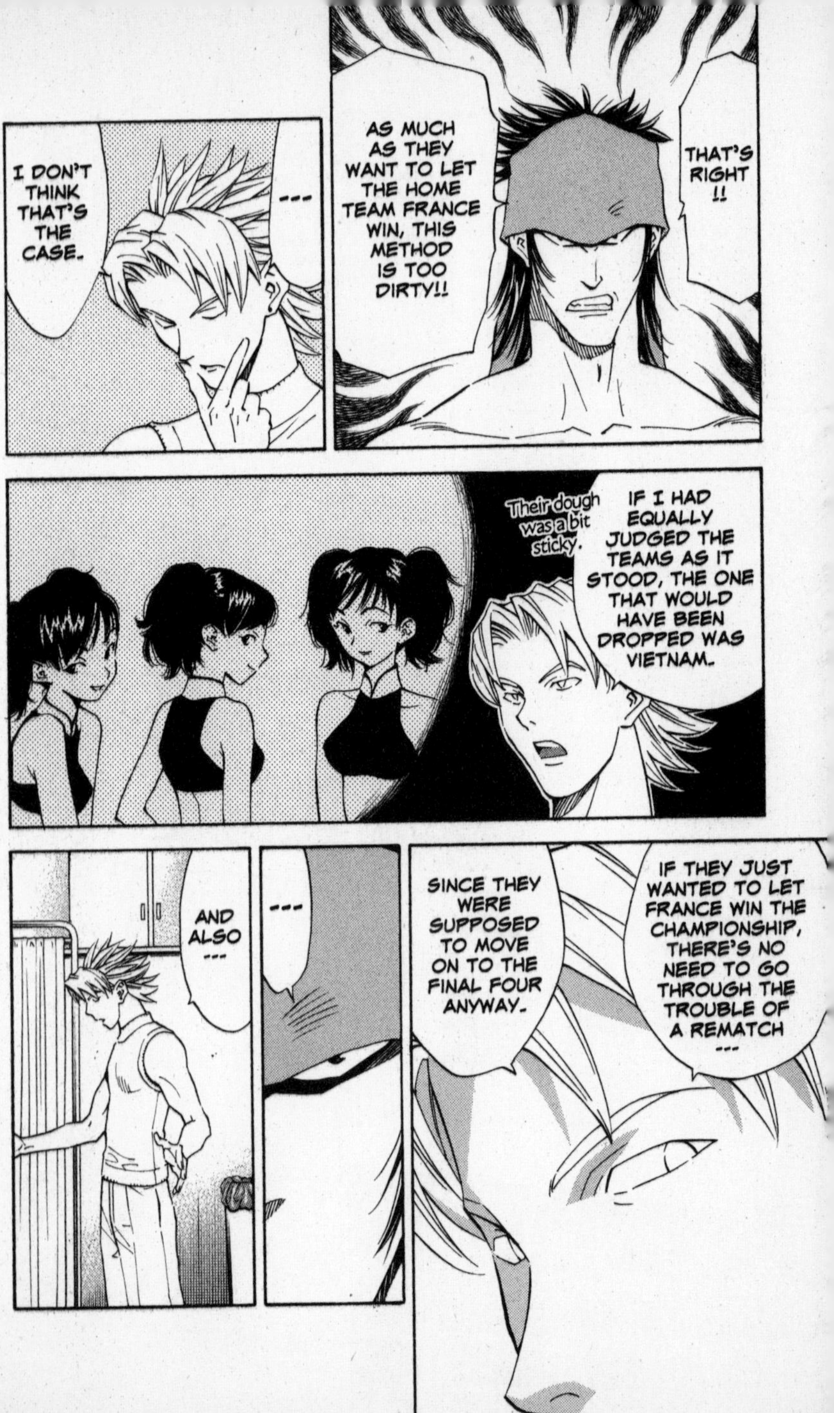
THAT'S RIGHT !!
AS MUCH AS THEY WANT TO LET THE HOME TEAM FRANCE WIN, THIS METHOD IS TOO DIRTY!!

I DON'T THINK THAT'S THE CASE.
IF I HAD EQUALLY JUDGED THE TEAMS AS IT STOOD, THE ONE THAT WOULD HAVE BEEN DROPPED WAS VIETNAM.
Their dough was a bit sticky.
IF THEY JUST WANTED TO LET FRANCE WIN THE CHAMPIONSHIP, THERE'S NO NEED TO GO THROUGH THE TROUBLE OF A REMATCH ---
SINCE THEY WERE SUPPOSED TO MOVE ON TO THE FINAL FOUR ANYWAY.

AND ALSO ---

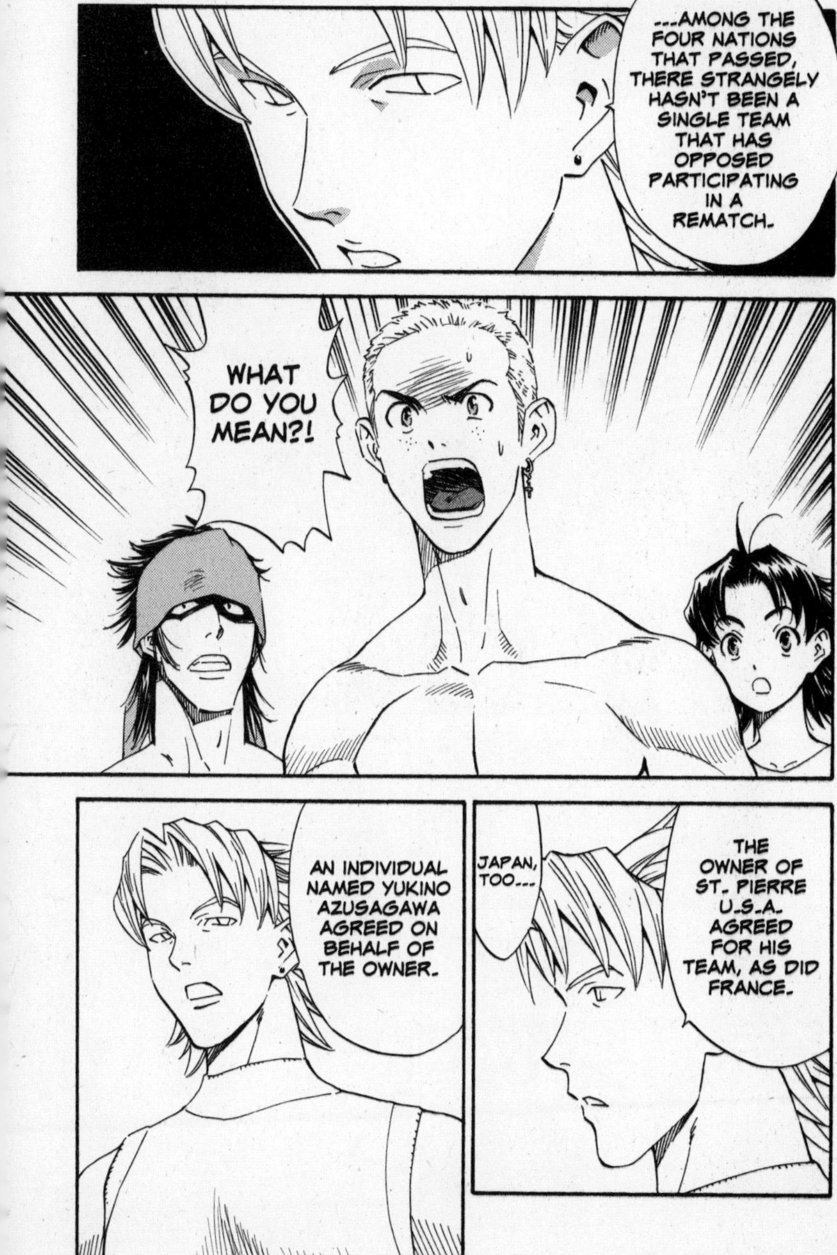
...AMONG THE FOUR NATIONS THAT PASSED, THERE STRANGELY HASN'T BEEN A SINGLE TEAM THAT HAS OPPOSED PARTICIPATING IN A REMATCH.
WHAT DO YOU MEAN?!
THE OWNER OF ST. PIERRE U.S.A. AGREED FOR HIS TEAM, AS DID FRANCE.
JAPAN, TOO...
AN INDIVIDUAL NAMED YUKINO AZUSAGAWA AGREED ON BEHALF OF THE OWNER.

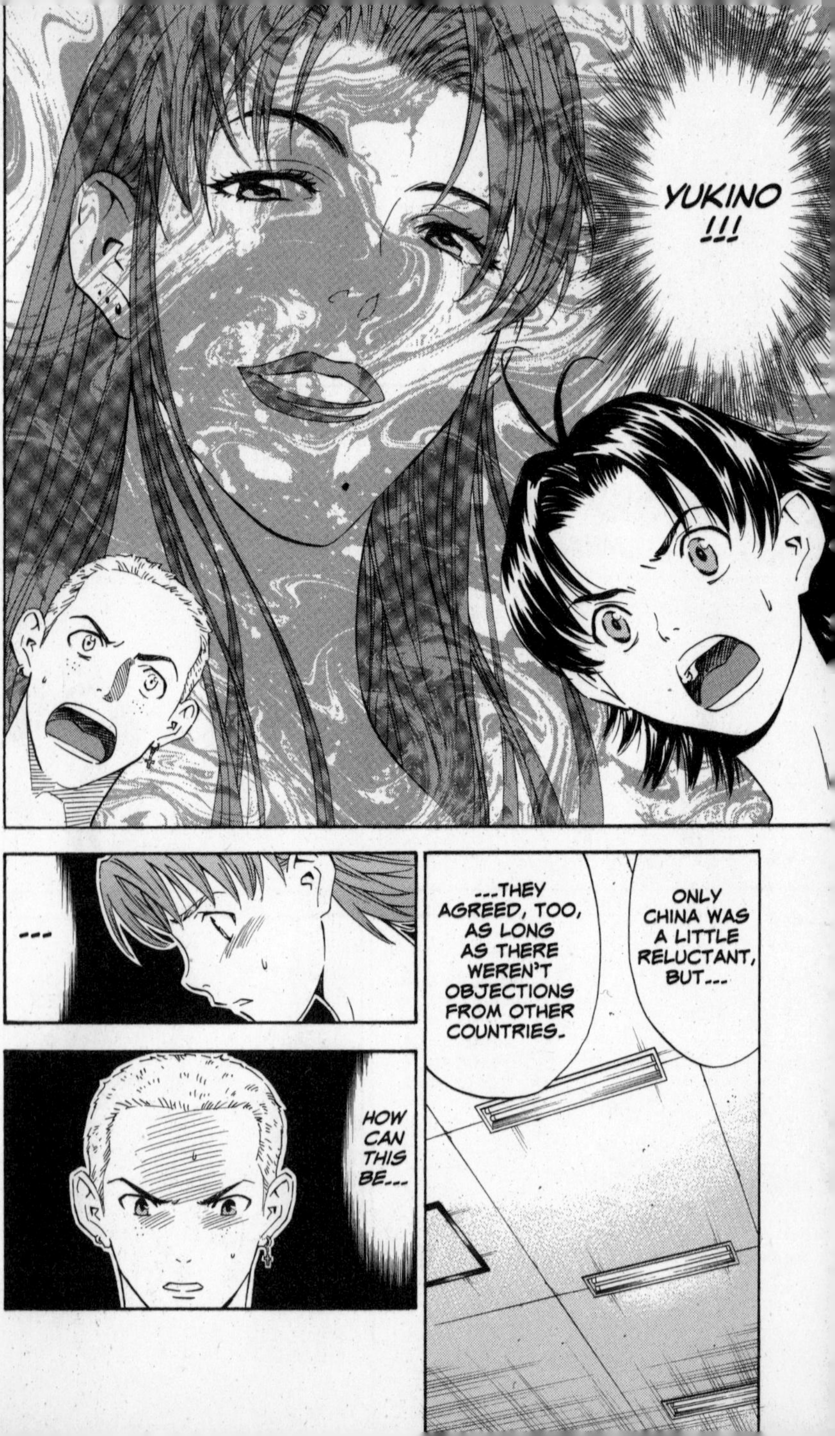
YUKINO !!!
ONLY CHINA WAS A LITTLE RELUCTANT, BUT...
...THEY AGREED, TOO, AS LONG AS THERE WEREN'T OBJECTIONS FROM OTHER COUNTRIES.
...
HOW CAN THIS BE...

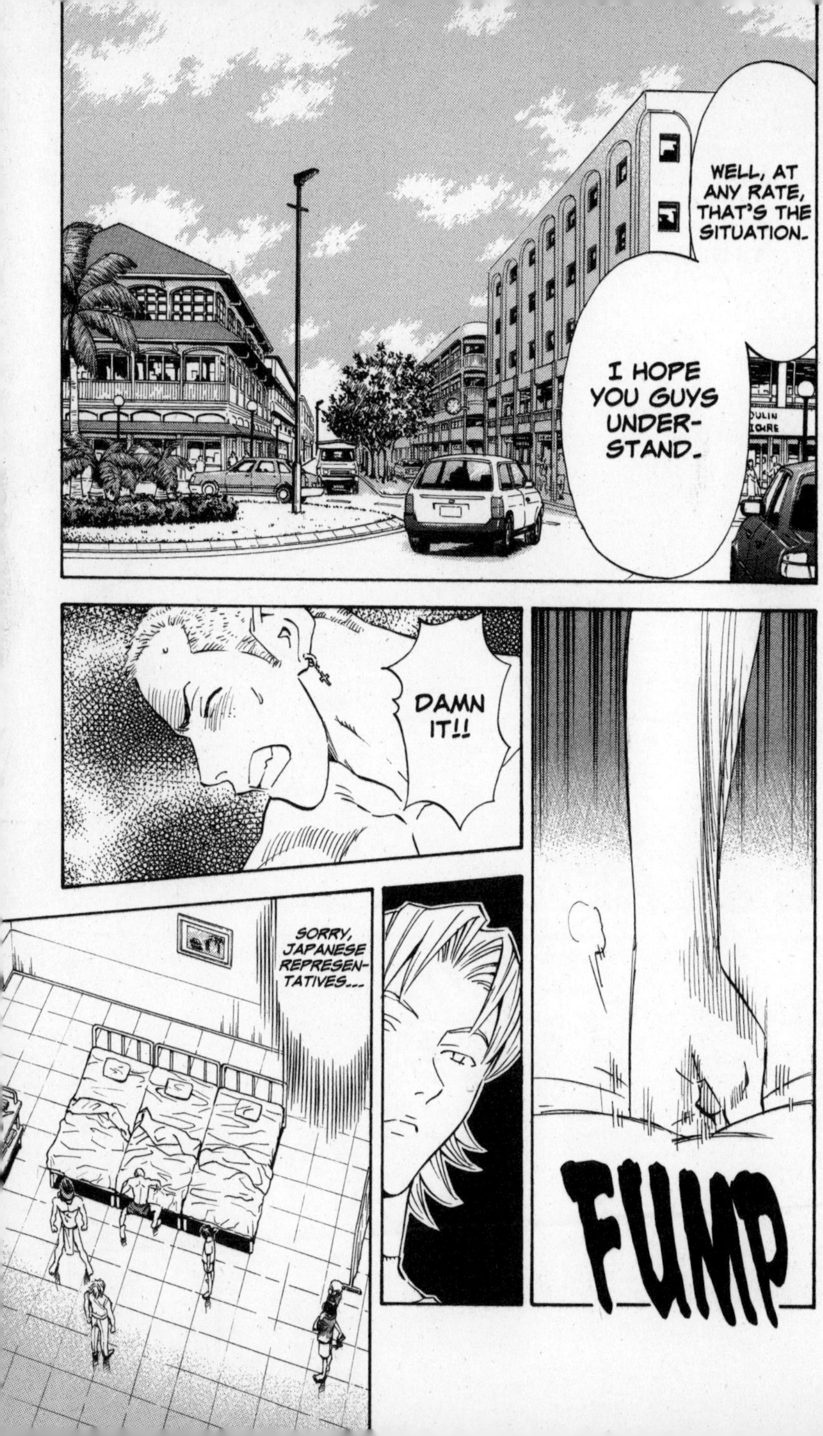
WELL, AT ANY RATE, THAT'S THE SITUATION.
I HOPE YOU GUYS UNDER-STAND.
FUMP
DAMN IT!!
SORRY, JAPANESE REPRESEN-TATIVES...

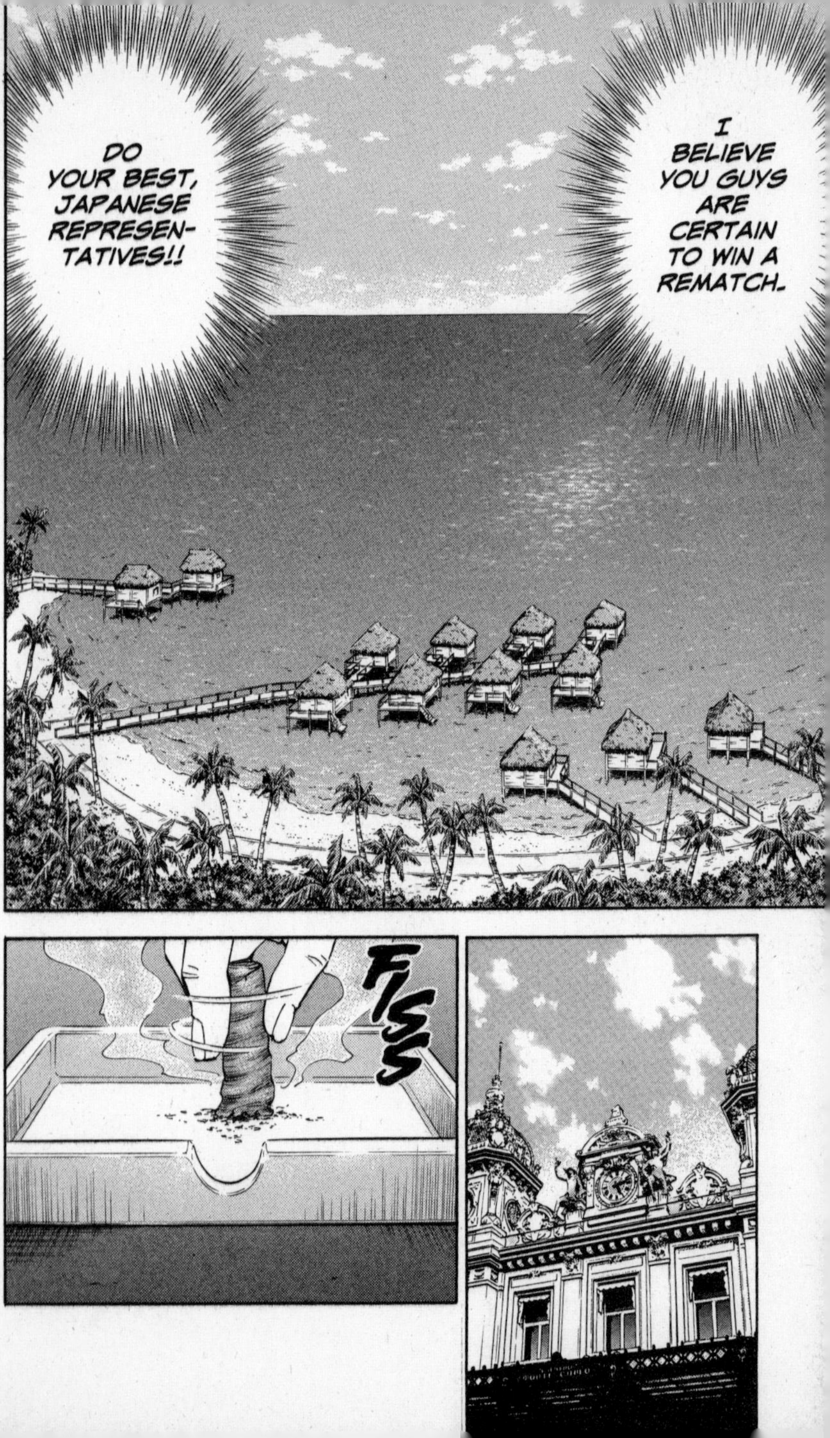
I BELIEVE YOU GUYS ARE CERTAIN TO WIN A REMATCH...
DO YOUR BEST, JAPANESE REPRESEN-TATIVES!!
FISS

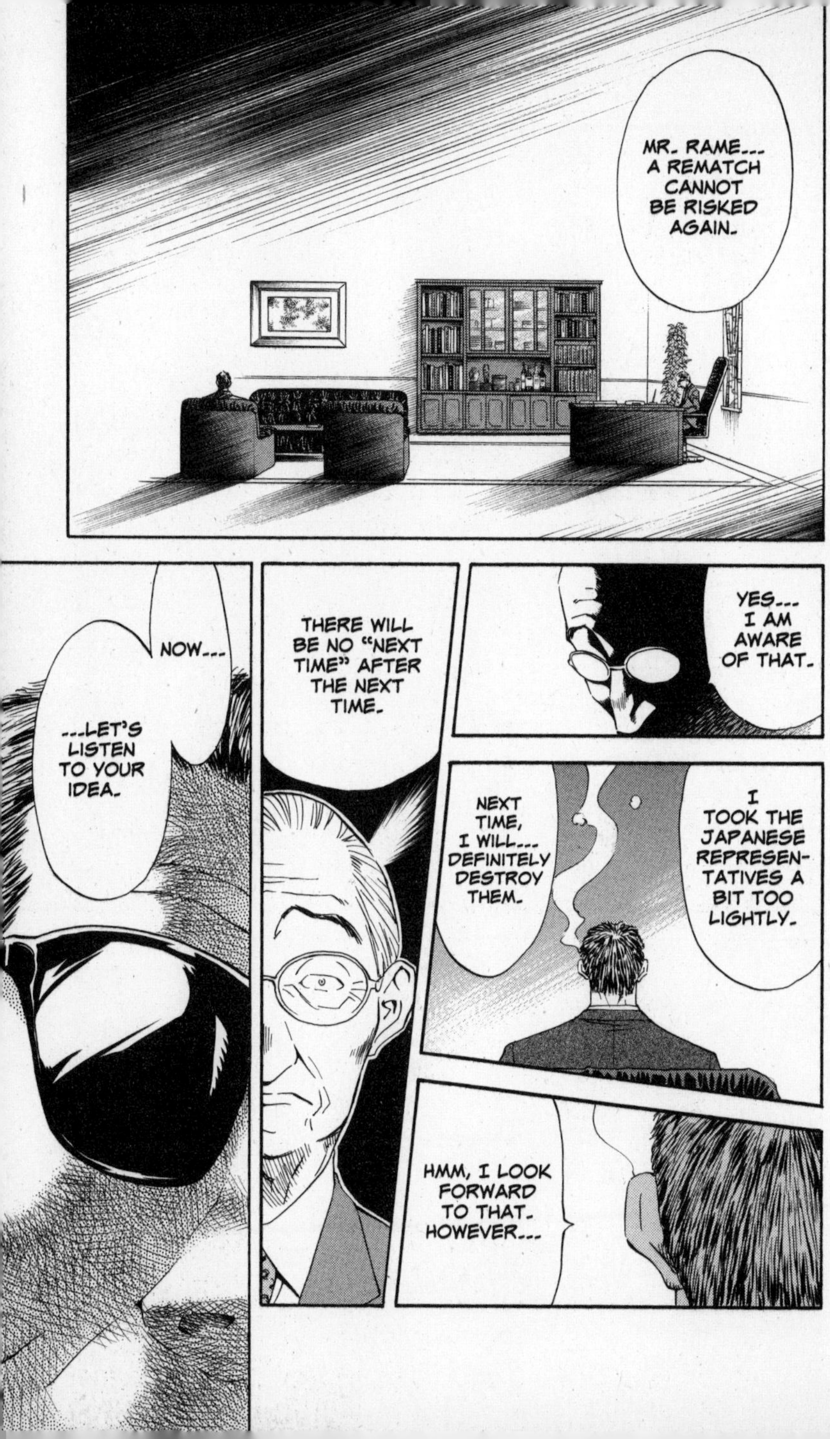
MR. RAME... A REMATCH CANNOT BE RISKED AGAIN.
YES... I AM AWARE OF THAT.
I TOOK THE JAPANESE REPRESEN-TATIVES A BIT TOO LIGHTLY.
NEXT TIME, I WILL... DEFINITELY DESTROY THEM.
HMM, I LOOK FORWARD TO THAT. HOWEVER...
THERE WILL BE NO "NEXT TIME" AFTER THE NEXT TIME.
NOW...
...LET'S LISTEN TO YOUR IDEA.

THE NEXT COMPETITION VENUE IS....

Y--- YES....

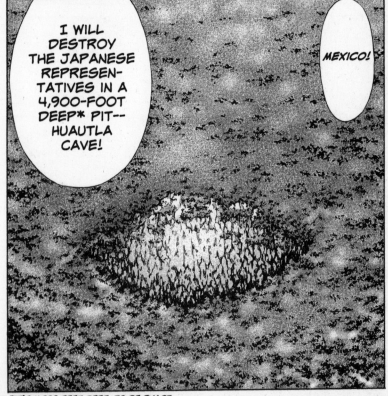

I WILL DESTROY THE JAPANESE REPRESENTATIVES IN A 4,900-FOOT DEEP* PIT-- HUAUTLA CAVE!

MEXICO!

*IT'S 4,839 FEET DEEP, TO BE EXACT.

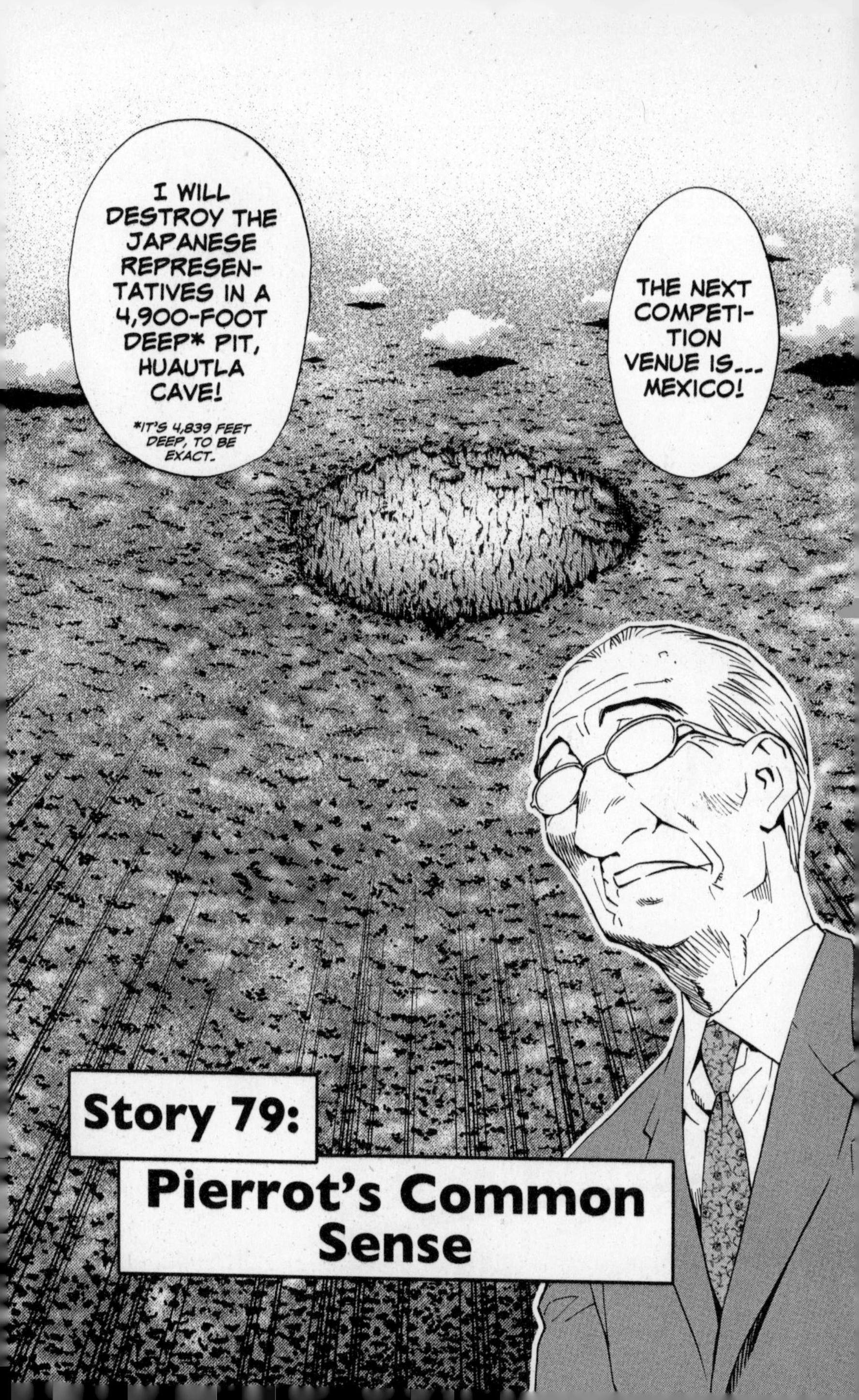
THE NEXT COMPETITION VENUE IS... MEXICO!
I WILL DESTROY THE JAPANESE REPRESENTATIVES IN A 4,900-FOOT DEEP* PIT, HUAUTLA CAVE!
*IT'S 4,839 FEET DEEP, TO BE EXACT.
Story 79:
Pierrot's Common Sense

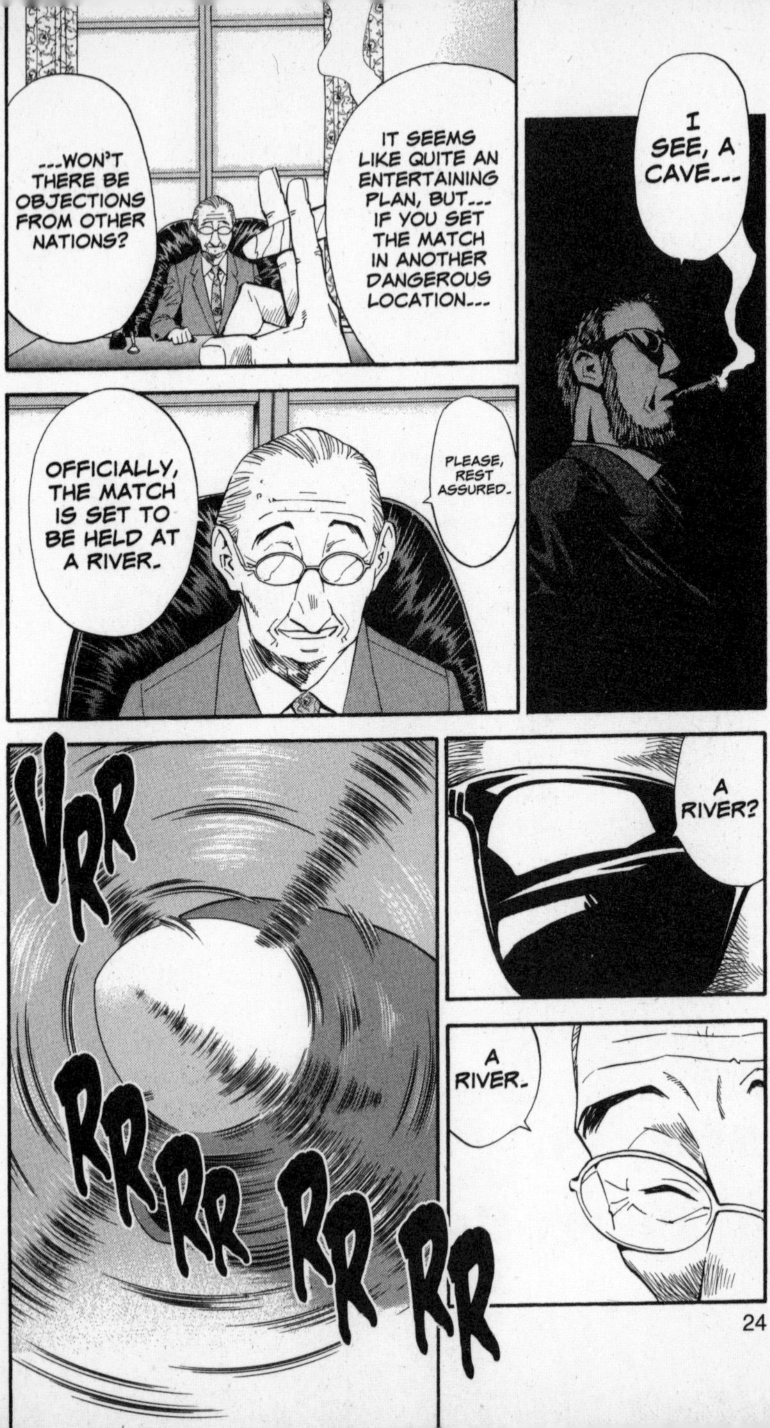
I SEE, A CAVE...
IT SEEMS LIKE QUITE AN ENTERTAINING PLAN, BUT... IF YOU SET THE MATCH IN ANOTHER DANGEROUS LOCATION...
...WON'T THERE BE OBJECTIONS FROM OTHER NATIONS?
PLEASE, REST ASSURED.
OFFICIALLY, THE MATCH IS SET TO BE HELD AT A RIVER.
A RIVER?
A RIVER.
VRRRRRRRRRR

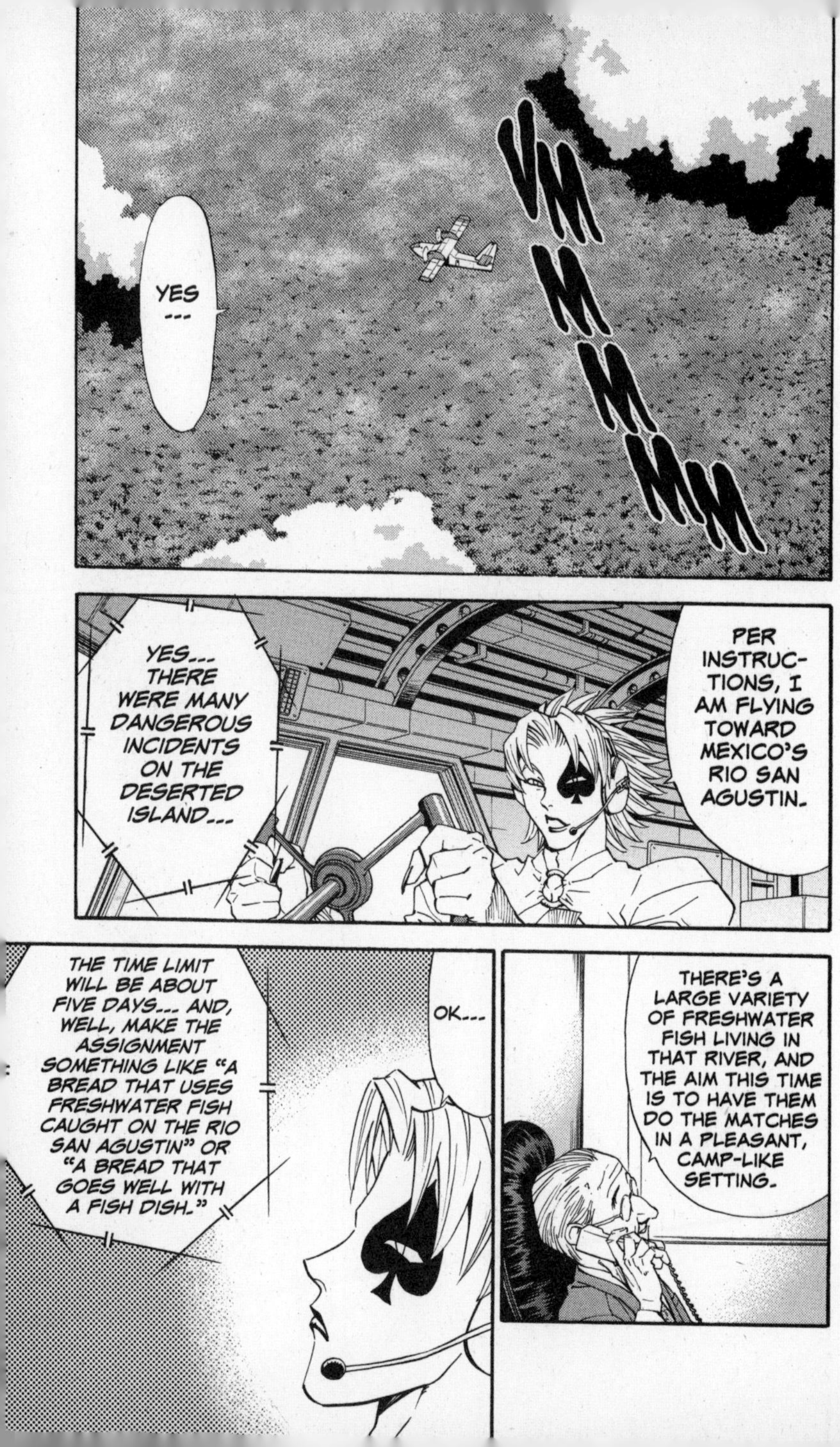
YES ---
VMMMMMM
PER INSTRUCTIONS, I AM FLYING TOWARD MEXICO'S RIO SAN AGUSTIN.
YES... THERE WERE MANY DANGEROUS INCIDENTS ON THE DESERTED ISLAND...
THERE'S A LARGE VARIETY OF FRESHWATER FISH LIVING IN THAT RIVER, AND THE AIM THIS TIME IS TO HAVE THEM DO THE MATCHES IN A PLEASANT, CAMP-LIKE SETTING.
OK---
THE TIME LIMIT WILL BE ABOUT FIVE DAYS... AND, WELL, MAKE THE ASSIGNMENT SOMETHING LIKE "A BREAD THAT USES FRESHWATER FISH CAUGHT ON THE RIO SAN AGUSTIN" OR "A BREAD THAT GOES WELL WITH A FISH DISH."

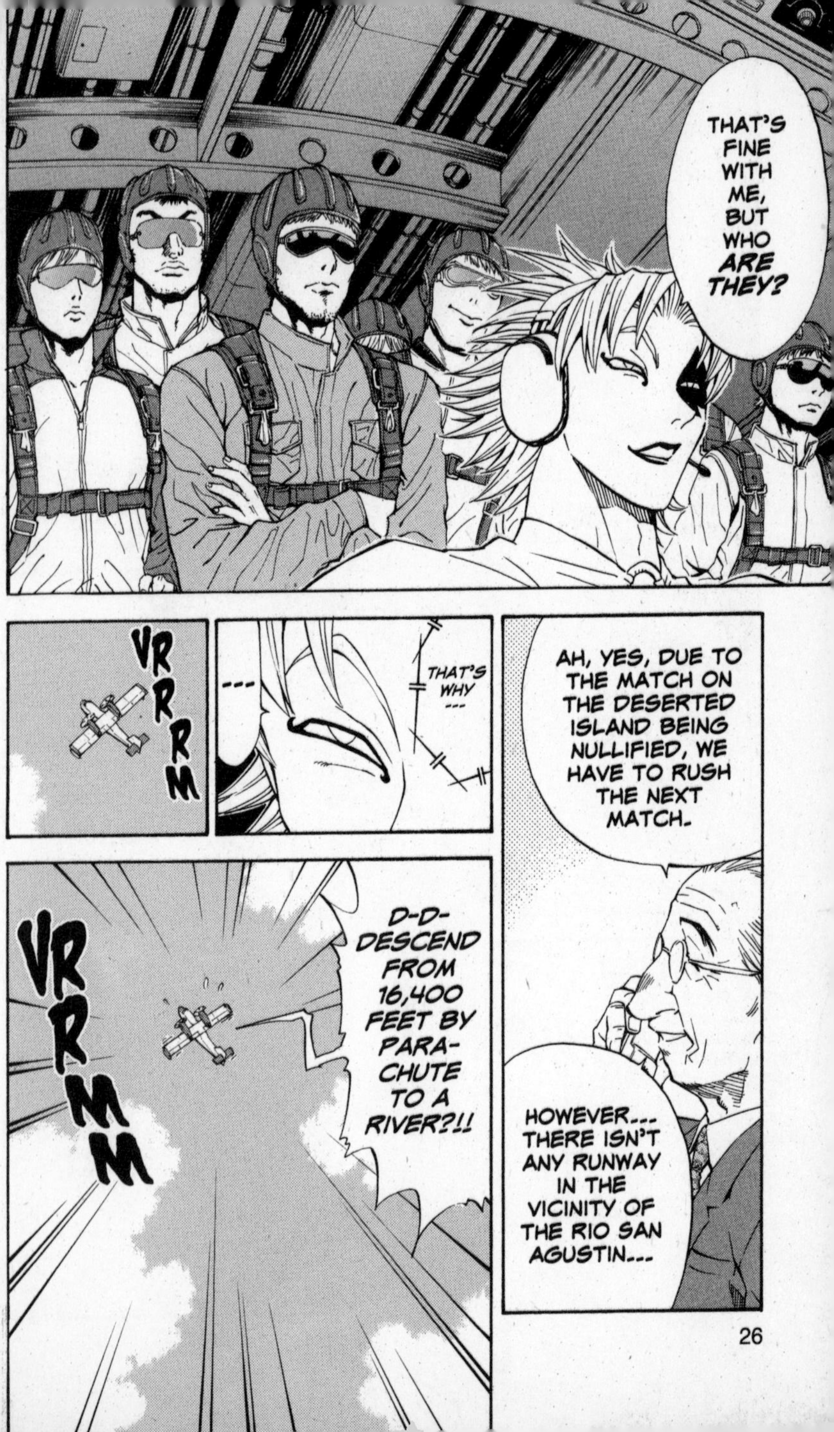
THAT'S FINE WITH ME, BUT WHO ARE THEY?
AH, YES, DUE TO THE MATCH ON THE DESERTED ISLAND BEING NULLIFIED, WE HAVE TO RUSH THE NEXT MATCH.
HOWEVER... THERE ISN'T ANY RUNWAY IN THE VICINITY OF THE RIO SAN AGUSTIN...
THAT'S WHY ---

VRRRM
VRRMM
D-D-DESCEND FROM 16,400 FEET BY PARA-CHUTE TO A RIVER?!!

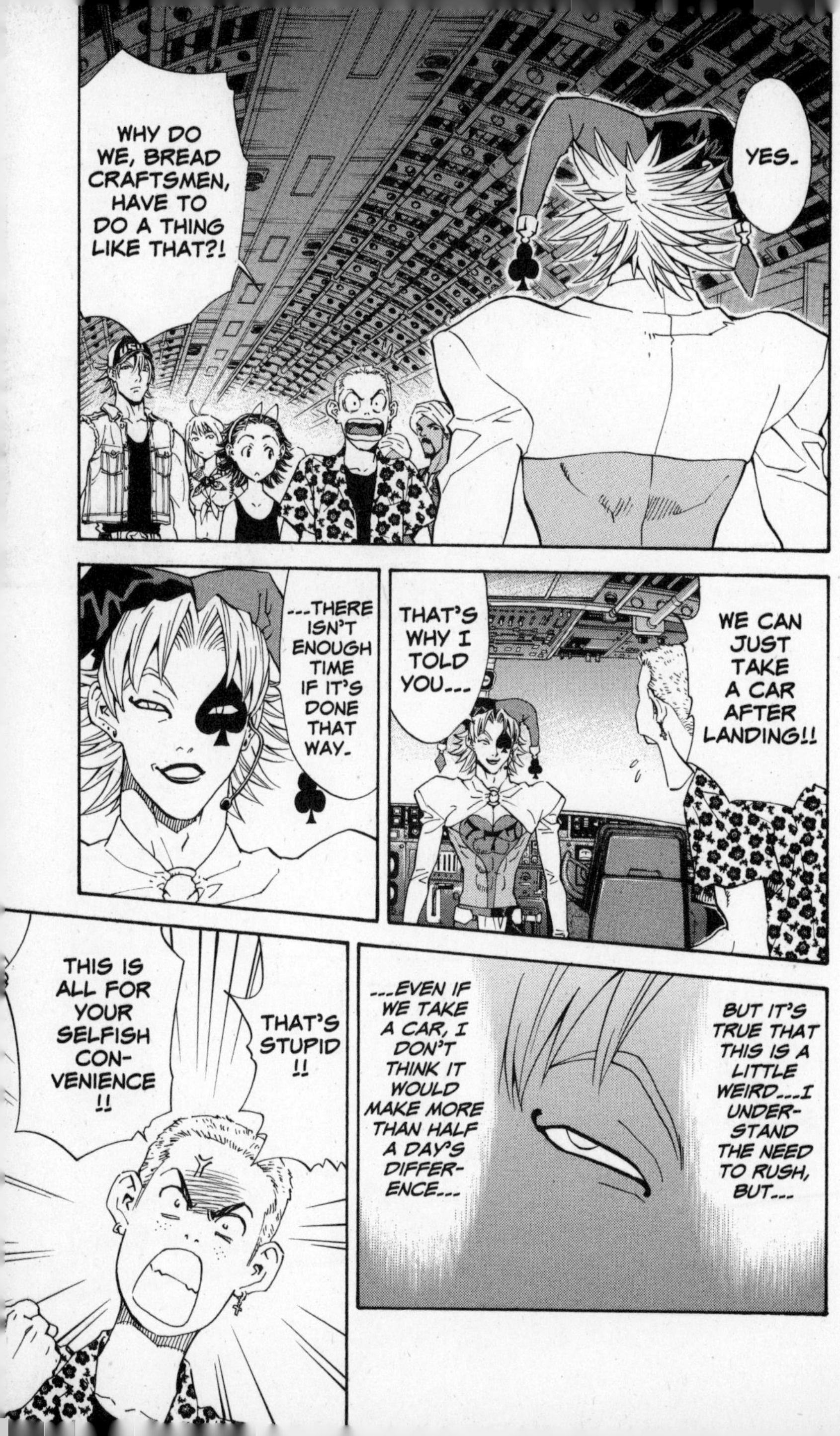
YES.
WHY DO WE, BREAD CRAFTSMEN, HAVE TO DO A THING LIKE THAT?!
WE CAN JUST TAKE A CAR AFTER LANDING!!
THAT'S WHY I TOLD YOU...
...THERE ISN'T ENOUGH TIME IF IT'S DONE THAT WAY.
BUT IT'S TRUE THAT THIS IS A LITTLE WEIRD... I UNDER-STAND THE NEED TO RUSH, BUT...
...EVEN IF WE TAKE A CAR, I DON'T THINK IT WOULD MAKE MORE THAN HALF A DAY'S DIFFER-ENCE...
THAT'S STUPID!!
THIS IS ALL FOR YOUR SELFISH CON-VENIENCE!!

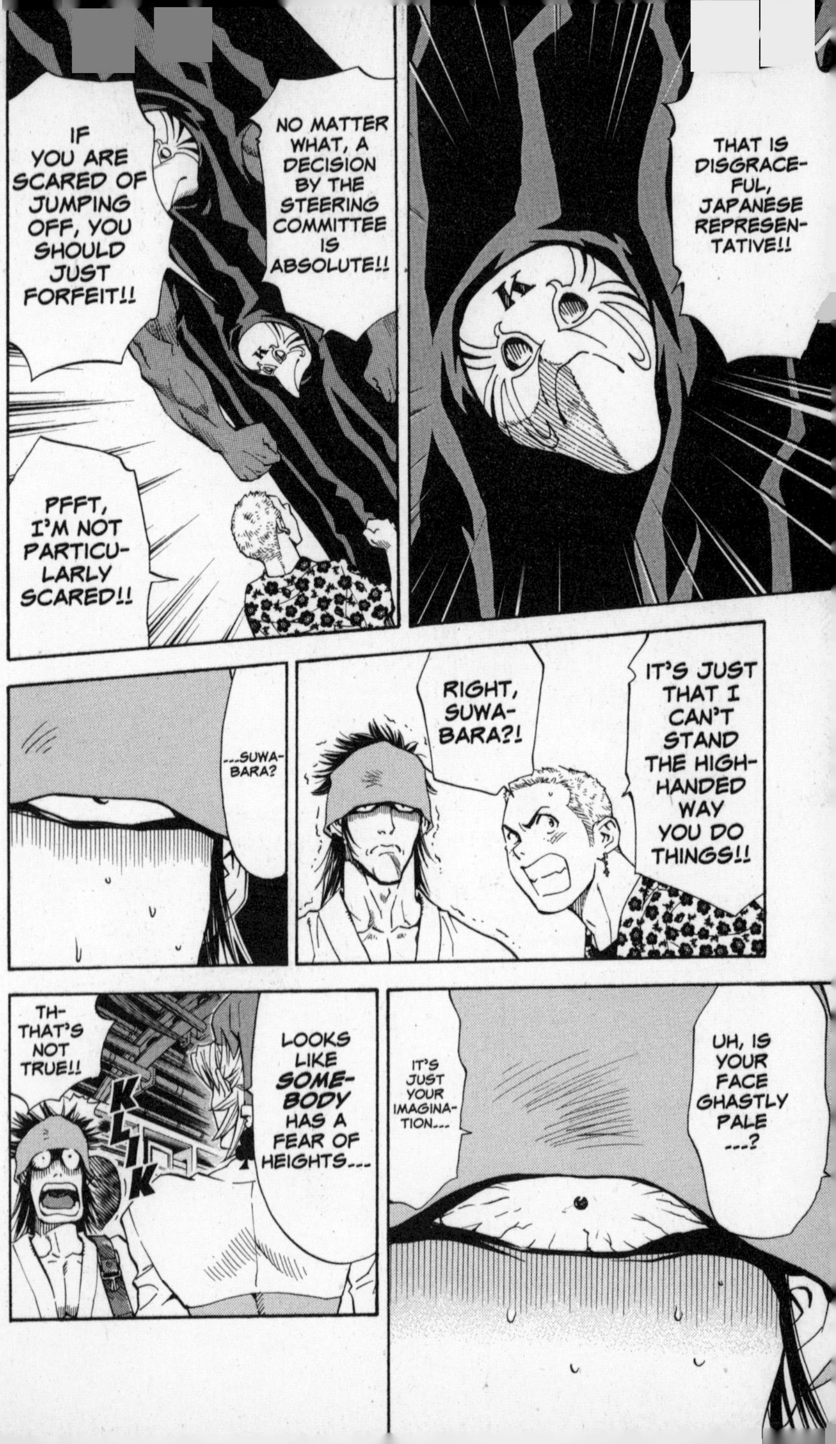
THAT IS DISGRACEFUL, JAPANESE REPRESENTATIVE!!
NO MATTER WHAT, A DECISION BY THE STEERING COMMITTEE IS ABSOLUTE!!
IF YOU ARE SCARED OF JUMPING OFF, YOU SHOULD JUST FORFEIT!!
PFFT, I'M NOT PARTICULARLY SCARED!!
IT'S JUST THAT I CAN'T STAND THE HIGH-HANDED WAY YOU DO THINGS!!
RIGHT, SUWABARA?!
...SUWABARA?
UH, IS YOUR FACE GHASTLY PALE ...?
IT'S JUST YOUR IMAGINATION...
LOOKS LIKE *SOMEBODY* HAS A FEAR OF HEIGHTS...
KLIK
TH-THAT'S NOT TRUE!!

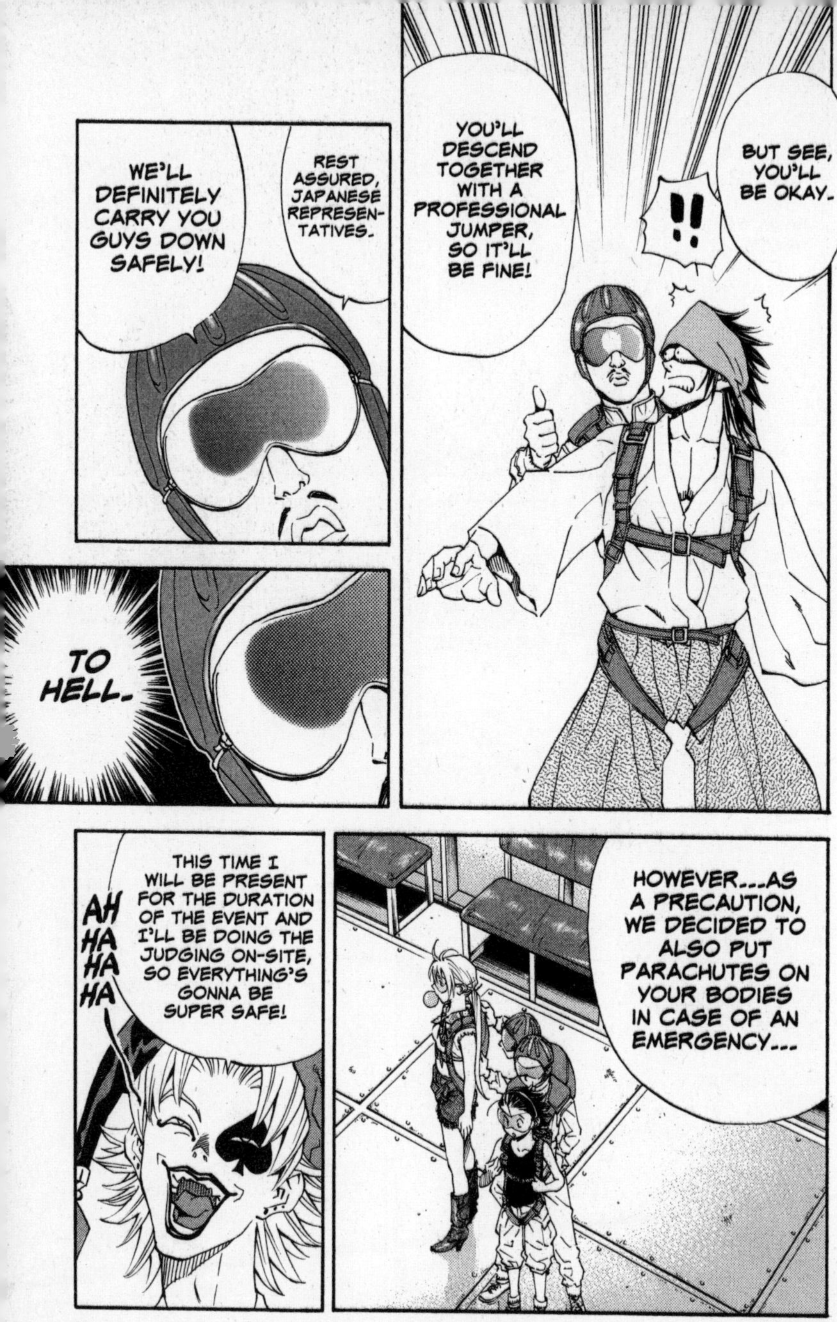
BUT SEE, YOU'LL BE OKAY.
!!
YOU'LL DESCEND TOGETHER WITH A PROFESSIONAL JUMPER, SO IT'LL BE FINE!
REST ASSURED, JAPANESE REPRESENTATIVES.
WE'LL DEFINITELY CARRY YOU GUYS DOWN SAFELY!
TO HELL.
HOWEVER...AS A PRECAUTION, WE DECIDED TO ALSO PUT PARACHUTES ON YOUR BODIES IN CASE OF AN EMERGENCY...
THIS TIME I WILL BE PRESENT FOR THE DURATION OF THE EVENT AND I'LL BE DOING THE JUDGING ON-SITE, SO EVERYTHING'S GONNA BE SUPER SAFE!
AH HA HA HA

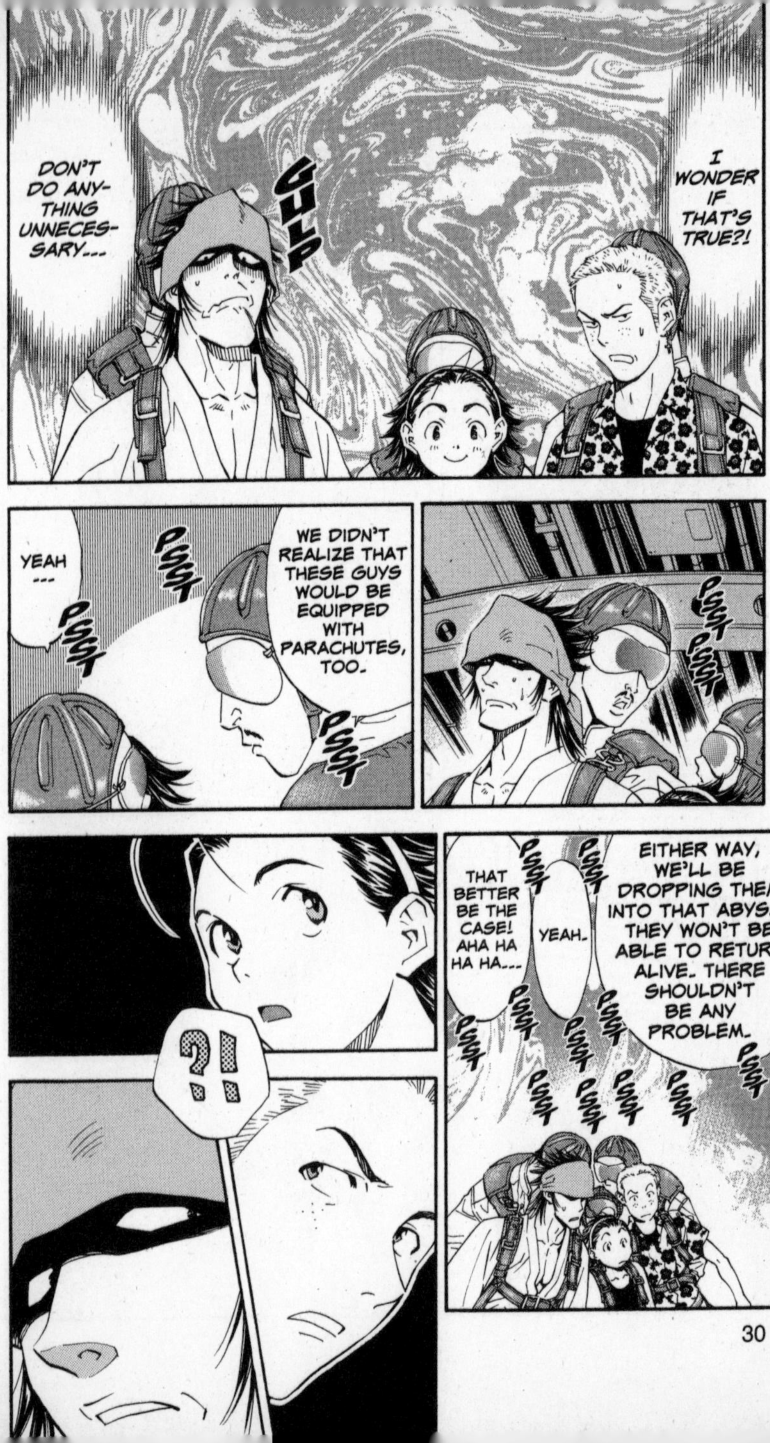
I WONDER IF THAT'S TRUE?!
GULP
DON'T DO ANY-THING UNNECES-SARY...
PSSST PSSST
WE DIDN'T REALIZE THAT THESE GUYS WOULD BE EQUIPPED WITH PARACHUTES, TOO.
PSSST PSSST PSSST
YEAH...
EITHER WAY, WE'LL BE DROPPING THEM INTO THAT ABYSS. THEY WON'T BE ABLE TO RETURN ALIVE. THERE SHOULDN'T BE ANY PROBLEM.
YEAH.
THAT BETTER BE THE CASE! AHA HA HA HA...
PSSST PSSST PSSST PSSST PSSST PSSST PSSST PSSST PSSST
?!

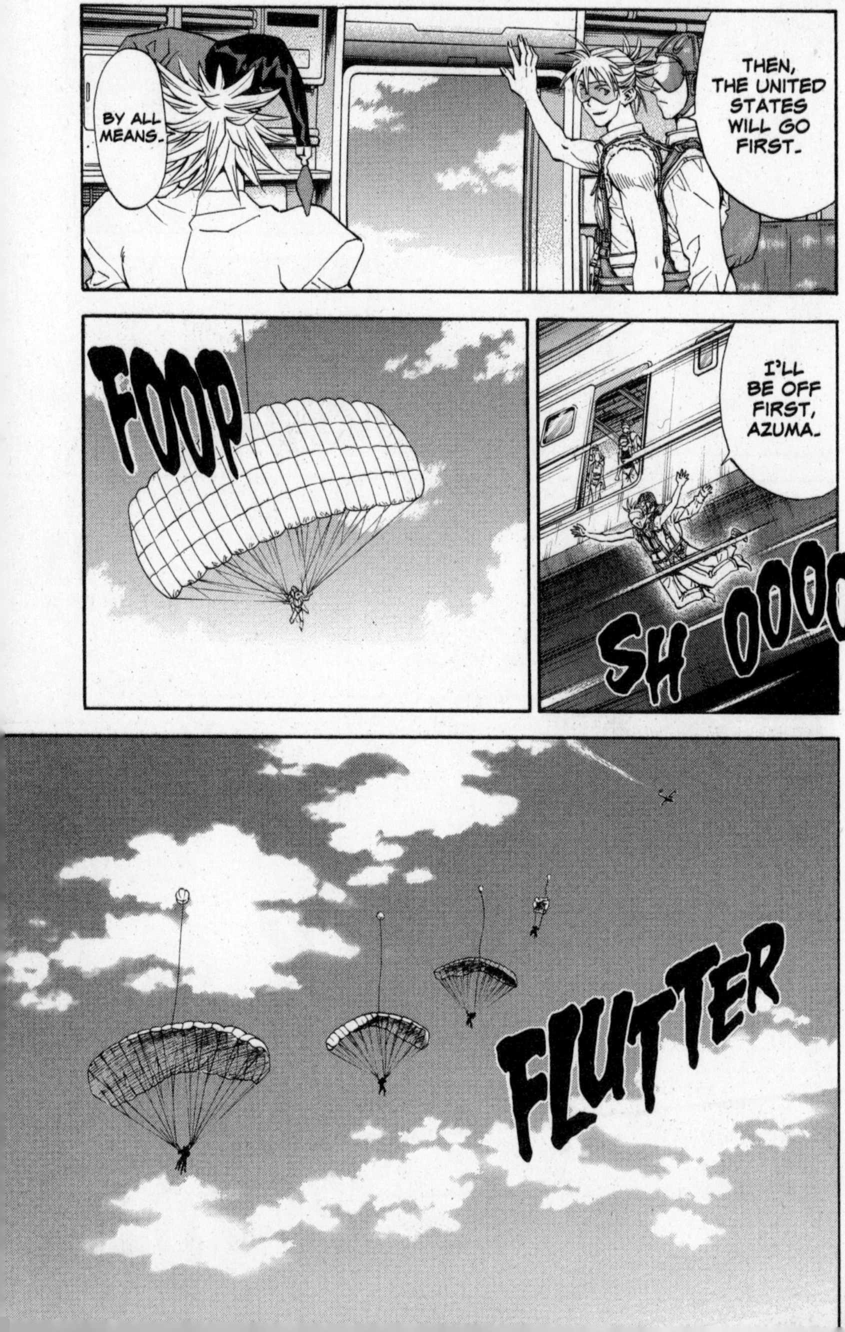
THEN, THE UNITED STATES WILL GO FIRST.
BY ALL MEANS.
I'LL BE OFF FIRST, AZUMA.
SH OOOO
FOOP
FLUTTER

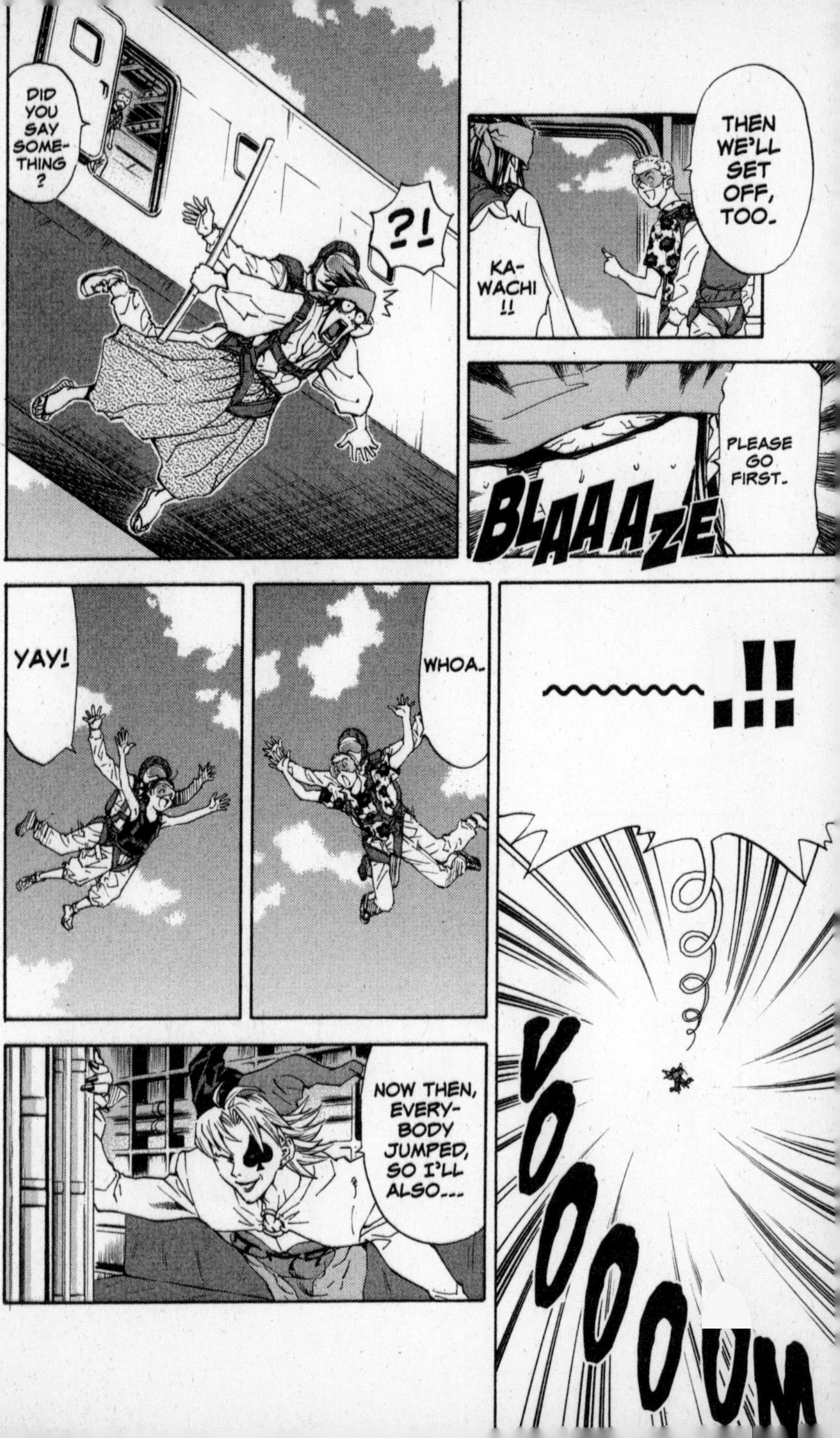
THEN WE'LL SET OFF, TOO.
KA-WACHI!!
PLEASE GO FIRST.
BLAAAZE
DID YOU SAY SOME-THING?
?!
~~~~~~~~~!!
VOOOOOOM
WHOA.
YAY!
NOW THEN, EVERY-BODY JUMPED, SO I'LL ALSO...
~~~~~~~~~

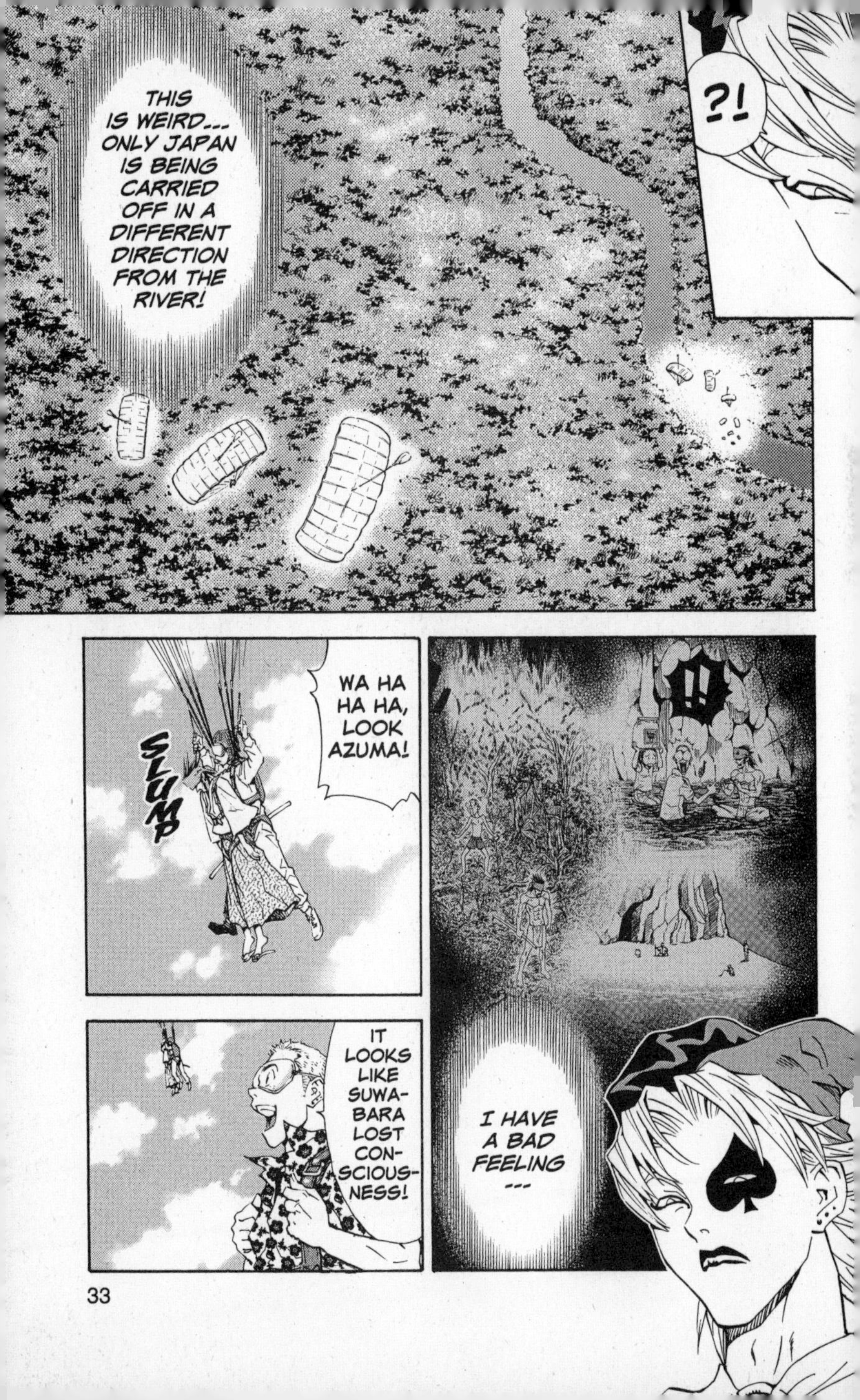
?!
THIS IS WEIRD... ONLY JAPAN IS BEING CARRIED OFF IN A DIFFERENT DIRECTION FROM THE RIVER!
!!
WA HA HA HA, LOOK AZUMA!
SLUMP
IT LOOKS LIKE SUWA-BARA LOST CON-SCIOUS-NESS!
I HAVE A BAD FEELING ...

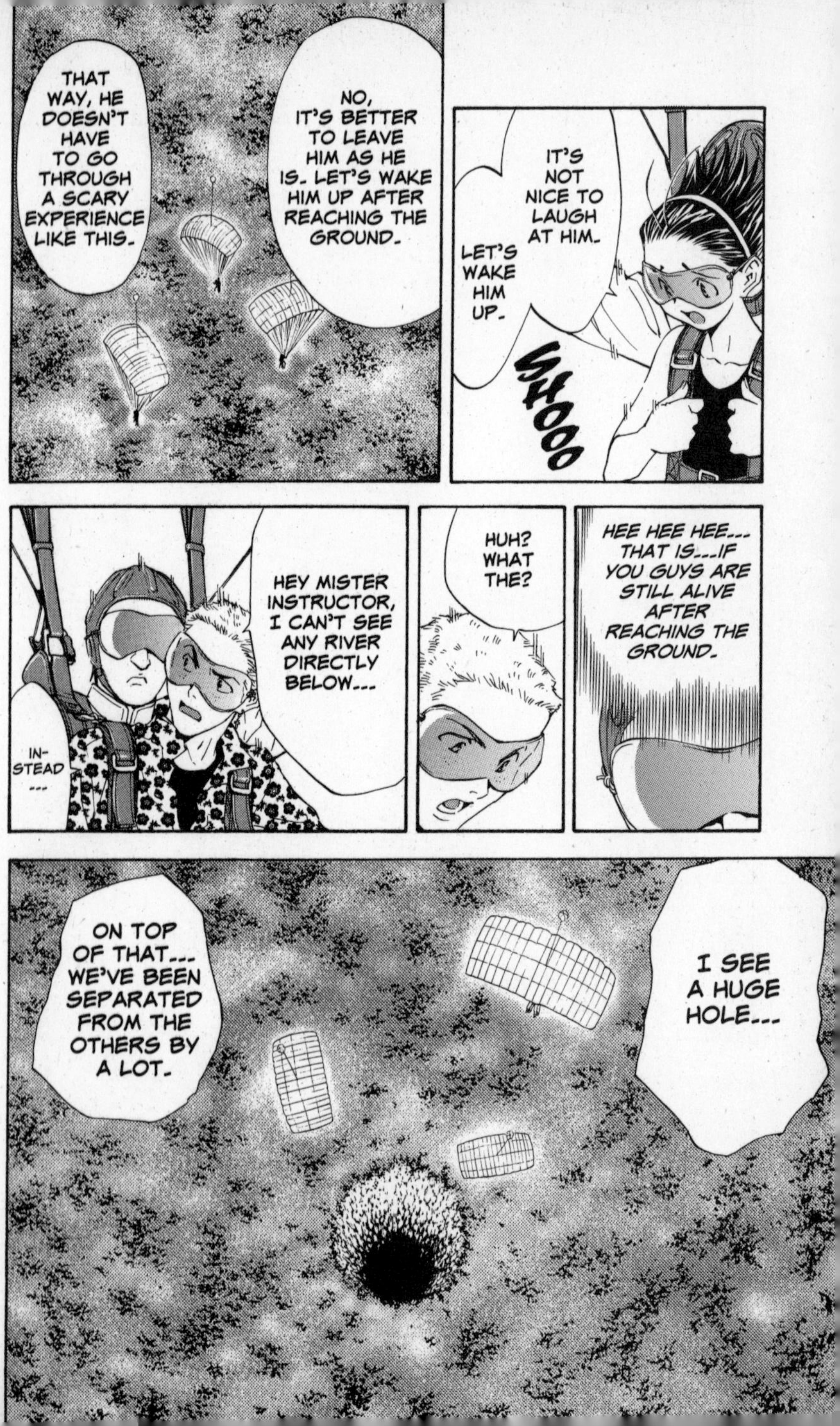
IT'S NOT NICE TO LAUGH AT HIM.
LET'S WAKE HIM UP.
SHOOO
NO, IT'S BETTER TO LEAVE HIM AS HE IS. LET'S WAKE HIM UP AFTER REACHING THE GROUND.
THAT WAY, HE DOESN'T HAVE TO GO THROUGH A SCARY EXPERIENCE LIKE THIS.
HEE HEE HEE... THAT IS...IF YOU GUYS ARE STILL ALIVE AFTER REACHING THE GROUND.
HUH? WHAT THE?
HEY MISTER INSTRUCTOR, I CAN'T SEE ANY RIVER DIRECTLY BELOW...
IN-STEAD...
I SEE A HUGE HOLE...
ON TOP OF THAT... WE'VE BEEN SEPARATED FROM THE OTHERS BY A LOT.

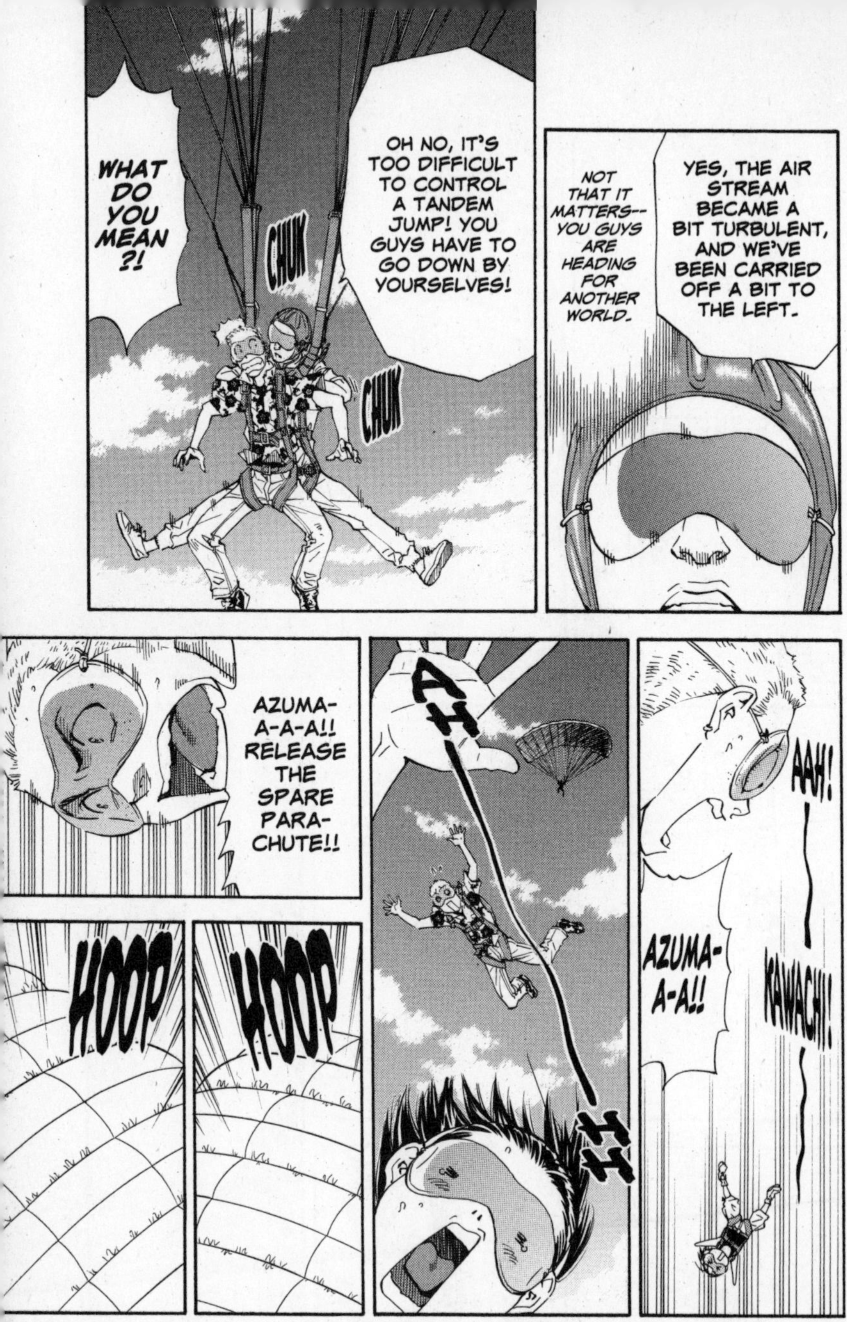
YES, THE AIR STREAM BECAME A BIT TURBULENT, AND WE'VE BEEN CARRIED OFF A BIT TO THE LEFT.
NOT THAT IT MATTERS-- YOU GUYS ARE HEADING FOR ANOTHER WORLD.
OH NO, IT'S TOO DIFFICULT TO CONTROL A TANDEM JUMP! YOU GUYS HAVE TO GO DOWN BY YOURSELVES!
CHUK
WHAT DO YOU MEAN?!
CHUK
AAH!
KAWACHI!
AZUMA-A-A!!
AH--!!
AZUMA-A-A-A!! RELEASE THE SPARE PARACHUTE!!
HOOP
HOOP

SIGH...

SHOO

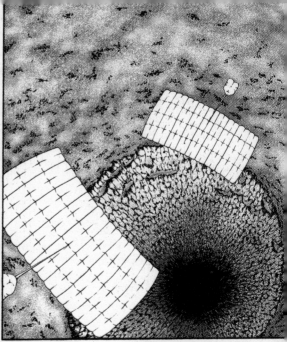

SHOOOO

SUWA-BARA!!!

SUWABARA IS STILL UNCON-SCIOUS!!!

HEY-Y-Y!!

WHAT ARE YOU DOING, KAWA-CHI?!

CHUK CHUK

36

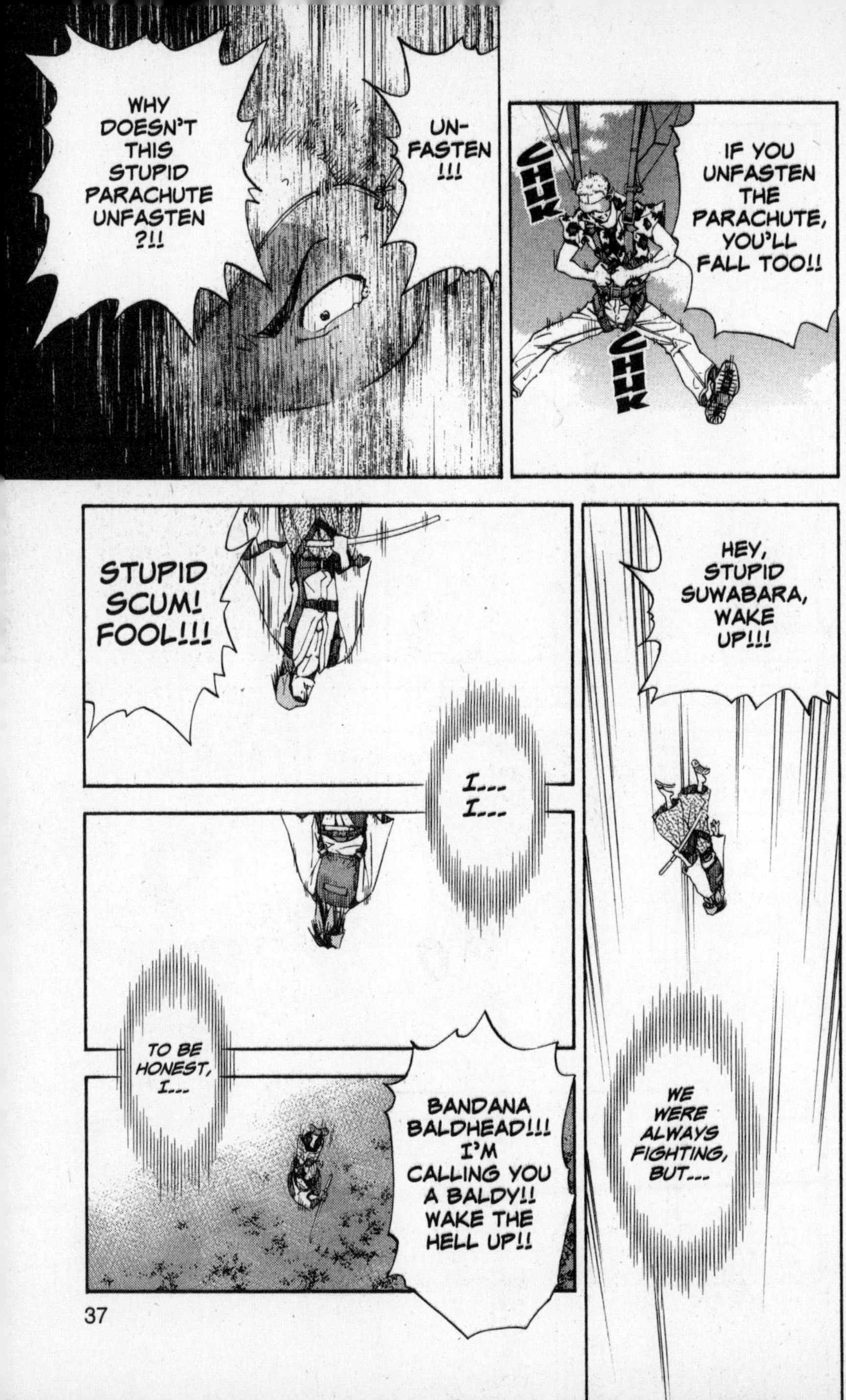
IF YOU UNFASTEN THE PARACHUTE, YOU'LL FALL TOO!!
CHUK
CHUK
UN-FASTEN!!!
WHY DOESN'T THIS STUPID PARACHUTE UNFASTEN?!!
HEY, STUPID SUWABARA, WAKE UP!!!
WE WERE ALWAYS FIGHTING, BUT...
STUPID SCUM! FOOL!!!
I... I...
TO BE HONEST, I...
BANDANA BALDHEAD!!! I'M CALLING YOU A BALDY!! WAKE THE HELL UP!!

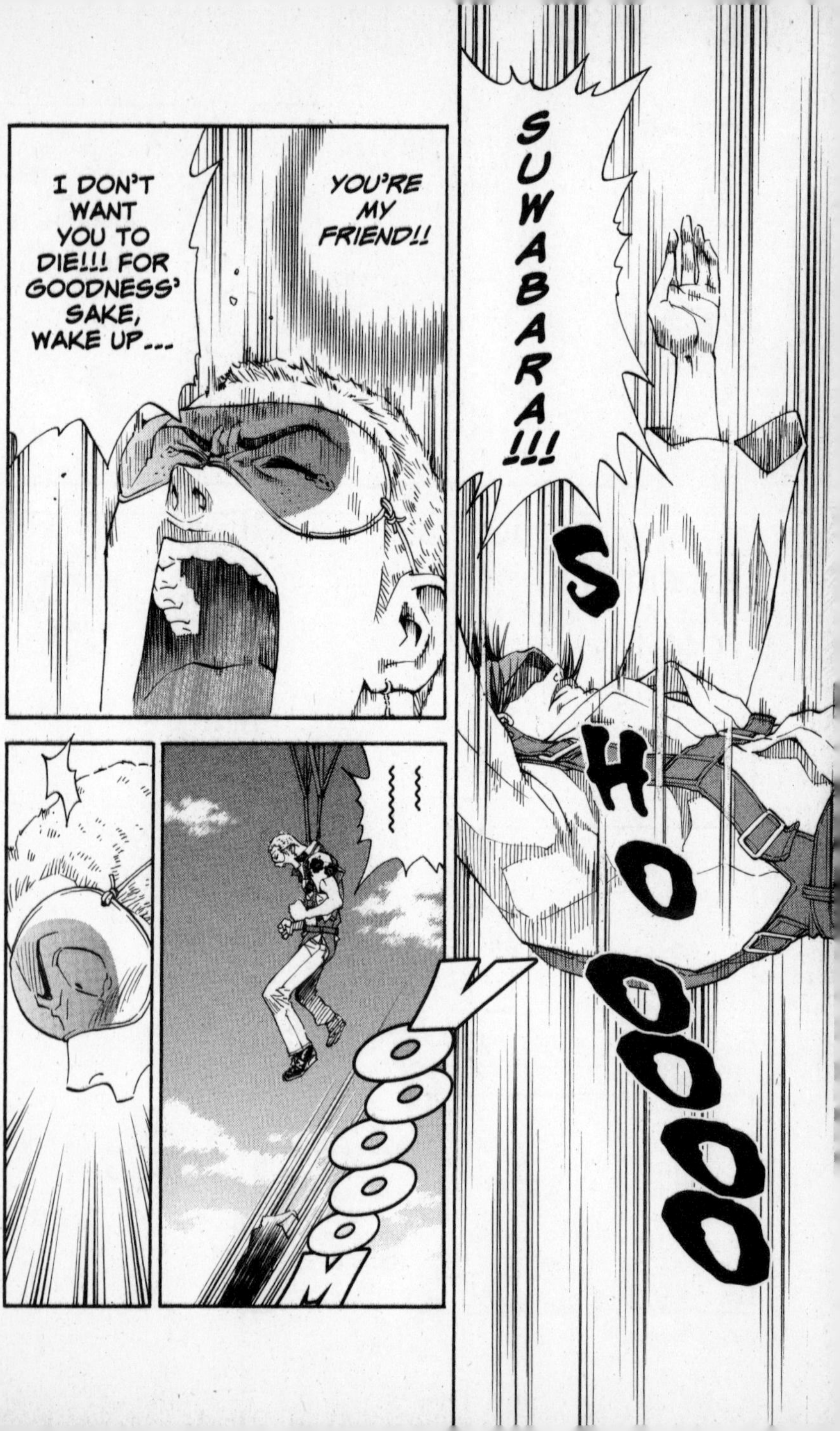
SUWABARA!!!
SHOOOOOO
YOU'RE MY FRIEND!!
I DON'T WANT YOU TO DIE!!! FOR GOODNESS' SAKE, WAKE UP...
VOOOOOOM

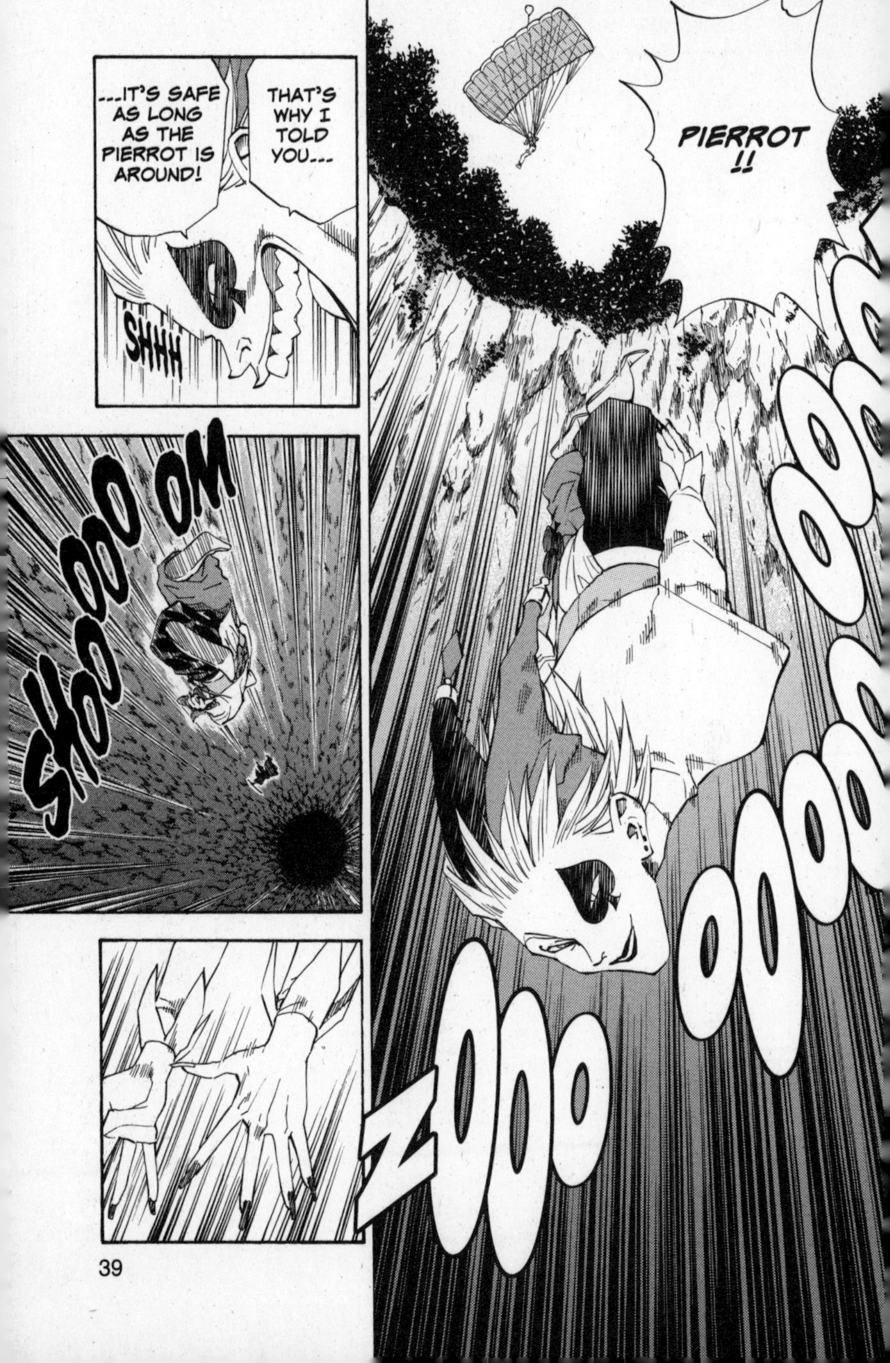
PIERROT !!
ZOOOOOOOOOOOOOOOO
THAT'S WHY I TOLD YOU...
...IT'S SAFE AS LONG AS THE PIERROT IS AROUND!
SHHH
SHOOOOOM

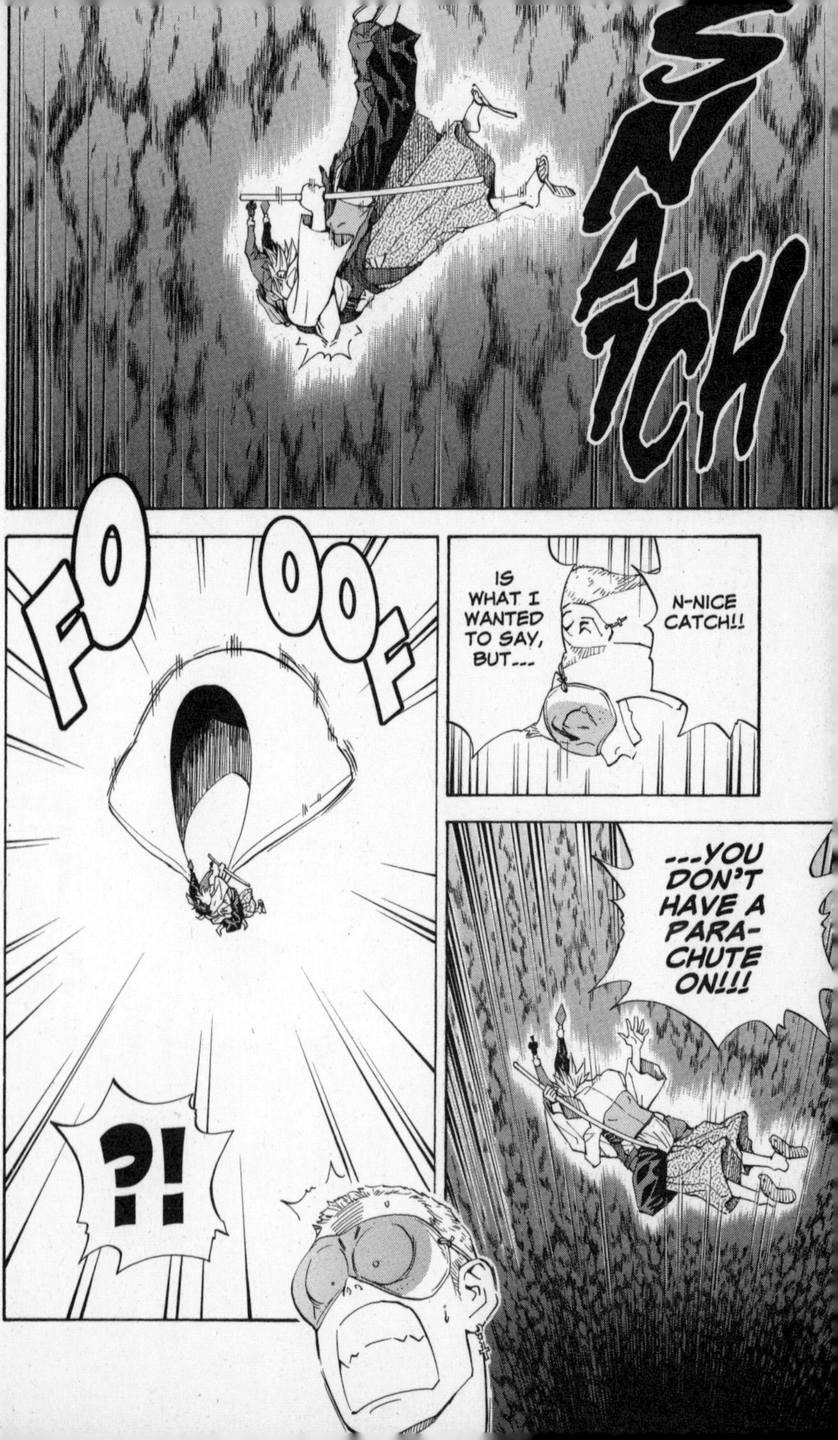
SNATCH
N-NICE CATCH!!
IS WHAT I WANTED TO SAY, BUT...
...YOU DON'T HAVE A PARA-CHUTE ON!!!
FOOOF
?!

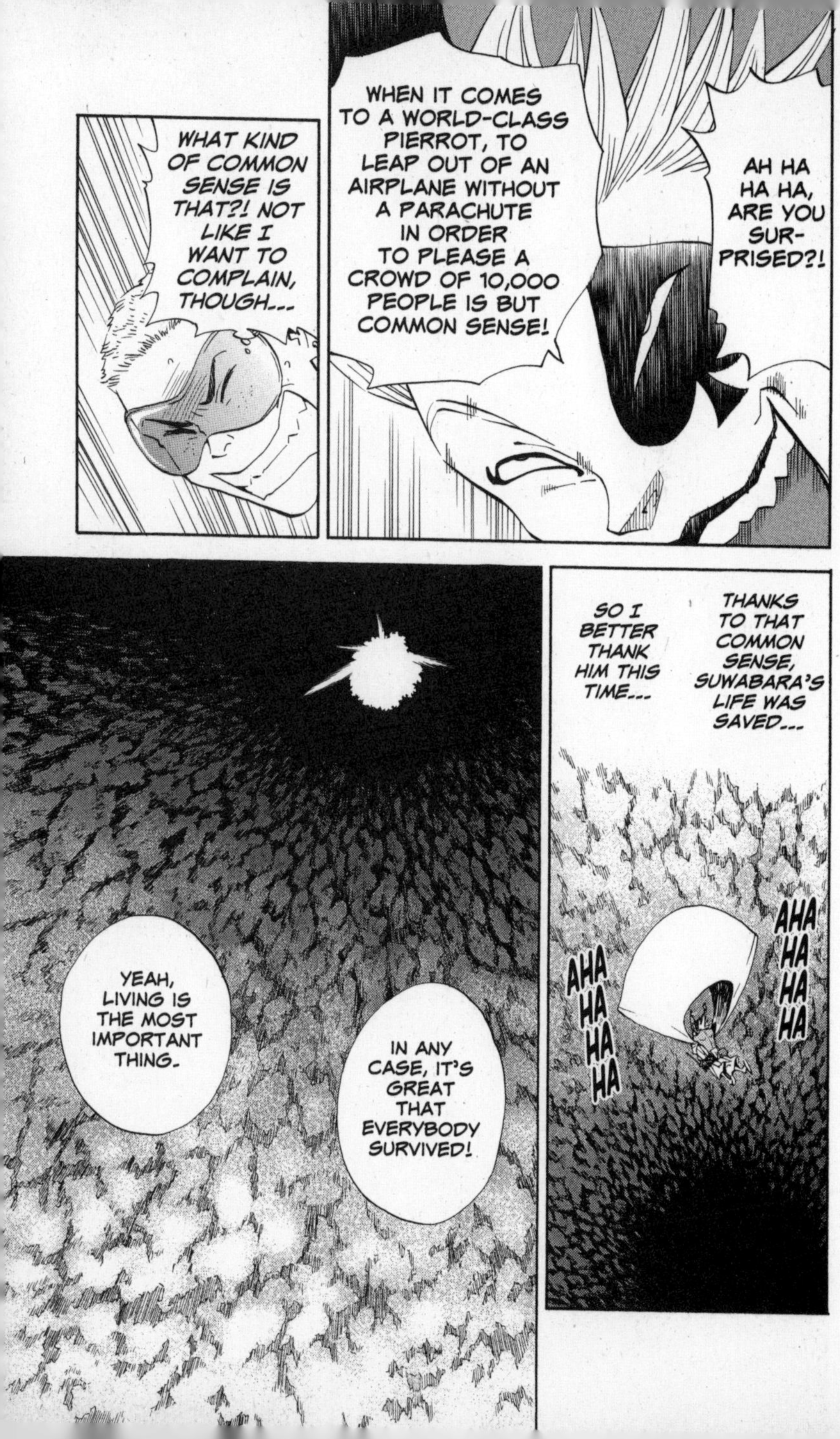
AH HA HA HA, ARE YOU SURPRISED?!
WHEN IT COMES TO A WORLD-CLASS PIERROT, TO LEAP OUT OF AN AIRPLANE WITHOUT A PARACHUTE IN ORDER TO PLEASE A CROWD OF 10,000 PEOPLE IS BUT COMMON SENSE!
WHAT KIND OF COMMON SENSE IS THAT?! NOT LIKE I WANT TO COMPLAIN, THOUGH...
THANKS TO THAT COMMON SENSE, SUWABARA'S LIFE WAS SAVED...
SO I BETTER THANK HIM THIS TIME...
AHA HA HA HA
AHA HA HA HA
IN ANY CASE, IT'S GREAT THAT EVERYBODY SURVIVED!
YEAH, LIVING IS THE MOST IMPORTANT THING.

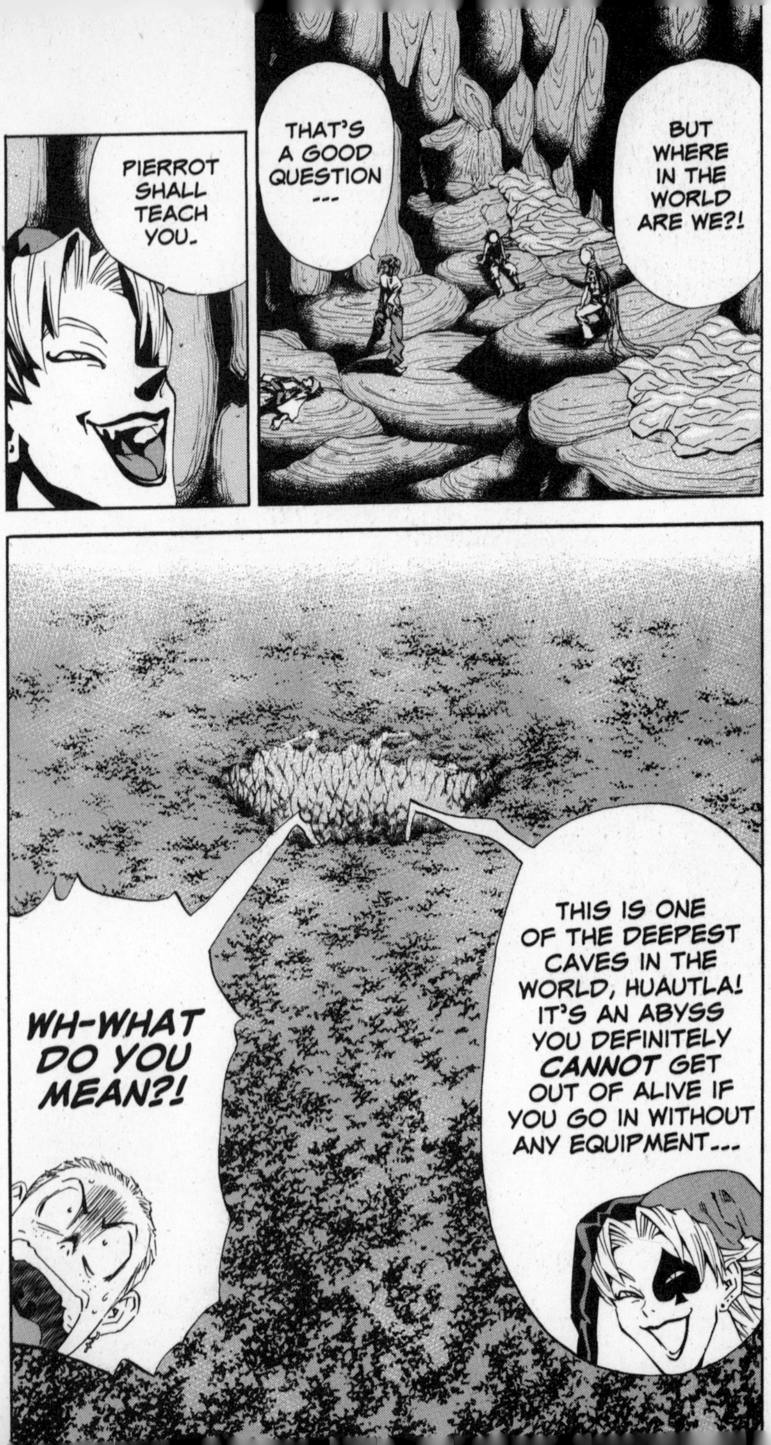
BUT WHERE IN THE WORLD ARE WE?!
THAT'S A GOOD QUESTION ---
PIERROT SHALL TEACH YOU.
THIS IS ONE OF THE DEEPEST CAVES IN THE WORLD, HUAUTLA! IT'S AN ABYSS YOU DEFINITELY CANNOT GET OUT OF ALIVE IF YOU GO IN WITHOUT ANY EQUIPMENT...
WH-WHAT DO YOU MEAN?!

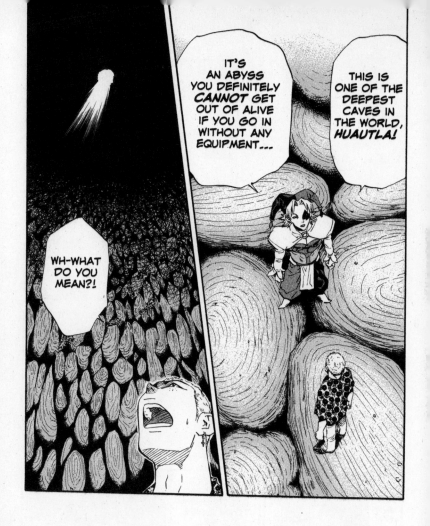

Story 80:

Nathalie ♪

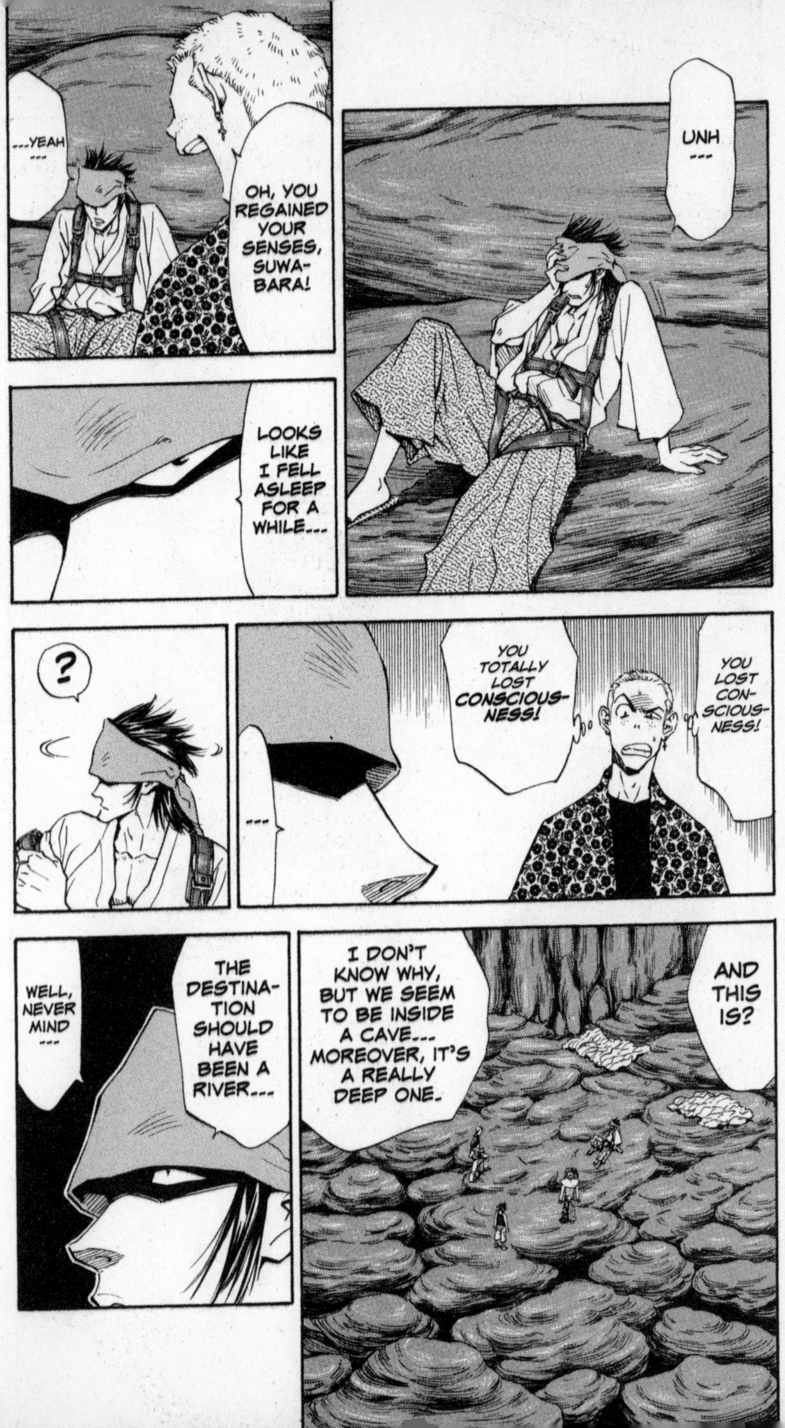
UNH ---
OH, YOU REGAINED YOUR SENSES, SUWA-BARA!
---YEAH ---
LOOKS LIKE I FELL ASLEEP FOR A WHILE---
YOU LOST CON-SCIOUS-NESS!
YOU TOTALLY LOST CONSCIOUS-NESS!

?
AND THIS IS?
I DON'T KNOW WHY, BUT WE SEEM TO BE INSIDE A CAVE--- MOREOVER, IT'S A REALLY DEEP ONE.
THE DESTINA-TION SHOULD HAVE BEEN A RIVER---
WELL, NEVER MIND ---

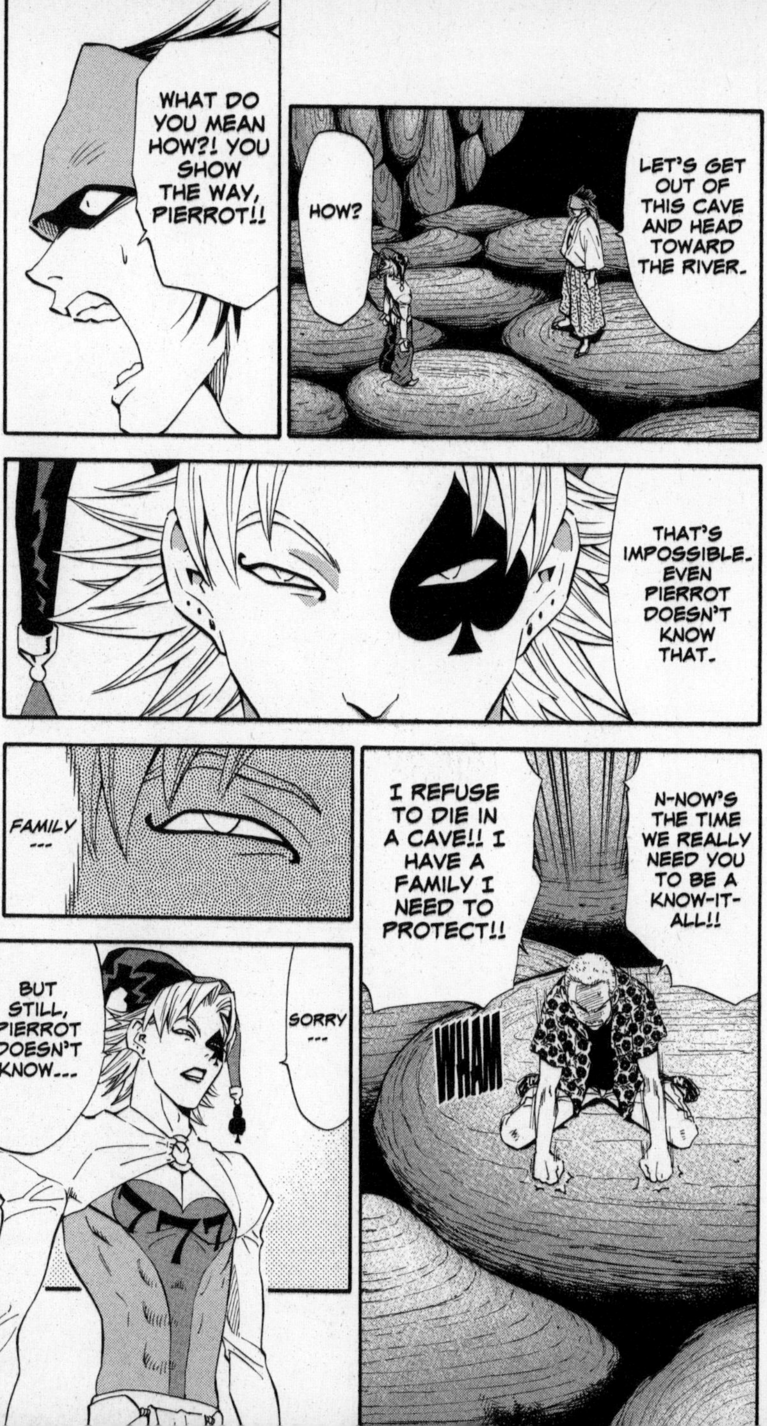
LET'S GET OUT OF THIS CAVE AND HEAD TOWARD THE RIVER.
HOW?
WHAT DO YOU MEAN HOW?! YOU SHOW THE WAY, PIERROT!!
THAT'S IMPOSSIBLE. EVEN PIERROT DOESN'T KNOW THAT.
N-NOW'S THE TIME WE REALLY NEED YOU TO BE A KNOW-IT-ALL!!
I REFUSE TO DIE IN A CAVE!! I HAVE A FAMILY I NEED TO PROTECT!!
WHAM
FAMILY...
SORRY...
BUT STILL, PIERROT DOESN'T KNOW...

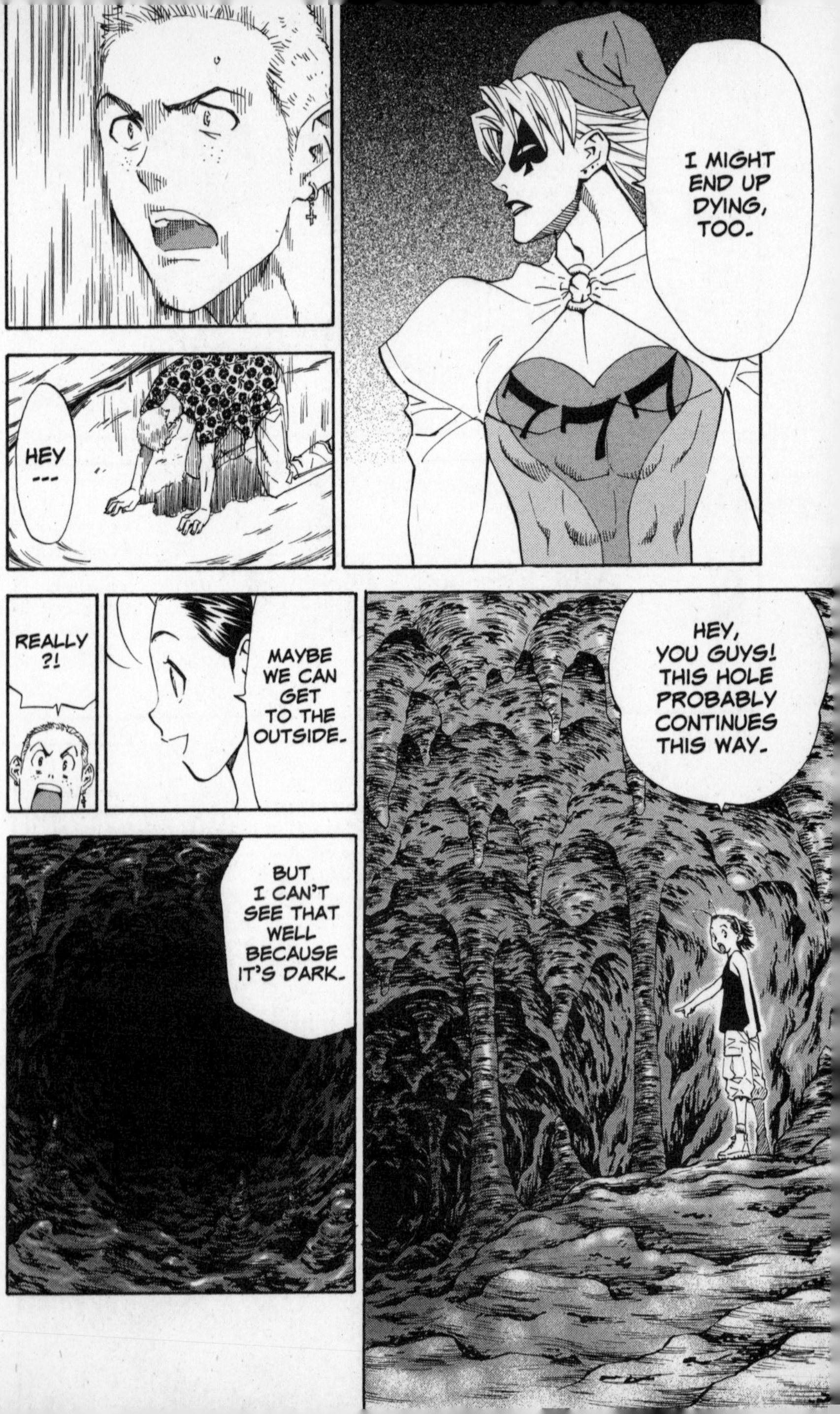
I MIGHT END UP DYING, TOO.
HEY ---
HEY, YOU GUYS! THIS HOLE PROBABLY CONTINUES THIS WAY.
MAYBE WE CAN GET TO THE OUTSIDE.
REALLY?!
BUT I CAN'T SEE THAT WELL BECAUSE IT'S DARK.

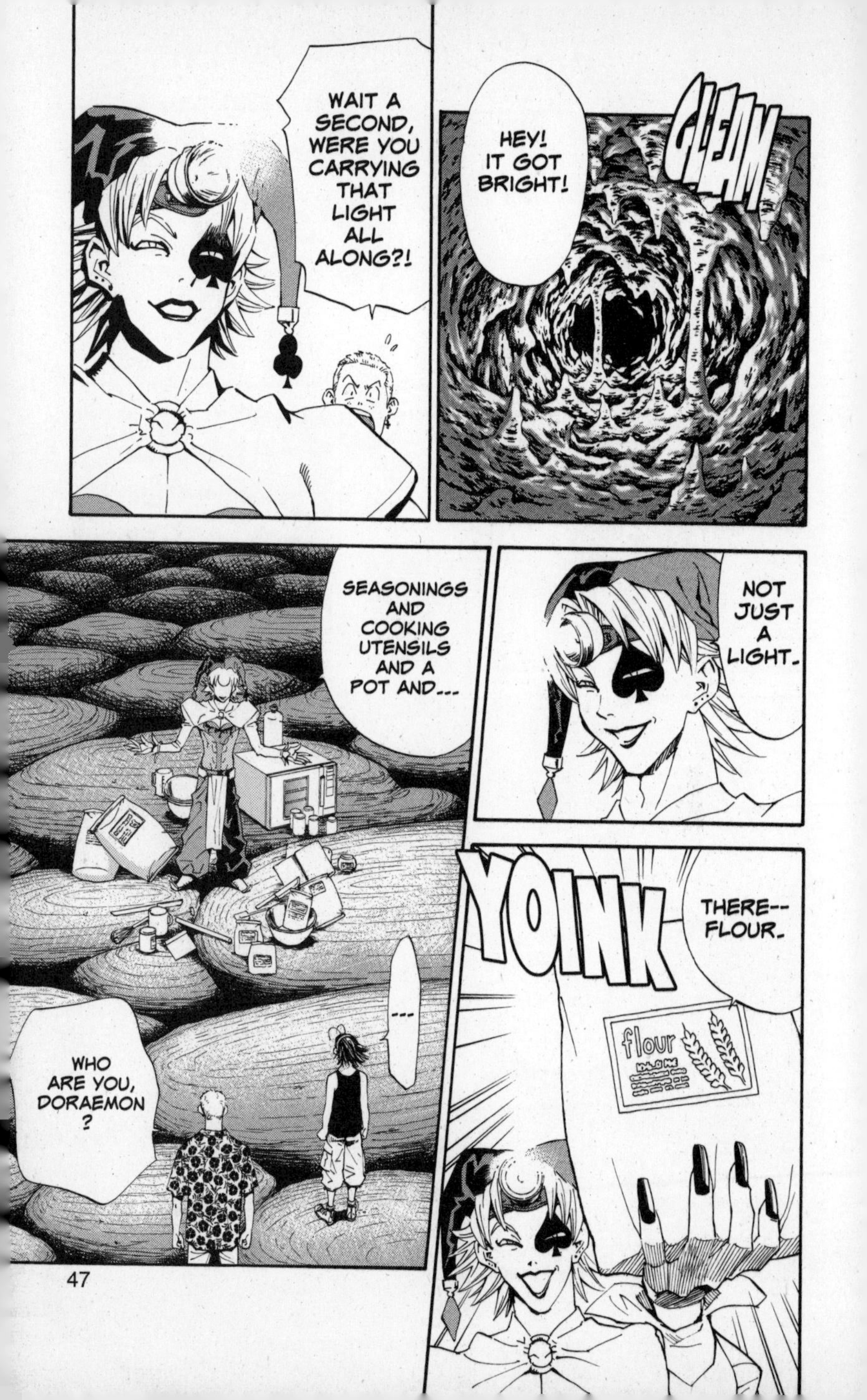
HEY! IT GOT BRIGHT!
GLEAM
WAIT A SECOND, WERE YOU CARRYING THAT LIGHT ALL ALONG?!
NOT JUST A LIGHT.
YOINK
THERE-- FLOUR.
flour
SEASONINGS AND COOKING UTENSILS AND A POT AND...
...
WHO ARE YOU, DORAEMON?

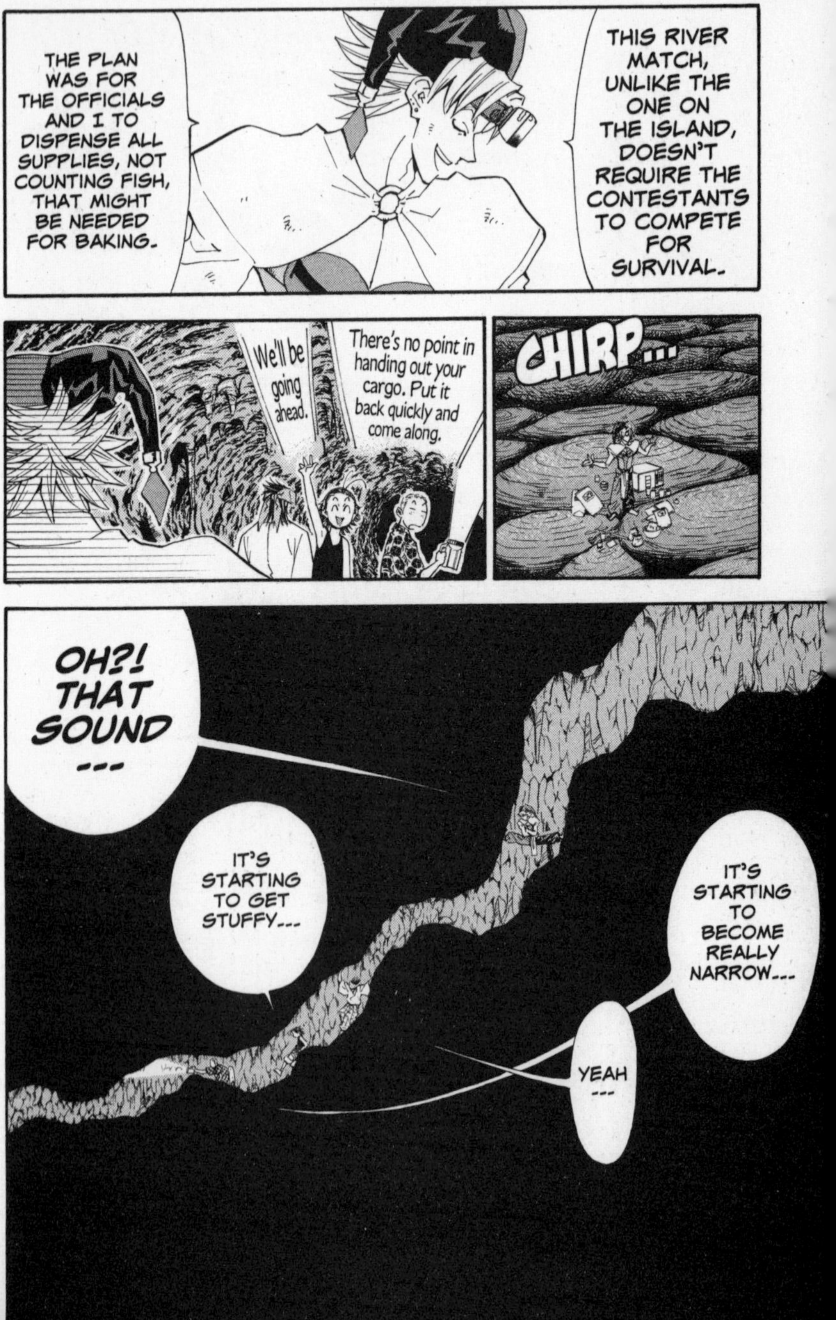
THIS RIVER MATCH, UNLIKE THE ONE ON THE ISLAND, DOESN'T REQUIRE THE CONTESTANTS TO COMPETE FOR SURVIVAL.
THE PLAN WAS FOR THE OFFICIALS AND I TO DISPENSE ALL SUPPLIES, NOT COUNTING FISH, THAT MIGHT BE NEEDED FOR BAKING.
CHIRP...
There's no point in handing out your cargo. Put it back quickly and come along.
We'll be going ahead.
OH?! THAT SOUND ---
IT'S STARTING TO BECOME REALLY NARROW---
IT'S STARTING TO GET STUFFY---
YEAH ---

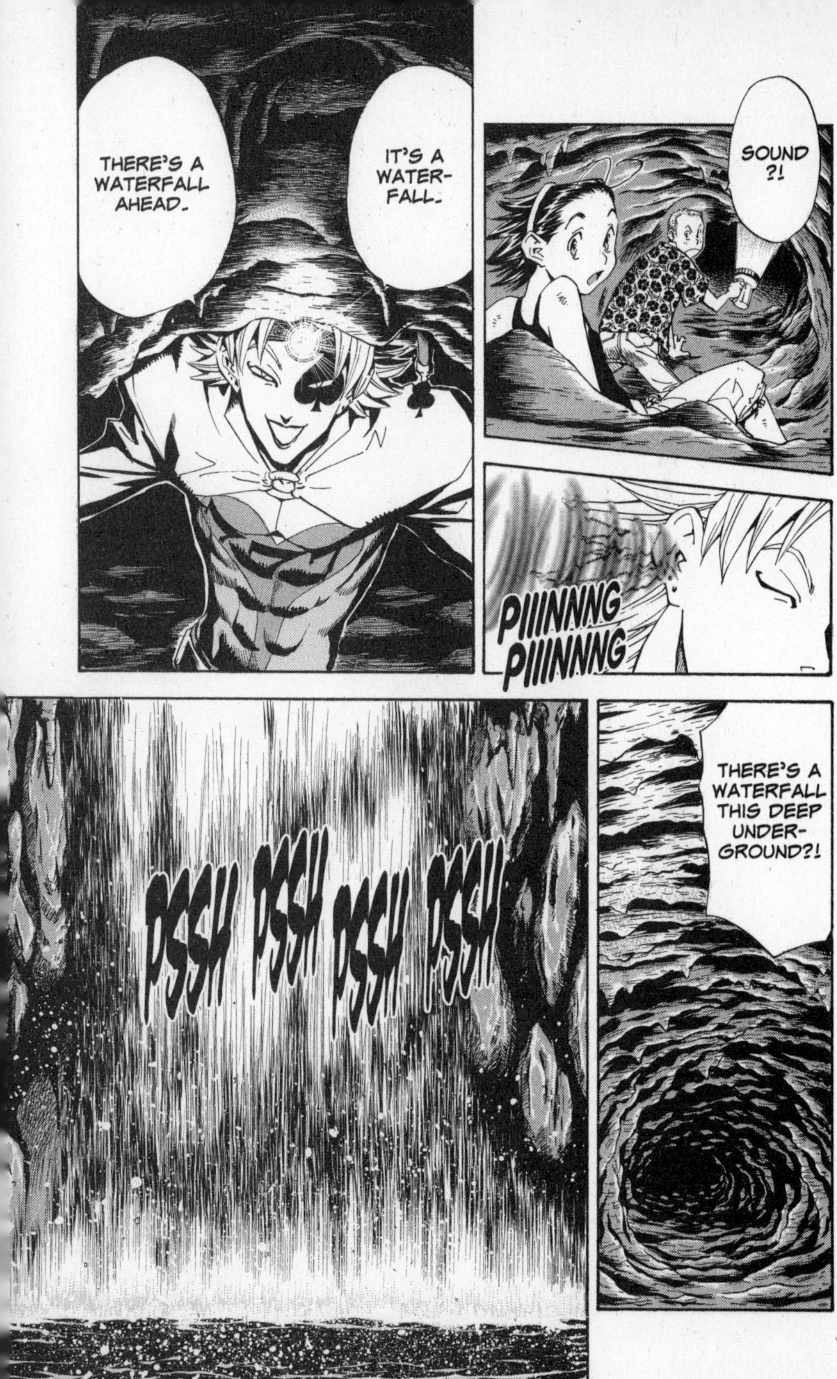
SOUND?!
PIIINNNG PIIINNNG
IT'S A WATER-FALL.
THERE'S A WATERFALL AHEAD.
THERE'S A WATERFALL THIS DEEP UNDER-GROUND?!
PSSH PSSH PSSH PSSH

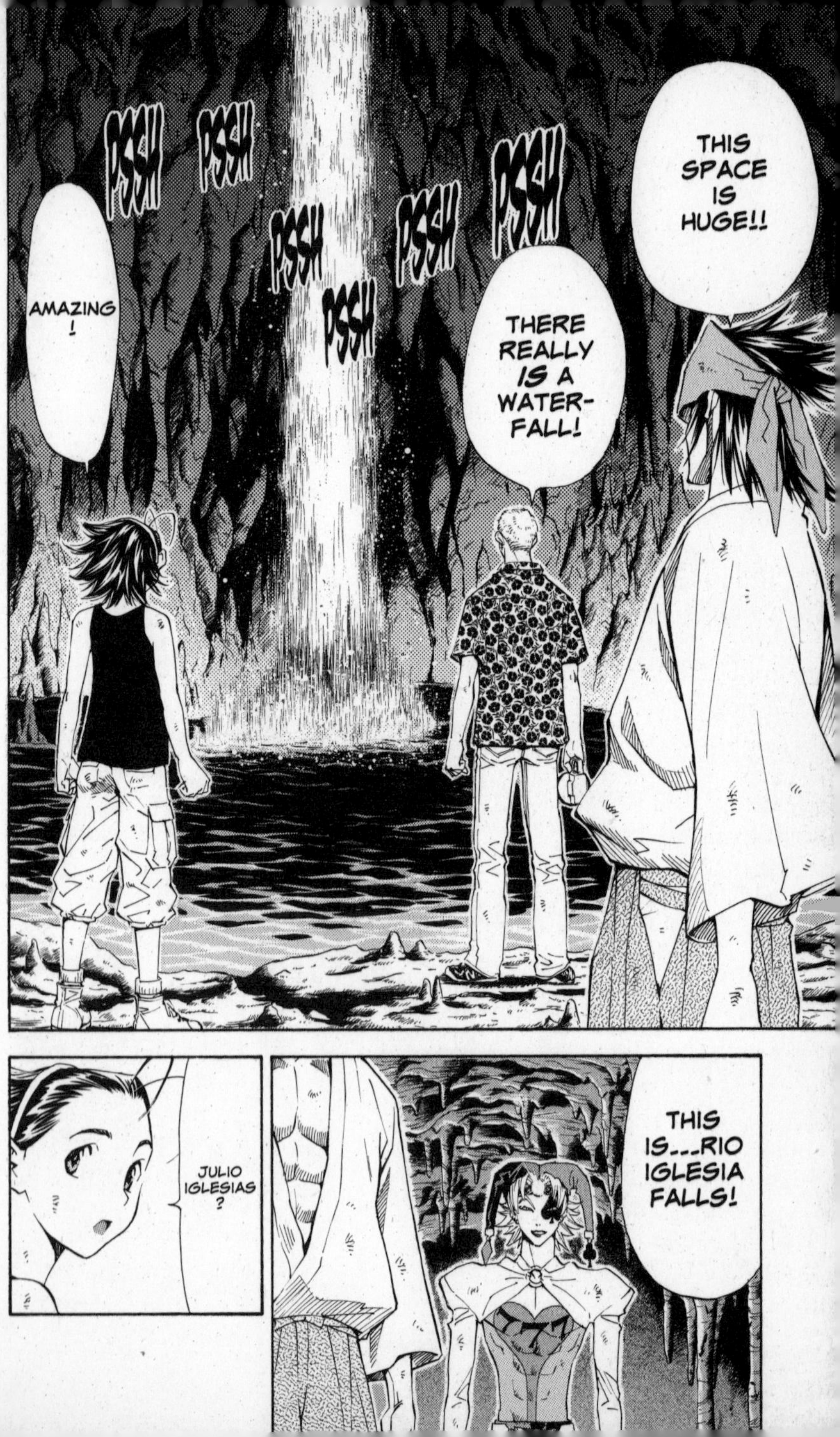
THIS SPACE IS HUGE!!
PSSH
PSSH
THERE REALLY IS A WATERFALL!
PSSH
PSSH
PSSH
PSSH
AMAZING!
THIS IS...RIO IGLESIA FALLS!
JULIO IGLESIAS?

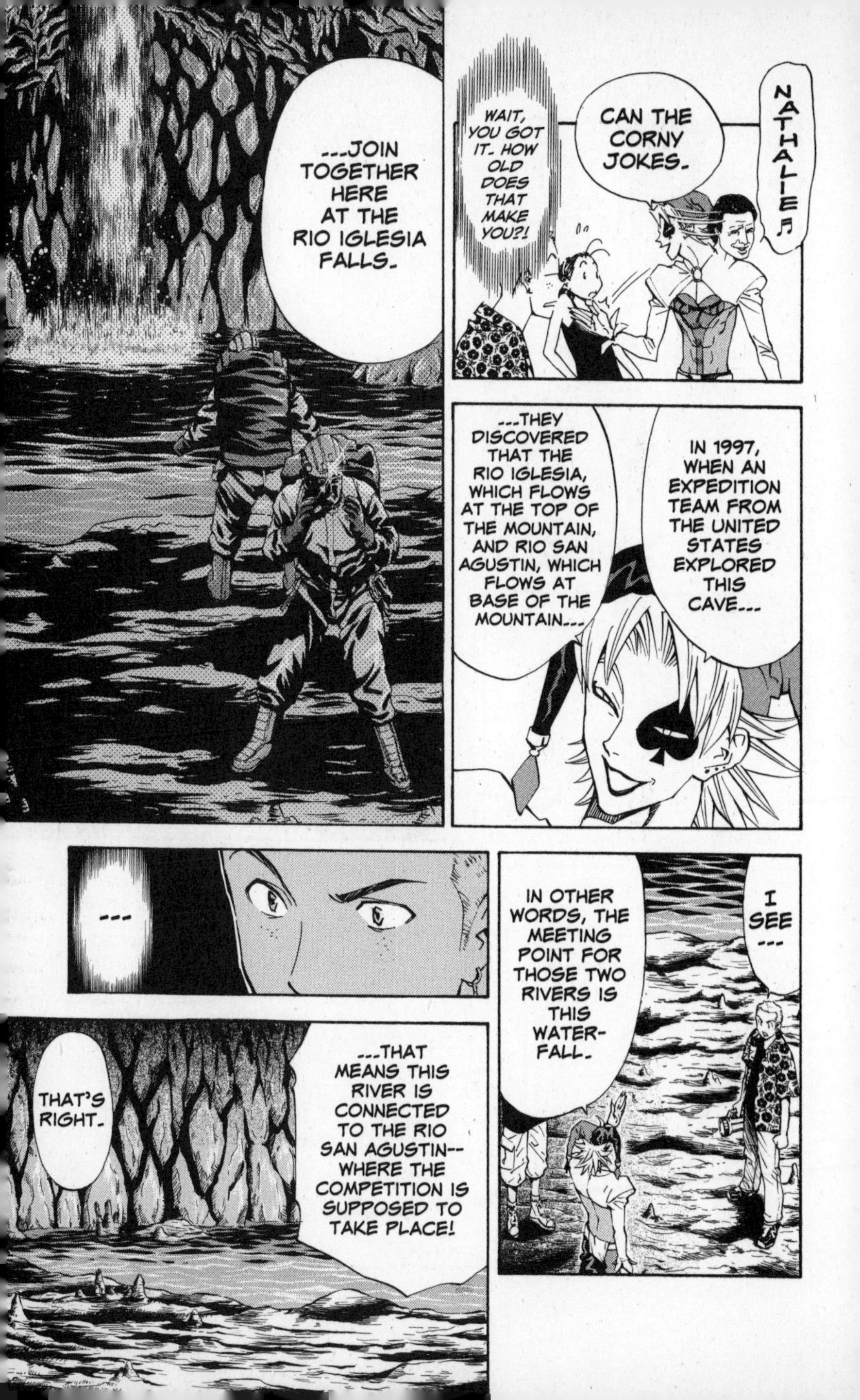

NATHALIE♪
CAN THE CORNY JOKES.
WAIT, YOU GOT IT. HOW OLD DOES THAT MAKE YOU?!
IN 1997, WHEN AN EXPEDITION TEAM FROM THE UNITED STATES EXPLORED THIS CAVE...
...THEY DISCOVERED THAT THE RIO IGLESIA, WHICH FLOWS AT THE TOP OF THE MOUNTAIN, AND RIO SAN AGUSTIN, WHICH FLOWS AT BASE OF THE MOUNTAIN...
...JOIN TOGETHER HERE AT THE RIO IGLESIA FALLS.
I SEE...
IN OTHER WORDS, THE MEETING POINT FOR THOSE TWO RIVERS IS THIS WATER-FALL.
...
...THAT MEANS THIS RIVER IS CONNECTED TO THE RIO SAN AGUSTIN--WHERE THE COMPETITION IS SUPPOSED TO TAKE PLACE!
THAT'S RIGHT.

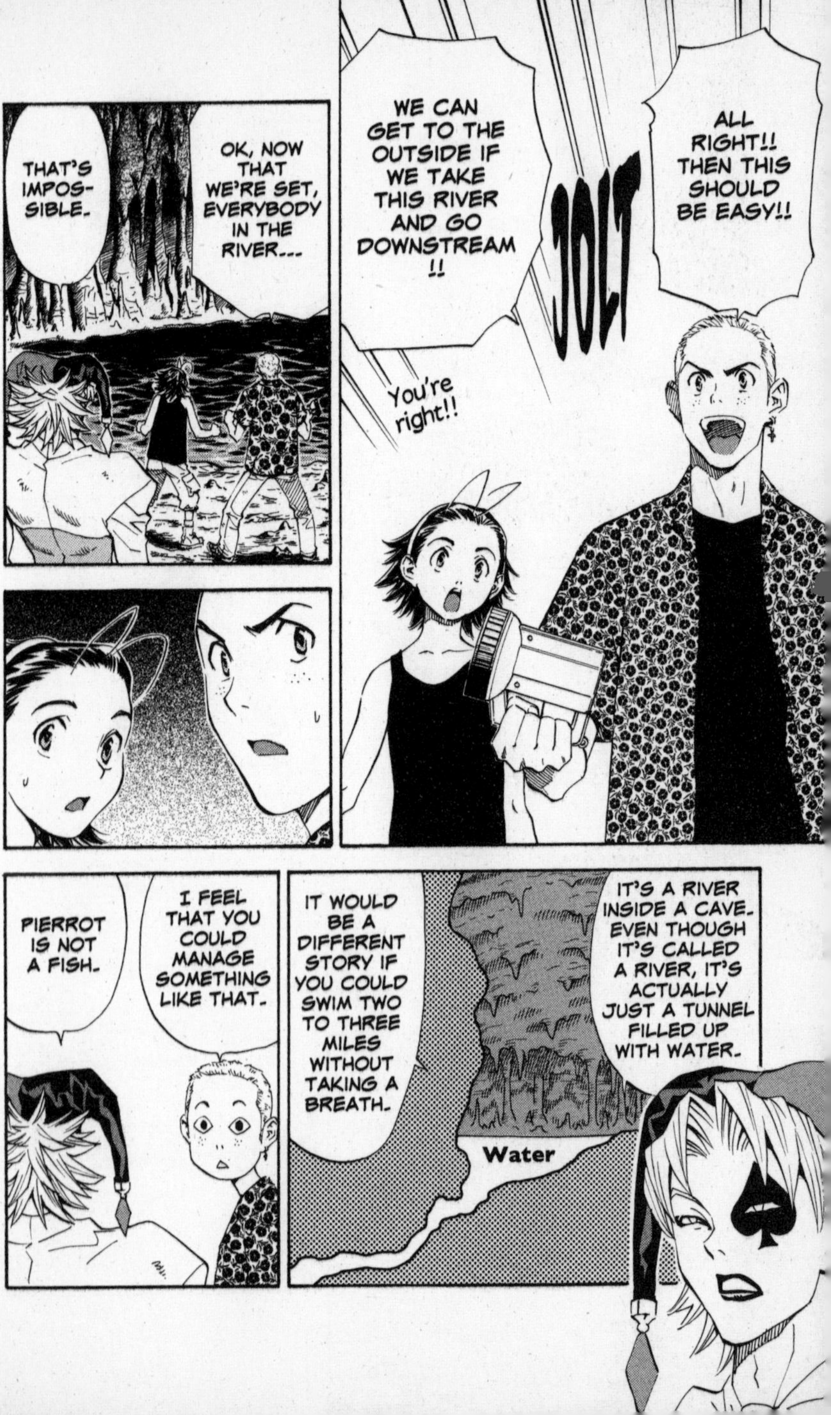
ALL RIGHT!! THEN THIS SHOULD BE EASY!!
JOLT
WE CAN GET TO THE OUTSIDE IF WE TAKE THIS RIVER AND GO DOWNSTREAM !!
You're right!!
OK, NOW THAT WE'RE SET, EVERYBODY IN THE RIVER...
THAT'S IMPOS-SIBLE.
IT'S A RIVER INSIDE A CAVE. EVEN THOUGH IT'S CALLED A RIVER, IT'S ACTUALLY JUST A TUNNEL FILLED UP WITH WATER.
Water
IT WOULD BE A DIFFERENT STORY IF YOU COULD SWIM TWO TO THREE MILES WITHOUT TAKING A BREATH.
I FEEL THAT YOU COULD MANAGE SOMETHING LIKE THAT.
PIERROT IS NOT A FISH.

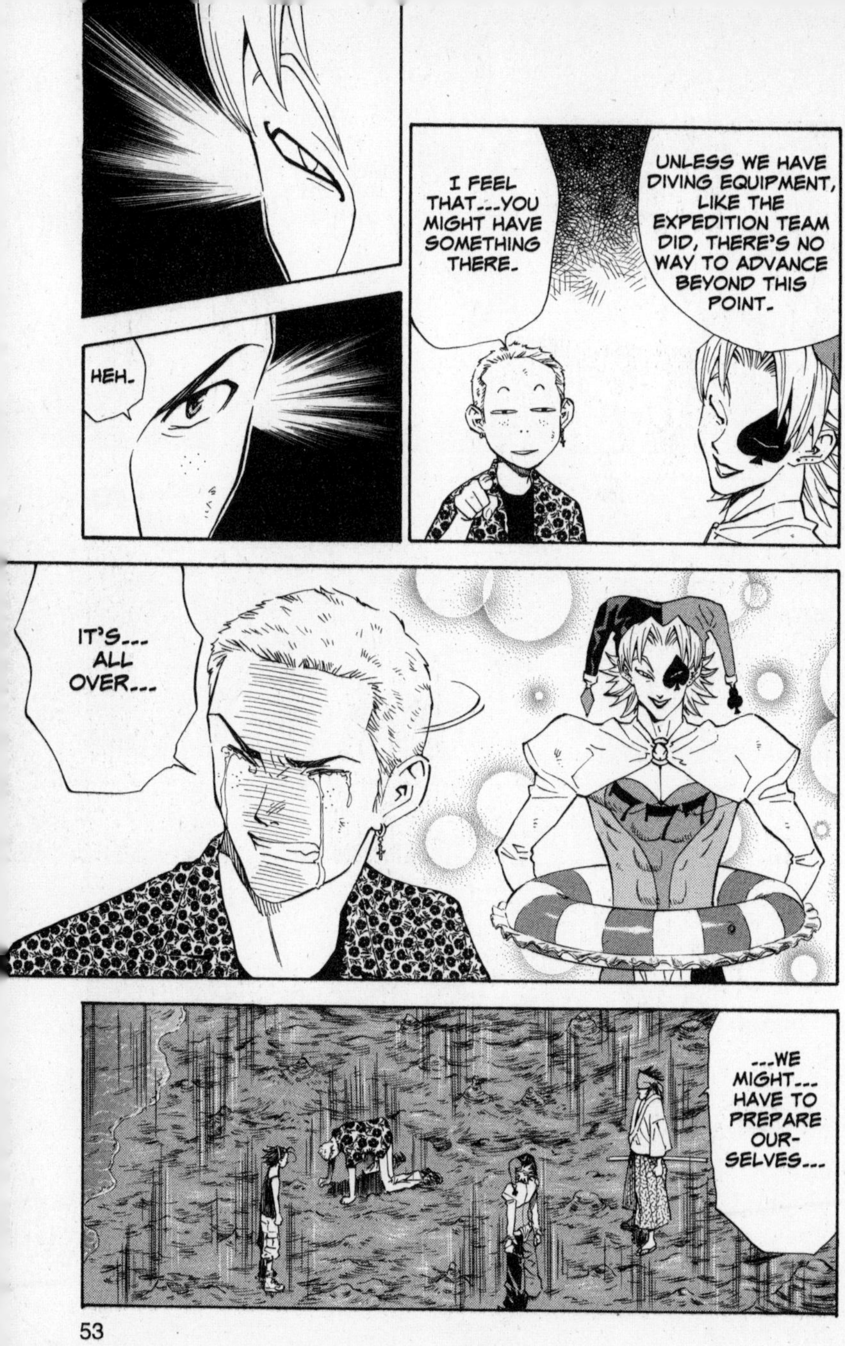
UNLESS WE HAVE DIVING EQUIPMENT, LIKE THE EXPEDITION TEAM DID, THERE'S NO WAY TO ADVANCE BEYOND THIS POINT.
I FEEL THAT...YOU MIGHT HAVE SOMETHING THERE.
HEH.
IT'S... ALL OVER...
...WE MIGHT... HAVE TO PREPARE OUR-SELVES...

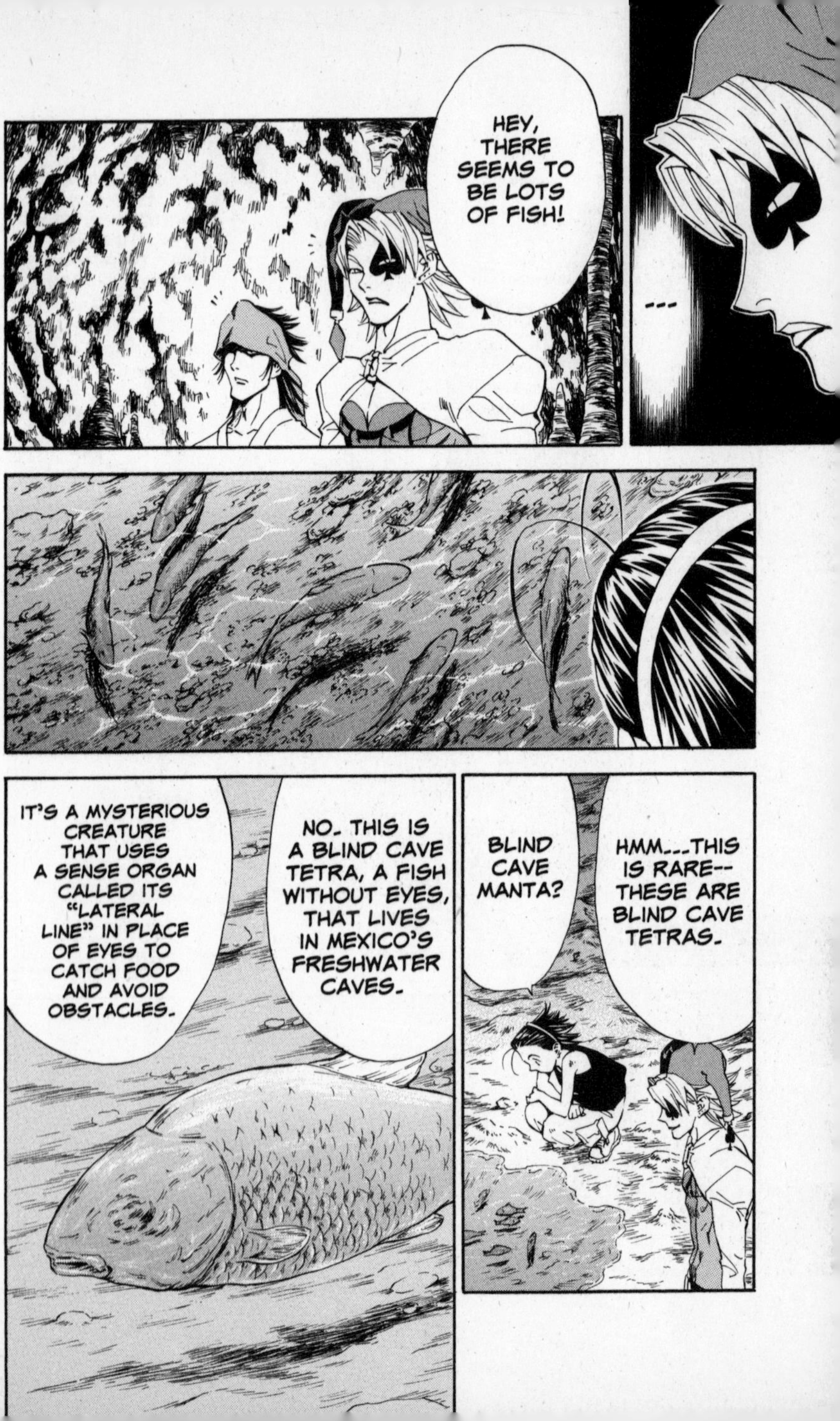
...
HEY, THERE SEEMS TO BE LOTS OF FISH!
HMM...THIS IS RARE-- THESE ARE BLIND CAVE TETRAS.
BLIND CAVE MANTA?
NO. THIS IS A BLIND CAVE TETRA, A FISH WITHOUT EYES, THAT LIVES IN MEXICO'S FRESHWATER CAVES.
IT'S A MYSTERIOUS CREATURE THAT USES A SENSE ORGAN CALLED ITS "LATERAL LINE" IN PLACE OF EYES TO CATCH FOOD AND AVOID OBSTACLES.

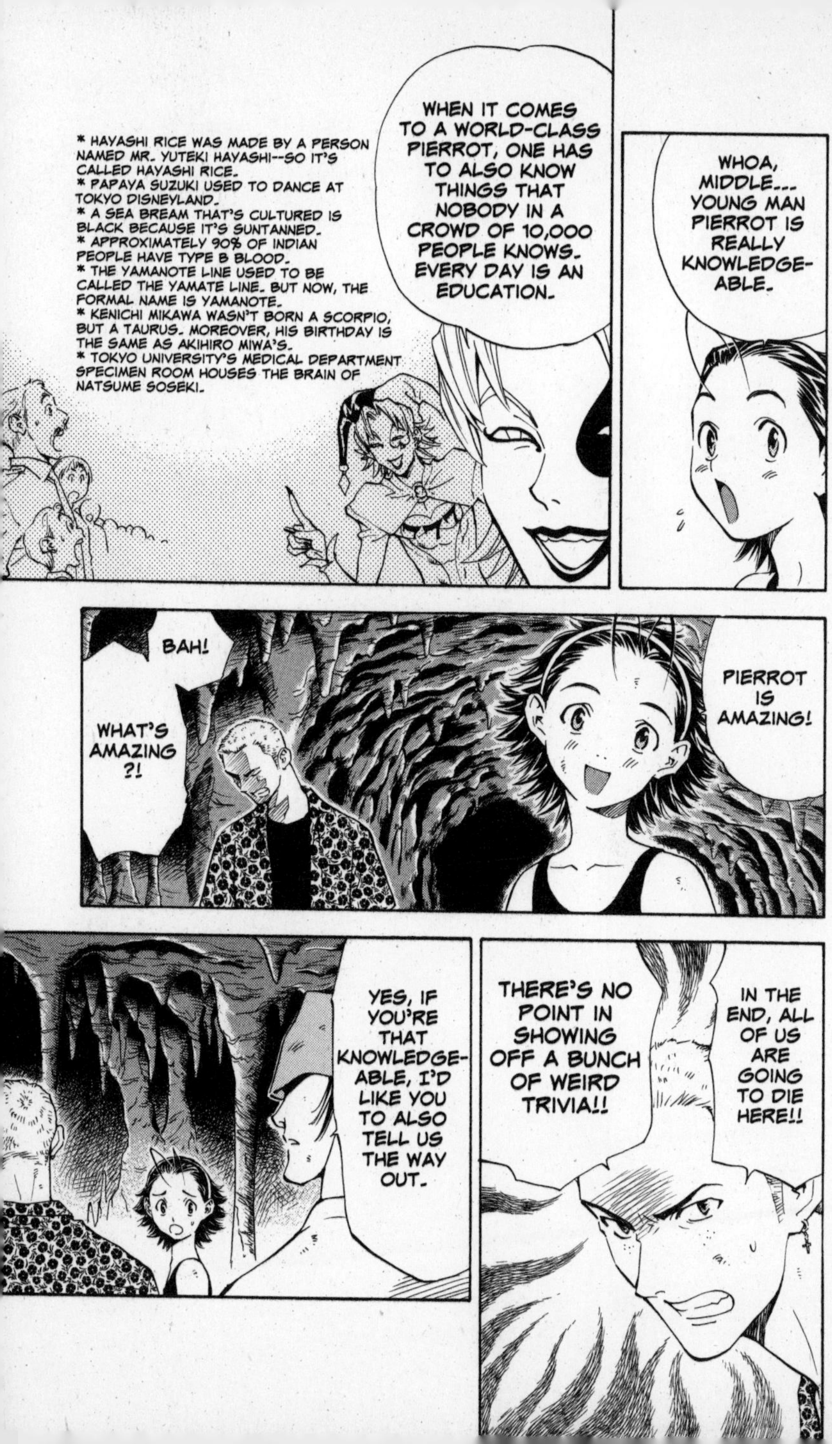
WHOA, MIDDLE... YOUNG MAN PIERROT IS REALLY KNOWLEDGE-ABLE.
WHEN IT COMES TO A WORLD-CLASS PIERROT, ONE HAS TO ALSO KNOW THINGS THAT NOBODY IN A CROWD OF 10,000 PEOPLE KNOWS. EVERY DAY IS AN EDUCATION.
* HAYASHI RICE WAS MADE BY A PERSON NAMED MR. YUTEKI HAYASHI--SO IT'S CALLED HAYASHI RICE.
* PAPAYA SUZUKI USED TO DANCE AT TOKYO DISNEYLAND.
* A SEA BREAM THAT'S CULTURED IS BLACK BECAUSE IT'S SUNTANNED.
* APPROXIMATELY 90% OF INDIAN PEOPLE HAVE TYPE B BLOOD.
* THE YAMANOTE LINE USED TO BE CALLED THE YAMATE LINE. BUT NOW, THE FORMAL NAME IS YAMANOTE.
* KENICHI MIKAWA WASN'T BORN A SCORPIO, BUT A TAURUS. MOREOVER, HIS BIRTHDAY IS THE SAME AS AKIHIRO MIWA'S.
* TOKYO UNIVERSITY'S MEDICAL DEPARTMENT SPECIMEN ROOM HOUSES THE BRAIN OF NATSUME SOSEKI.
PIERROT IS AMAZING!
BAH!
WHAT'S AMAZING ?!
IN THE END, ALL OF US ARE GOING TO DIE HERE!!
THERE'S NO POINT IN SHOWING OFF A BUNCH OF WEIRD TRIVIA!!
YES, IF YOU'RE THAT KNOWLEDGE-ABLE, I'D LIKE YOU TO ALSO TELL US THE WAY OUT.

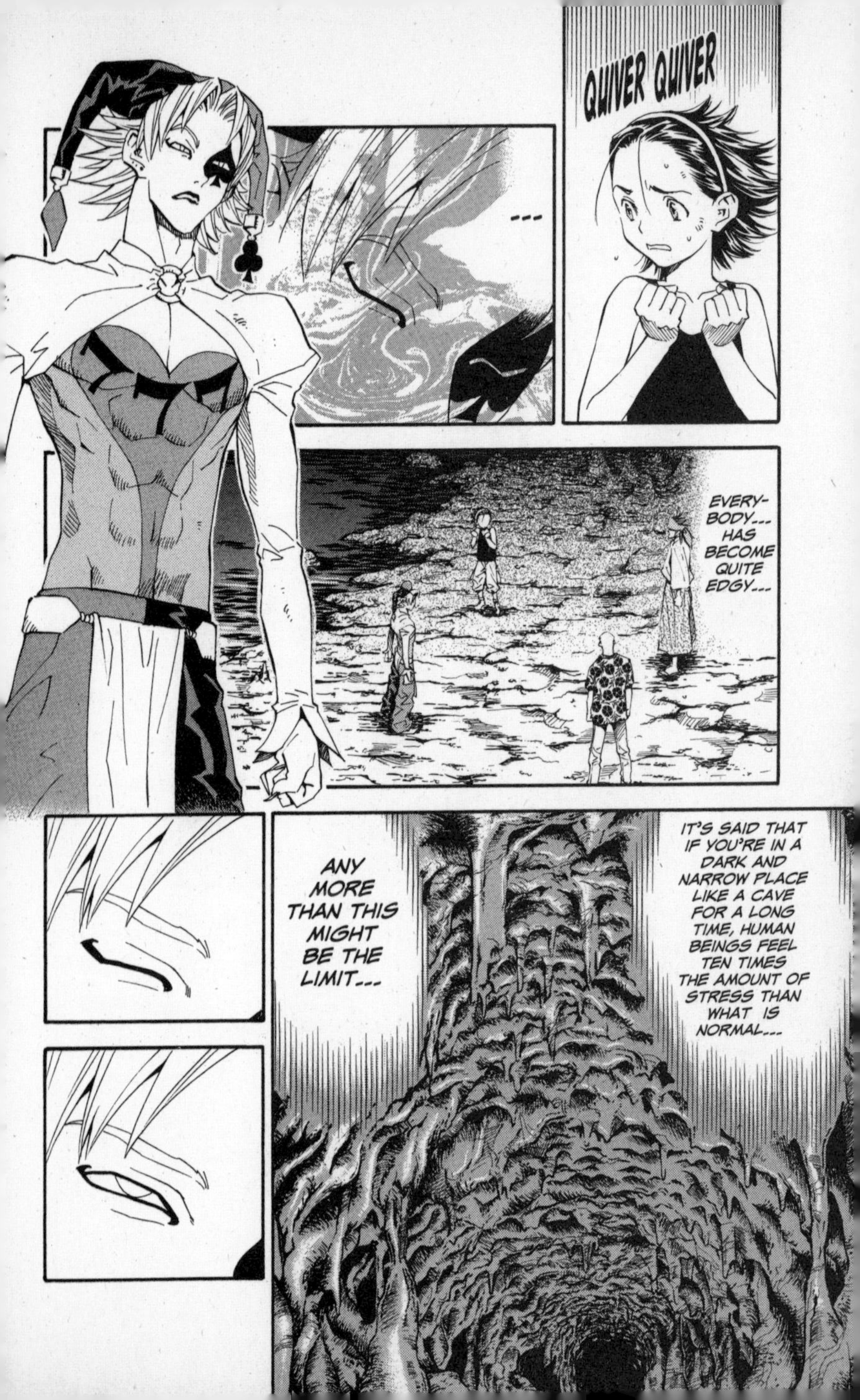
QUIVER QUIVER
...
EVERYBODY... HAS BECOME QUITE EDGY...
IT'S SAID THAT IF YOU'RE IN A DARK AND NARROW PLACE LIKE A CAVE FOR A LONG TIME, HUMAN BEINGS FEEL TEN TIMES THE AMOUNT OF STRESS THAN WHAT IS NORMAL...
ANY MORE THAN THIS MIGHT BE THE LIMIT...

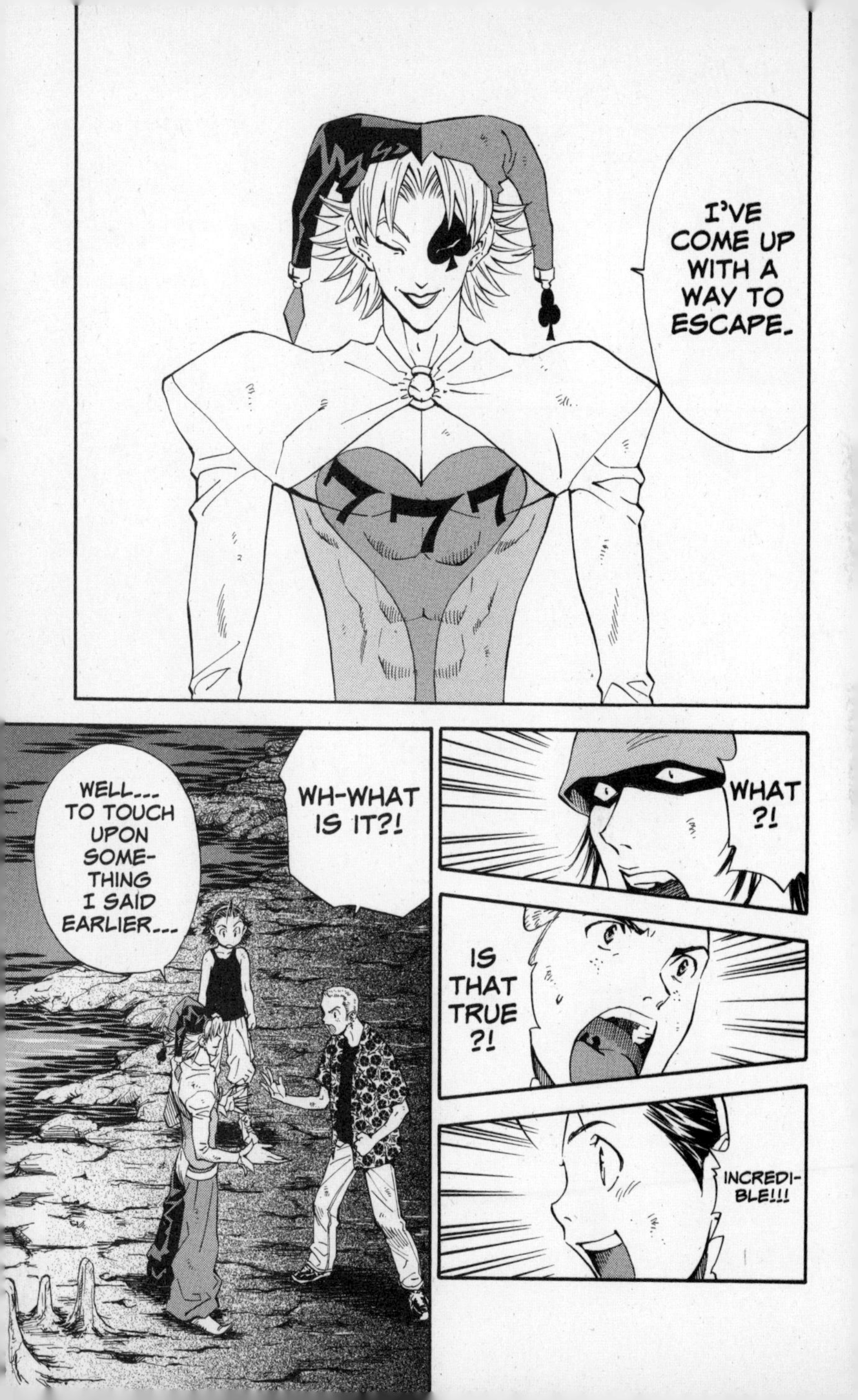
I'VE COME UP WITH A WAY TO ESCAPE.
WHAT ?!
IS THAT TRUE ?!
INCREDIBLE!!!
WH-WHAT IS IT?!
WELL... TO TOUCH UPON SOMETHING I SAID EARLIER...

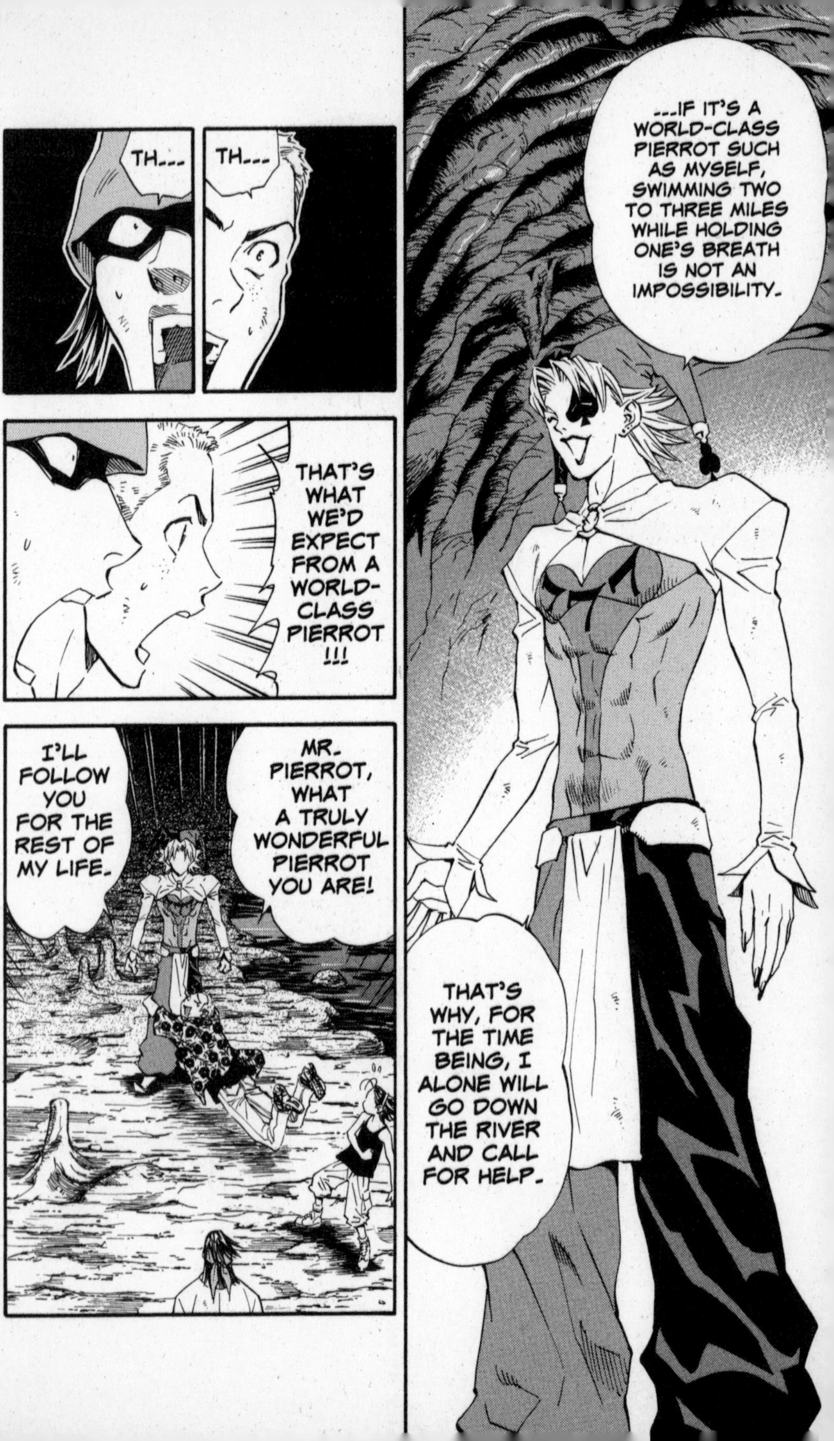
...IF IT'S A WORLD-CLASS PIERROT SUCH AS MYSELF, SWIMMING TWO TO THREE MILES WHILE HOLDING ONE'S BREATH IS NOT AN IMPOSSIBILITY.
THAT'S WHY, FOR THE TIME BEING, I ALONE WILL GO DOWN THE RIVER AND CALL FOR HELP.
TH...
TH...
THAT'S WHAT WE'D EXPECT FROM A WORLD-CLASS PIERROT!!!
MR. PIERROT, WHAT A TRULY WONDERFUL PIERROT YOU ARE!
I'LL FOLLOW YOU FOR THE REST OF MY LIFE.

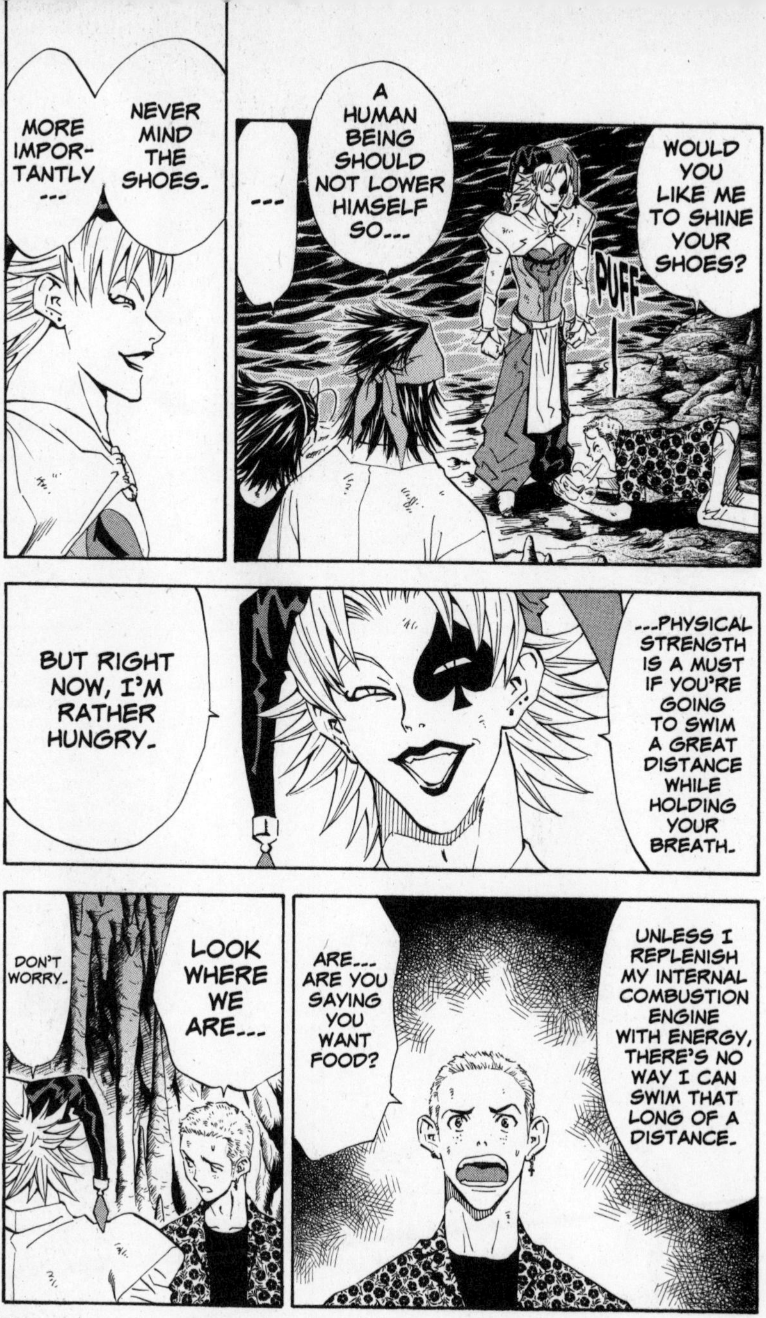

WOULD YOU LIKE ME TO SHINE YOUR SHOES?
PUFF
A HUMAN BEING SHOULD NOT LOWER HIMSELF SO...
...
NEVER MIND THE SHOES.
MORE IMPOR-TANTLY ...
...PHYSICAL STRENGTH IS A MUST IF YOU'RE GOING TO SWIM A GREAT DISTANCE WHILE HOLDING YOUR BREATH.
BUT RIGHT NOW, I'M RATHER HUNGRY.
UNLESS I REPLENISH MY INTERNAL COMBUSTION ENGINE WITH ENERGY, THERE'S NO WAY I CAN SWIM THAT LONG OF A DISTANCE.
ARE... ARE YOU SAYING YOU WANT FOOD?
LOOK WHERE WE ARE...
DON'T WORRY.

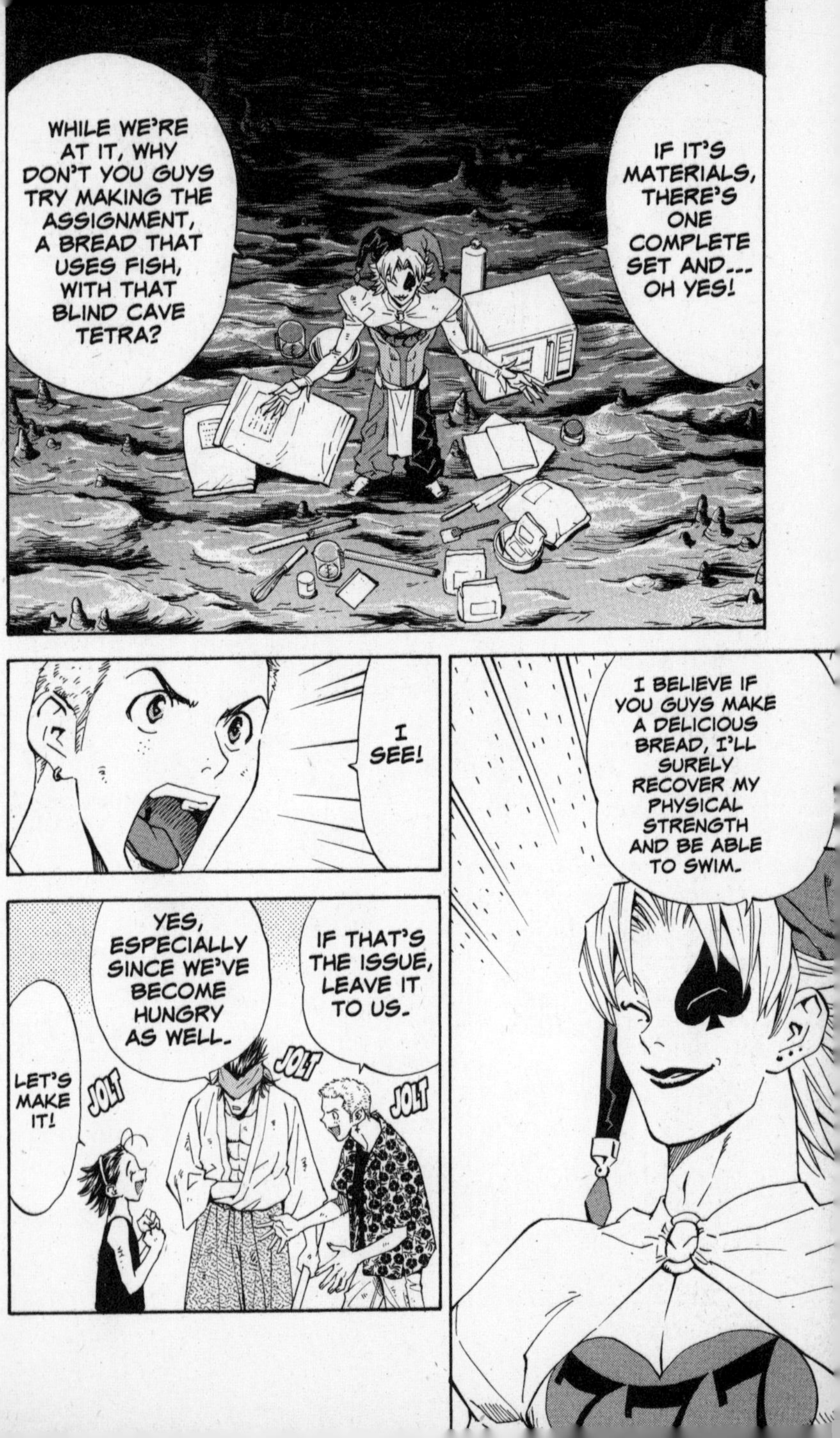
IF IT'S MATERIALS, THERE'S ONE COMPLETE SET AND... OH YES!
WHILE WE'RE AT IT, WHY DON'T YOU GUYS TRY MAKING THE ASSIGNMENT, A BREAD THAT USES FISH, WITH THAT BLIND CAVE TETRA?
I BELIEVE IF YOU GUYS MAKE A DELICIOUS BREAD, I'LL SURELY RECOVER MY PHYSICAL STRENGTH AND BE ABLE TO SWIM.
I SEE!
IF THAT'S THE ISSUE, LEAVE IT TO US.
JOLT
YES, ESPECIALLY SINCE WE'VE BECOME HUNGRY AS WELL.
JOLT
LET'S MAKE IT!
JOLT

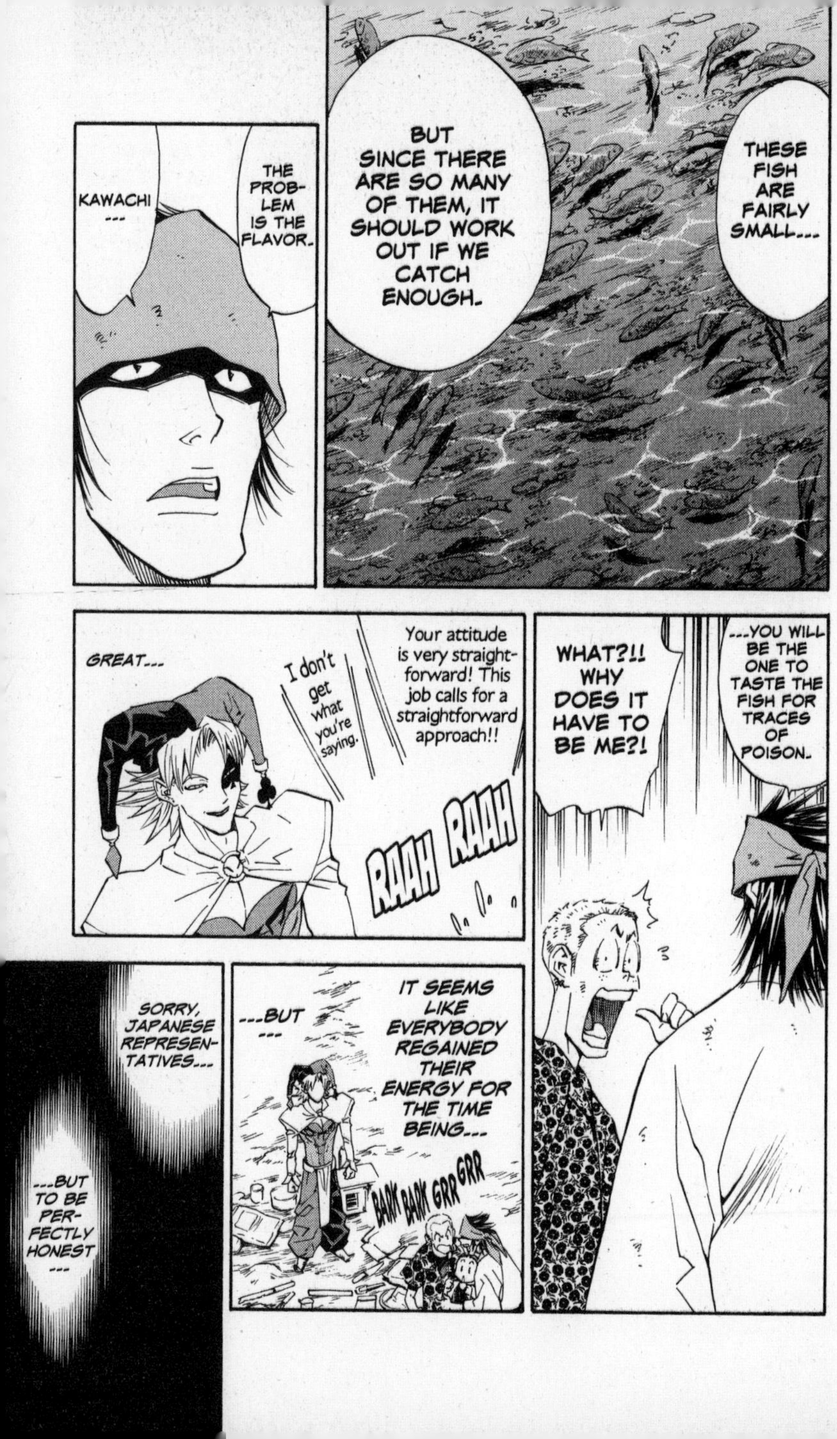
THESE FISH ARE FAIRLY SMALL...
BUT SINCE THERE ARE SO MANY OF THEM, IT SHOULD WORK OUT IF WE CATCH ENOUGH.
THE PROB-LEM IS THE FLAVOR.
KAWACHI...
...YOU WILL BE THE ONE TO TASTE THE FISH FOR TRACES OF POISON.
WHAT?!! WHY DOES IT HAVE TO BE ME?!
Your attitude is very straight-forward! This job calls for a straightforward approach!!
I don't get what you're saying.
RAAH RAAH
GREAT...
IT SEEMS LIKE EVERYBODY REGAINED THEIR ENERGY FOR THE TIME BEING...
...BUT...
BARK BARK GRR GRR
SORRY, JAPANESE REPRESEN-TATIVES...
...BUT TO BE PER-FECTLY HONEST...

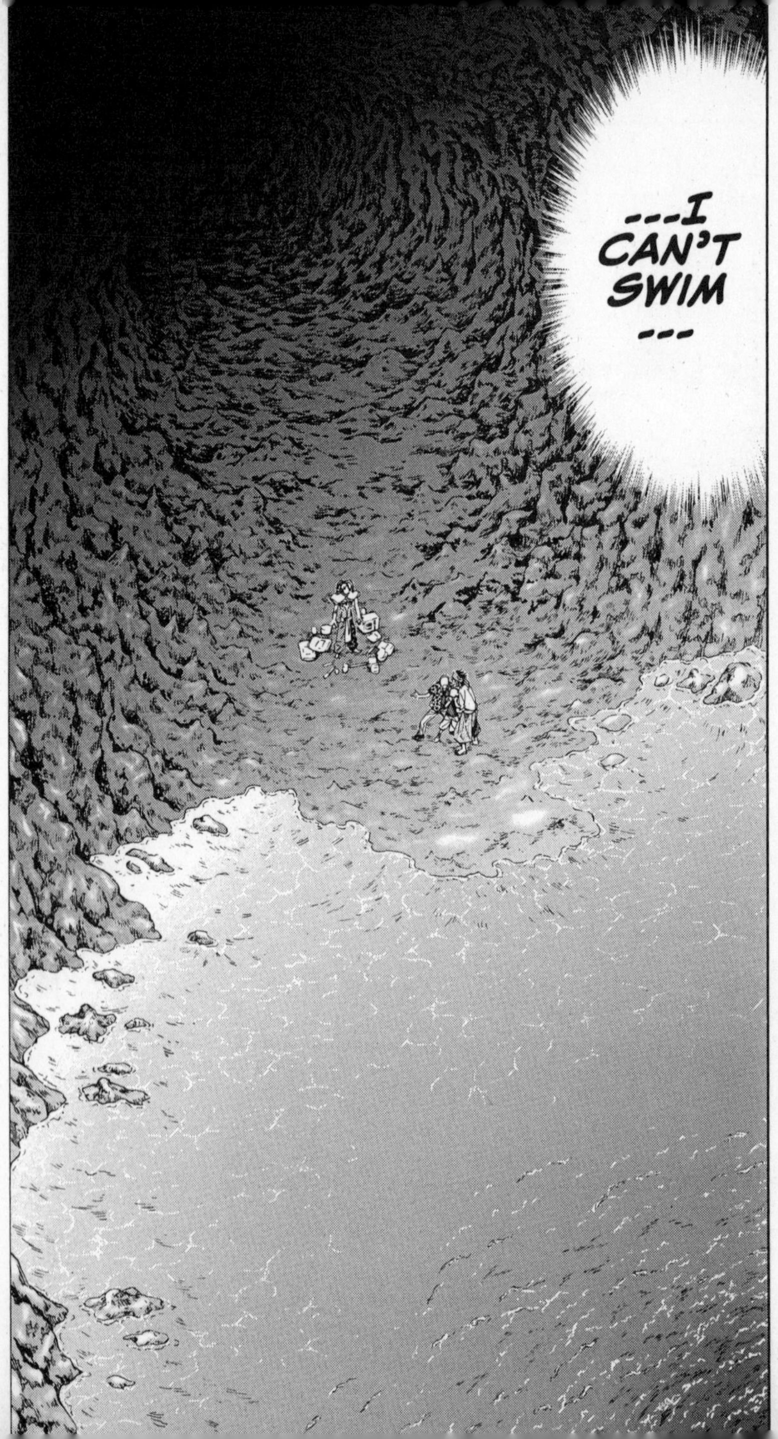
---I CAN'T SWIM ---

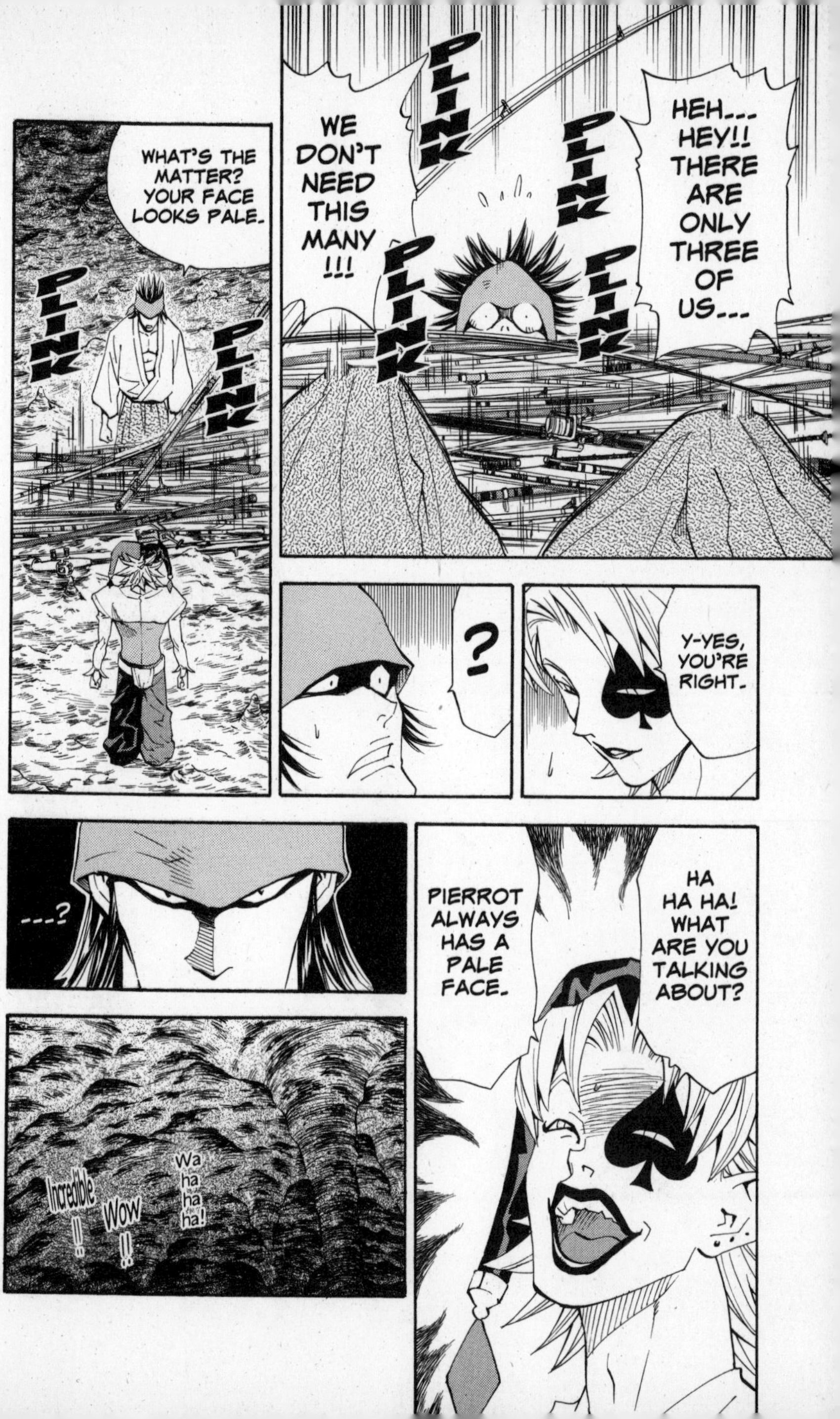
HEH... HEY!! THERE ARE ONLY THREE OF US...
PLINK
PLINK
PLINK
PLINK
WE DON'T NEED THIS MANY!!!
Y-YES, YOU'RE RIGHT.
?
WHAT'S THE MATTER? YOUR FACE LOOKS PALE.
PLINK
PLINK
HA HA HA! WHAT ARE YOU TALKING ABOUT?
PIERROT ALWAYS HAS A PALE FACE.
...?
Wa ha ha ha!
Wow!!
Incredible!!

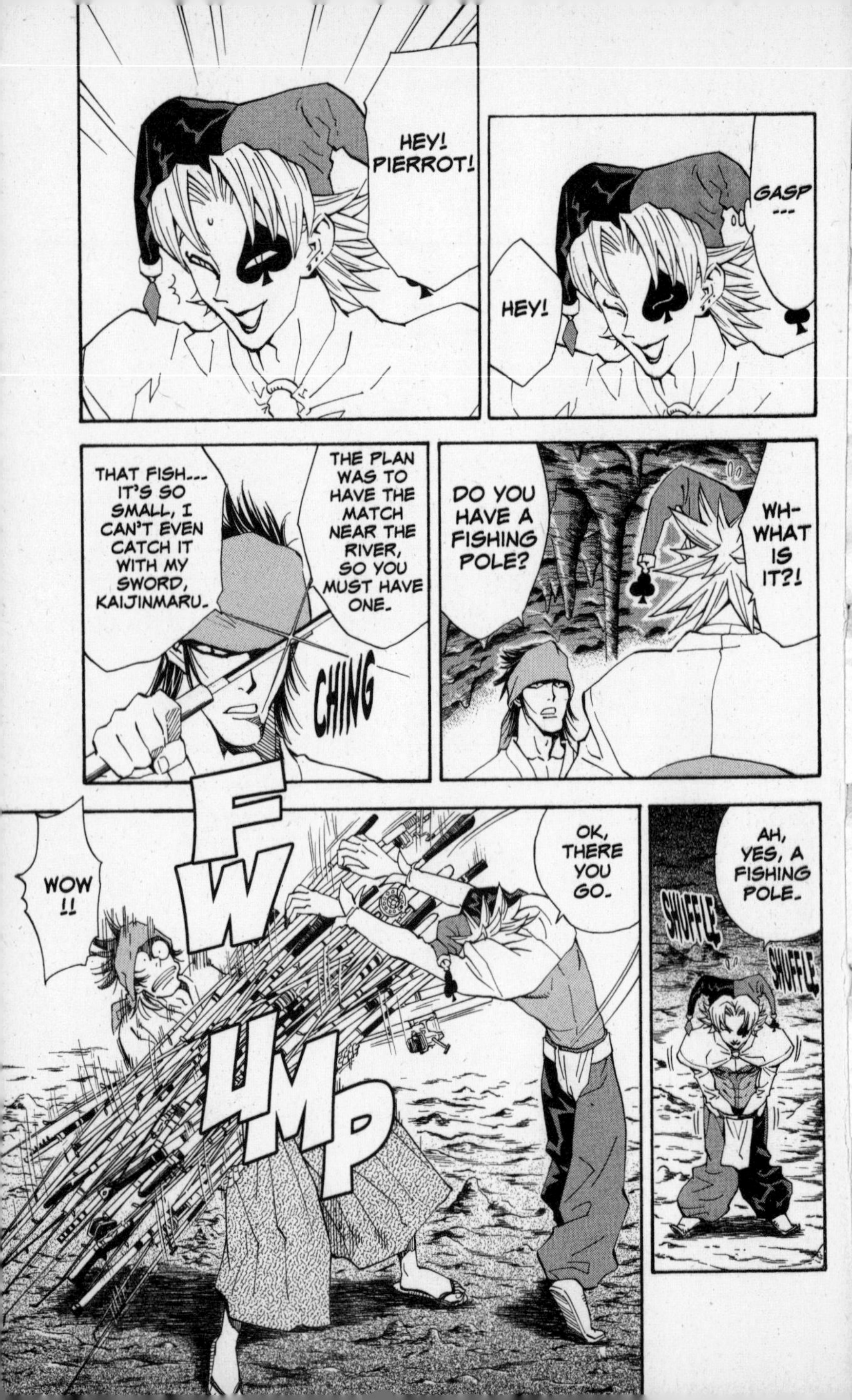
GASP ...
HEY!
HEY! PIERROT!
WH-WHAT IS IT?!
DO YOU HAVE A FISHING POLE?
THE PLAN WAS TO HAVE THE MATCH NEAR THE RIVER, SO YOU MUST HAVE ONE.
CHING
THAT FISH... IT'S SO SMALL, I CAN'T EVEN CATCH IT WITH MY SWORD, KAIJINMARU.
AH, YES, A FISHING POLE.
SHUFFLE
SHUFFLE
OK, THERE YOU GO.
FWUMP
WOW !!

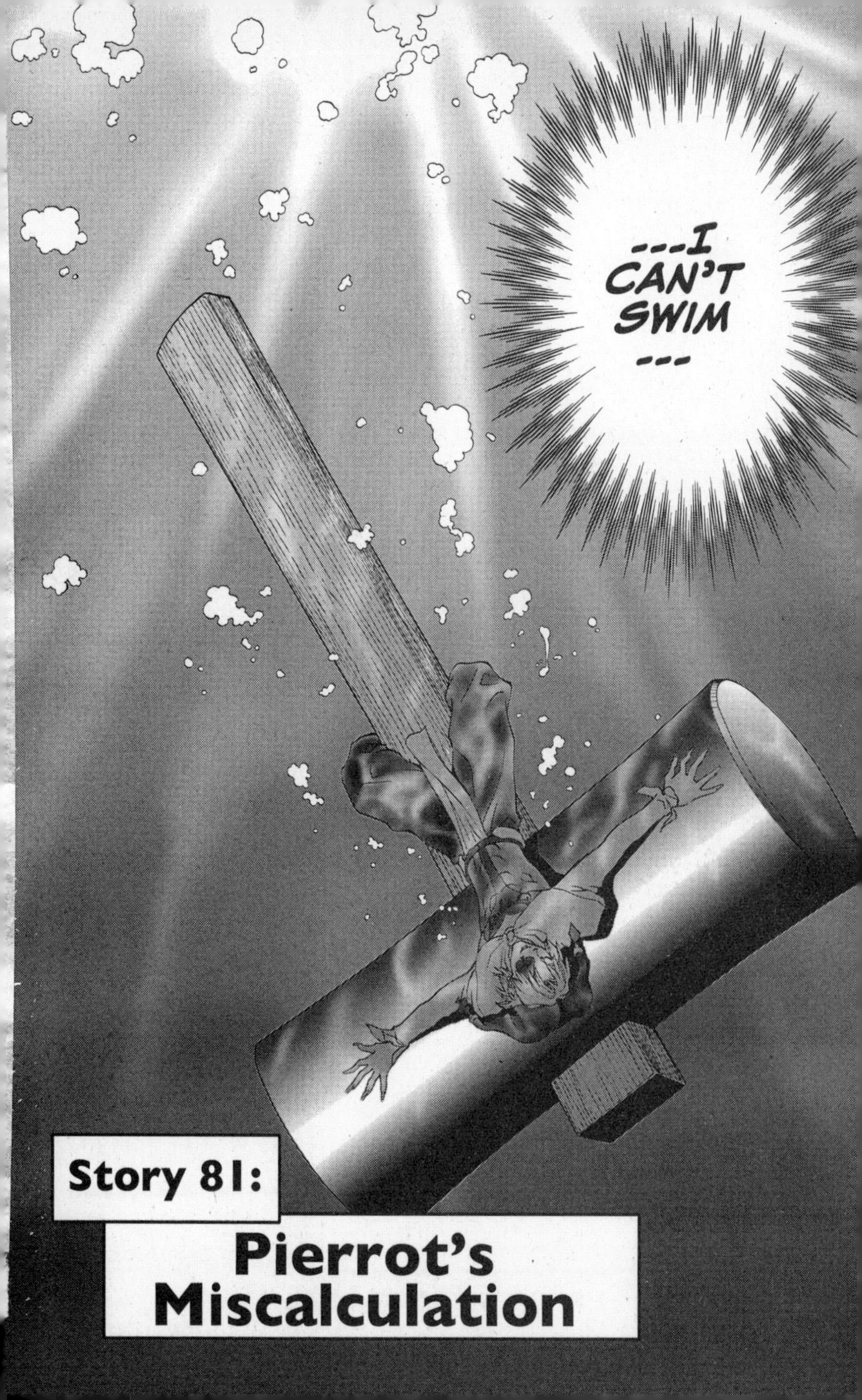
---I CAN'T SWIM ---

Story 81: Pierrot's Miscalculation

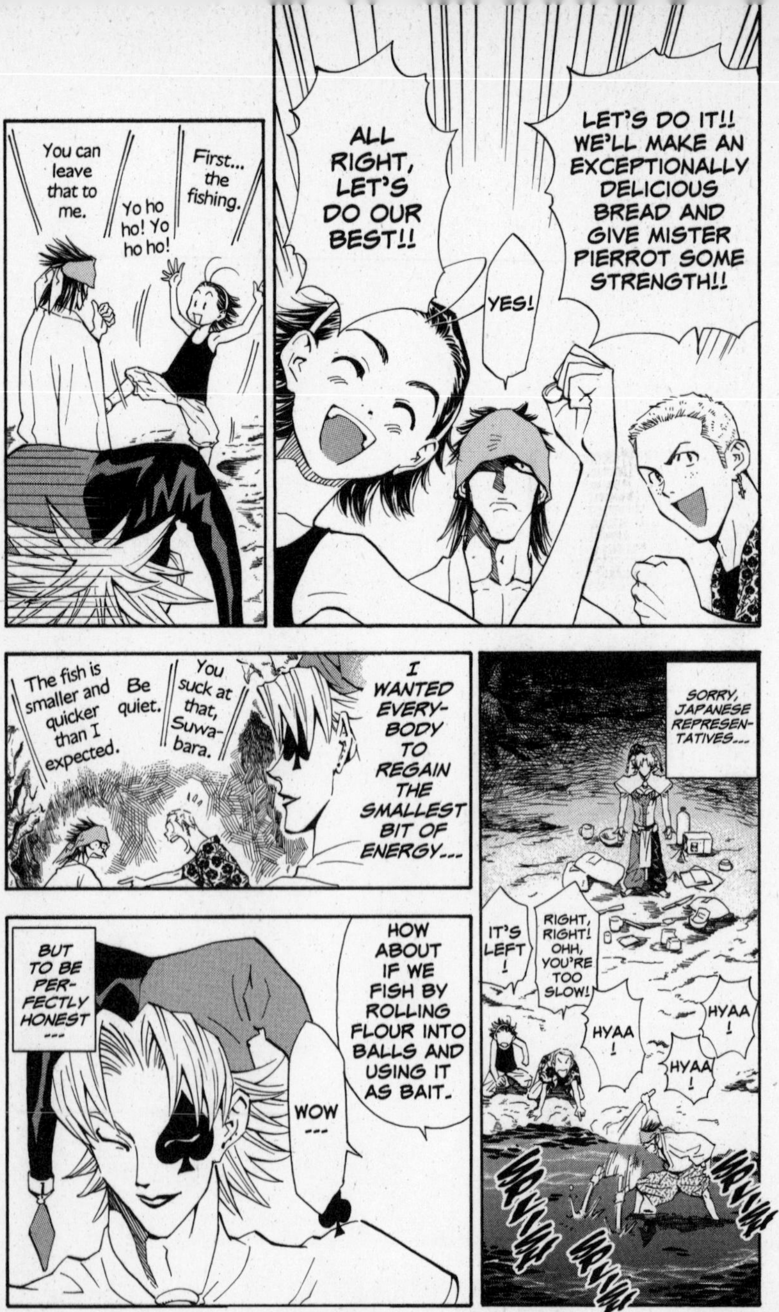
LET'S DO IT!! WE'LL MAKE AN EXCEPTIONALLY DELICIOUS BREAD AND GIVE MISTER PIERROT SOME STRENGTH!!
ALL RIGHT, LET'S DO OUR BEST!!
YES!
First... the fishing.
You can leave that to me.
Yo ho ho! Yo ho ho!
SORRY, JAPANESE REPRESENTATIVES...
RIGHT, RIGHT! OHH, YOU'RE TOO SLOW!
IT'S LEFT!
HYAA!
HYAA!
HYAA!
I WANTED EVERYBODY TO REGAIN THE SMALLEST BIT OF ENERGY...
You suck at that, Suwabara.
Be quiet.
The fish is smaller and quicker than I expected.
HOW ABOUT IF WE FISH BY ROLLING FLOUR INTO BALLS AND USING IT AS BAIT.
WOW...
BUT TO BE PERFECTLY HONEST...

Story 81: Pierrot's Miscalculation

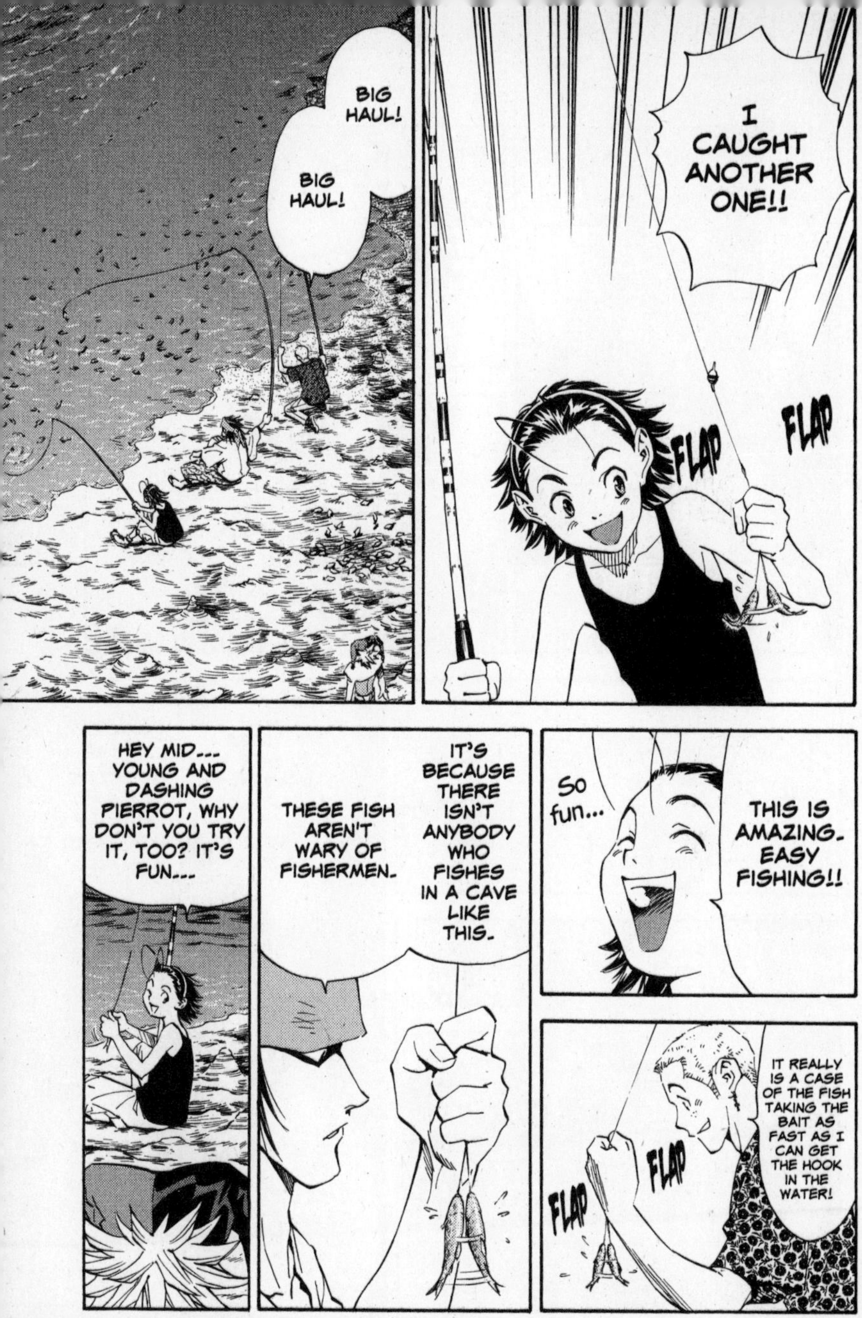

I CAUGHT ANOTHER ONE!!
FLAP
FLAP
BIG HAUL!
BIG HAUL!
THIS IS AMAZING. EASY FISHING!!
So fun...
IT REALLY IS A CASE OF THE FISH TAKING THE BAIT AS FAST AS I CAN GET THE HOOK IN THE WATER!
FLAP
FLAP
IT'S BECAUSE THERE ISN'T ANYBODY WHO FISHES IN A CAVE LIKE THIS.
THESE FISH AREN'T WARY OF FISHERMEN.
HEY MID... YOUNG AND DASHING PIERROT, WHY DON'T YOU TRY IT, TOO? IT'S FUN...

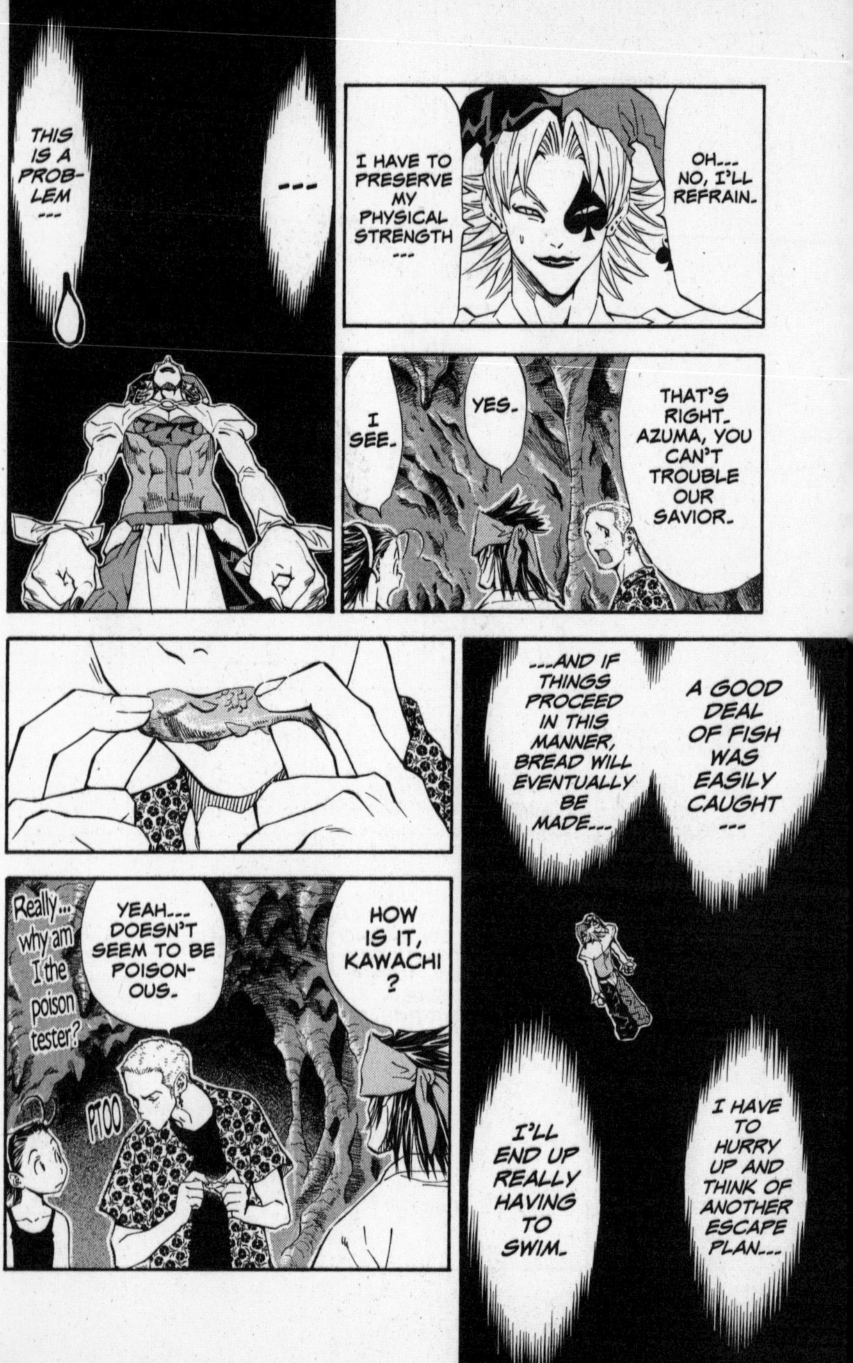
OH... NO, I'LL REFRAIN.
I HAVE TO PRESERVE MY PHYSICAL STRENGTH...
THAT'S RIGHT. AZUMA, YOU CAN'T TROUBLE OUR SAVIOR.
YES.
I SEE.
...
THIS IS A PROB-LEM...
A GOOD DEAL OF FISH WAS EASILY CAUGHT...
...AND IF THINGS PROCEED IN THIS MANNER, BREAD WILL EVENTUALLY BE MADE...
I HAVE TO HURRY UP AND THINK OF ANOTHER ESCAPE PLAN...
I'LL END UP REALLY HAVING TO SWIM.
HOW IS IT, KAWACHI?
YEAH... DOESN'T SEEM TO BE POISON-OUS.
Really... why am I the poison tester?
PTOO

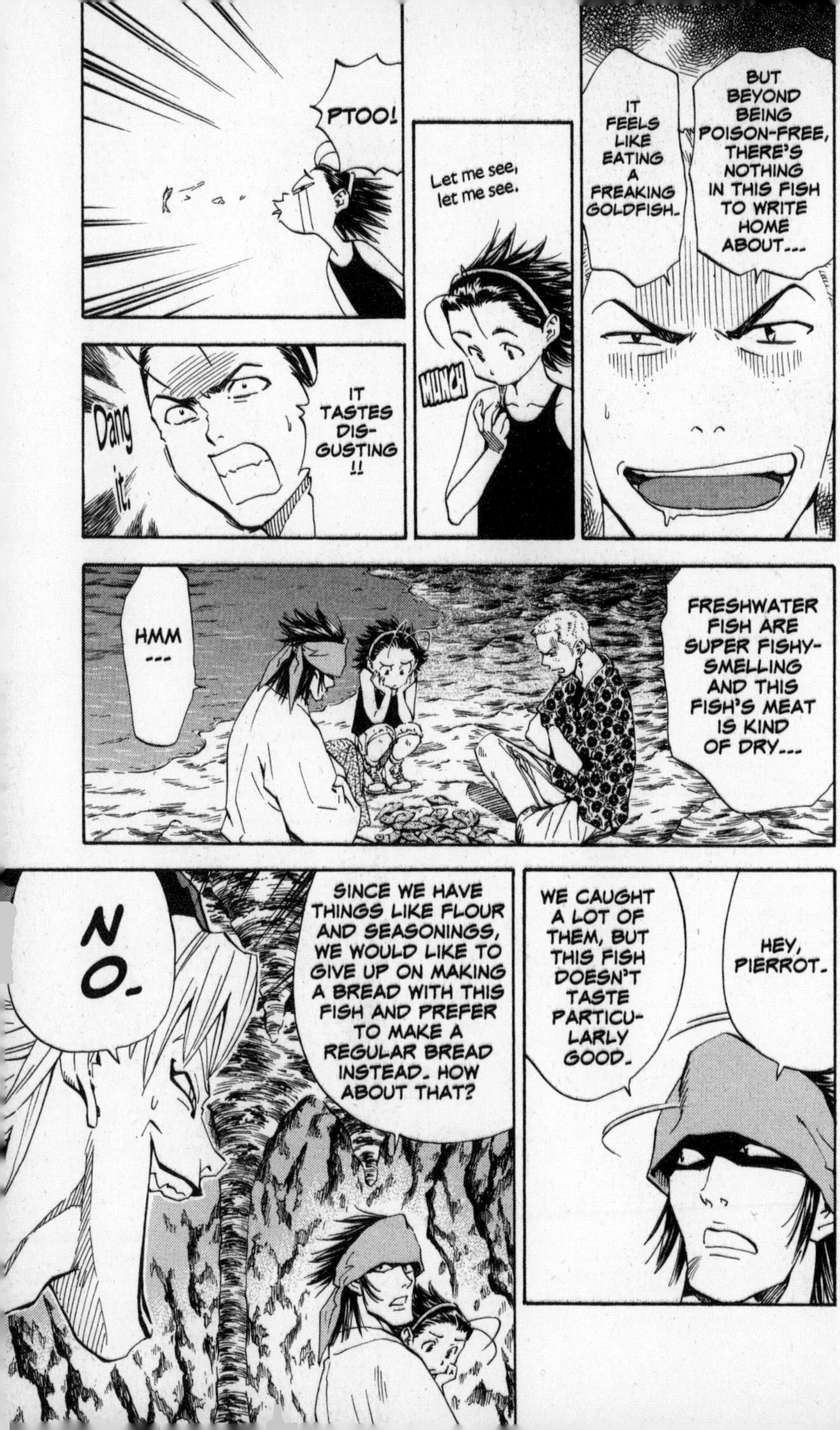

BUT BEYOND BEING POISON-FREE, THERE'S NOTHING IN THIS FISH TO WRITE HOME ABOUT...
IT FEELS LIKE EATING A FREAKING GOLDFISH.
Let me see, let me see.
MUNCH
PTOO!
Dang it.
IT TASTES DIS-GUSTING!!
FRESHWATER FISH ARE SUPER FISHY-SMELLING AND THIS FISH'S MEAT IS KIND OF DRY...
HMM...
HEY, PIERROT.
WE CAUGHT A LOT OF THEM, BUT THIS FISH DOESN'T TASTE PARTICU-LARLY GOOD.
SINCE WE HAVE THINGS LIKE FLOUR AND SEASONINGS, WE WOULD LIKE TO GIVE UP ON MAKING A BREAD WITH THIS FISH AND PREFER TO MAKE A REGULAR BREAD INSTEAD. HOW ABOUT THAT?
NO.

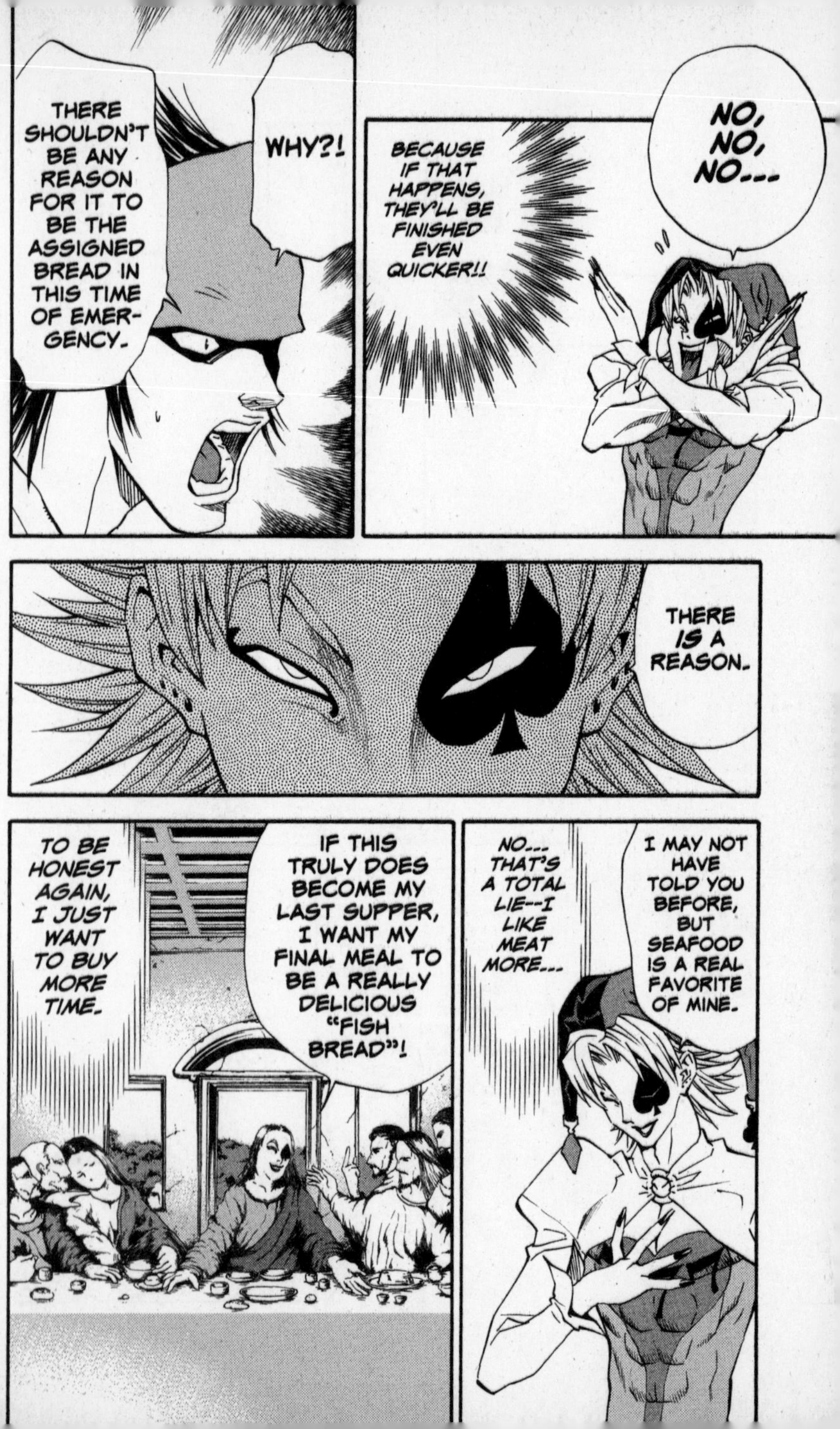
NO, NO, NO...
BECAUSE IF THAT HAPPENS, THEY'LL BE FINISHED EVEN QUICKER!!
WHY?!
THERE SHOULDN'T BE ANY REASON FOR IT TO BE THE ASSIGNED BREAD IN THIS TIME OF EMERGENCY.
THERE *IS* A REASON.
I MAY NOT HAVE TOLD YOU BEFORE, BUT SEAFOOD IS A REAL FAVORITE OF MINE.
NO... THAT'S A TOTAL LIE--I LIKE MEAT MORE...
IF THIS TRULY DOES BECOME MY LAST SUPPER, I WANT MY FINAL MEAL TO BE A REALLY DELICIOUS "FISH BREAD"!
TO BE HONEST AGAIN, I JUST WANT TO BUY MORE TIME.

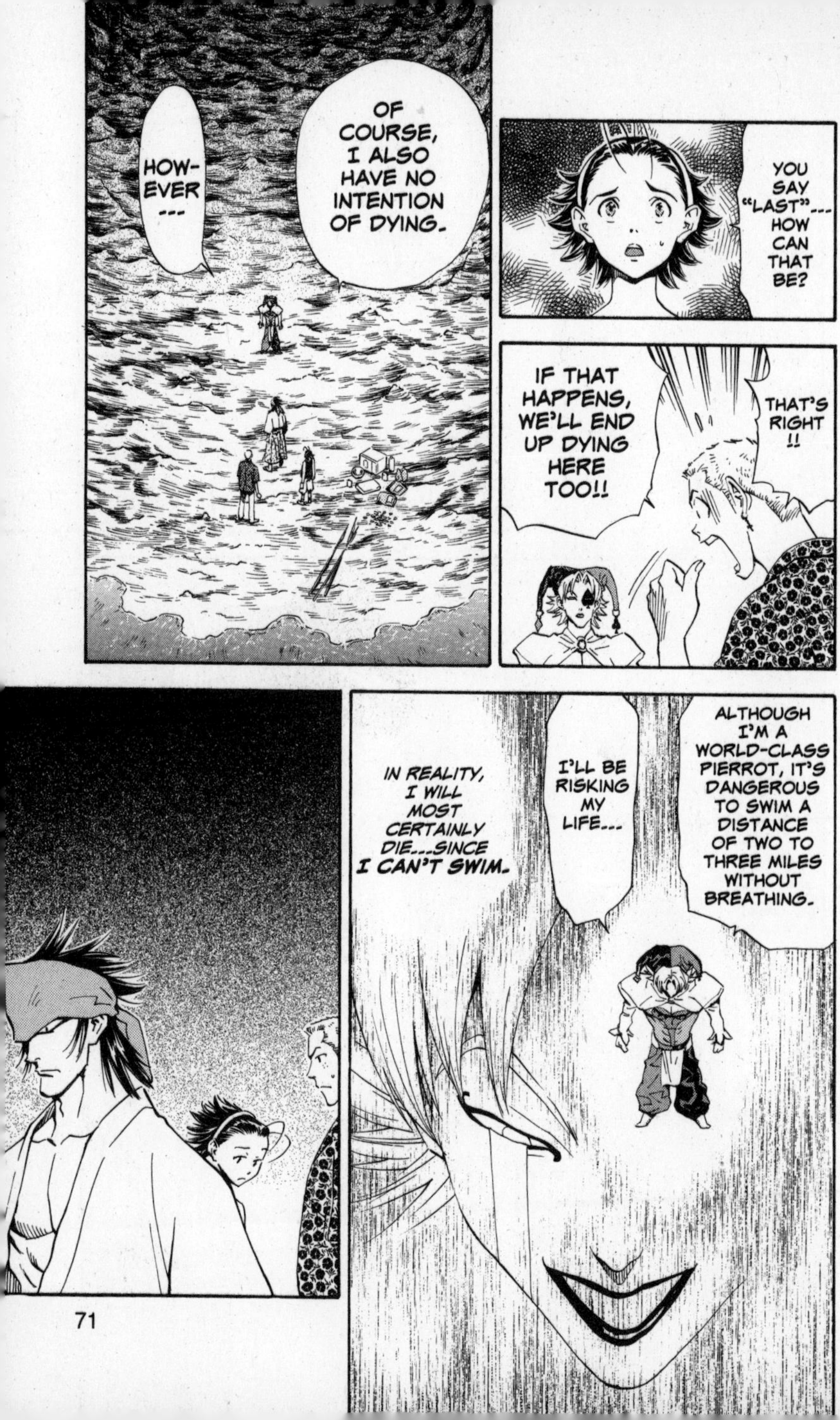
YOU SAY "LAST"... HOW CAN THAT BE?
THAT'S RIGHT!!
IF THAT HAPPENS, WE'LL END UP DYING HERE TOO!!
OF COURSE, I ALSO HAVE NO INTENTION OF DYING.
HOW-EVER...
ALTHOUGH I'M A WORLD-CLASS PIERROT, IT'S DANGEROUS TO SWIM A DISTANCE OF TWO TO THREE MILES WITHOUT BREATHING.
I'LL BE RISKING MY LIFE...
IN REALITY, I WILL MOST CERTAINLY DIE...SINCE I CAN'T SWIM.

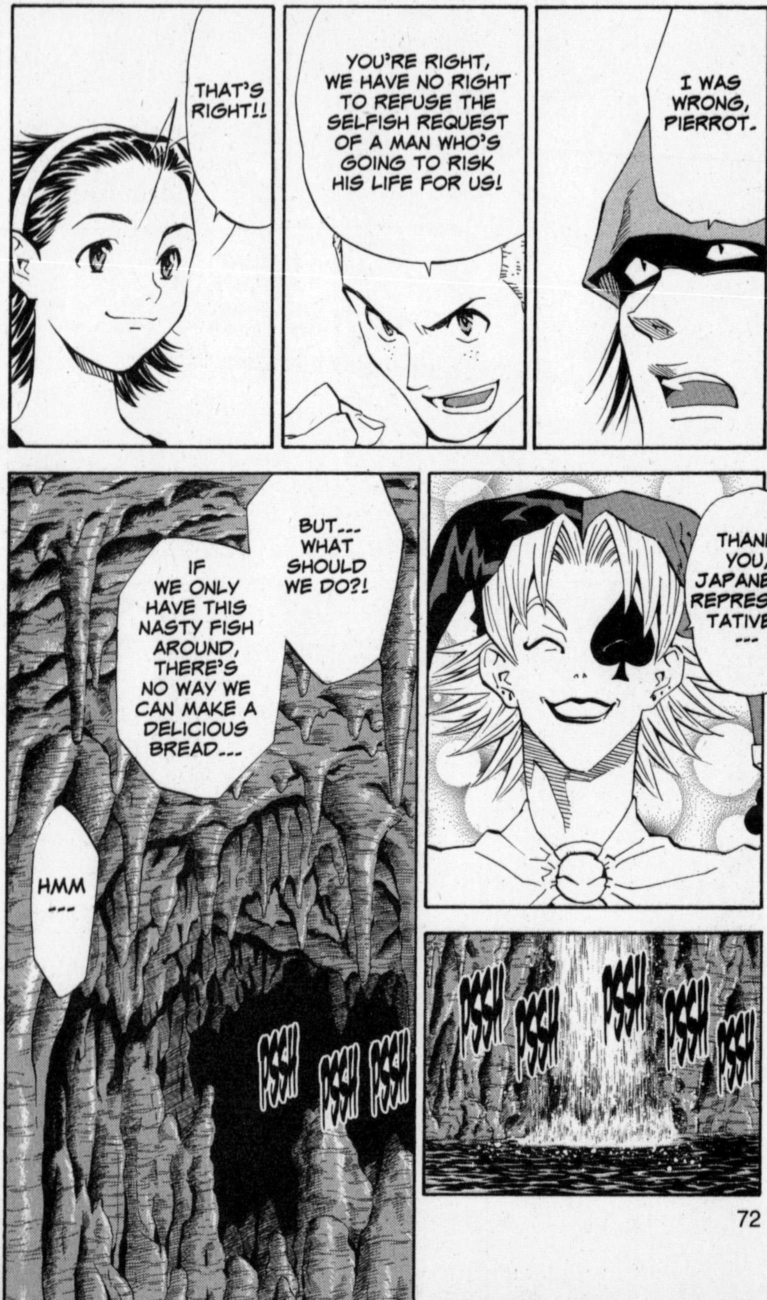
I WAS WRONG, PIERROT.
YOU'RE RIGHT, WE HAVE NO RIGHT TO REFUSE THE SELFISH REQUEST OF A MAN WHO'S GOING TO RISK HIS LIFE FOR US!
THAT'S RIGHT!!
THANK YOU, JAPANESE REPRESEN-TATIVES...
PSSH PSSH PSSH PSSH PSSH
BUT... WHAT SHOULD WE DO?!
IF WE ONLY HAVE THIS NASTY FISH AROUND, THERE'S NO WAY WE CAN MAKE A DELICIOUS BREAD...
HMM...
PSSH PSSH PSSH

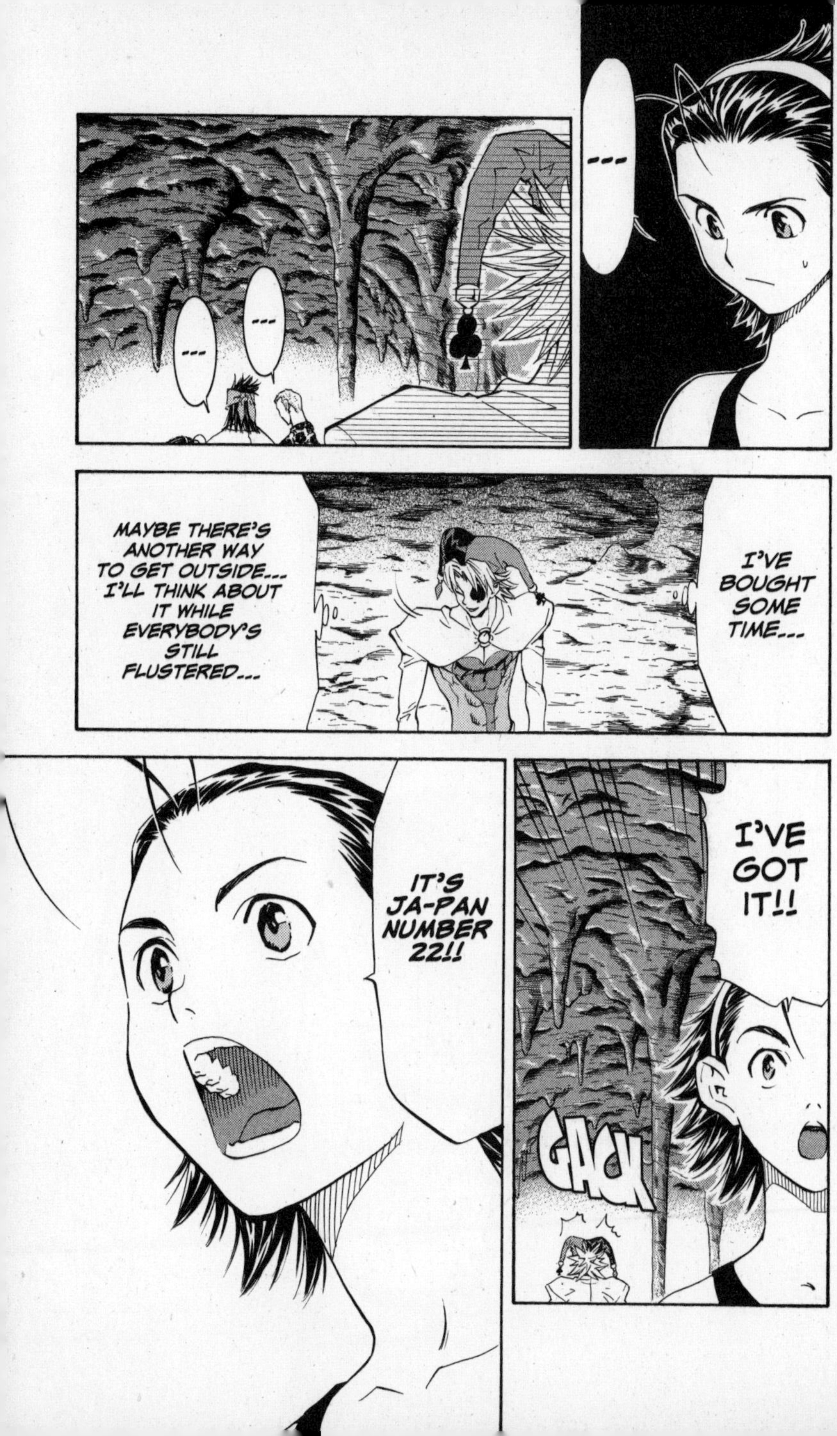
...
...
...
I'VE BOUGHT SOME TIME...
MAYBE THERE'S ANOTHER WAY TO GET OUTSIDE... I'LL THINK ABOUT IT WHILE EVERYBODY'S STILL FLUSTERED...
I'VE GOT IT!!
GACK
IT'S JA-PAN NUMBER 22!!

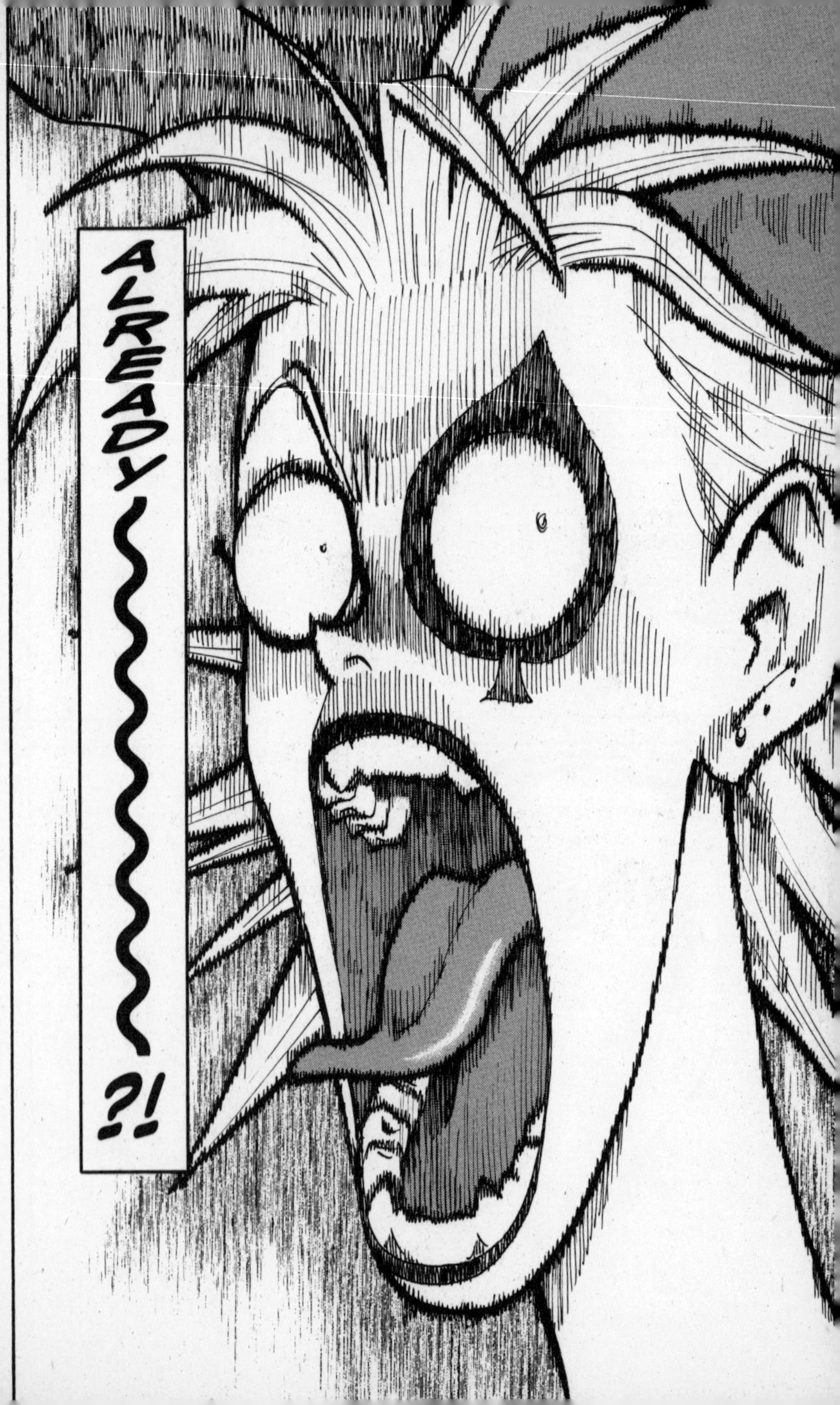
ALREADY~~~?!

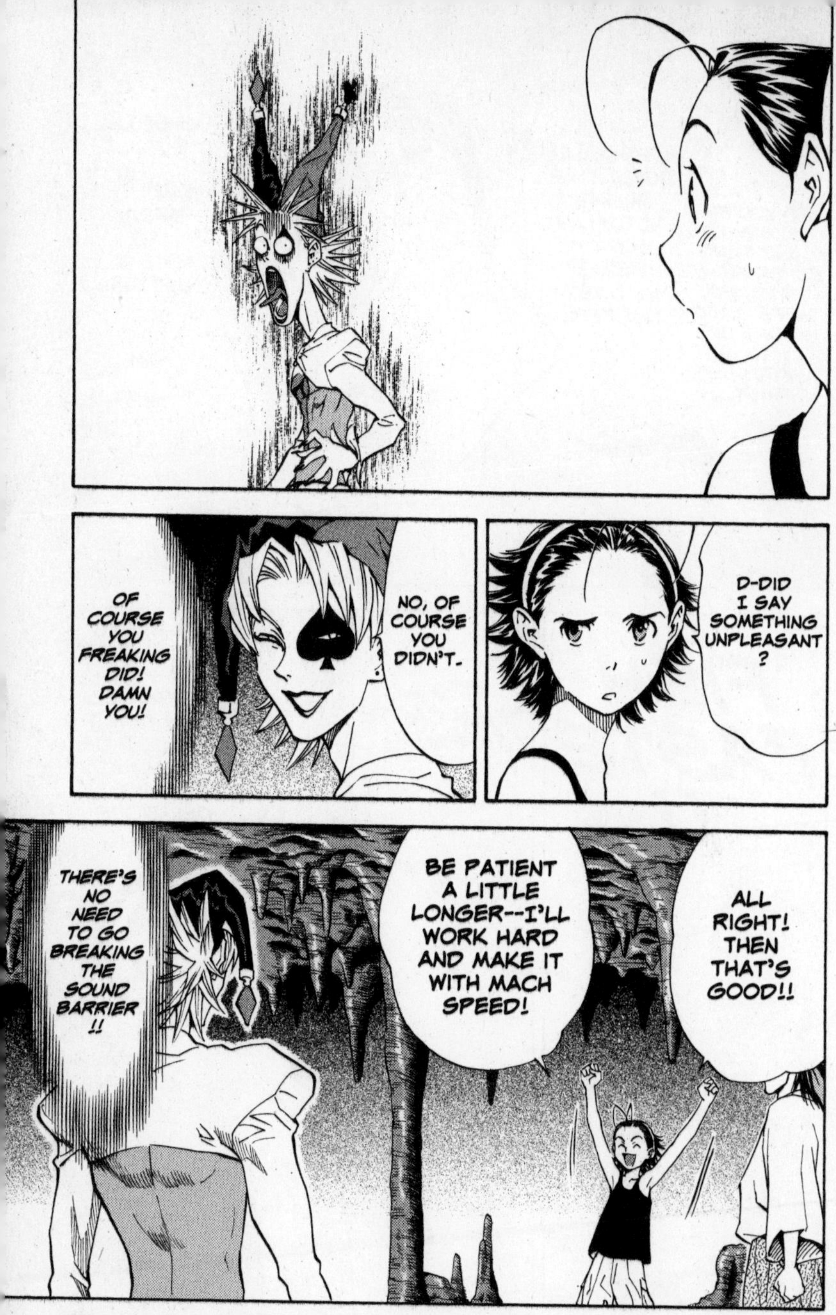
D-DID I SAY SOMETHING UNPLEASANT?
NO, OF COURSE YOU DIDN'T.
OF COURSE YOU FREAKING DID! DAMN YOU!
ALL RIGHT! THEN THAT'S GOOD!!
BE PATIENT A LITTLE LONGER--I'LL WORK HARD AND MAKE IT WITH MACH SPEED!
THERE'S NO NEED TO GO BREAKING THE SOUND BARRIER!!

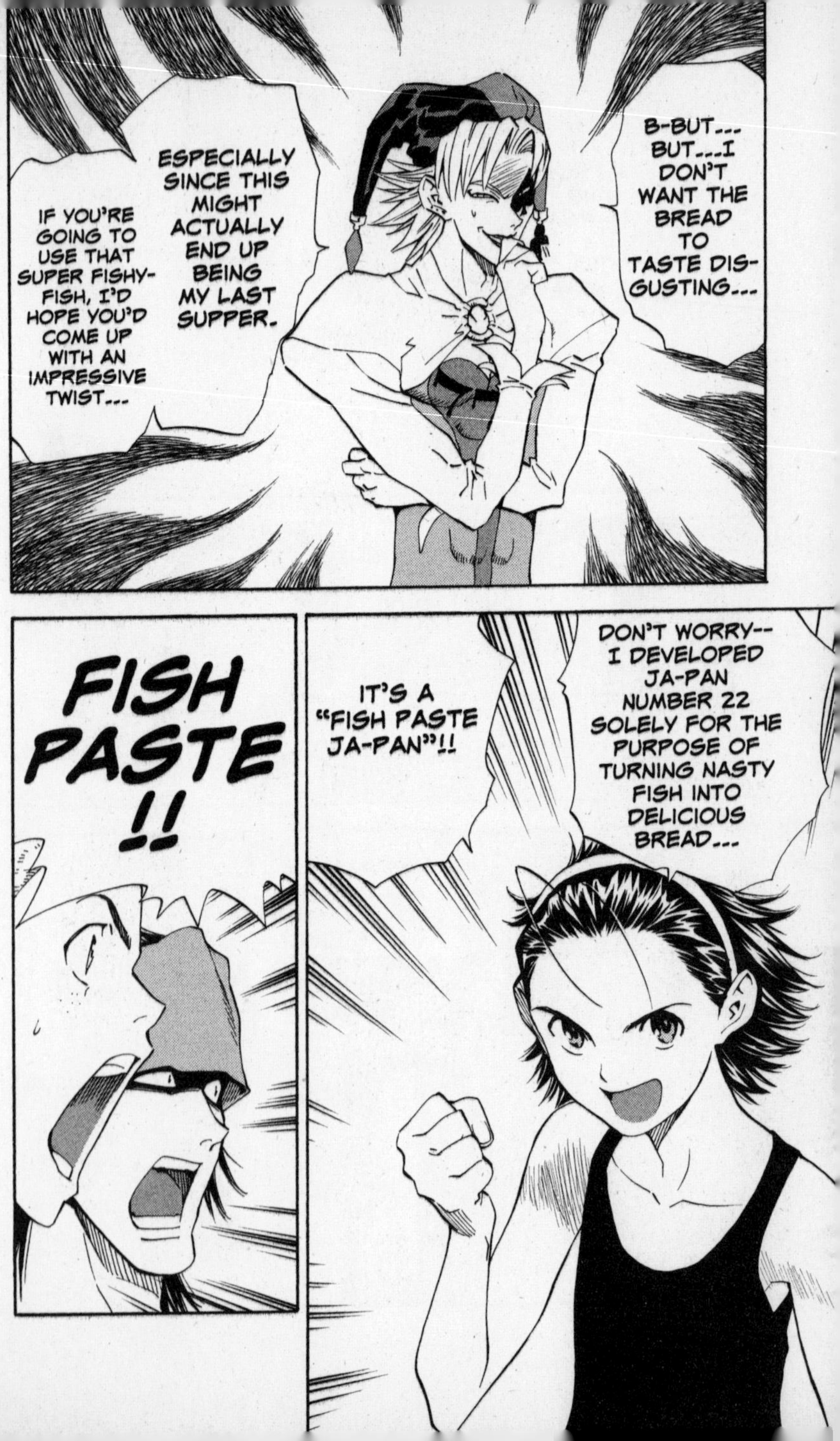
B-BUT... BUT...I DON'T WANT THE BREAD TO TASTE DISGUSTING...
ESPECIALLY SINCE THIS MIGHT ACTUALLY END UP BEING MY LAST SUPPER.
IF YOU'RE GOING TO USE THAT SUPER FISHY-FISH, I'D HOPE YOU'D COME UP WITH AN IMPRESSIVE TWIST...
DON'T WORRY-- I DEVELOPED JA-PAN NUMBER 22 SOLELY FOR THE PURPOSE OF TURNING NASTY FISH INTO DELICIOUS BREAD...
IT'S A "FISH PASTE JA-PAN"!!
FISH PASTE !!

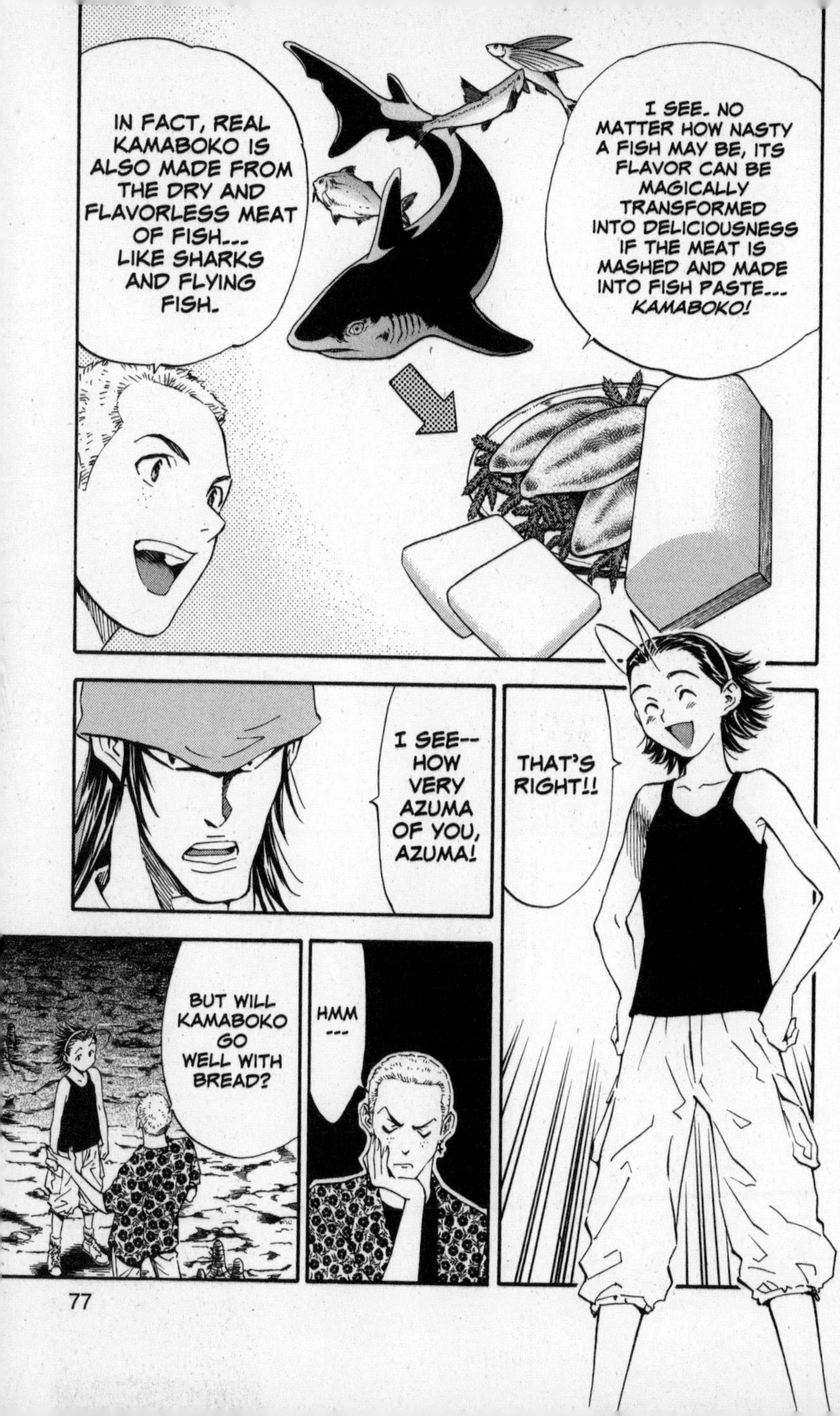
IN FACT, REAL KAMABOKO IS ALSO MADE FROM THE DRY AND FLAVORLESS MEAT OF FISH... LIKE SHARKS AND FLYING FISH.
I SEE. NO MATTER HOW NASTY A FISH MAY BE, ITS FLAVOR CAN BE MAGICALLY TRANSFORMED INTO DELICIOUSNESS IF THE MEAT IS MASHED AND MADE INTO FISH PASTE... *KAMABOKO!*
THAT'S RIGHT!!
I SEE-- HOW VERY AZUMA OF YOU, AZUMA!
HMM---
BUT WILL KAMABOKO GO WELL WITH BREAD?

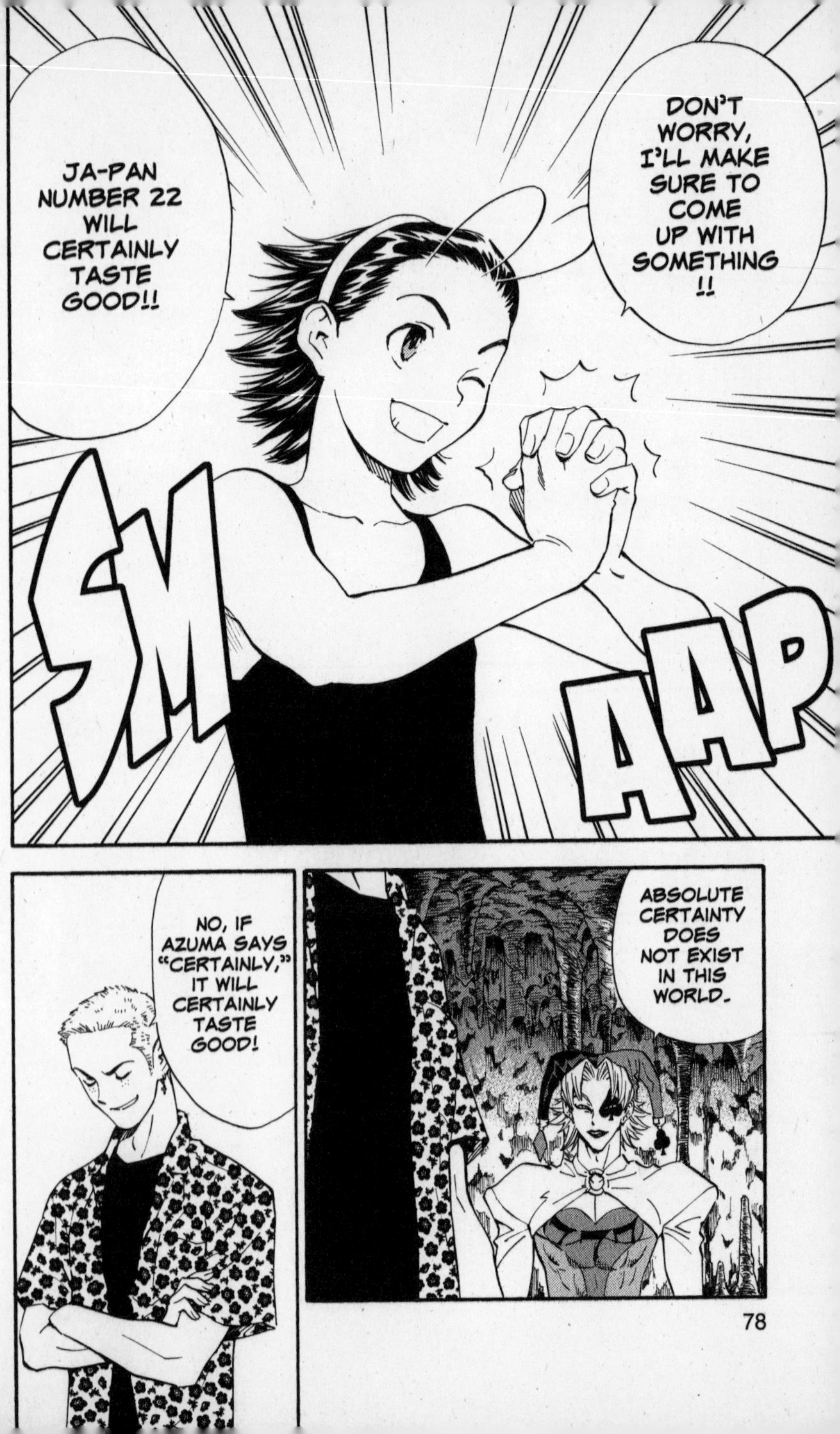
DON'T WORRY, I'LL MAKE SURE TO COME UP WITH SOMETHING !!
JA-PAN NUMBER 22 WILL CERTAINLY TASTE GOOD!!
SMAAP
ABSOLUTE CERTAINTY DOES NOT EXIST IN THIS WORLD.
NO, IF AZUMA SAYS "CERTAINLY," IT WILL CERTAINLY TASTE GOOD!

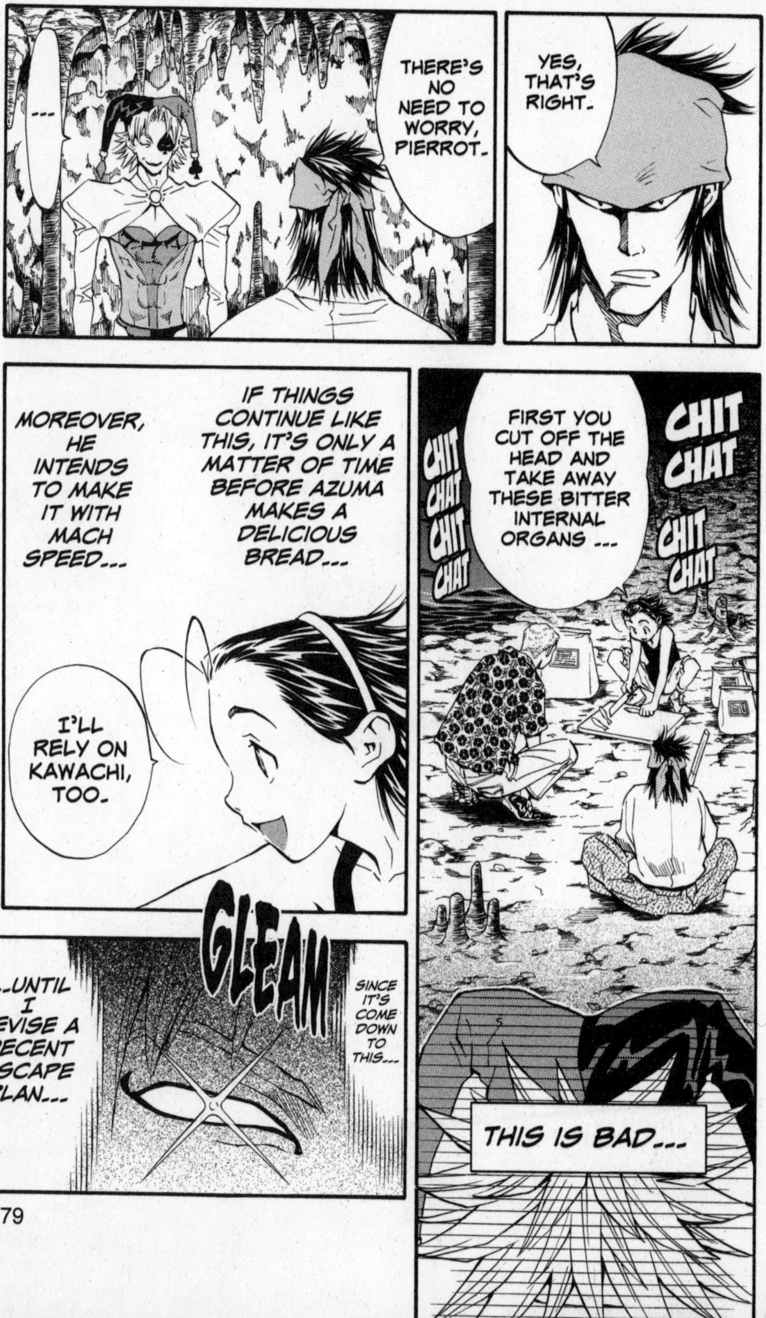
YES, THAT'S RIGHT.
THERE'S NO NEED TO WORRY, PIERROT.
...
CHIT CHAT
FIRST YOU CUT OFF THE HEAD AND TAKE AWAY THESE BITTER INTERNAL ORGANS ...
CHIT CHAT
CHIT CHAT CHIT CHAT
THIS IS BAD...
IF THINGS CONTINUE LIKE THIS, IT'S ONLY A MATTER OF TIME BEFORE AZUMA MAKES A DELICIOUS BREAD...
MOREOVER, HE INTENDS TO MAKE IT WITH MACH SPEED...
I'LL RELY ON KAWACHI, TOO.
GLEAM
SINCE IT'S COME DOWN TO THIS...
...UNTIL I DEVISE A DECENT ESCAPE PLAN...

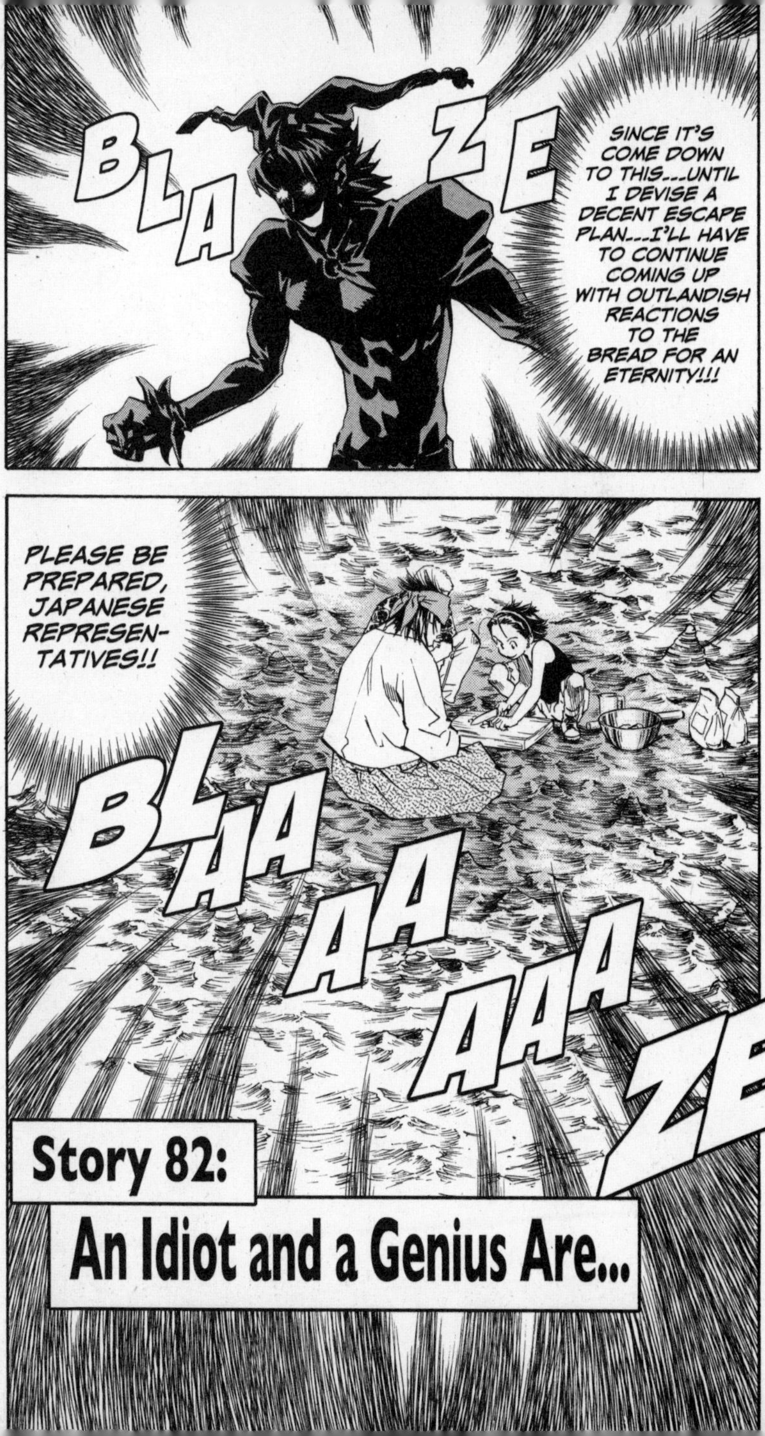
SINCE IT'S COME DOWN TO THIS...UNTIL I DEVISE A DECENT ESCAPE PLAN...I'LL HAVE TO CONTINUE COMING UP WITH OUTLANDISH REACTIONS TO THE BREAD FOR AN ETERNITY!!!
BLAZE
PLEASE BE PREPARED, JAPANESE REPRESEN-TATIVES!!
BLAAAAAAAZE
Story 82:
An Idiot and a Genius Are...

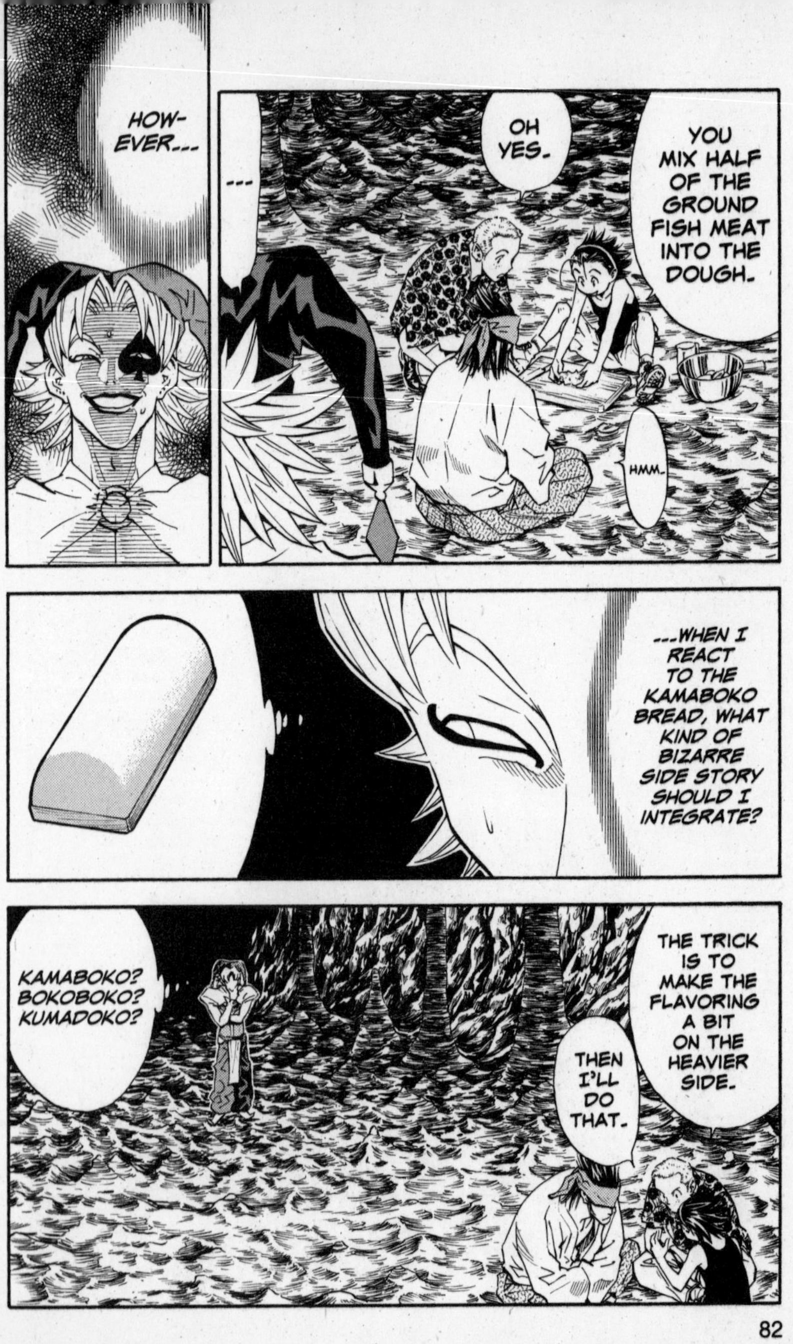
YOU MIX HALF OF THE GROUND FISH MEAT INTO THE DOUGH.
OH YES.
...
HMM.
HOW-EVER...
...WHEN I REACT TO THE KAMABOKO BREAD, WHAT KIND OF BIZARRE SIDE STORY SHOULD I INTEGRATE?
THE TRICK IS TO MAKE THE FLAVORING A BIT ON THE HEAVIER SIDE.
THEN I'LL DO THAT.
KAMABOKO? BOKOBOKO? KUMADOKO?

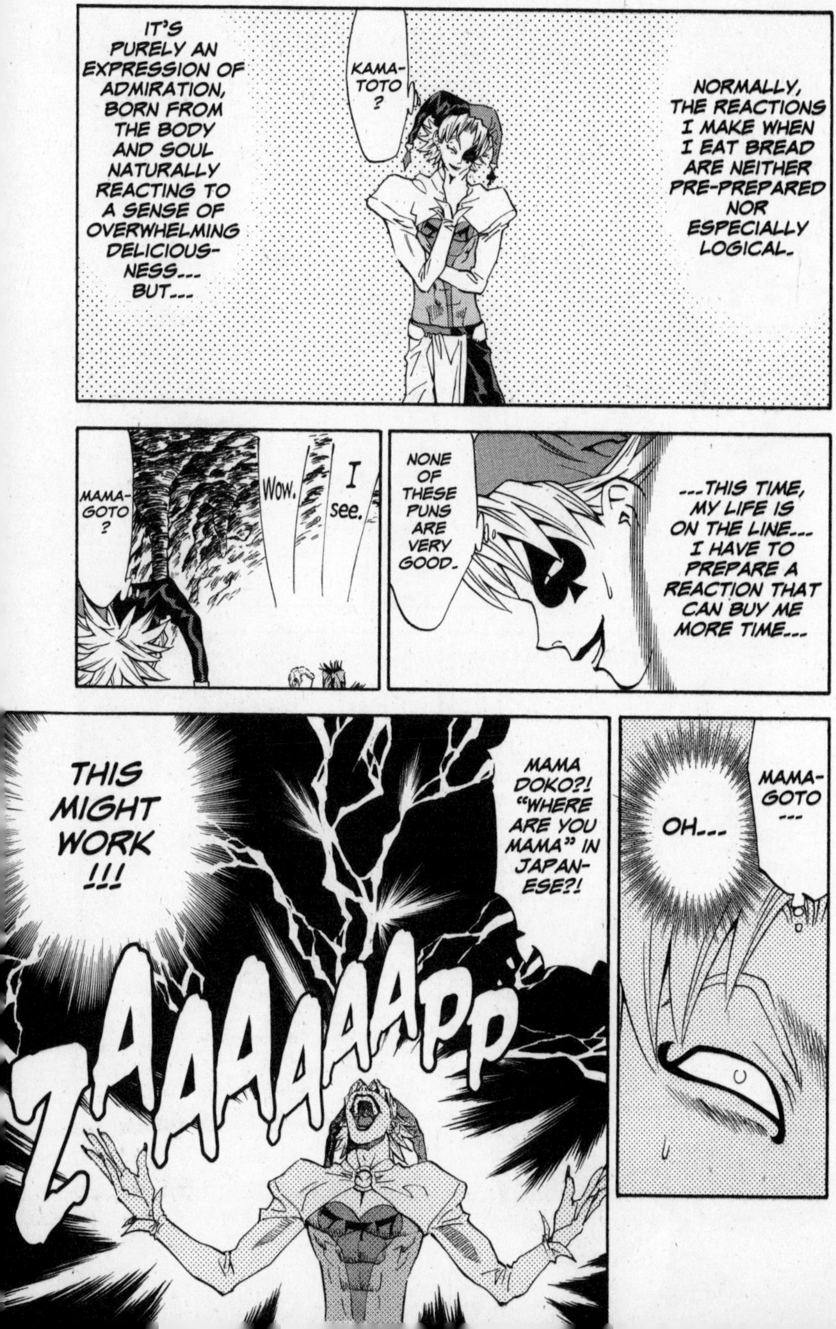
KAMA-TOTO?
NORMALLY, THE REACTIONS I MAKE WHEN I EAT BREAD ARE NEITHER PRE-PREPARED NOR ESPECIALLY LOGICAL.
IT'S PURELY AN EXPRESSION OF ADMIRATION, BORN FROM THE BODY AND SOUL NATURALLY REACTING TO A SENSE OF OVERWHELMING DELICIOUS-NESS... BUT...
...THIS TIME, MY LIFE IS ON THE LINE... I HAVE TO PREPARE A REACTION THAT CAN BUY ME MORE TIME...
NONE OF THESE PUNS ARE VERY GOOD.
I see.
Wow.
MAMA-GOTO?
MAMA-GOTO...
OH...
MAMA DOKO?! "WHERE ARE YOU MAMA" IN JAPAN-ESE?!
THIS MIGHT WORK!!!
ZAAAAAAPP

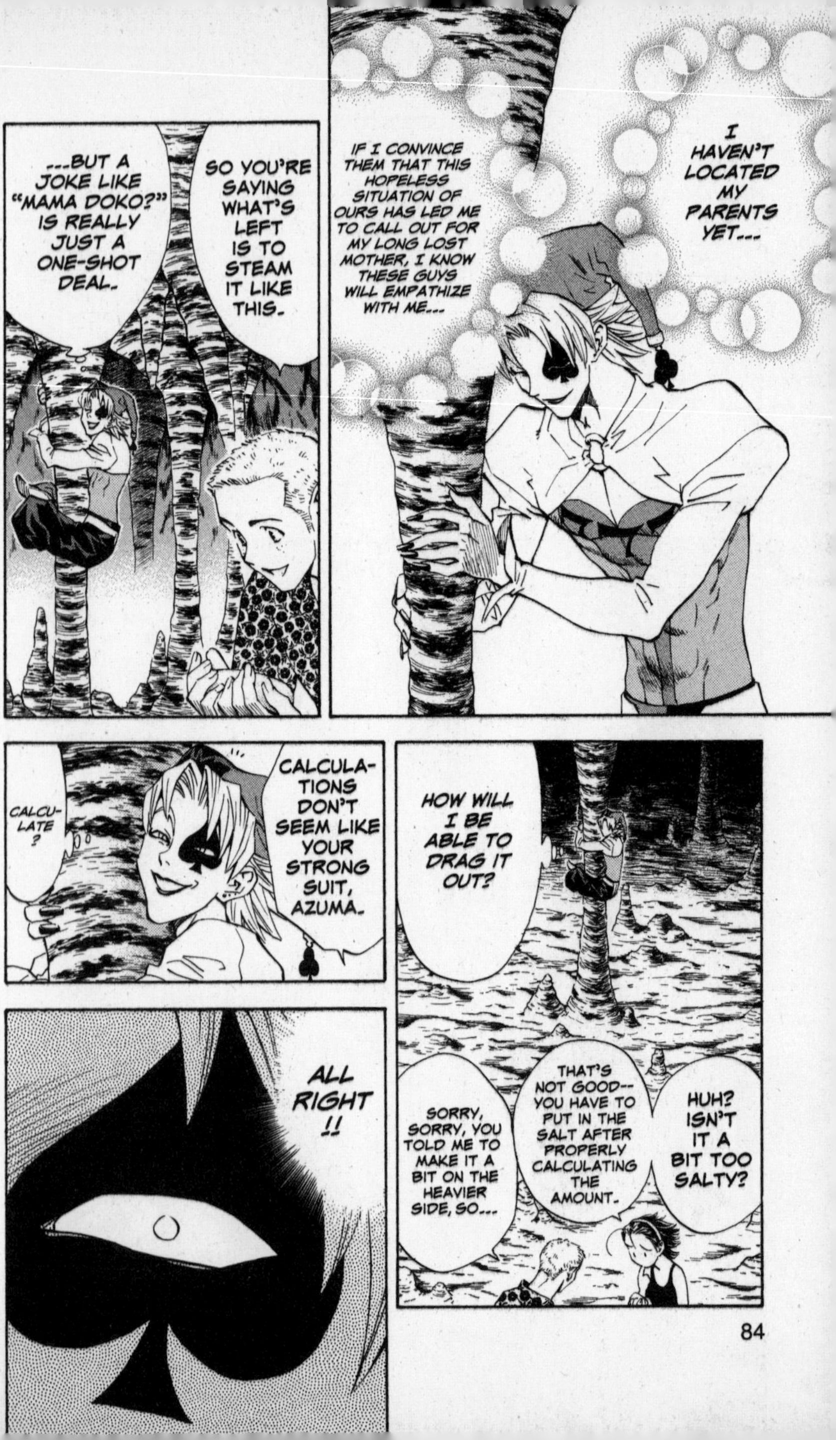
I HAVEN'T LOCATED MY PARENTS YET...
IF I CONVINCE THEM THAT THIS HOPELESS SITUATION OF OURS HAS LED ME TO CALL OUT FOR MY LONG LOST MOTHER, I KNOW THESE GUYS WILL EMPATHIZE WITH ME...
SO YOU'RE SAYING WHAT'S LEFT IS TO STEAM IT LIKE THIS.
...BUT A JOKE LIKE "MAMA DOKO?" IS REALLY JUST A ONE-SHOT DEAL.
HOW WILL I BE ABLE TO DRAG IT OUT?
HUH? ISN'T IT A BIT TOO SALTY?
THAT'S NOT GOOD-- YOU HAVE TO PUT IN THE SALT AFTER PROPERLY CALCULATING THE AMOUNT.
SORRY, SORRY, YOU TOLD ME TO MAKE IT A BIT ON THE HEAVIER SIDE, SO...
CALCULATIONS DON'T SEEM LIKE YOUR STRONG SUIT, AZUMA.
CALCULATE?
ALL RIGHT !!

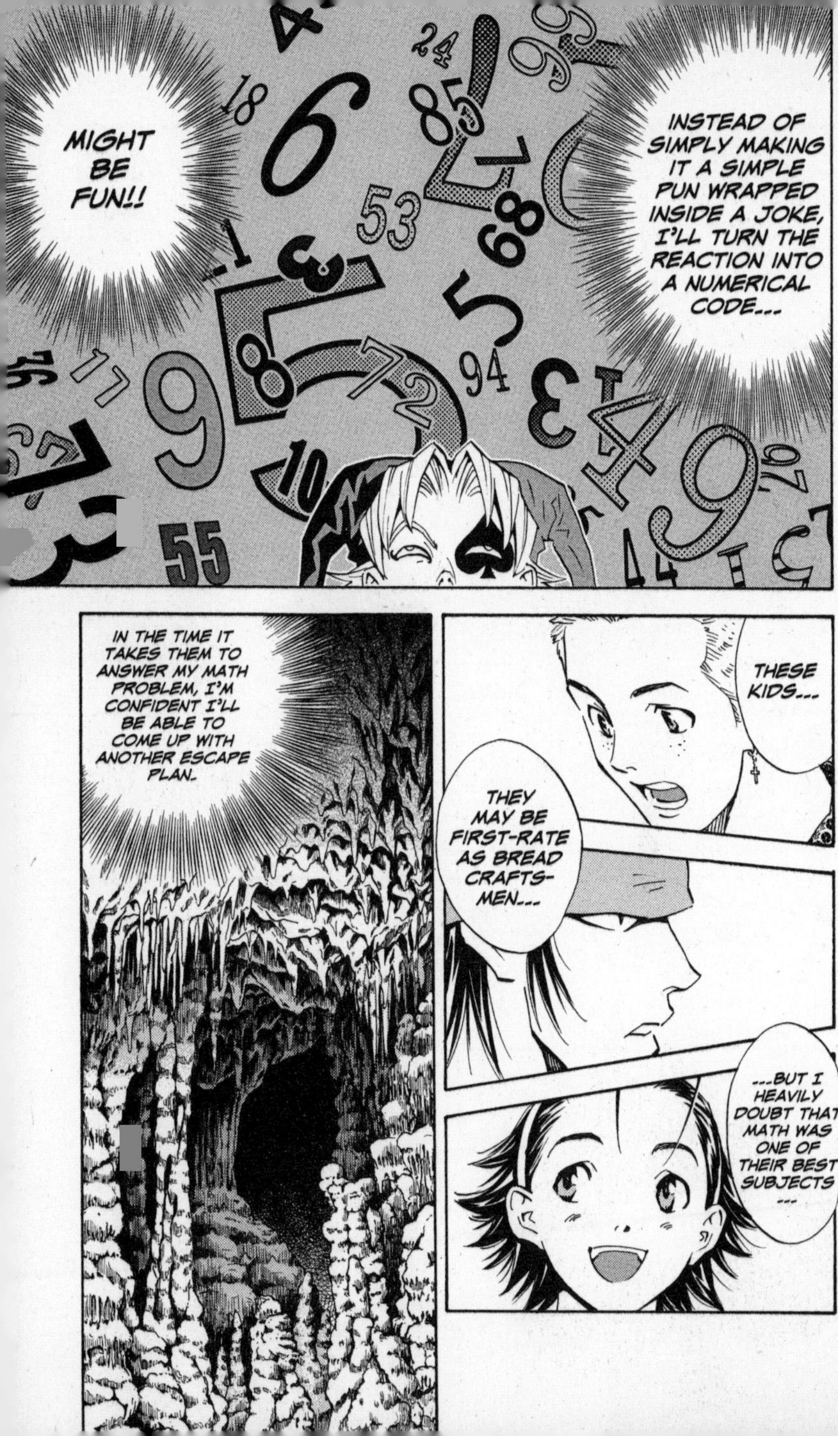
INSTEAD OF SIMPLY MAKING IT A SIMPLE PUN WRAPPED INSIDE A JOKE, I'LL TURN THE REACTION INTO A NUMERICAL CODE...
MIGHT BE FUN!!
THESE KIDS...
THEY MAY BE FIRST-RATE AS BREAD CRAFTS-MEN...
...BUT I HEAVILY DOUBT THAT MATH WAS ONE OF THEIR BEST SUBJECTS...
IN THE TIME IT TAKES THEM TO ANSWER MY MATH PROBLEM, I'M CONFIDENT I'LL BE ABLE TO COME UP WITH ANOTHER ESCAPE PLAN.

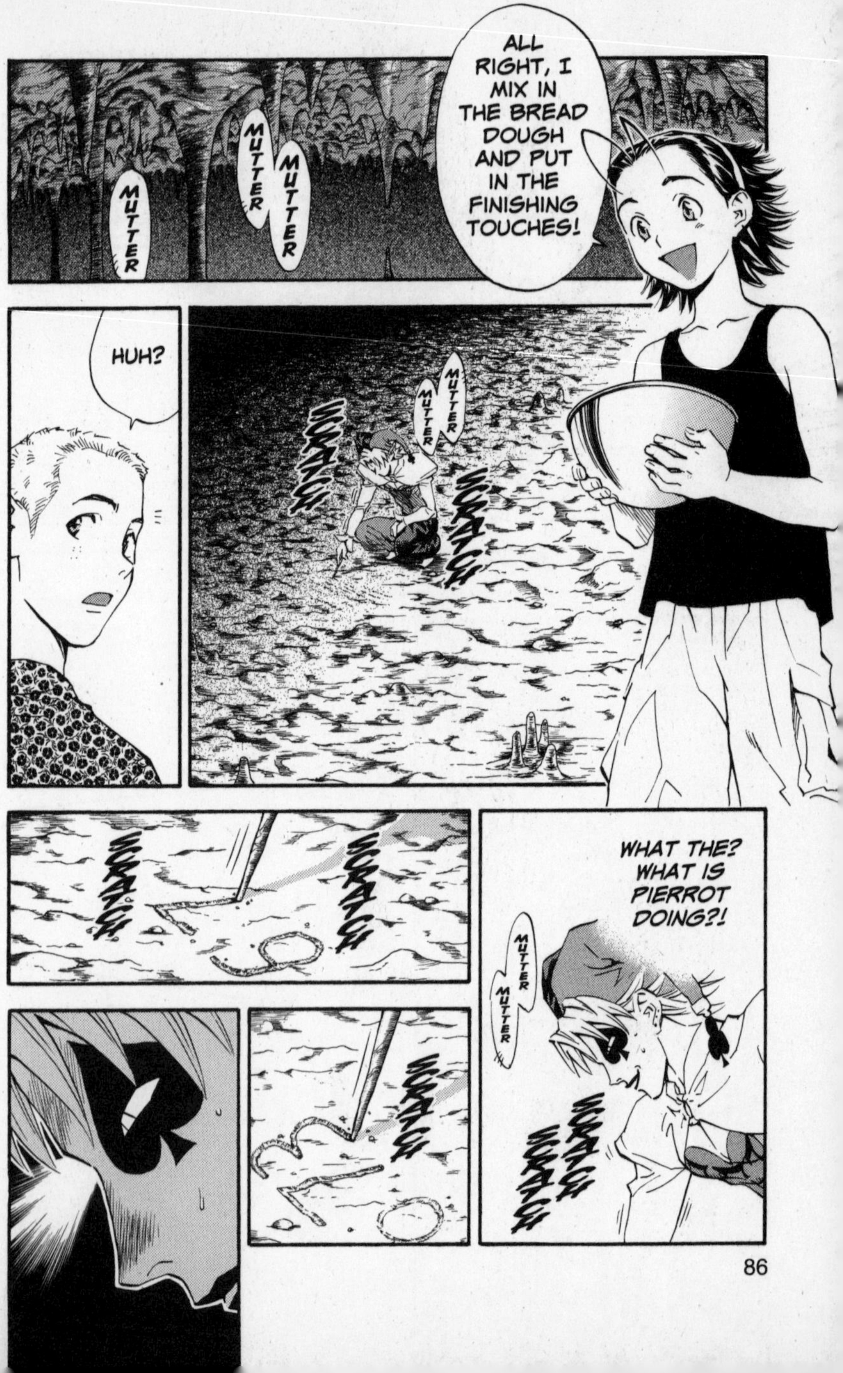
ALL RIGHT, I MIX IN THE BREAD DOUGH AND PUT IN THE FINISHING TOUCHES!
MUTTER
MUTTER
MUTTER
MUTTER
MUTTER
SCRATCH
SCRATCH
HUH?
WHAT THE? WHAT IS PIERROT DOING?!
MUTTER
MUTTER
SCRATCH
SCRATCH
SCRATCH
SCRATCH
SCRATCH

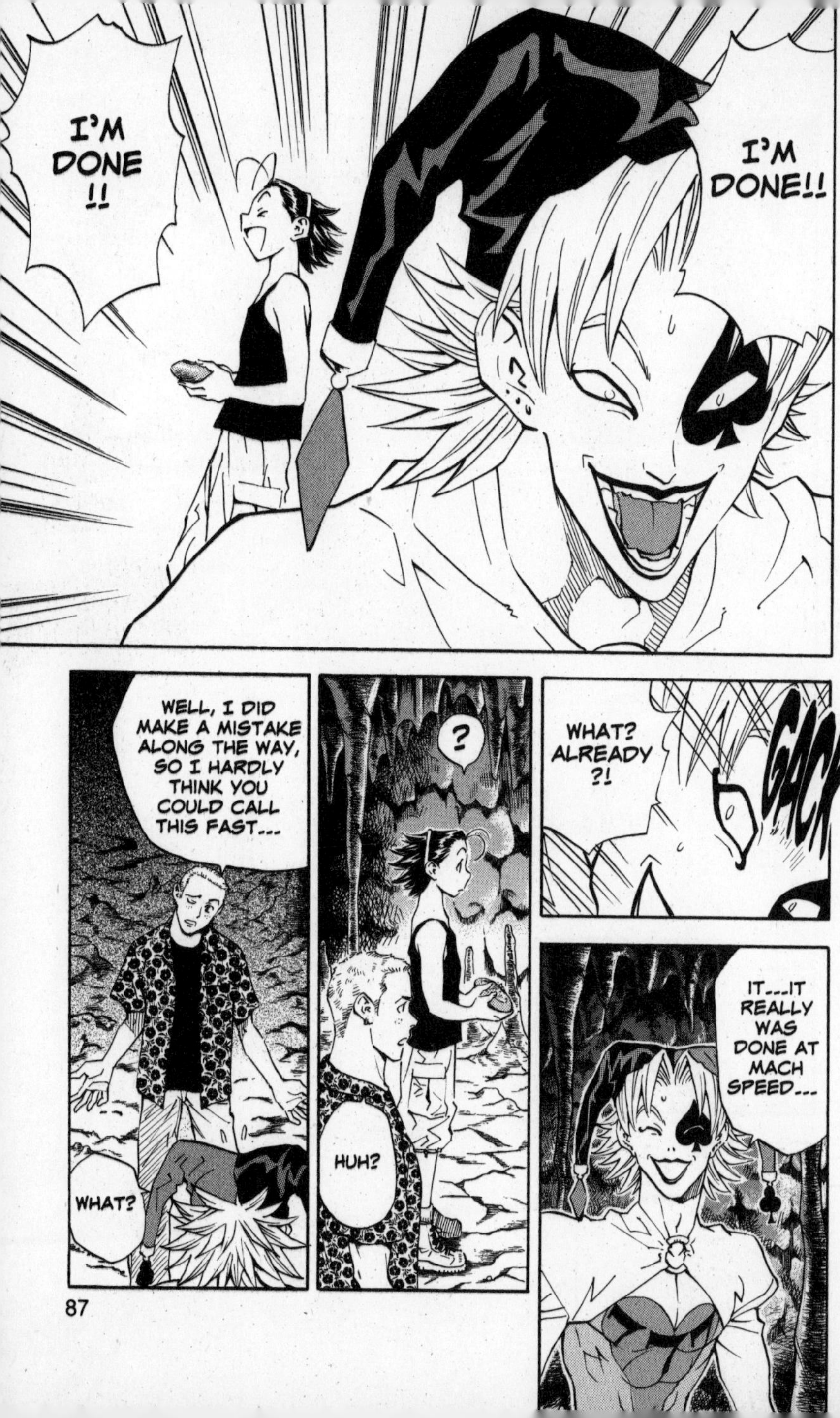
I'M DONE!!
I'M DONE !!
WHAT? ALREADY ?!
GACK
IT...IT REALLY WAS DONE AT MACH SPEED...
?
HUH?
WELL, I DID MAKE A MISTAKE ALONG THE WAY, SO I HARDLY THINK YOU COULD CALL THIS FAST...
WHAT?

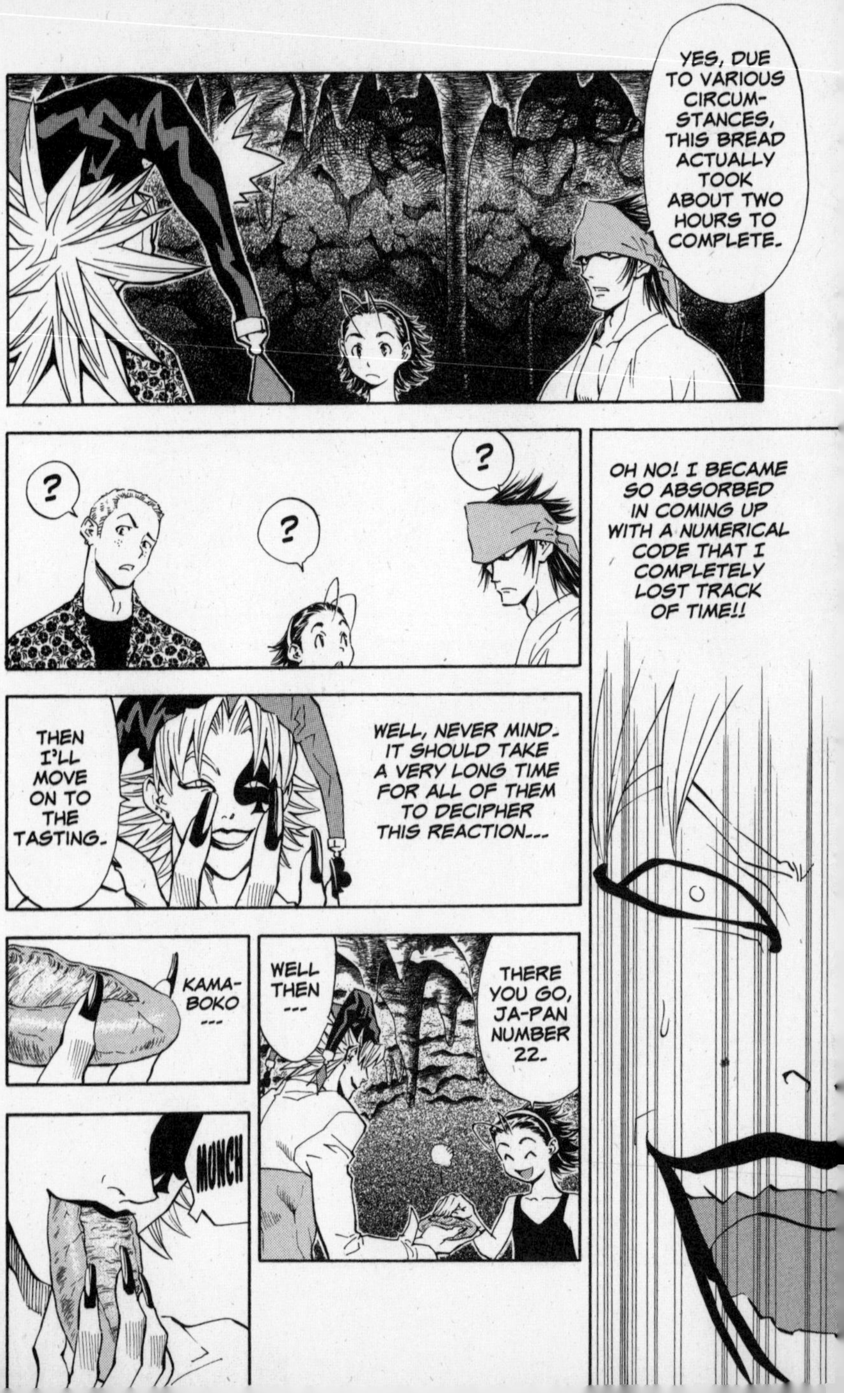
YES, DUE TO VARIOUS CIRCUM-STANCES, THIS BREAD ACTUALLY TOOK ABOUT TWO HOURS TO COMPLETE.
OH NO! I BECAME SO ABSORBED IN COMING UP WITH A NUMERICAL CODE THAT I COMPLETELY LOST TRACK OF TIME!!
?
?
?
WELL, NEVER MIND. IT SHOULD TAKE A VERY LONG TIME FOR ALL OF THEM TO DECIPHER THIS REACTION...
THEN I'LL MOVE ON TO THE TASTING.
THERE YOU GO, JA-PAN NUMBER 22.
WELL THEN ---
KAMA-BOKO ---
MUNCH

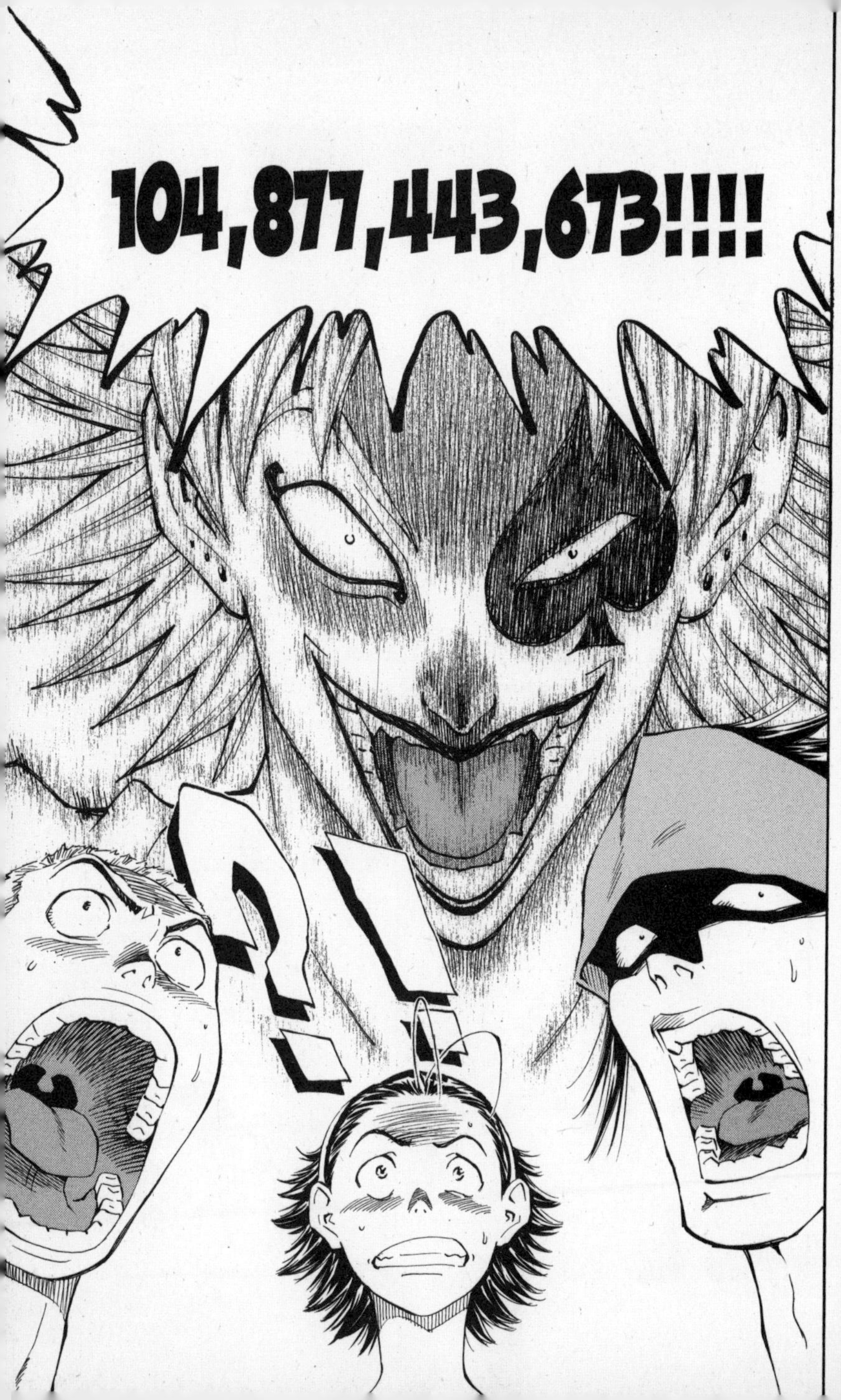
104,877,443,673!!!!
?!

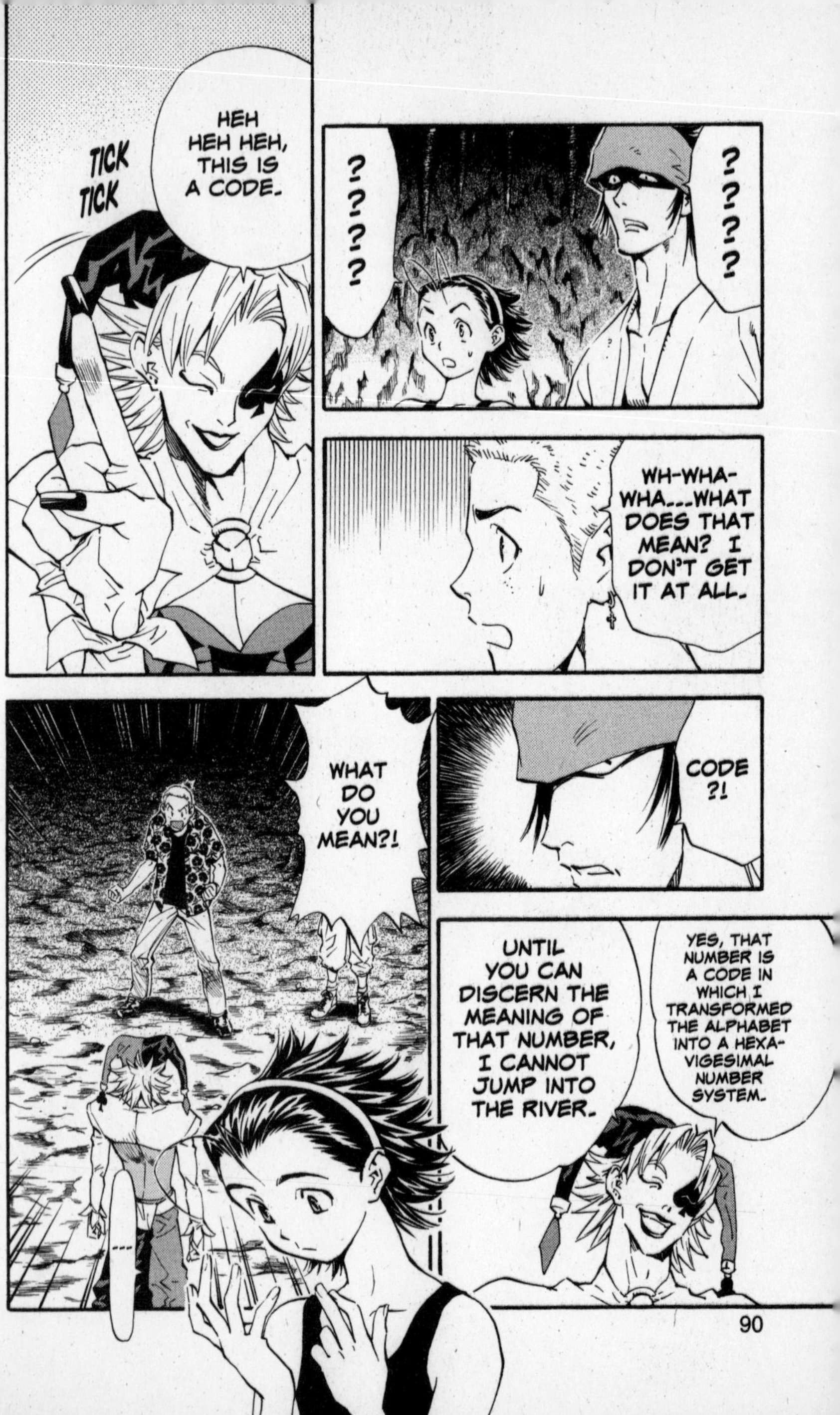

?????
?????
WH-WHA-WHA...WHAT DOES THAT MEAN? I DON'T GET IT AT ALL.
TICK TICK
HEH HEH HEH, THIS IS A CODE.
CODE?!
YES, THAT NUMBER IS A CODE IN WHICH I TRANSFORMED THE ALPHABET INTO A HEXA-VIGESIMAL NUMBER SYSTEM.
UNTIL YOU CAN DISCERN THE MEANING OF THAT NUMBER, I CANNOT JUMP INTO THE RIVER.
WHAT DO YOU MEAN?!
...

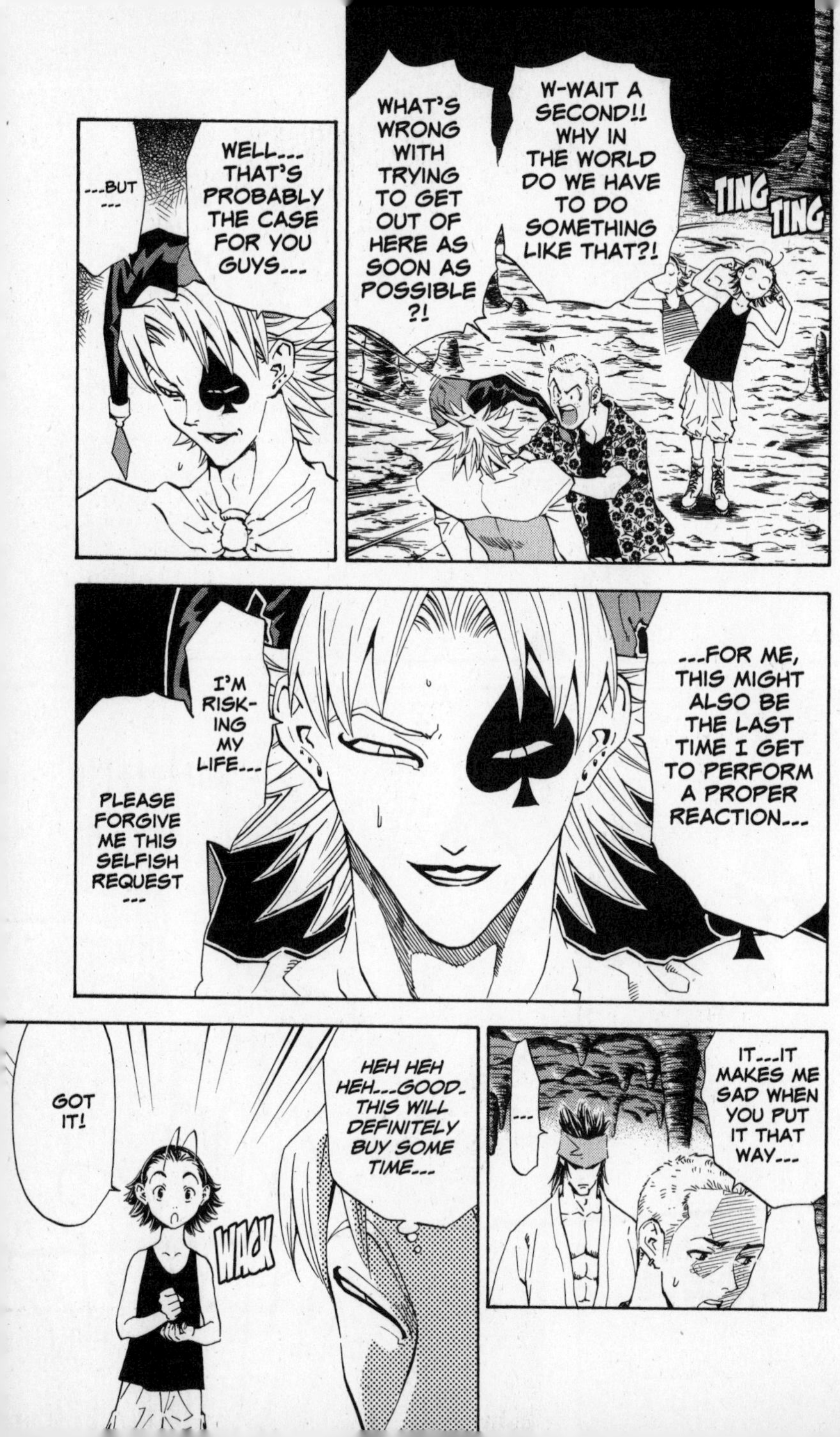
W-WAIT A SECOND!! WHY IN THE WORLD DO WE HAVE TO DO SOMETHING LIKE THAT?!
TING TING
WHAT'S WRONG WITH TRYING TO GET OUT OF HERE AS SOON AS POSSIBLE?!
WELL... THAT'S PROBABLY THE CASE FOR YOU GUYS...
...BUT ...
...FOR ME, THIS MIGHT ALSO BE THE LAST TIME I GET TO PERFORM A PROPER REACTION...
I'M RISKING MY LIFE...
PLEASE FORGIVE ME THIS SELFISH REQUEST...
IT...IT MAKES ME SAD WHEN YOU PUT IT THAT WAY...
...
HEH HEH HEH...GOOD. THIS WILL DEFINITELY BUY SOME TIME...
GOT IT!
WHACK

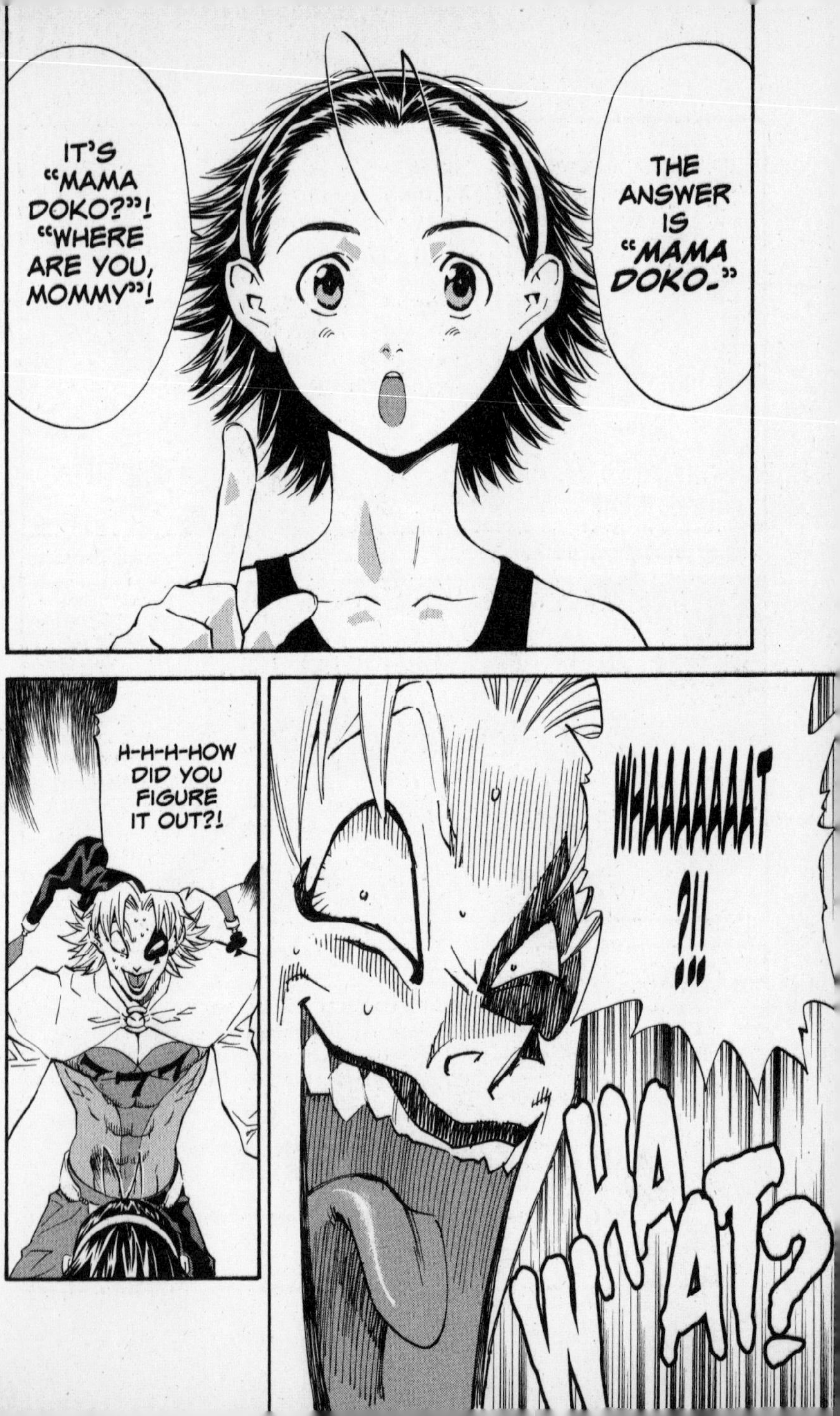
THE ANSWER IS "MAMA DOKO-"
IT'S "MAMA DOKO?"! "WHERE ARE YOU, MOMMY"!
WHAAAAAAAT ?!!
WHAT?
H-H-H-HOW DID YOU FIGURE IT OUT?!

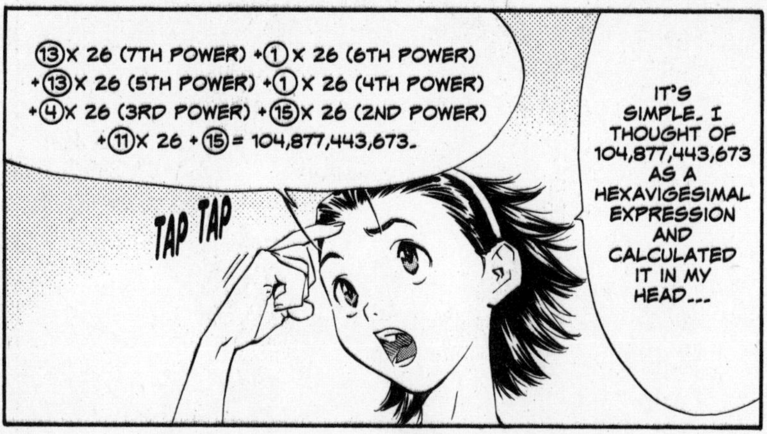
IT'S SIMPLE. I THOUGHT OF 104,877,443,673 AS A HEXAVIGESIMAL EXPRESSION AND CALCULATED IT IN MY HEAD...
⑬X 26 (7TH POWER) +①X 26 (6TH POWER) +⑬X 26 (5TH POWER) +①X 26 (4TH POWER) +④X 26 (3RD POWER) +⑮X 26 (2ND POWER) +⑪X 26 +⑮= 104,877,443,673.
TAP TAP

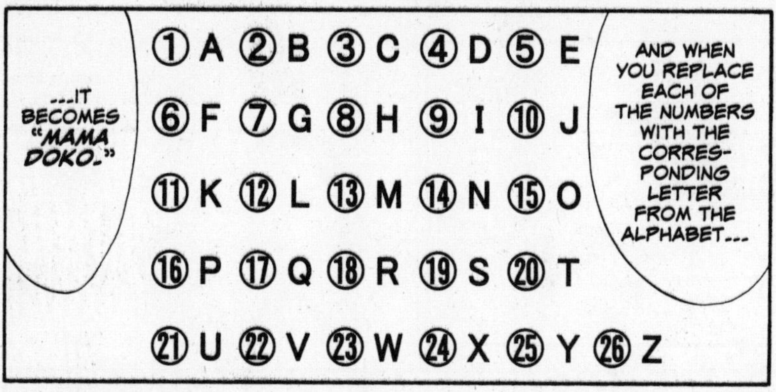
AND WHEN YOU REPLACE EACH OF THE NUMBERS WITH THE CORRES-PONDING LETTER FROM THE ALPHABET...
①A ②B ③C ④D ⑤E
⑥F ⑦G ⑧H ⑨I ⑩J
⑪K ⑫L ⑬M ⑭N ⑮O
⑯P ⑰Q ⑱R ⑲S ⑳T
㉑U ㉒V ㉓W ㉔X ㉕Y ㉖Z
...IT BECOMES "MAMA DOKO."

Supplementary Explanation

This manner of calculating is called "message encryption." RSA, which you're probably familiar with if you use a computer or the Internet, is also made with this manner of "message encryption."

Incidentally, if you want to send a message like DOG, it goes something like this: D =④, O =⑮, G =⑦.

It ends up becoming ④ x 26 (2nd power) +⑮ x 26 +⑦ = 3101.

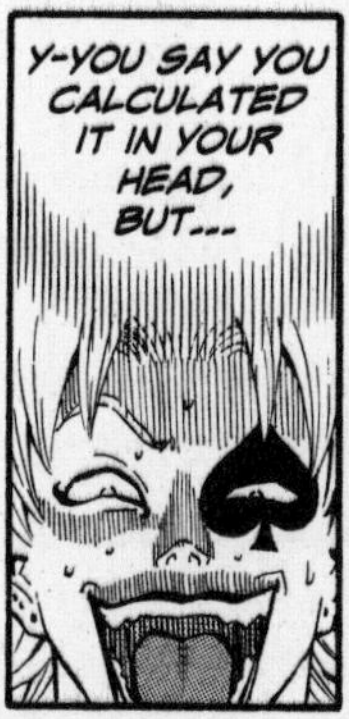
Y-YOU SAY YOU CALCULATED IT IN YOUR HEAD, BUT...

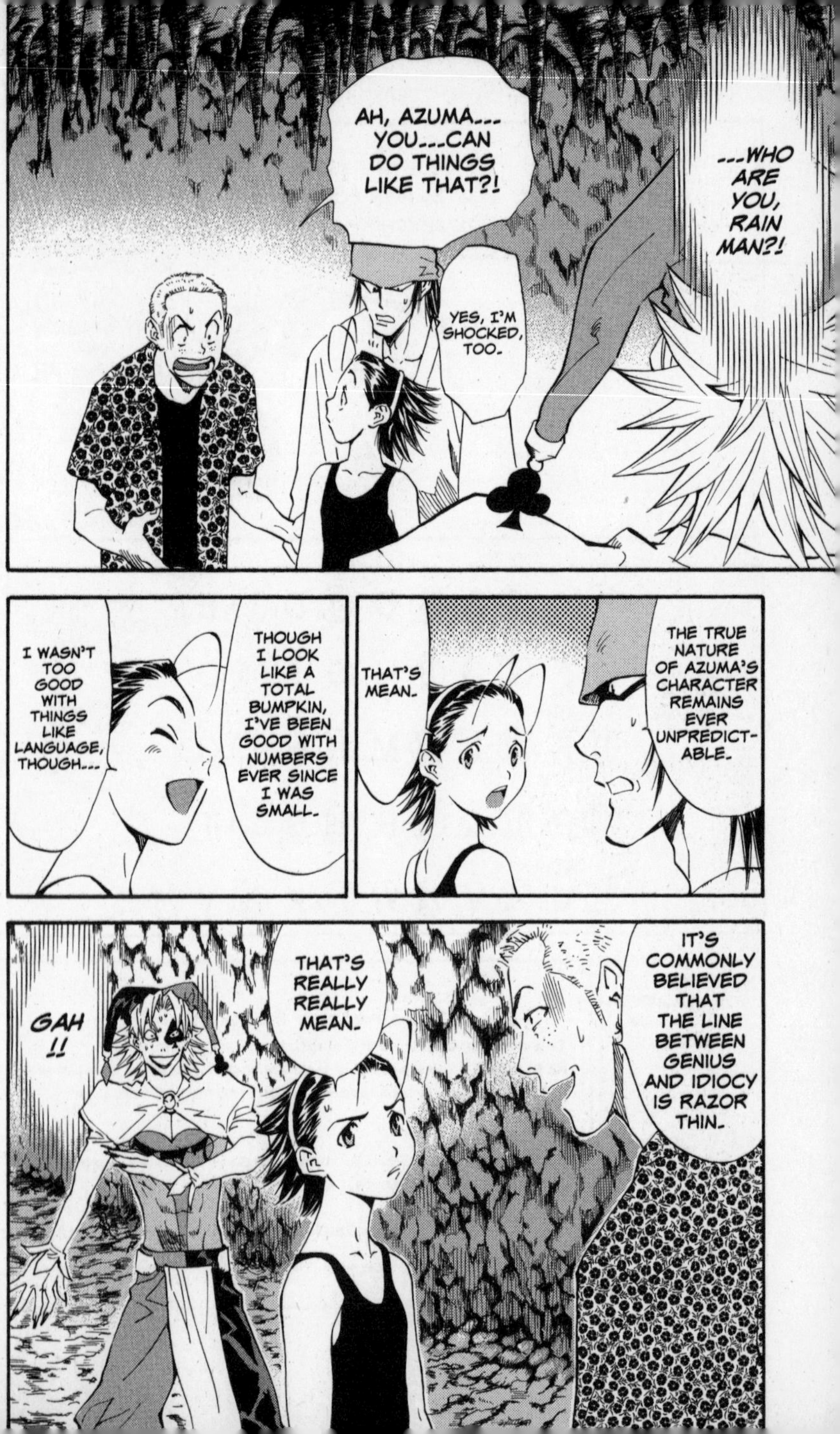
...WHO ARE YOU, RAIN MAN?!
AH, AZUMA... YOU...CAN DO THINGS LIKE THAT?!
YES, I'M SHOCKED, TOO.
THE TRUE NATURE OF AZUMA'S CHARACTER REMAINS EVER UNPREDICT-ABLE.
THAT'S MEAN.
THOUGH I LOOK LIKE A TOTAL BUMPKIN, I'VE BEEN GOOD WITH NUMBERS EVER SINCE I WAS SMALL.
I WASN'T TOO GOOD WITH THINGS LIKE LANGUAGE, THOUGH...
IT'S COMMONLY BELIEVED THAT THE LINE BETWEEN GENIUS AND IDIOCY IS RAZOR THIN.
THAT'S REALLY REALLY MEAN.
GAH !!

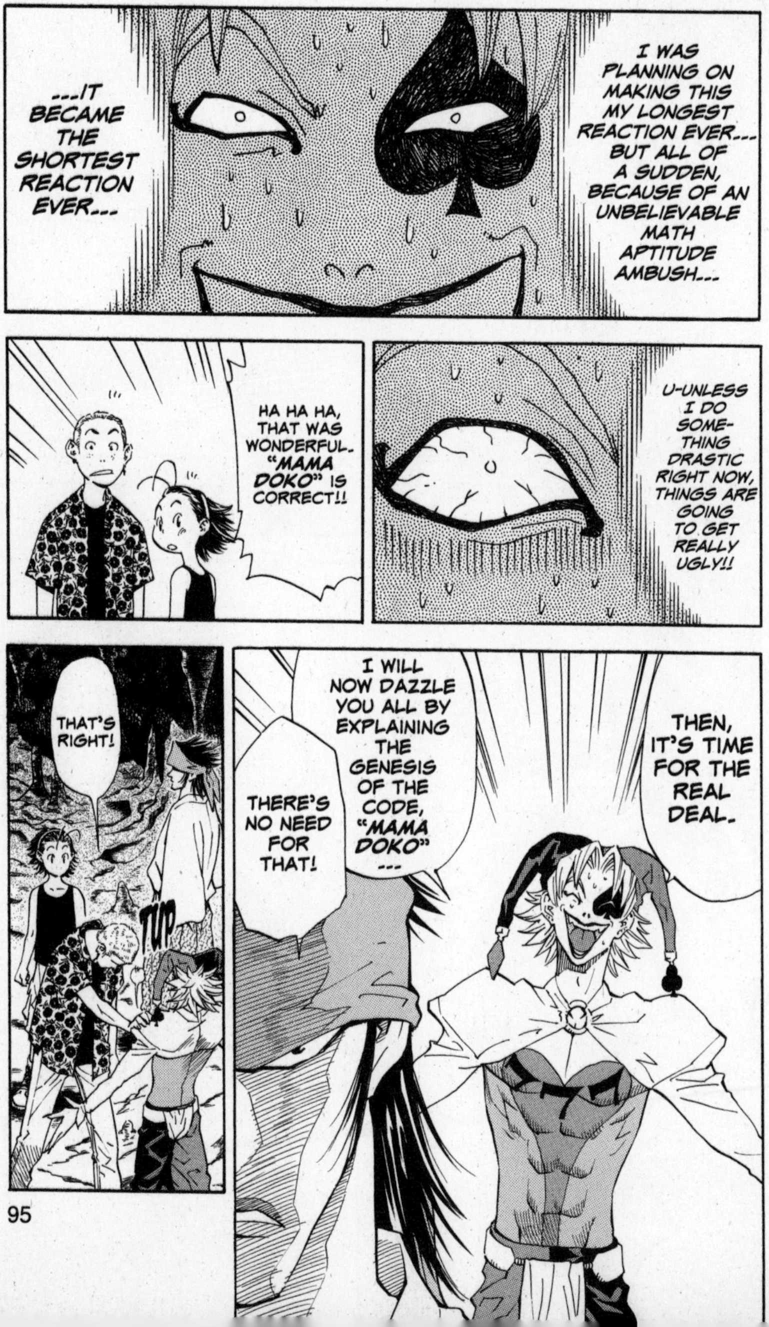
I WAS PLANNING ON MAKING THIS MY LONGEST REACTION EVER... BUT ALL OF A SUDDEN, BECAUSE OF AN UNBELIEVABLE MATH APTITUDE AMBUSH...
...IT BECAME THE SHORTEST REACTION EVER...
U-UNLESS I DO SOME-THING DRASTIC RIGHT NOW, THINGS ARE GOING TO GET REALLY UGLY!!
HA HA HA, THAT WAS WONDERFUL. "MAMA DOKO" IS CORRECT!!
THEN, IT'S TIME FOR THE REAL DEAL.
I WILL NOW DAZZLE YOU ALL BY EXPLAINING THE GENESIS OF THE CODE, "MAMA DOKO"...
THERE'S NO NEED FOR THAT!
THAT'S RIGHT!
TUP

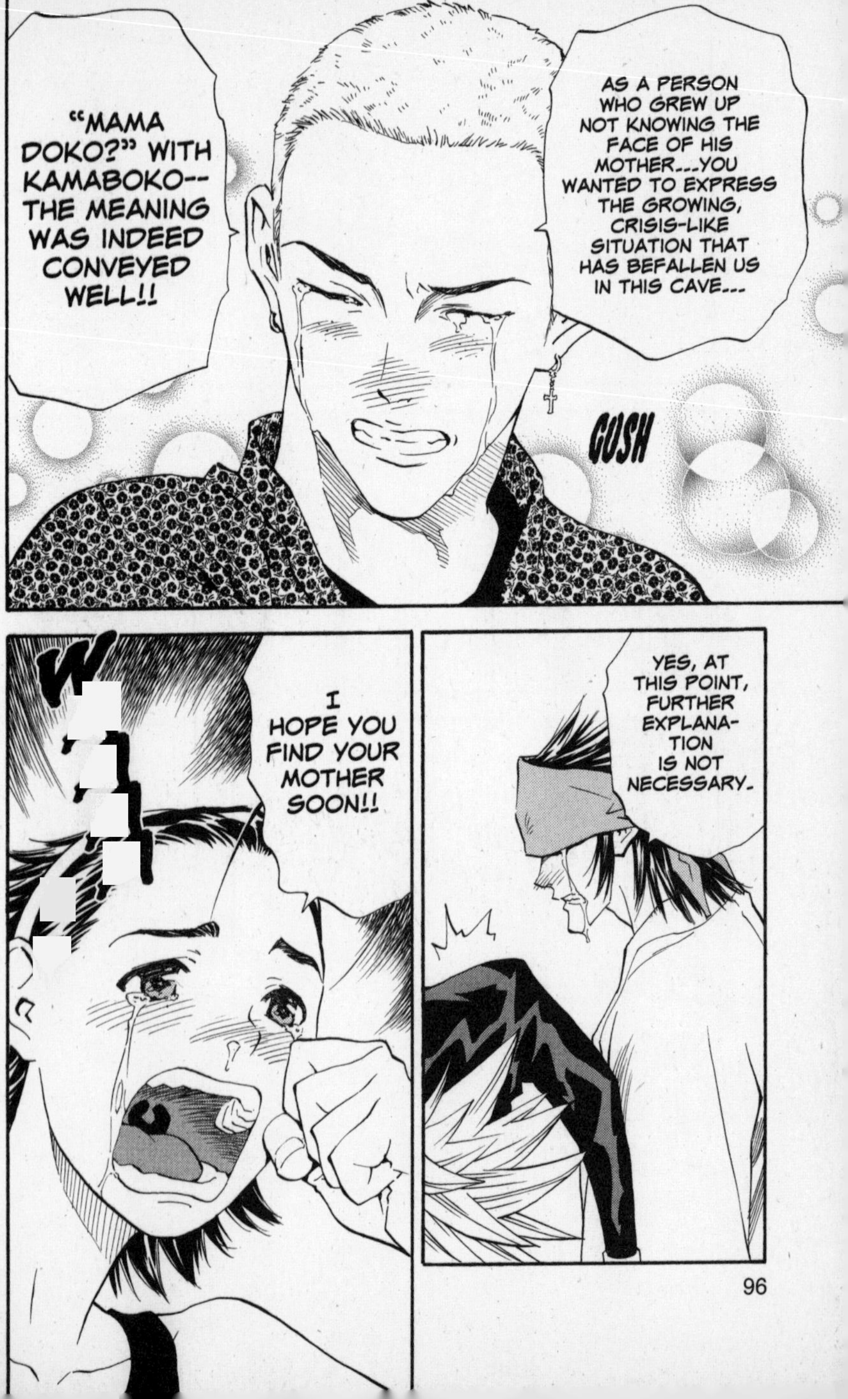
AS A PERSON WHO GREW UP NOT KNOWING THE FACE OF HIS MOTHER...YOU WANTED TO EXPRESS THE GROWING, CRISIS-LIKE SITUATION THAT HAS BEFALLEN US IN THIS CAVE...
"MAMA DOKO?" WITH KAMABOKO-- THE MEANING WAS INDEED CONVEYED WELL!!
GUSH
YES, AT THIS POINT, FURTHER EXPLANATION IS NOT NECESSARY.
I HOPE YOU FIND YOUR MOTHER SOON!!
W

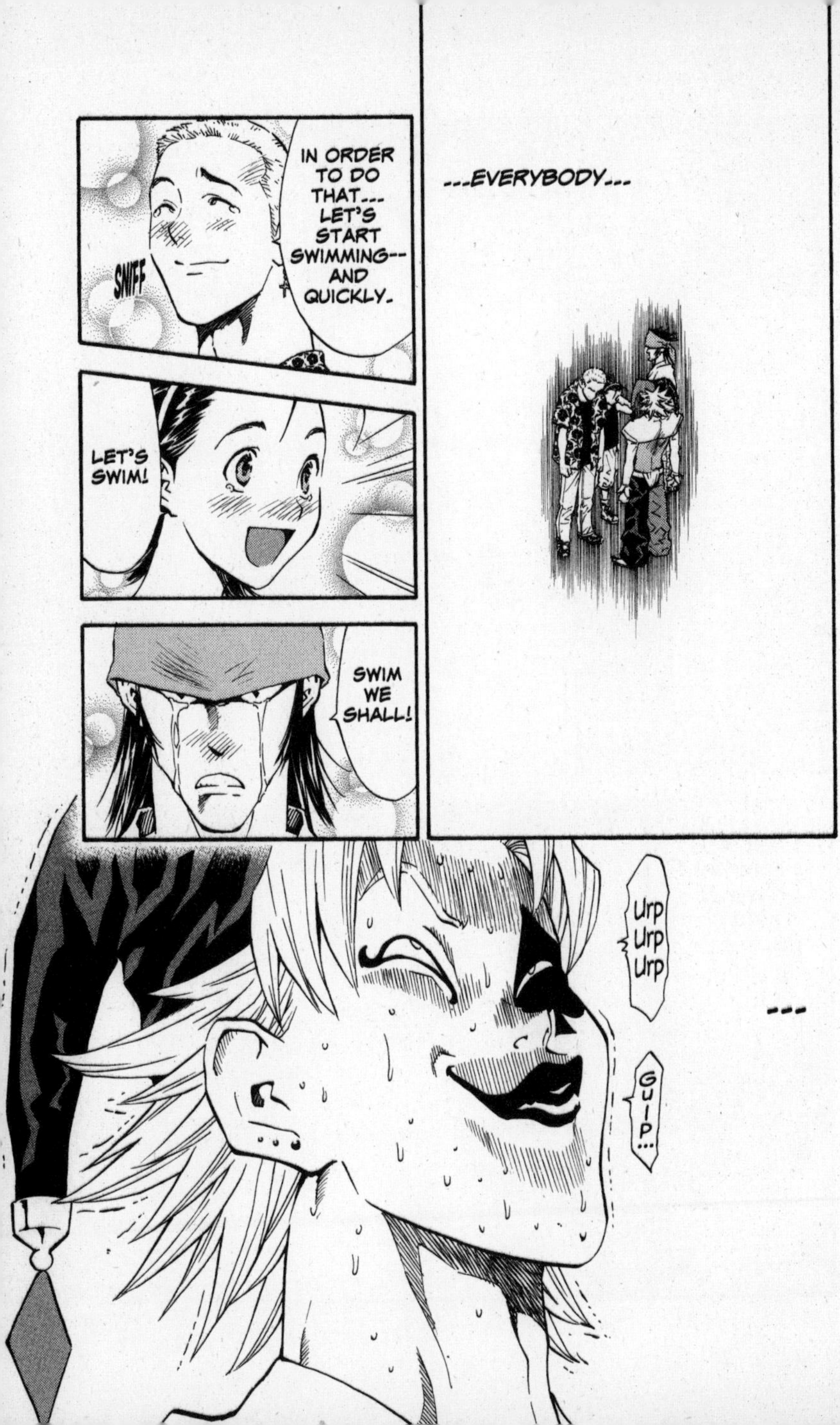
...EVERYBODY...
IN ORDER TO DO THAT... LET'S START SWIMMING-- AND QUICKLY.
SNIFF
LET'S SWIM!
SWIM WE SHALL!
...
Urp Urp Urp
Gulp...

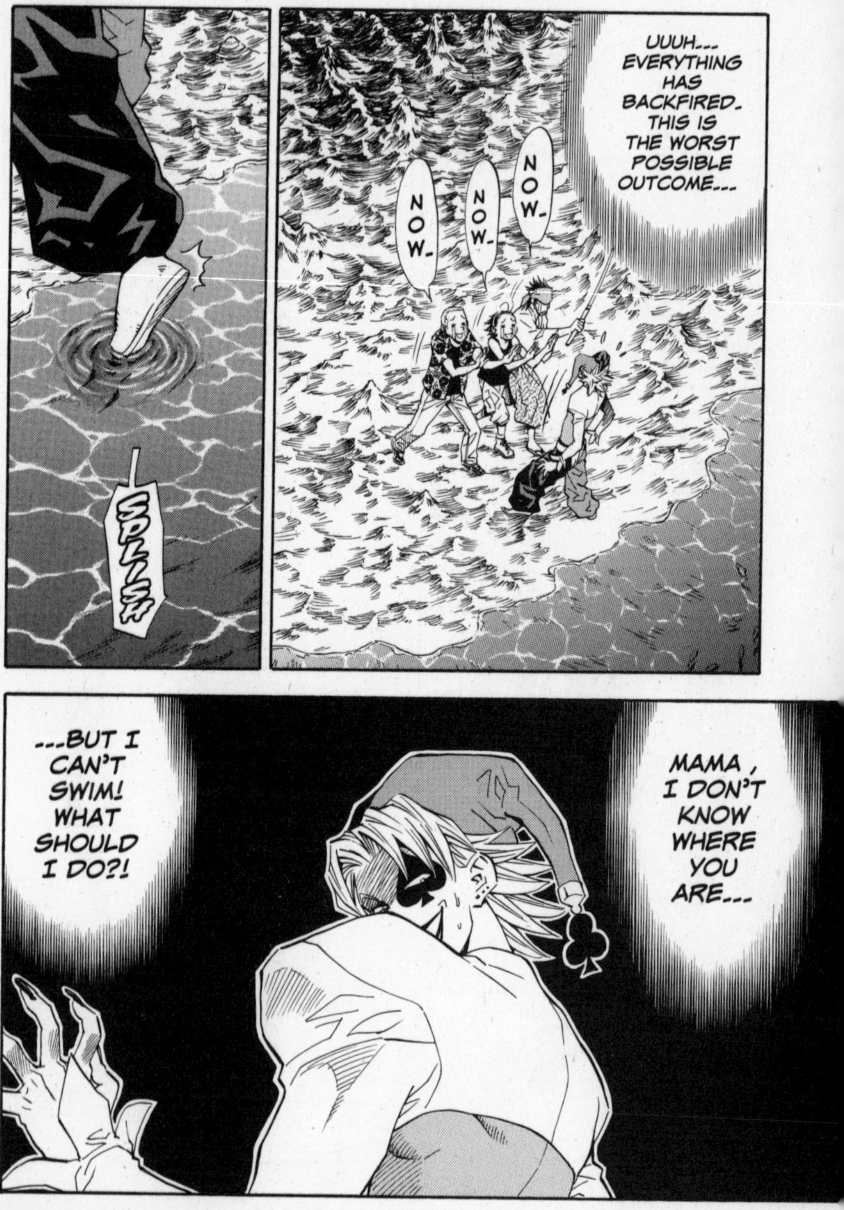
UUUH... EVERYTHING HAS BACKFIRED. THIS IS THE WORST POSSIBLE OUTCOME...
NOW..
NOW..
NOW..
SPLISH
MAMA, I DON'T KNOW WHERE YOU ARE...
...BUT I CAN'T SWIM! WHAT SHOULD I DO?!

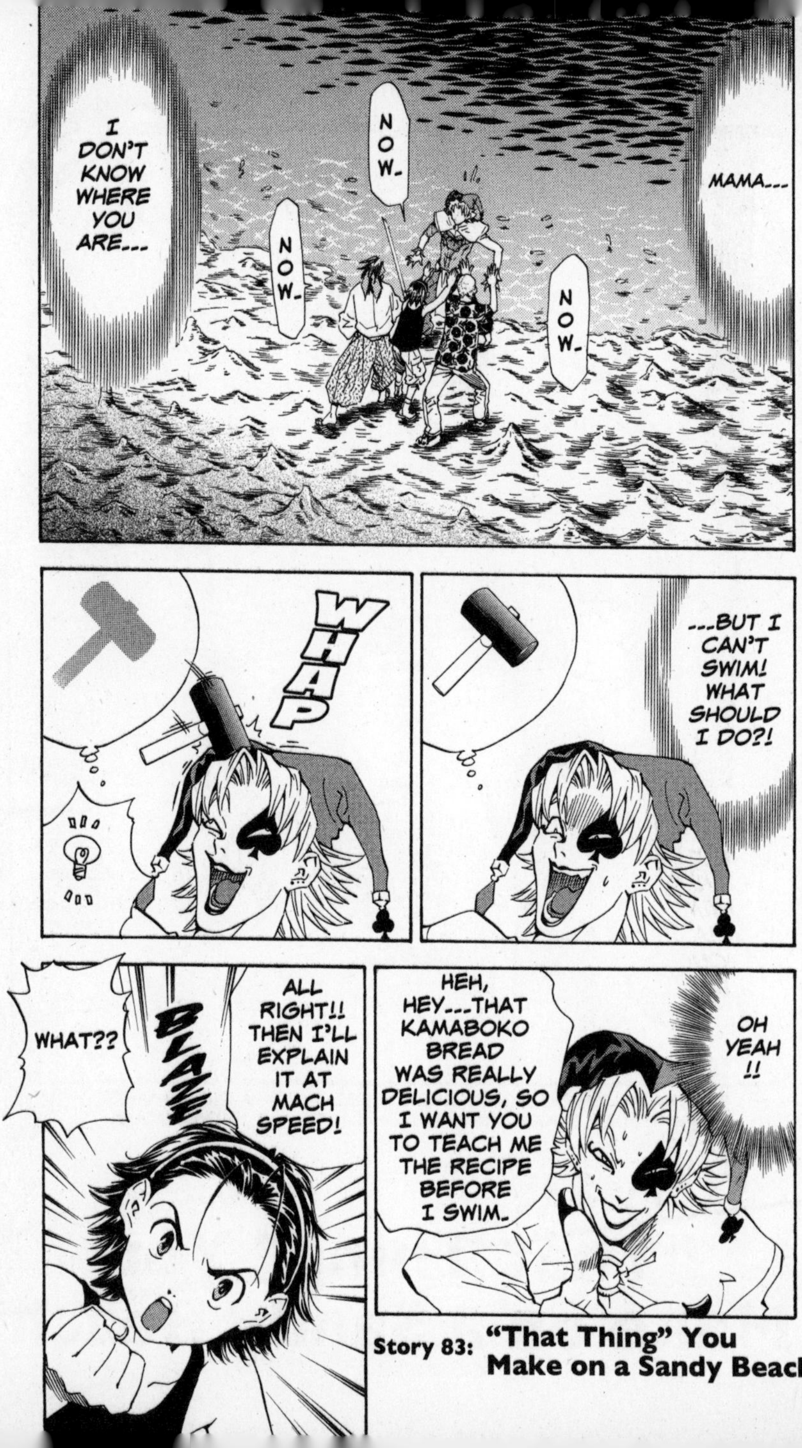
MAMA...
NOW.
NOW.
NOW.
I DON'T KNOW WHERE YOU ARE...
...BUT I CAN'T SWIM! WHAT SHOULD I DO?!
WHAP
OH YEAH!!
HEH, HEY...THAT KAMABOKO BREAD WAS REALLY DELICIOUS, SO I WANT YOU TO TEACH ME THE RECIPE BEFORE I SWIM.
ALL RIGHT!! THEN I'LL EXPLAIN IT AT MACH SPEED!
BLAZE
WHAT??

Story 83: **"That Thing" You Make on a Sandy Beach**

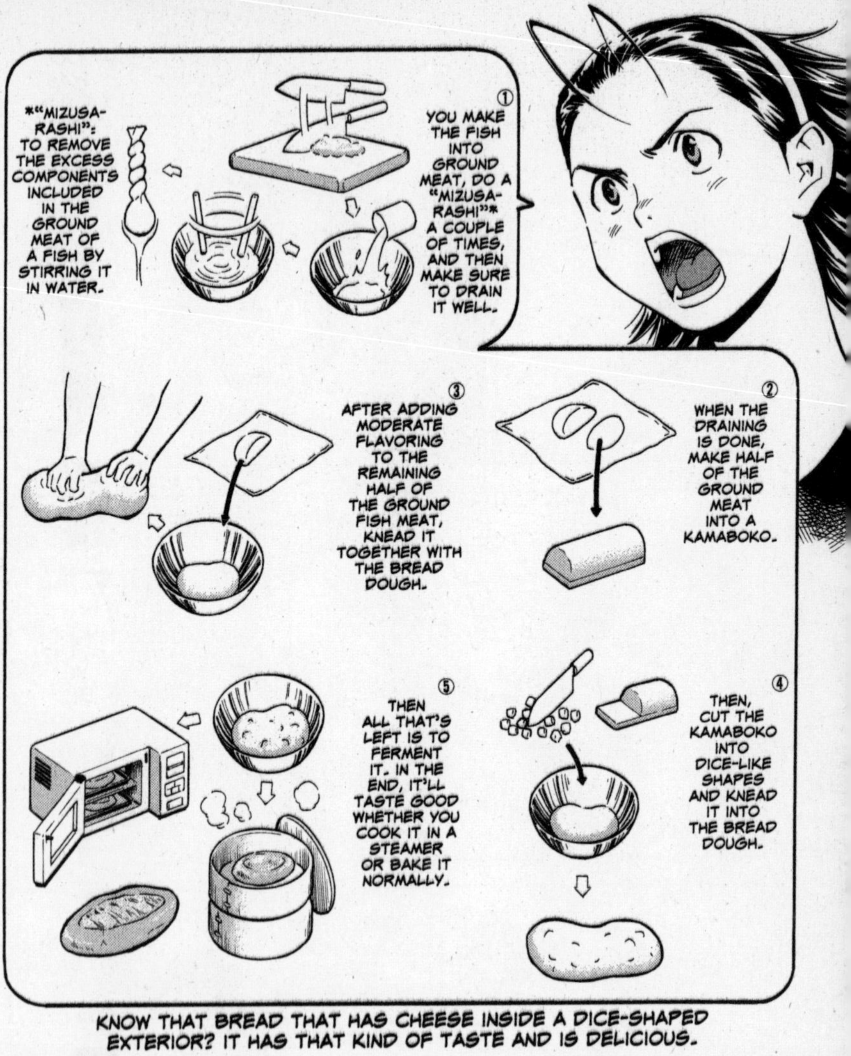
① YOU MAKE THE FISH INTO GROUND MEAT, DO A "MIZUSA-RASHI"* A COUPLE OF TIMES, AND THEN MAKE SURE TO DRAIN IT WELL.
*"MIZUSA-RASHI": TO REMOVE THE EXCESS COMPONENTS INCLUDED IN THE GROUND MEAT OF A FISH BY STIRRING IT IN WATER.
② WHEN THE DRAINING IS DONE, MAKE HALF OF THE GROUND MEAT INTO A KAMABOKO.
③ AFTER ADDING MODERATE FLAVORING TO THE REMAINING HALF OF THE GROUND FISH MEAT, KNEAD IT TOGETHER WITH THE BREAD DOUGH.
④ THEN, CUT THE KAMABOKO INTO DICE-LIKE SHAPES AND KNEAD IT INTO THE BREAD DOUGH.
⑤ THEN ALL THAT'S LEFT IS TO FERMENT IT. IN THE END, IT'LL TASTE GOOD WHETHER YOU COOK IT IN A STEAMER OR BAKE IT NORMALLY.
KNOW THAT BREAD THAT HAS CHEESE INSIDE A DICE-SHAPED EXTERIOR? IT HAS THAT KIND OF TASTE AND IS DELICIOUS.

Story 83:
"That Thing" You Make on a Sandy Beach

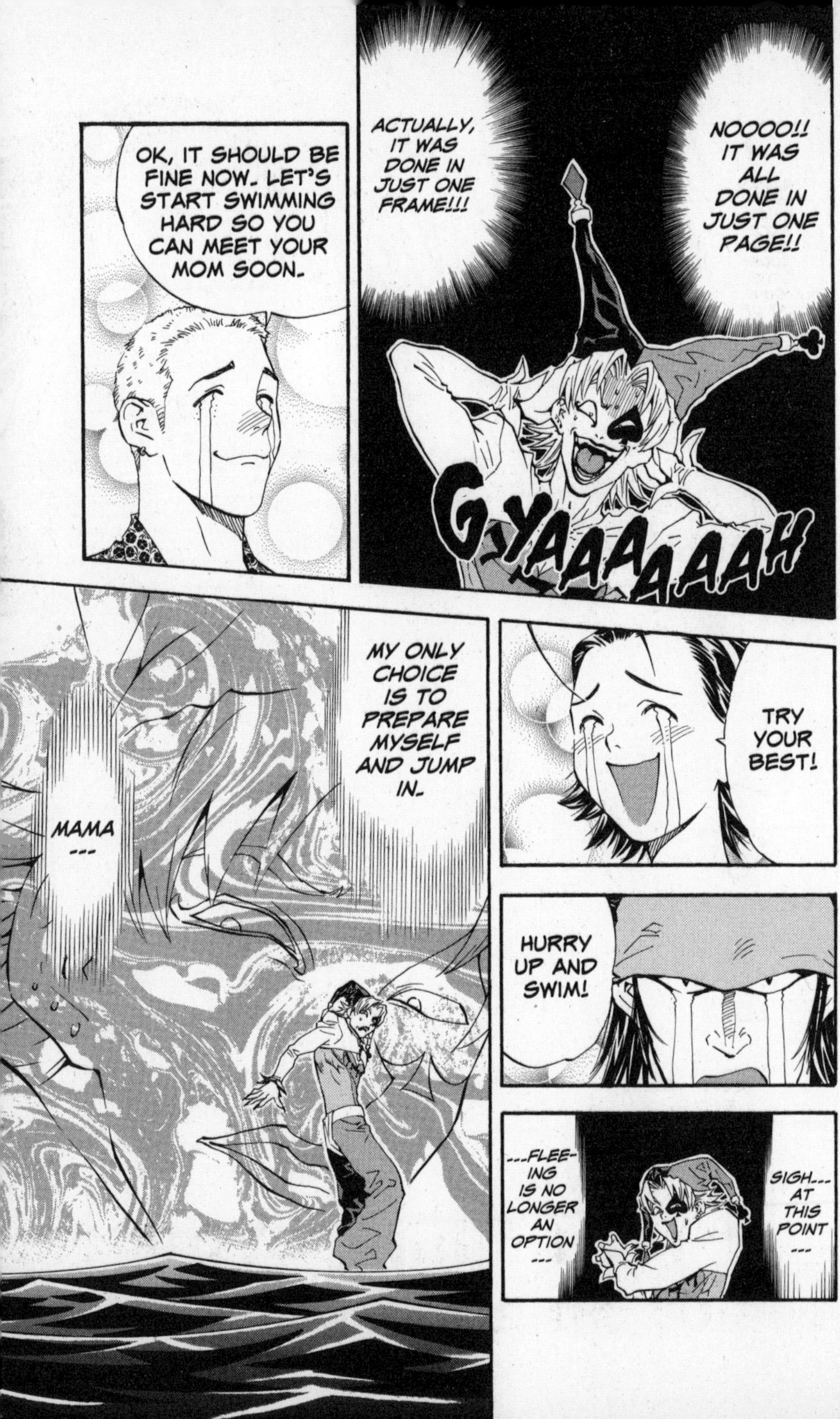
NOOOO!! IT WAS ALL DONE IN JUST ONE PAGE!!
ACTUALLY, IT WAS DONE IN JUST ONE FRAME!!!
GYAAAAAAH
OK, IT SHOULD BE FINE NOW. LET'S START SWIMMING HARD SO YOU CAN MEET YOUR MOM SOON.
TRY YOUR BEST!
HURRY UP AND SWIM!
SIGH... AT THIS POINT ...
...FLEE-ING IS NO LONGER AN OPTION ...
MY ONLY CHOICE IS TO PREPARE MYSELF AND JUMP IN.
MAMA ...

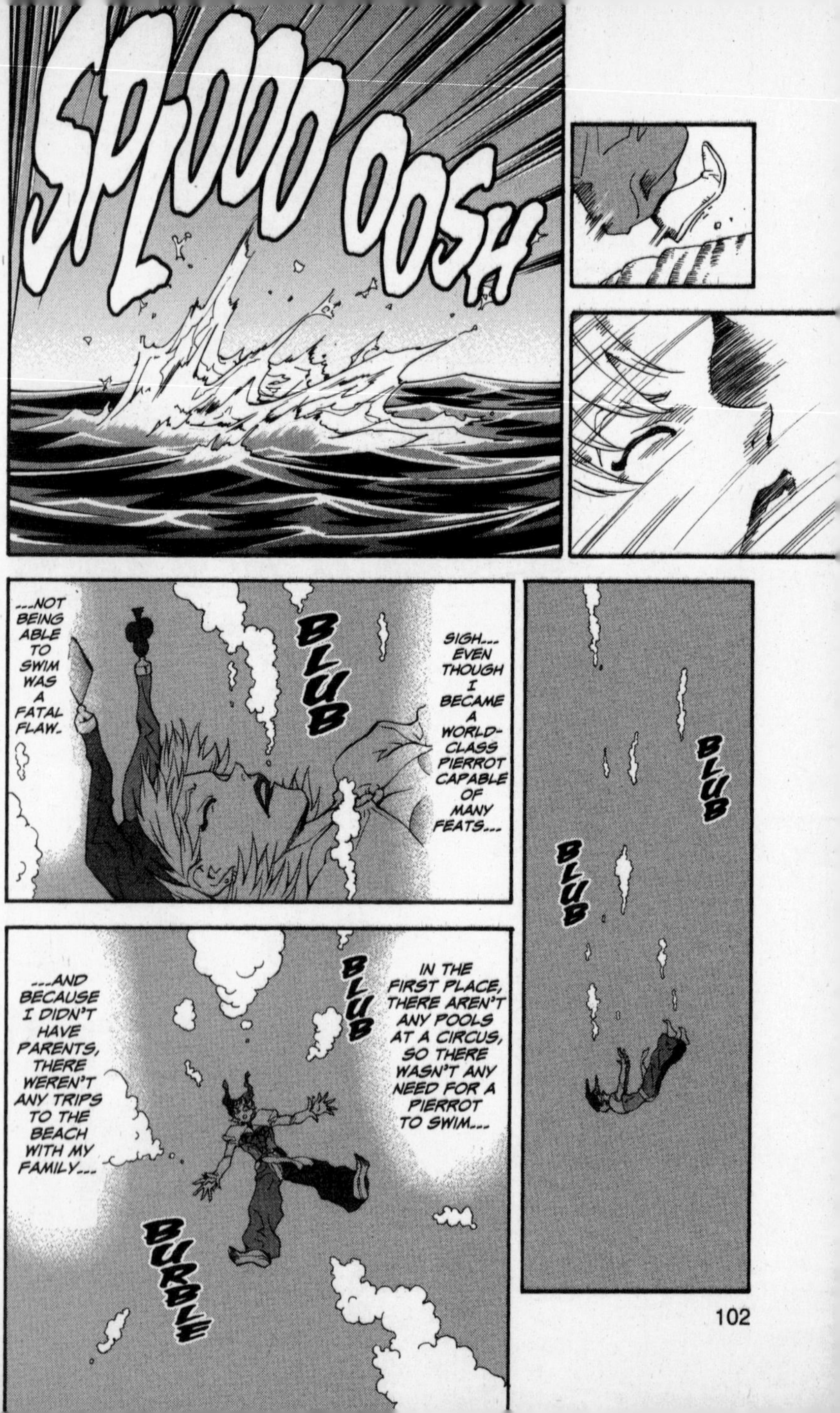
SPLOOOO OOSH
BLUB
BLUB
BLUB
SIGH... EVEN THOUGH I BECAME A WORLD-CLASS PIERROT CAPABLE OF MANY FEATS...
...NOT BEING ABLE TO SWIM WAS A FATAL FLAW.
BLUB
IN THE FIRST PLACE, THERE AREN'T ANY POOLS AT A CIRCUS, SO THERE WASN'T ANY NEED FOR A PIERROT TO SWIM...
...AND BECAUSE I DIDN'T HAVE PARENTS, THERE WEREN'T ANY TRIPS TO THE BEACH WITH MY FAMILY...
BURBLE

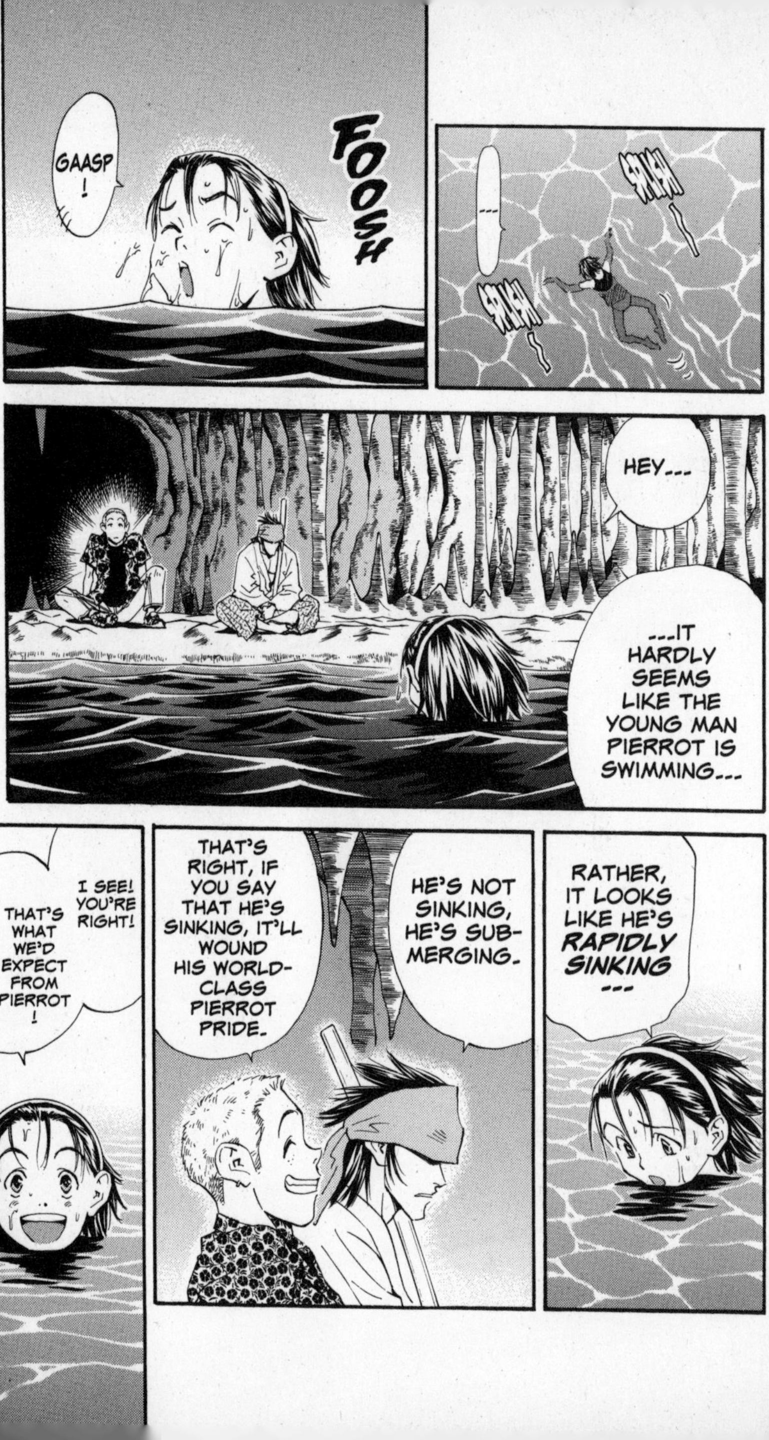
...
GAASP!
FOOSH
HEY...
...IT HARDLY SEEMS LIKE THE YOUNG MAN PIERROT IS SWIMMING...
RATHER, IT LOOKS LIKE HE'S RAPIDLY SINKING...
HE'S NOT SINKING, HE'S SUBMERGING.
THAT'S RIGHT, IF YOU SAY THAT HE'S SINKING, IT'LL WOUND HIS WORLD-CLASS PIERROT PRIDE.
I SEE! YOU'RE RIGHT!
THAT'S WHAT WE'D EXPECT FROM PIERROT!

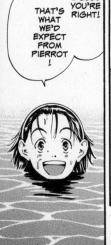

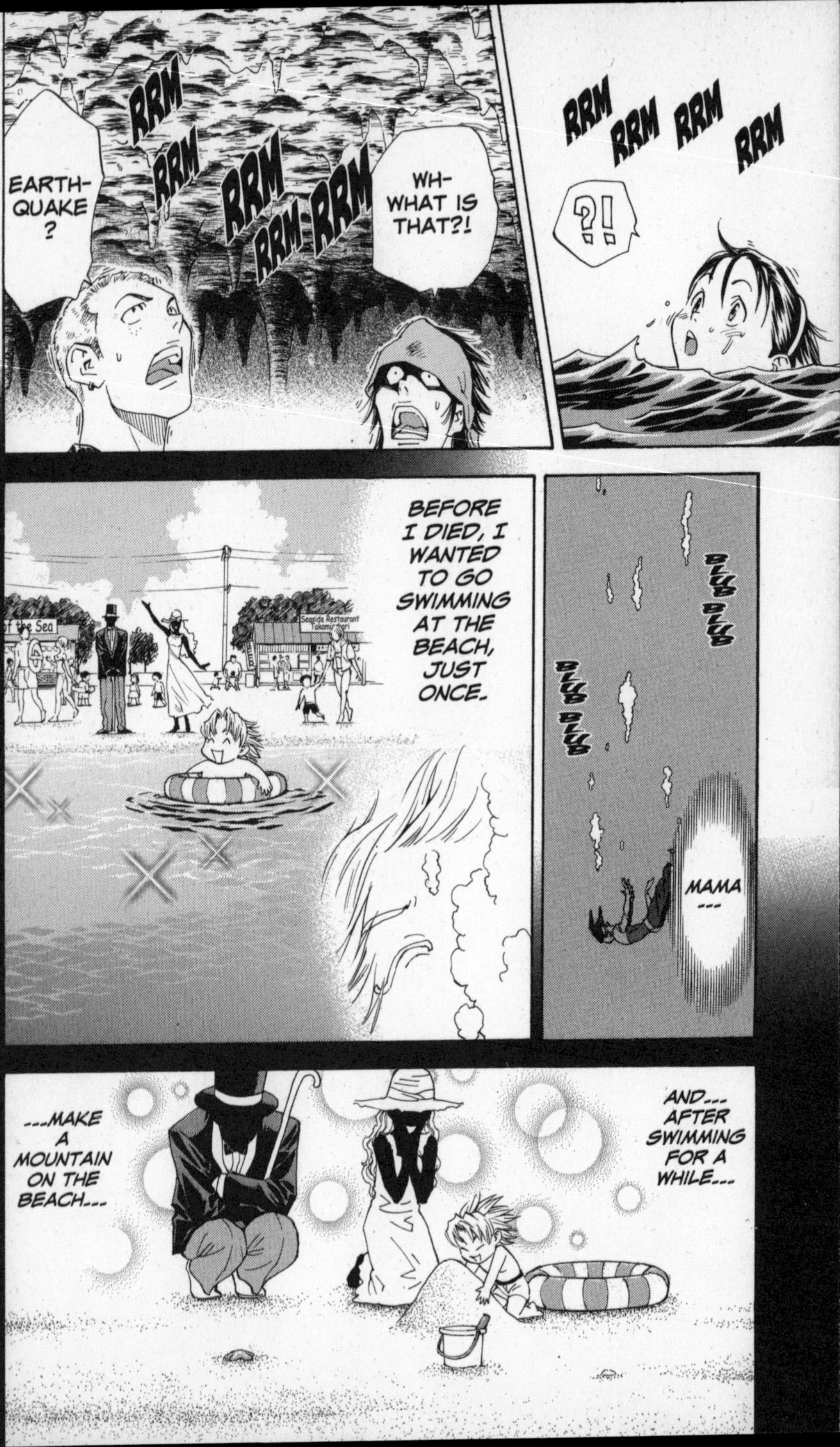
RRM RRM RRM RRM
?!
WH- WHAT IS THAT?!
RRM RRM RRM RRM RRM
EARTH-QUAKE?
BLUB BLUB
BLUB BLUB
MAMA---
BEFORE I DIED, I WANTED TO GO SWIMMING AT THE BEACH, JUST ONCE.
Seaside Restaurant
of the Sea
AND... AFTER SWIMMING FOR A WHILE...
...MAKE A MOUNTAIN ON THE BEACH...

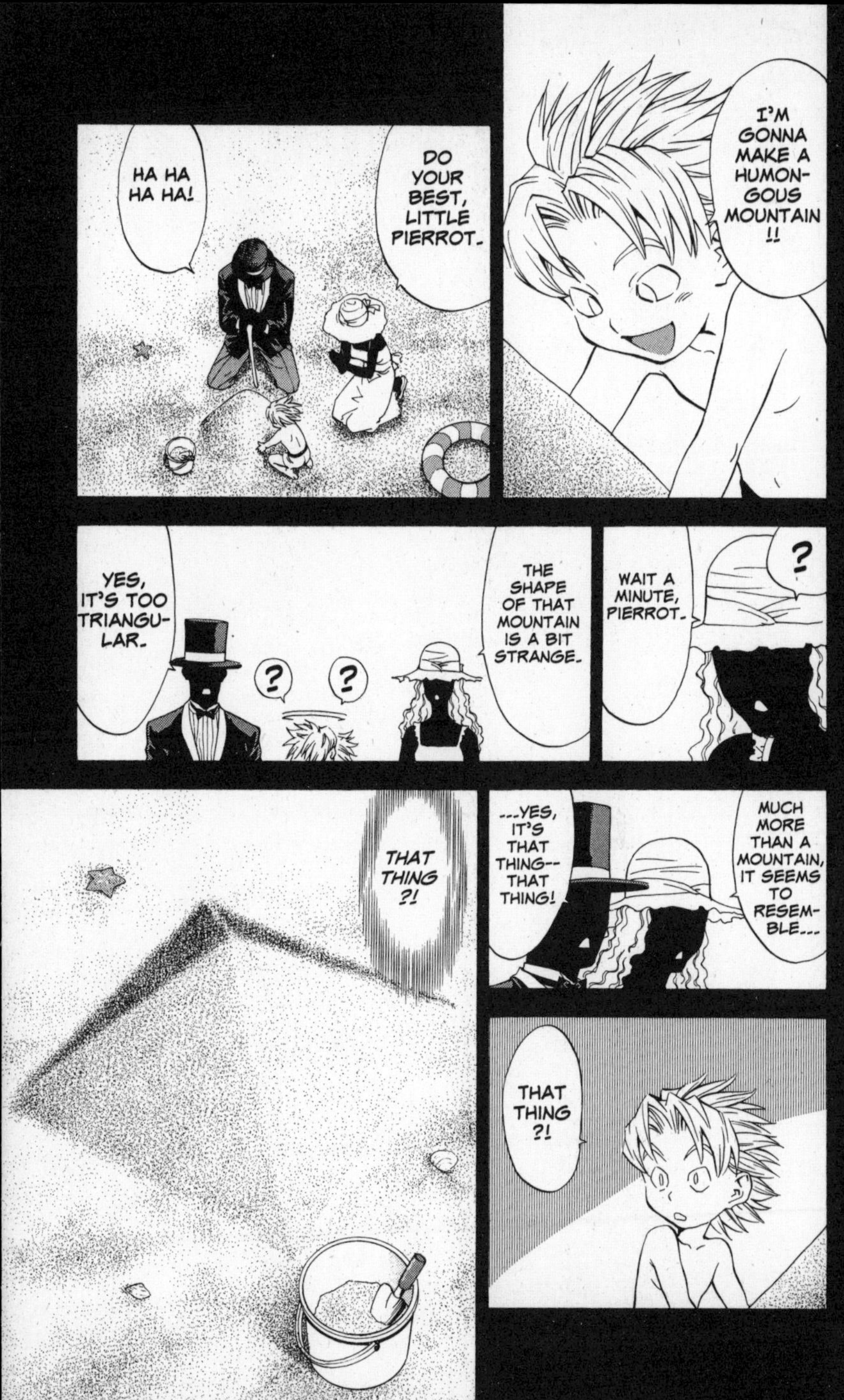
I'M GONNA MAKE A HUMON-GOUS MOUNTAIN !!
DO YOUR BEST, LITTLE PIERROT.
HA HA HA HA!
?
WAIT A MINUTE, PIERROT.
THE SHAPE OF THAT MOUNTAIN IS A BIT STRANGE.
?
?
YES, IT'S TOO TRIANGU-LAR.
MUCH MORE THAN A MOUNTAIN, IT SEEMS TO RESEMB-LE...
...YES, IT'S THAT THING--THAT THING!
THAT THING ?!
THAT THING ?!

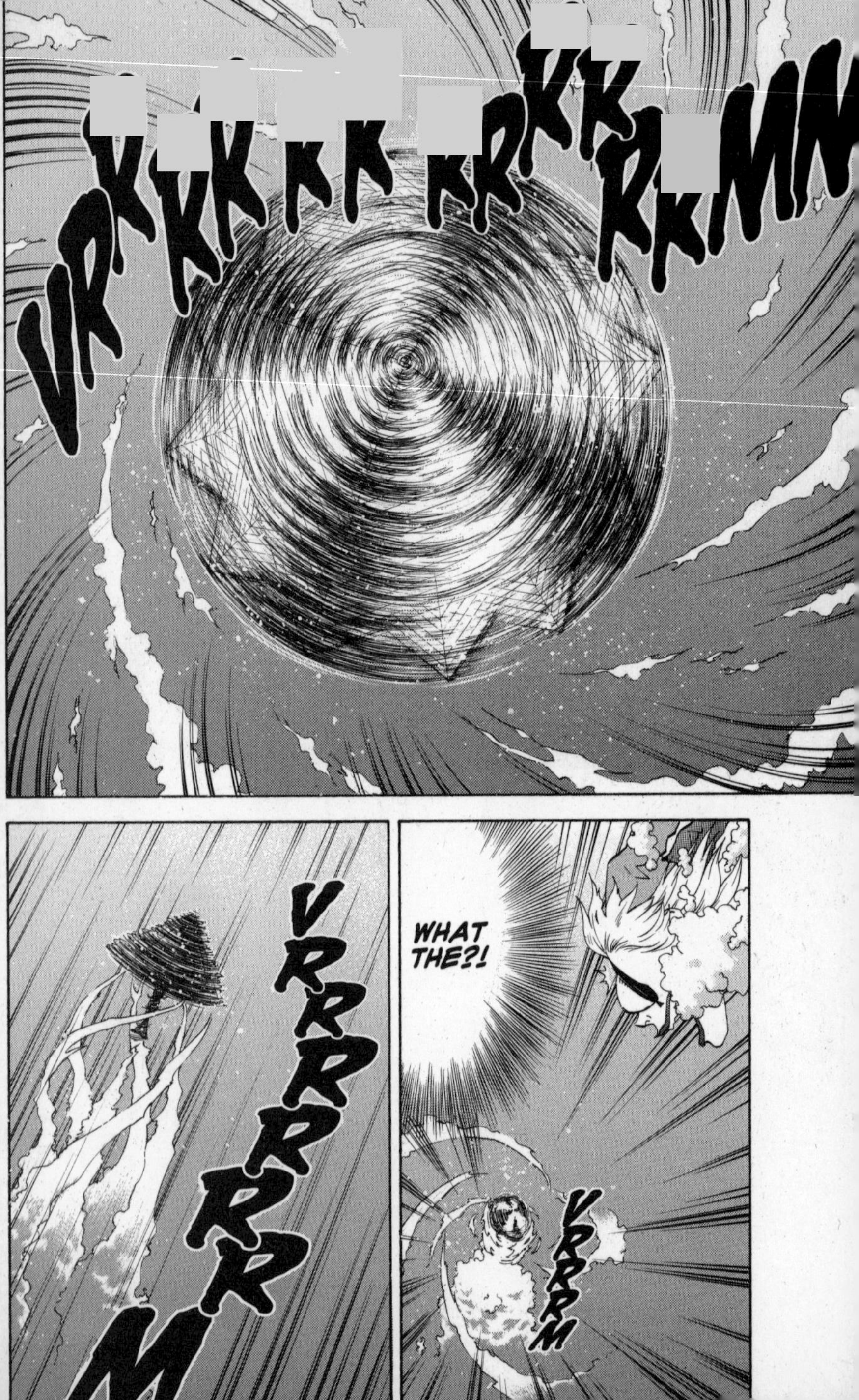
WHAT THE?!
VRRRM
VRRRRRRRM

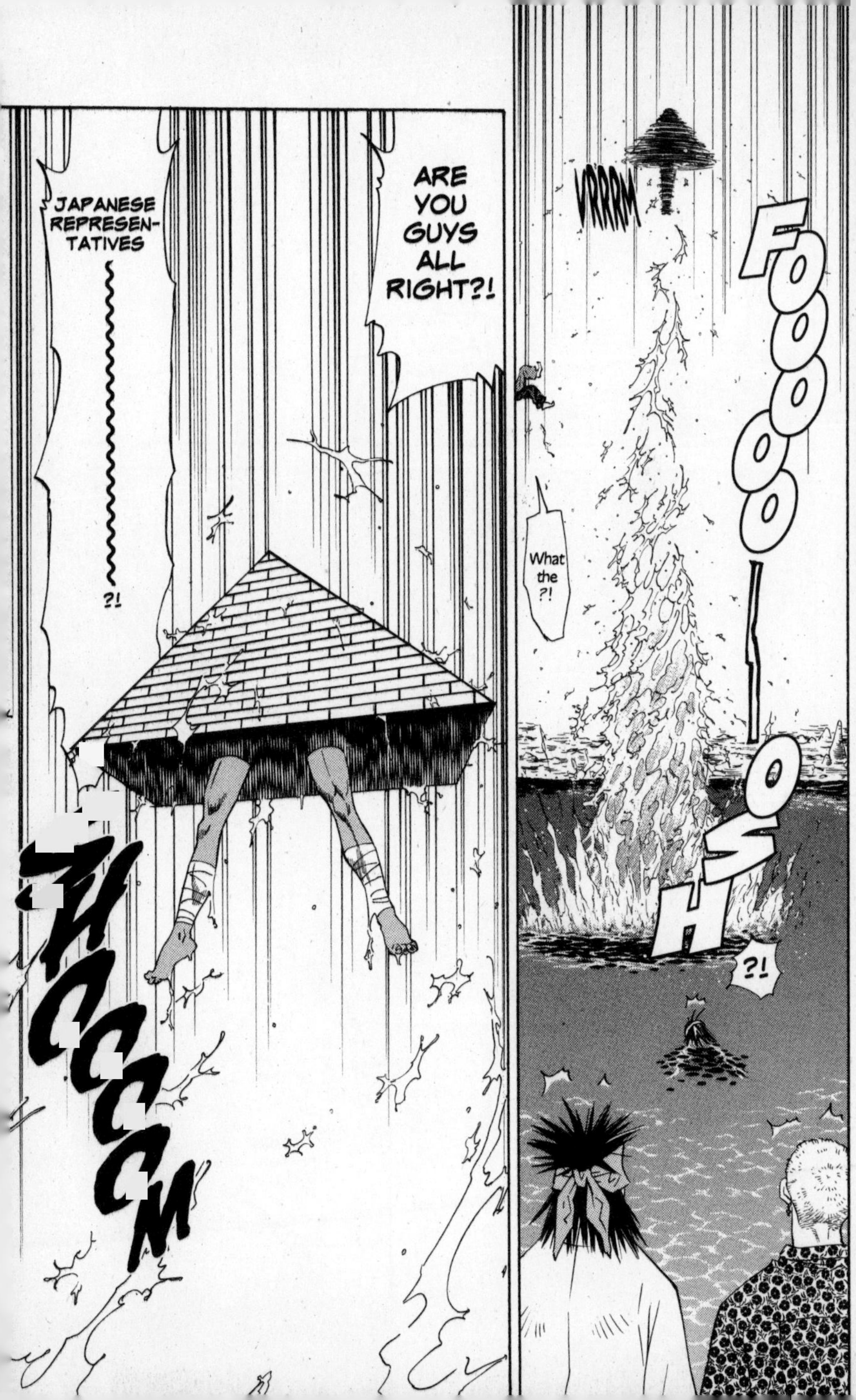
VRRRM
FOOOOO—OSH
What the ?!
?!
ARE YOU GUYS ALL RIGHT?!
JAPANESE REPRESEN-TATIVES ~ ?!

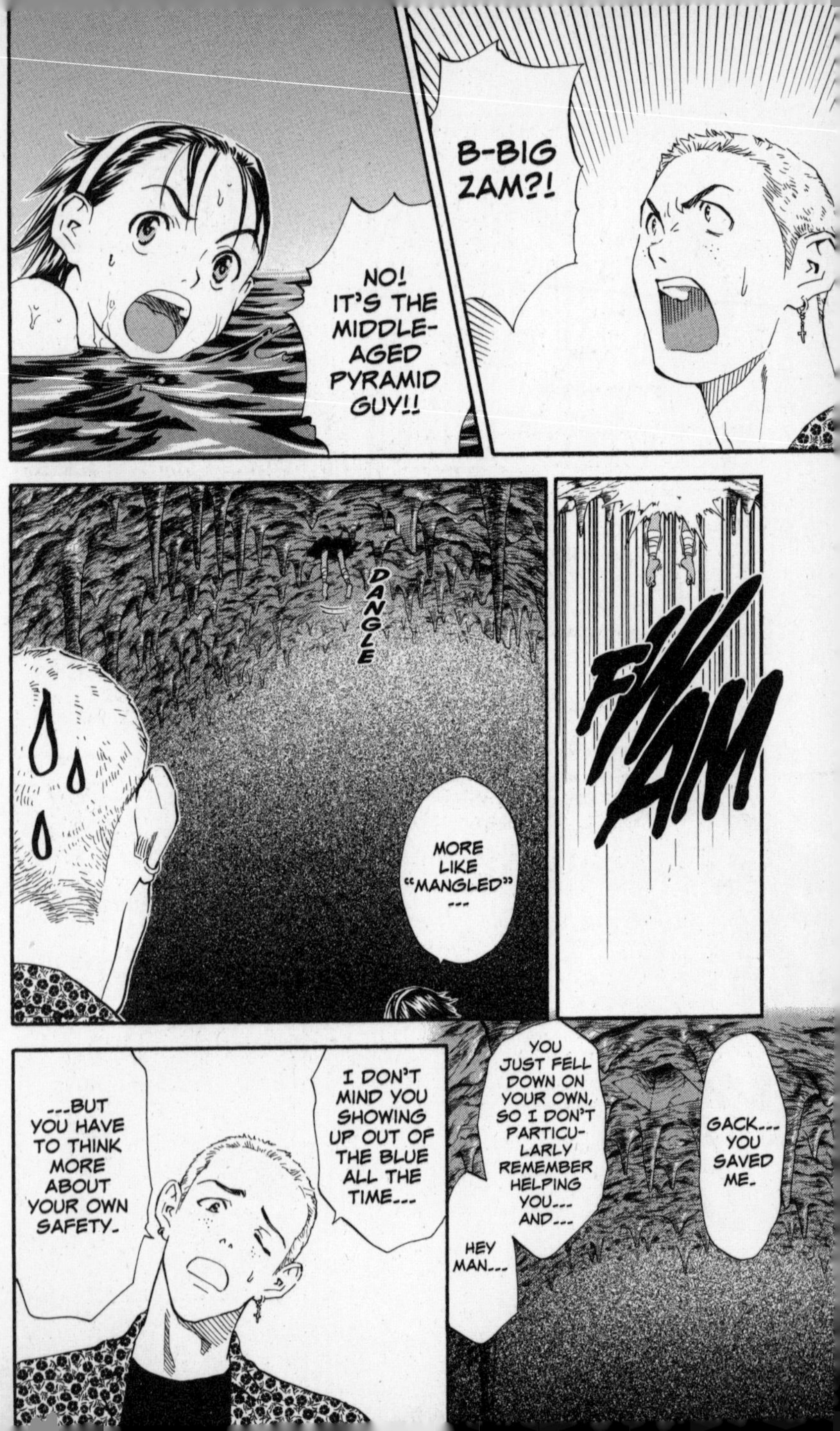
B-BIG ZAM?!
NO! IT'S THE MIDDLE-AGED PYRAMID GUY!!
FWAM
DANGLE
MORE LIKE "MANGLED"...
GACK... YOU SAVED ME.
YOU JUST FELL DOWN ON YOUR OWN, SO I DON'T PARTICULARLY REMEMBER HELPING YOU... AND...
HEY MAN...
I DON'T MIND YOU SHOWING UP OUT OF THE BLUE ALL THE TIME...
...BUT YOU HAVE TO THINK MORE ABOUT YOUR OWN SAFETY.

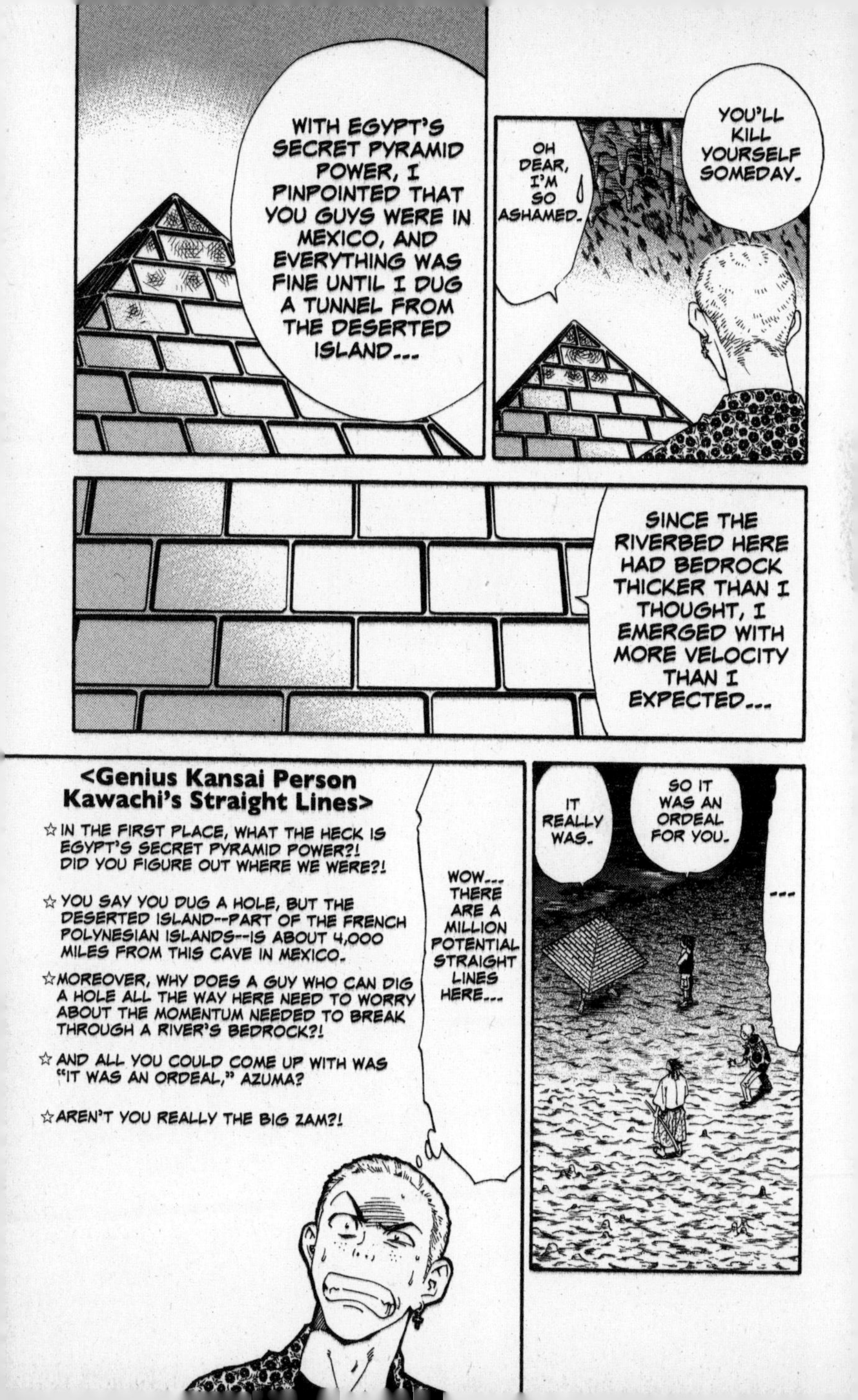
YOU'LL KILL YOURSELF SOMEDAY.
OH DEAR, I'M SO ASHAMED.
WITH EGYPT'S SECRET PYRAMID POWER, I PINPOINTED THAT YOU GUYS WERE IN MEXICO, AND EVERYTHING WAS FINE UNTIL I DUG A TUNNEL FROM THE DESERTED ISLAND...
SINCE THE RIVERBED HERE HAD BEDROCK THICKER THAN I THOUGHT, I EMERGED WITH MORE VELOCITY THAN I EXPECTED...
SO IT WAS AN ORDEAL FOR YOU.
IT REALLY WAS.
...
WOW... THERE ARE A MILLION POTENTIAL STRAIGHT LINES HERE...
<Genius Kansai Person Kawachi's Straight Lines>
☆ IN THE FIRST PLACE, WHAT THE HECK IS EGYPT'S SECRET PYRAMID POWER?! DID YOU FIGURE OUT WHERE WE WERE?!
☆ YOU SAY YOU DUG A HOLE, BUT THE DESERTED ISLAND--PART OF THE FRENCH POLYNESIAN ISLANDS--IS ABOUT 4,000 MILES FROM THIS CAVE IN MEXICO.
☆ MOREOVER, WHY DOES A GUY WHO CAN DIG A HOLE ALL THE WAY HERE NEED TO WORRY ABOUT THE MOMENTUM NEEDED TO BREAK THROUGH A RIVER'S BEDROCK?!
☆ AND ALL YOU COULD COME UP WITH WAS "IT WAS AN ORDEAL," AZUMA?
☆ AREN'T YOU REALLY THE BIG ZAM?!

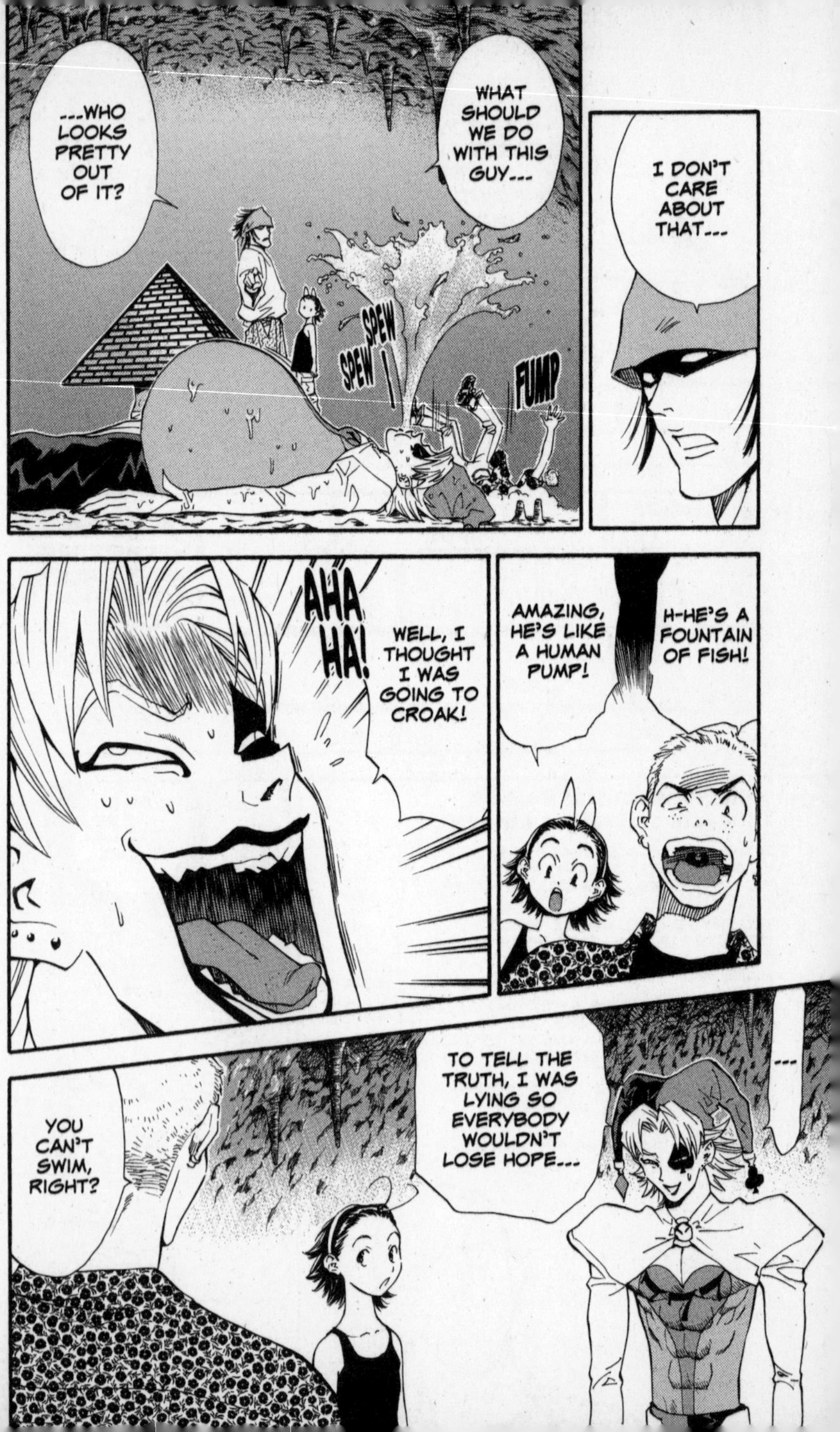
I DON'T CARE ABOUT THAT...
WHAT SHOULD WE DO WITH THIS GUY...
...WHO LOOKS PRETTY OUT OF IT?
FUMP
SPEW SPEW
H-HE'S A FOUNTAIN OF FISH!
AMAZING, HE'S LIKE A HUMAN PUMP!
WELL, I THOUGHT I WAS GOING TO CROAK!
AHA HA!
...
TO TELL THE TRUTH, I WAS LYING SO EVERYBODY WOULDN'T LOSE HOPE...
YOU CAN'T SWIM, RIGHT?

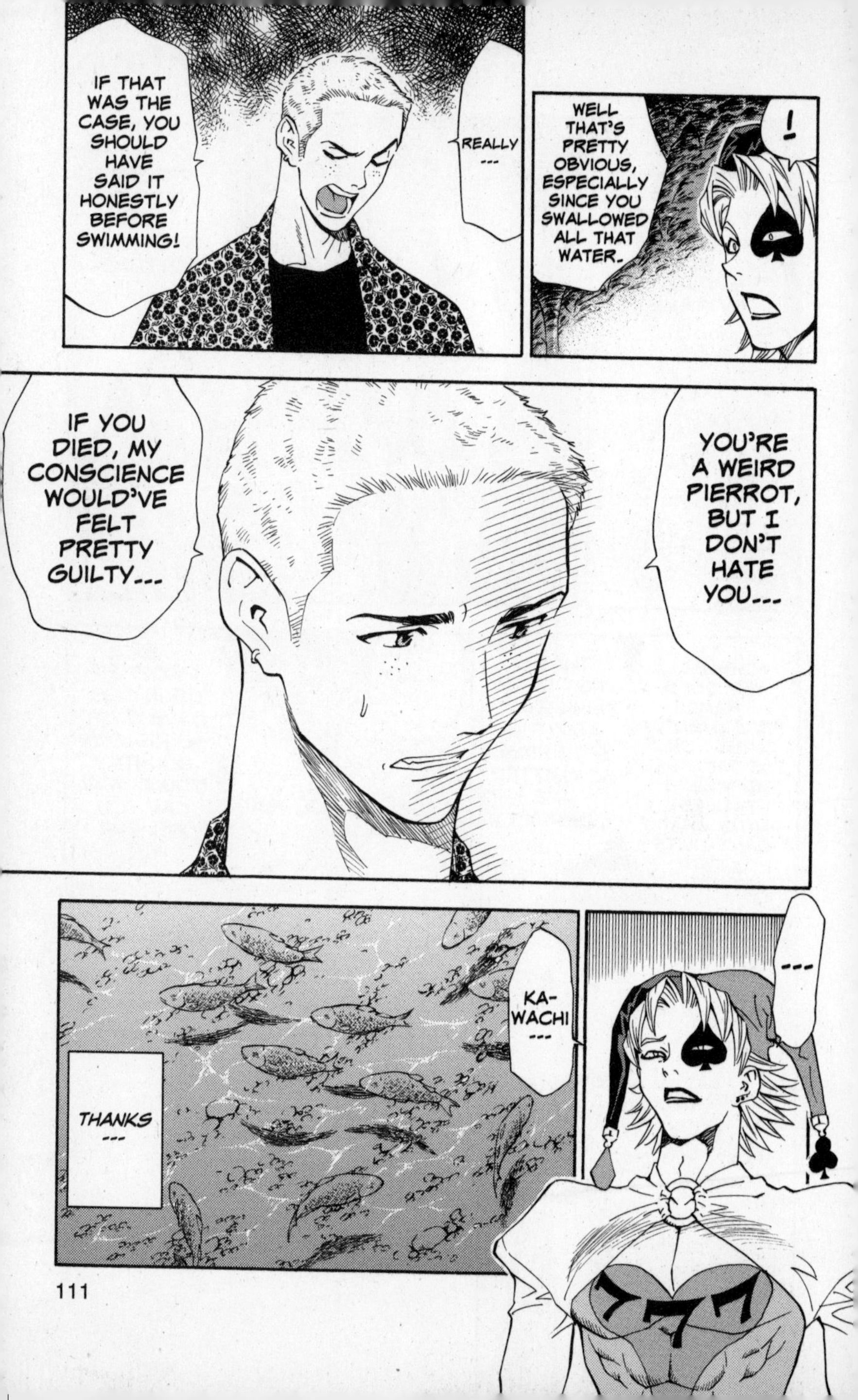
!
WELL THAT'S PRETTY OBVIOUS, ESPECIALLY SINCE YOU SWALLOWED ALL THAT WATER.
REALLY ---
IF THAT WAS THE CASE, YOU SHOULD HAVE SAID IT HONESTLY BEFORE SWIMMING!
YOU'RE A WEIRD PIERROT, BUT I DON'T HATE YOU...
IF YOU DIED, MY CONSCIENCE WOULD'VE FELT PRETTY GUILTY...

KA-WACHI ---
THANKS ---

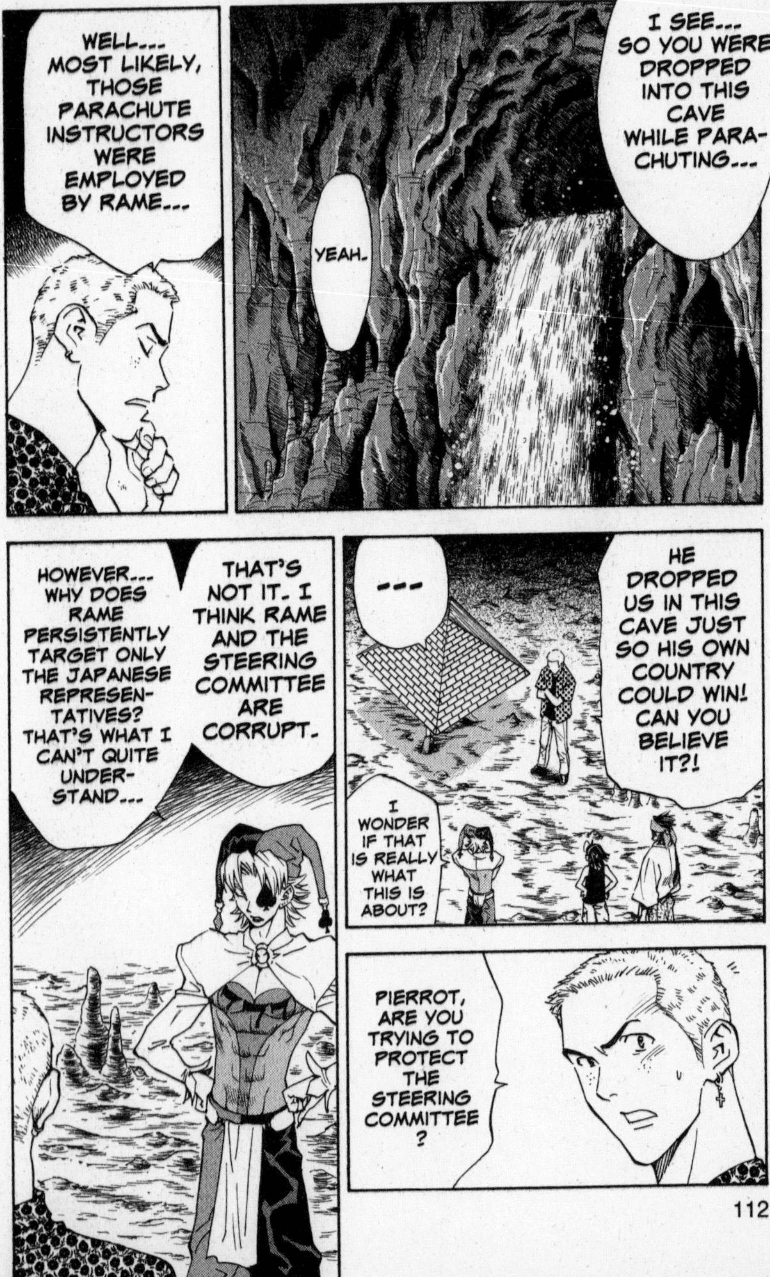
I SEE... SO YOU WERE DROPPED INTO THIS CAVE WHILE PARA-CHUTING...
YEAH.
WELL... MOST LIKELY, THOSE PARACHUTE INSTRUCTORS WERE EMPLOYED BY RAME...
HE DROPPED US IN THIS CAVE JUST SO HIS OWN COUNTRY COULD WIN! CAN YOU BELIEVE IT?!
...
I WONDER IF THAT IS REALLY WHAT THIS IS ABOUT?
PIERROT, ARE YOU TRYING TO PROTECT THE STEERING COMMITTEE?
THAT'S NOT IT. I THINK RAME AND THE STEERING COMMITTEE ARE CORRUPT.
HOWEVER... WHY DOES RAME PERSISTENTLY TARGET ONLY THE JAPANESE REPRESEN-TATIVES? THAT'S WHAT I CAN'T QUITE UNDER-STAND...

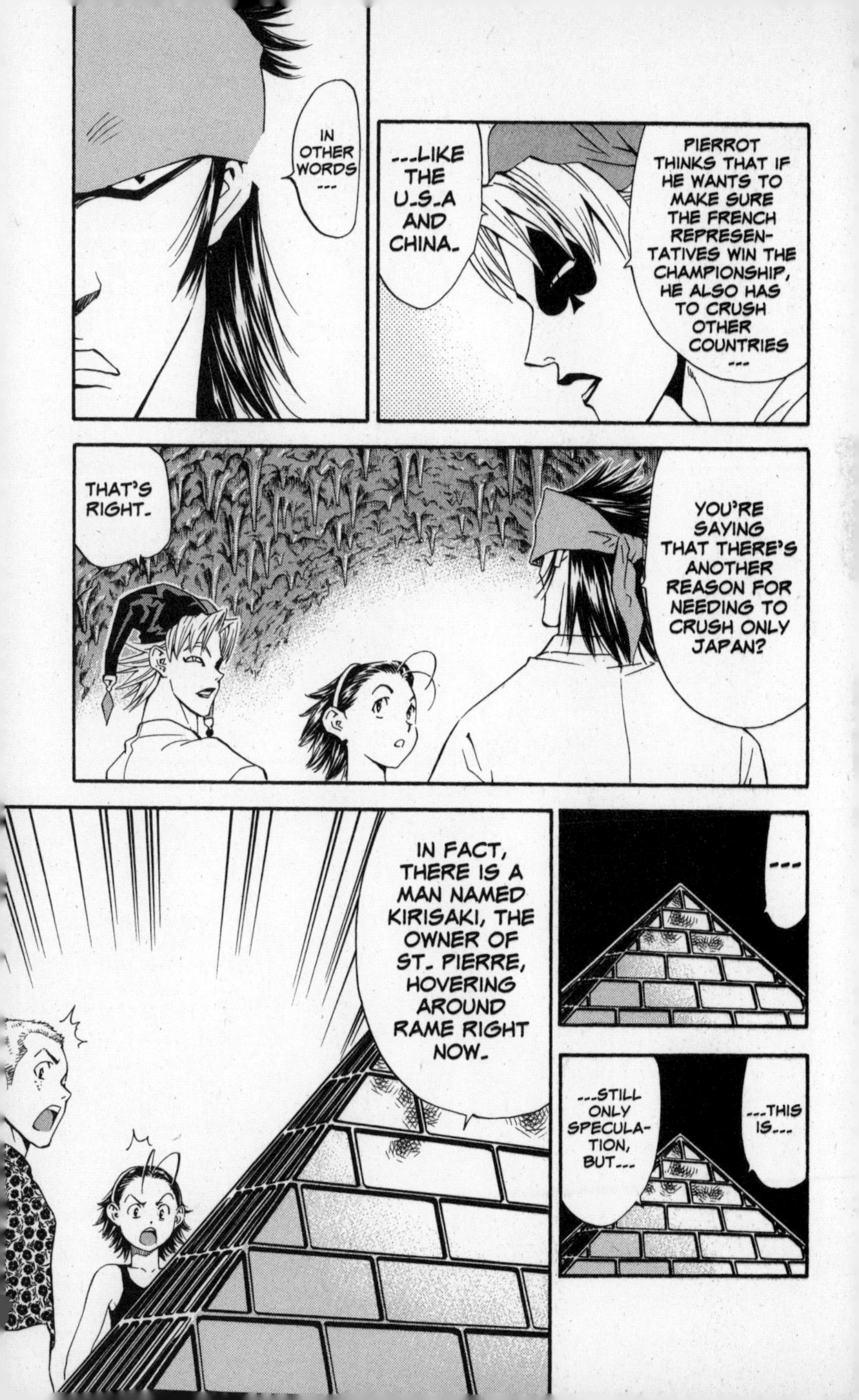
PIERROT THINKS THAT IF HE WANTS TO MAKE SURE THE FRENCH REPRESEN-TATIVES WIN THE CHAMPIONSHIP, HE ALSO HAS TO CRUSH OTHER COUNTRIES...
...LIKE THE U.S.A AND CHINA.
IN OTHER WORDS...
YOU'RE SAYING THAT THERE'S ANOTHER REASON FOR NEEDING TO CRUSH ONLY JAPAN?
THAT'S RIGHT.
...
...THIS IS...
...STILL ONLY SPECULA-TION, BUT...
IN FACT, THERE IS A MAN NAMED KIRISAKI, THE OWNER OF ST. PIERRE, HOVERING AROUND RAME RIGHT NOW.

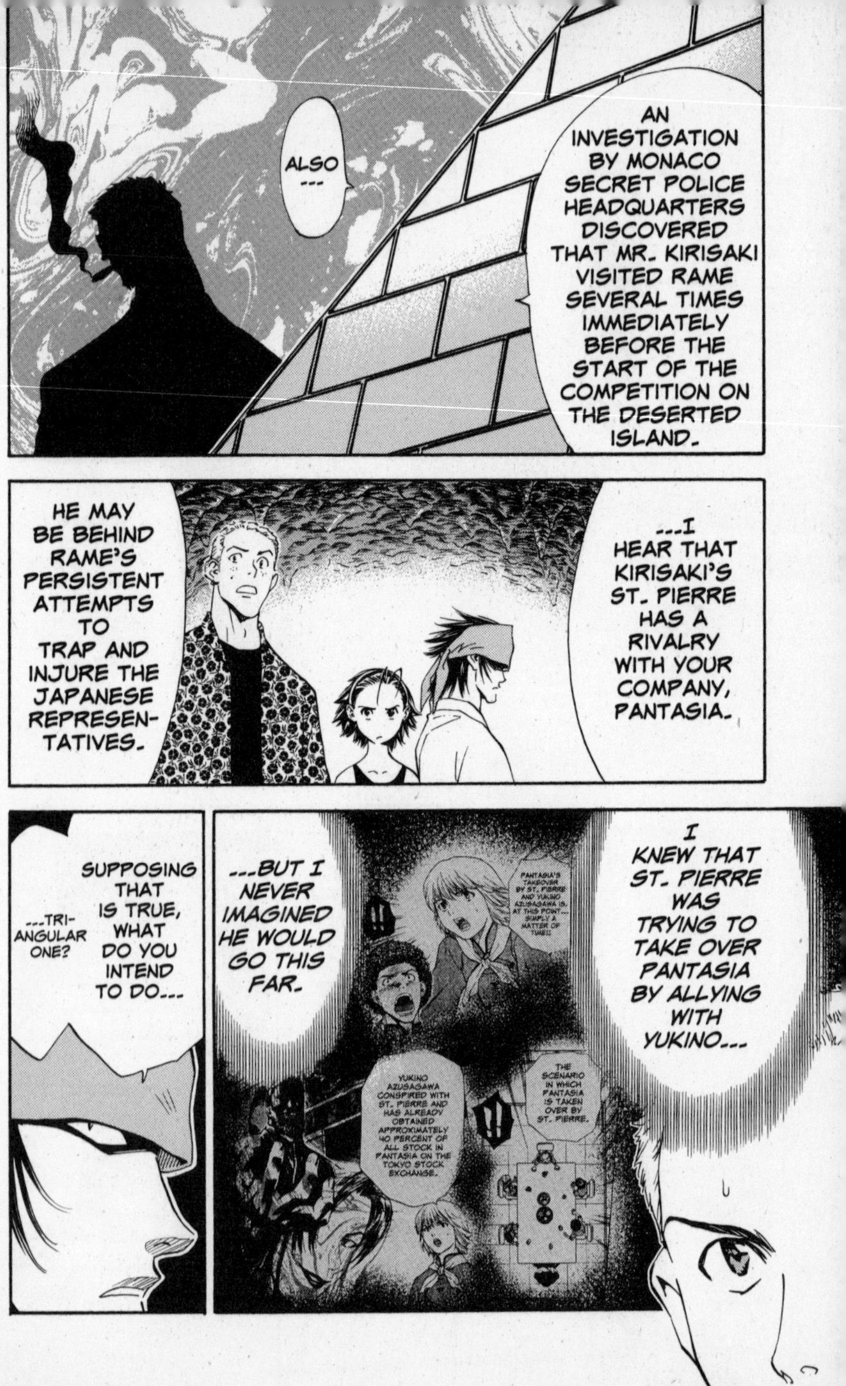
AN INVESTIGATION BY MONACO SECRET POLICE HEADQUARTERS DISCOVERED THAT MR. KIRISAKI VISITED RAME SEVERAL TIMES IMMEDIATELY BEFORE THE START OF THE COMPETITION ON THE DESERTED ISLAND.
ALSO ---
...I HEAR THAT KIRISAKI'S ST. PIERRE HAS A RIVALRY WITH YOUR COMPANY, PANTASIA.
HE MAY BE BEHIND RAME'S PERSISTENT ATTEMPTS TO TRAP AND INJURE THE JAPANESE REPRESEN-TATIVES.
I KNEW THAT ST. PIERRE WAS TRYING TO TAKE OVER PANTASIA BY ALLYING WITH YUKINO...
PANTASIA'S TAKEOVER BY ST. PIERRE AND YUKINO AZUSAGAWA IS, AT THIS POINT... SIMPLY A MATTER OF TIME!!
!!
...BUT I NEVER IMAGINED HE WOULD GO THIS FAR.
THE SCENARIO IN WHICH PANTASIA IS TAKEN OVER BY ST. PIERRE.
!!
YUKINO AZUSAGAWA CONSPIRED WITH ST. PIERRE AND HAS ALREADY OBTAINED APPROXIMATELY 40 PERCENT OF ALL STOCK IN PANTASIA ON THE TOKYO STOCK EXCHANGE.
SUPPOSING THAT IS TRUE, WHAT DO YOU INTEND TO DO...
...TRI-ANGULAR ONE?

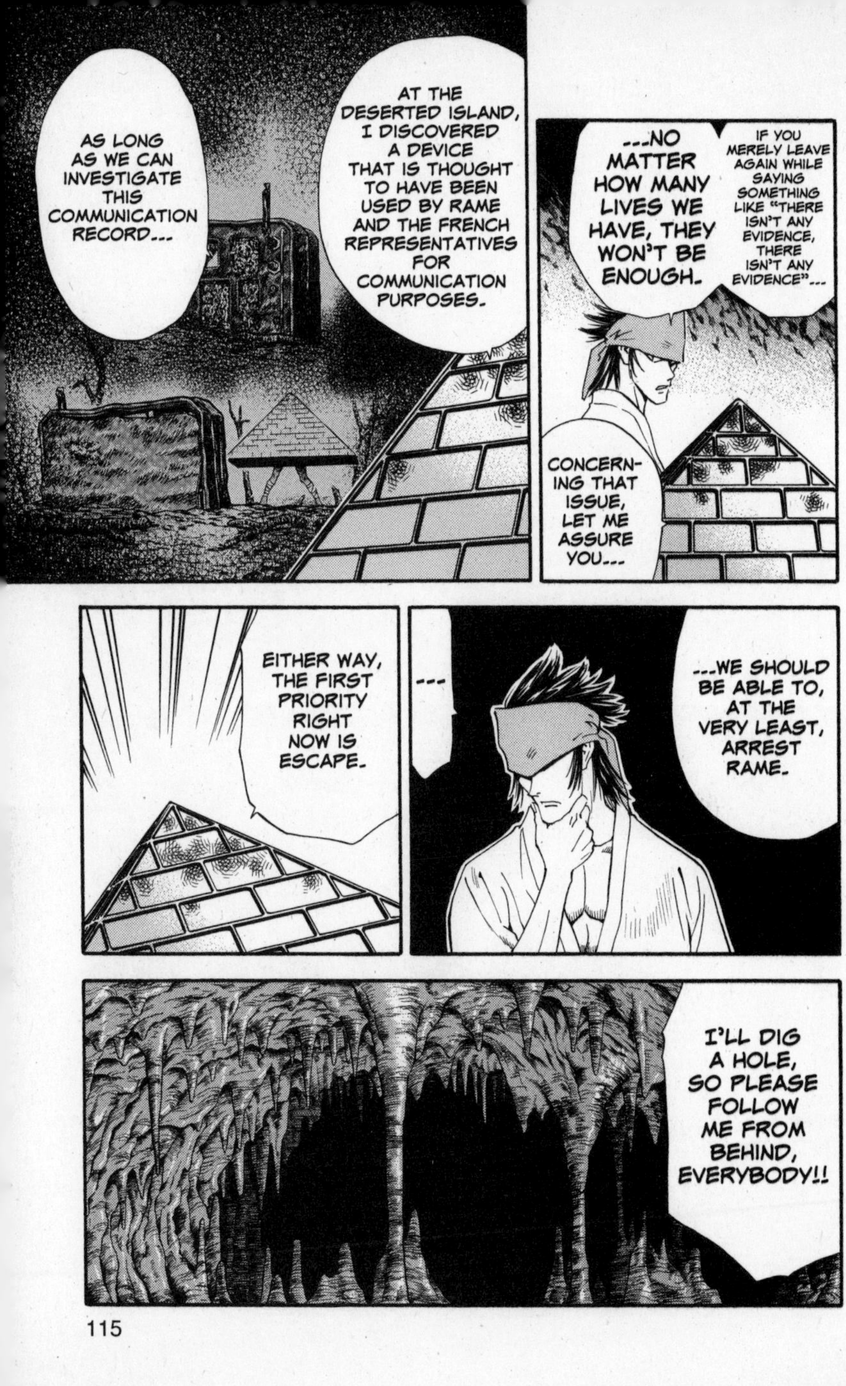
IF YOU MERELY LEAVE AGAIN WHILE SAYING SOMETHING LIKE "THERE ISN'T ANY EVIDENCE, THERE ISN'T ANY EVIDENCE"...
...NO MATTER HOW MANY LIVES WE HAVE, THEY WON'T BE ENOUGH.
CONCERNING THAT ISSUE, LET ME ASSURE YOU...
AT THE DESERTED ISLAND, I DISCOVERED A DEVICE THAT IS THOUGHT TO HAVE BEEN USED BY RAME AND THE FRENCH REPRESENTATIVES FOR COMMUNICATION PURPOSES.
AS LONG AS WE CAN INVESTIGATE THIS COMMUNICATION RECORD...
...WE SHOULD BE ABLE TO, AT THE VERY LEAST, ARREST RAME.
...
EITHER WAY, THE FIRST PRIORITY RIGHT NOW IS ESCAPE.
I'LL DIG A HOLE, SO PLEASE FOLLOW ME FROM BEHIND, EVERYBODY!!

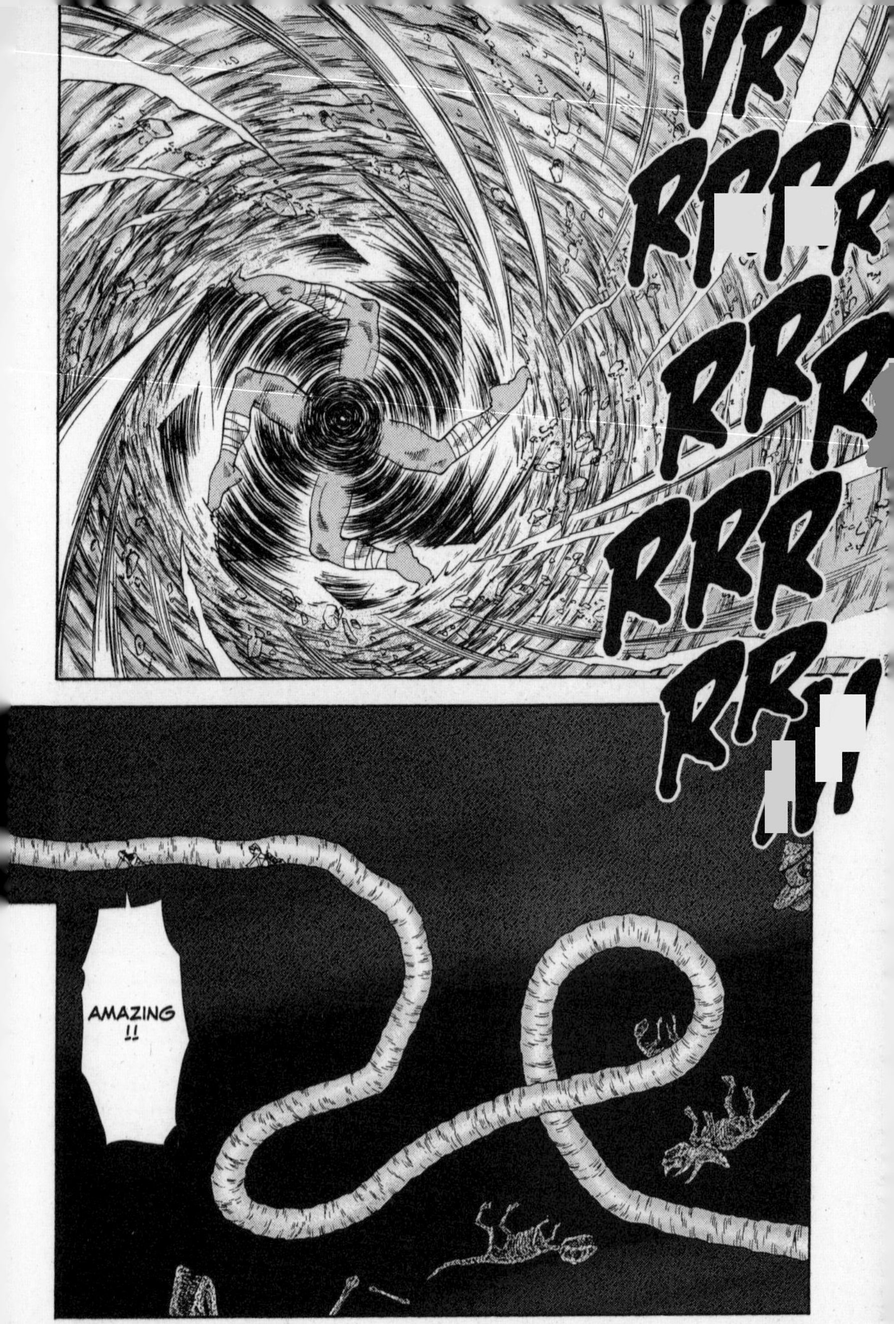
VRRRRRRRRRRRRR!!
AMAZING !!

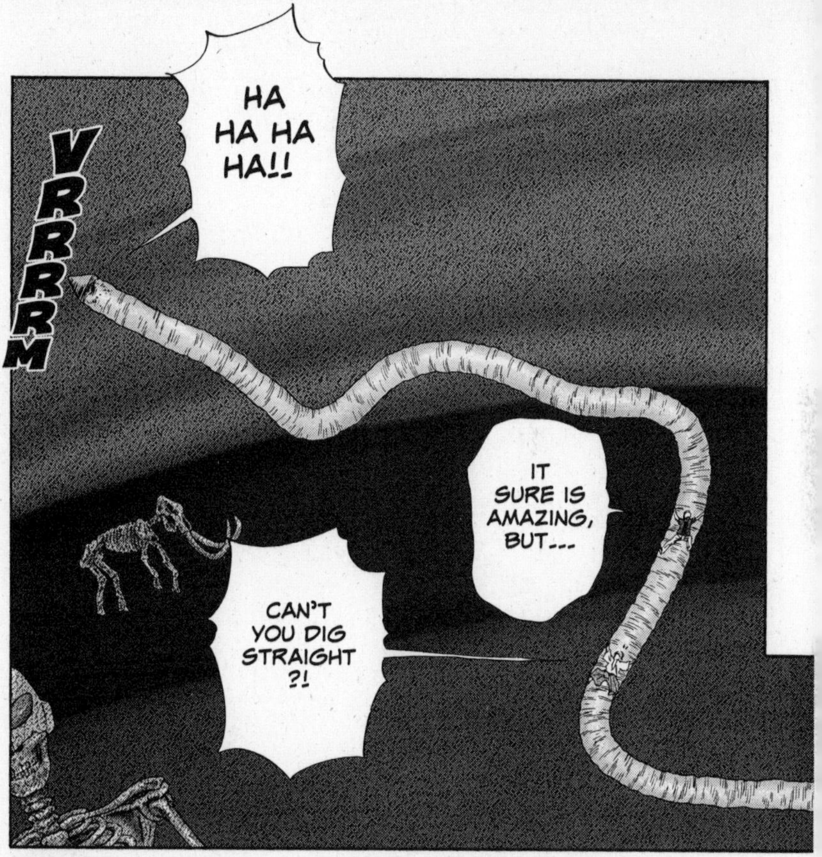
HA HA HA HA!!
VRRRRM
IT SURE IS AMAZING, BUT...
CAN'T YOU DIG STRAIGHT?!
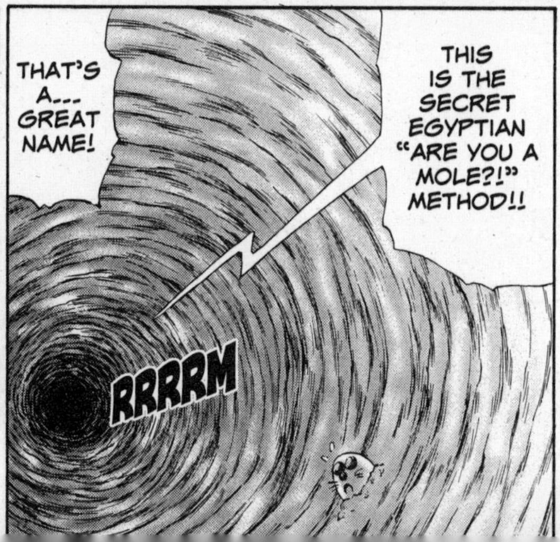
THIS IS THE SECRET EGYPTIAN "ARE YOU A MOLE?!" METHOD!!
THAT'S A... GREAT NAME!
RRRRM
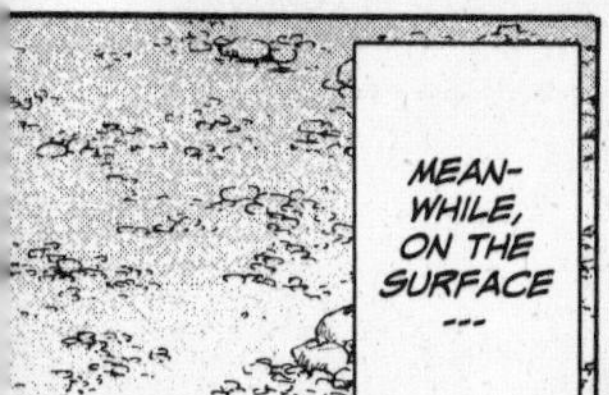
MEAN-WHILE, ON THE SURFACE...

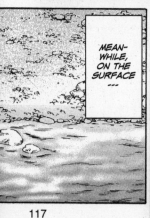

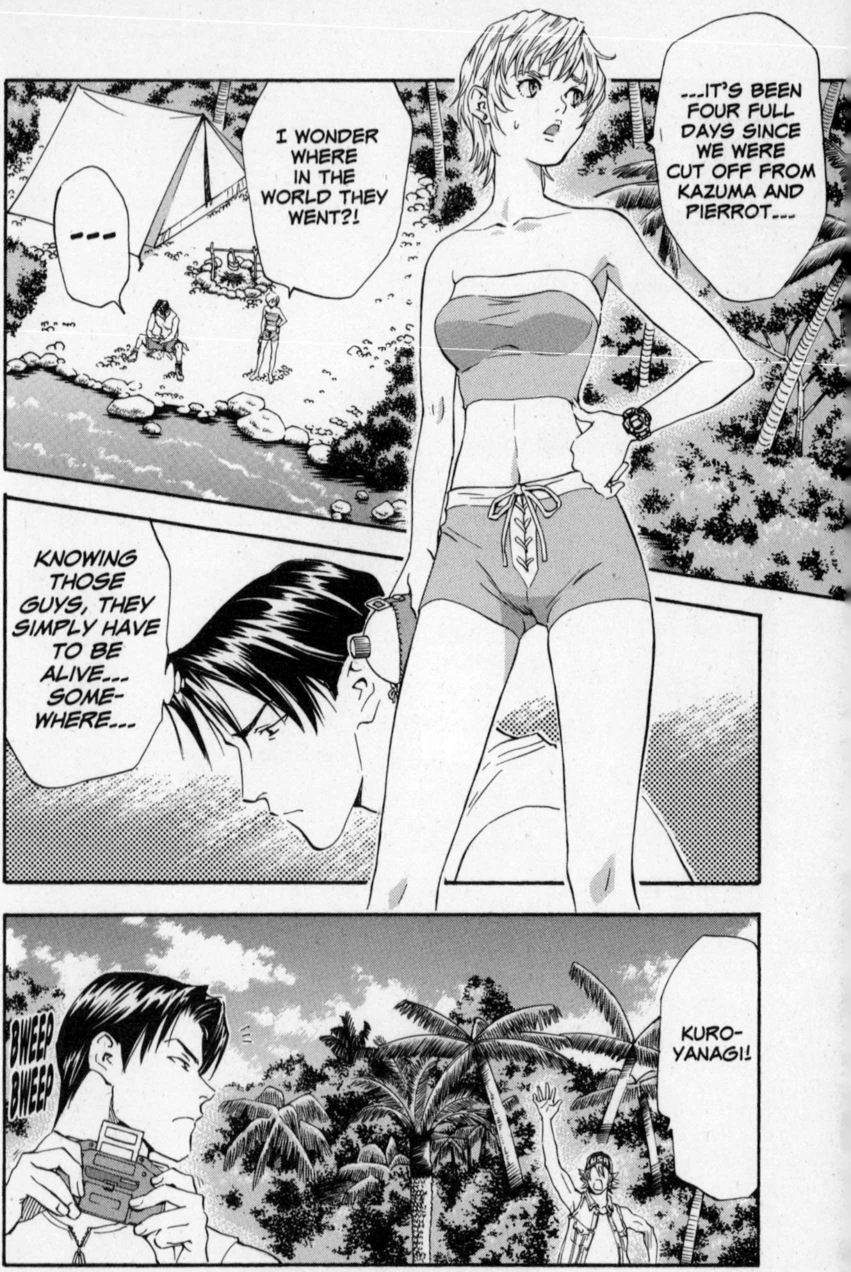
...IT'S BEEN FOUR FULL DAYS SINCE WE WERE CUT OFF FROM KAZUMA AND PIERROT...
I WONDER WHERE IN THE WORLD THEY WENT?!
...
KNOWING THOSE GUYS, THEY SIMPLY HAVE TO BE ALIVE... SOME-WHERE...
KURO-YANAGI!
BWEEP BWEEP

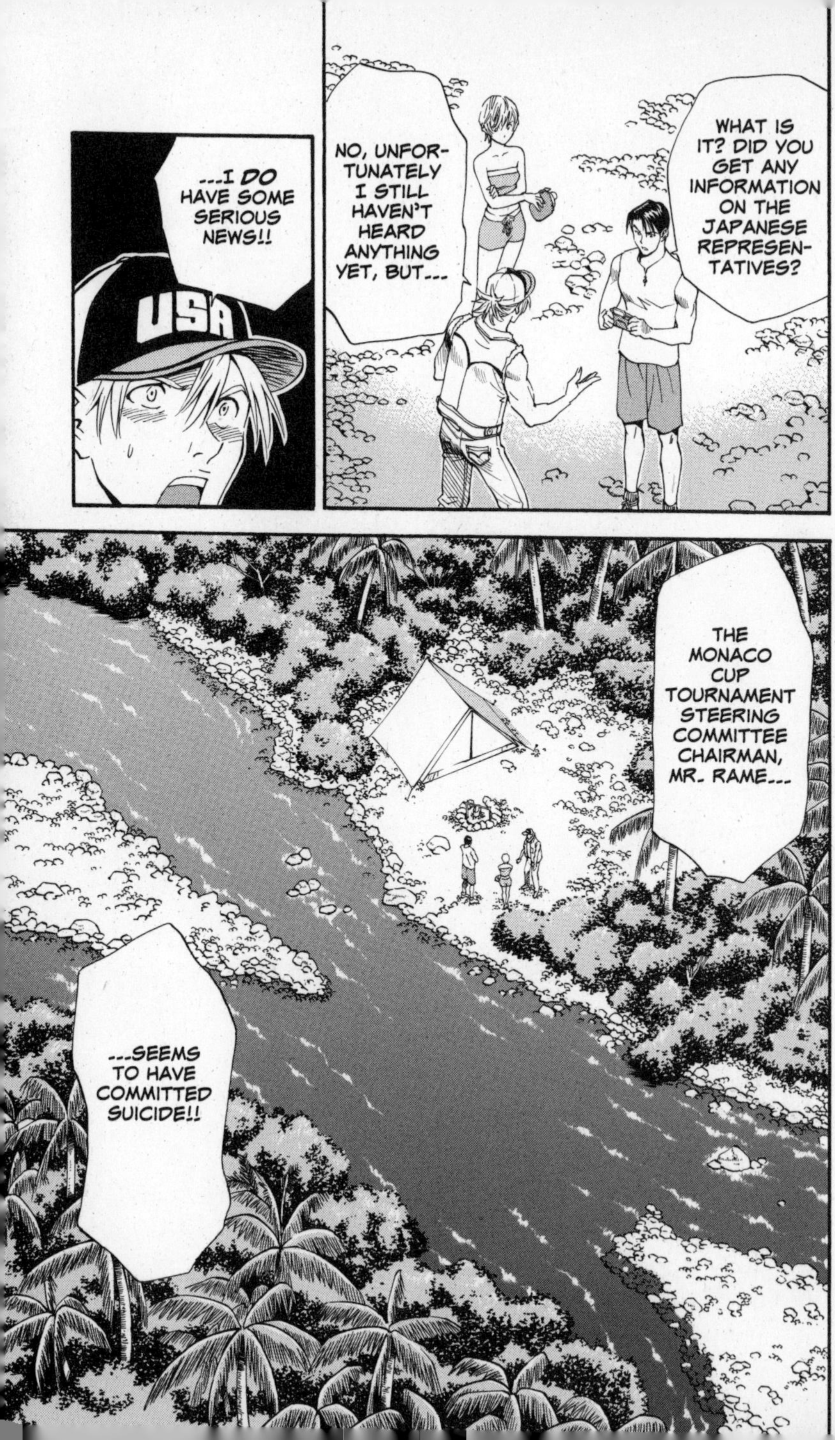
WHAT IS IT? DID YOU GET ANY INFORMATION ON THE JAPANESE REPRESEN-TATIVES?
NO, UNFOR-TUNATELY I STILL HAVEN'T HEARD ANYTHING YET, BUT...
...I DO HAVE SOME SERIOUS NEWS!!
THE MONACO CUP TOURNAMENT STEERING COMMITTEE CHAIRMAN, MR. RAME...
...SEEMS TO HAVE COMMITTED SUICIDE!!

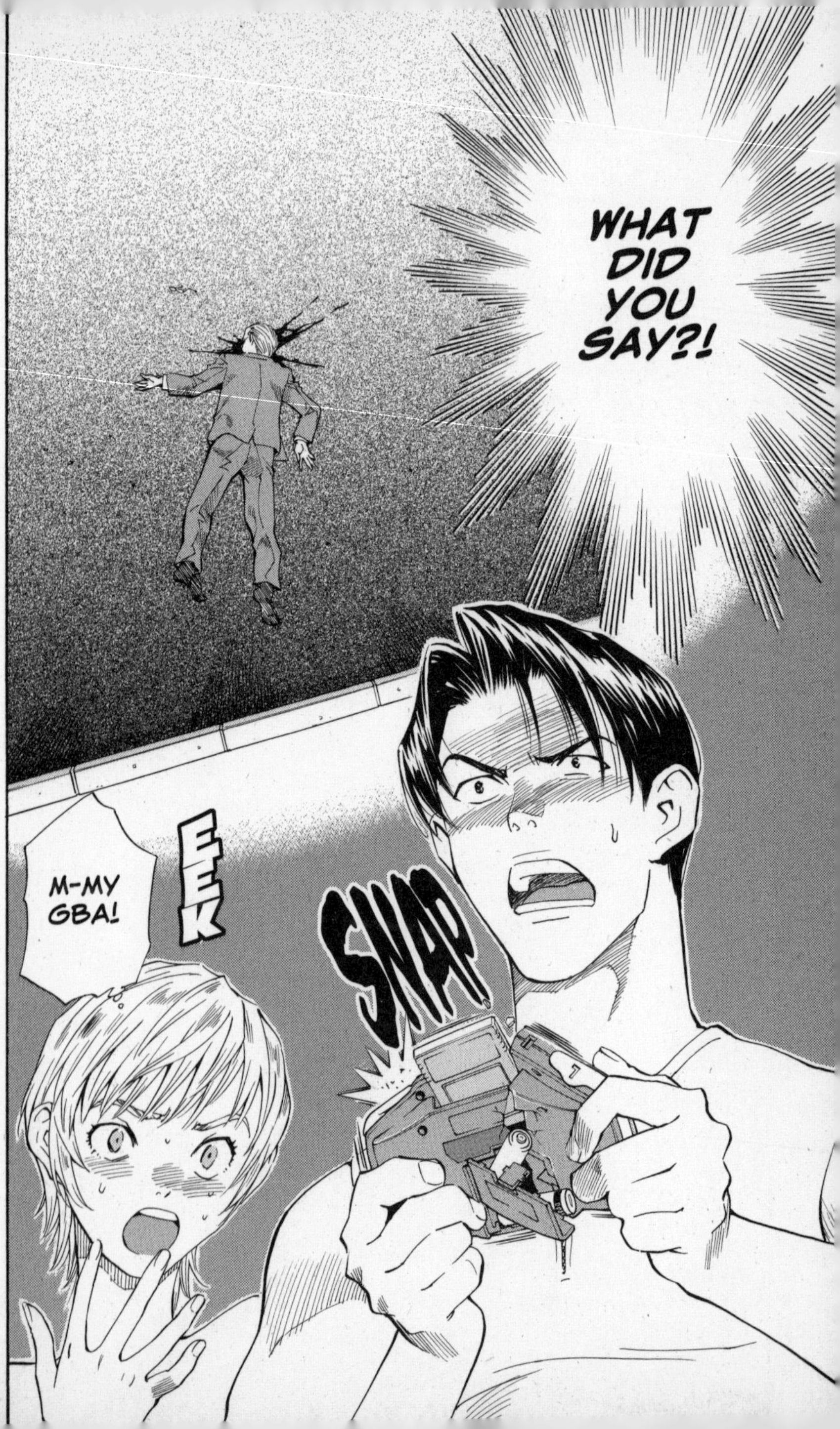
WHAT DID YOU SAY?!
SNAP
EEK
M-MY GBA!

Story 84: King of Monaco

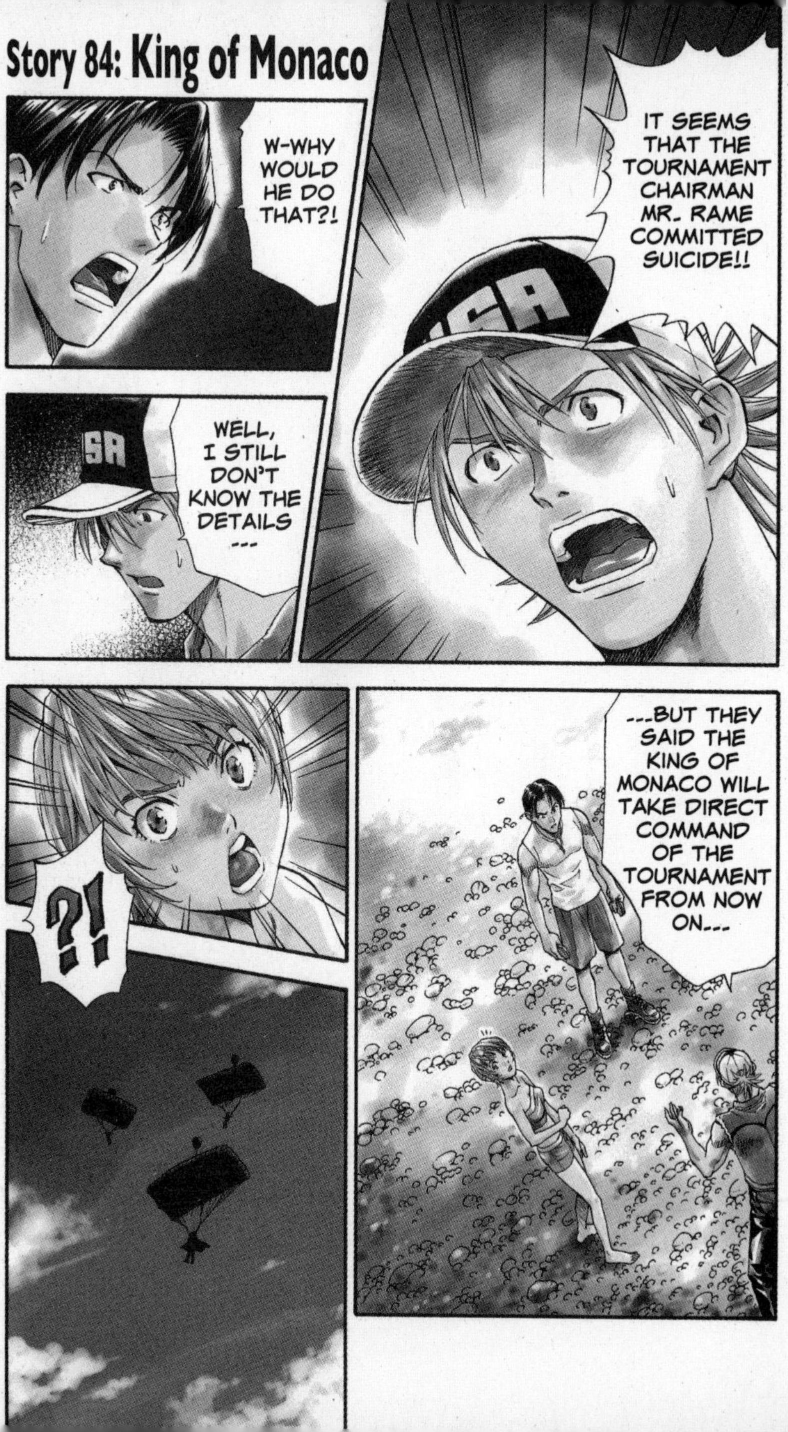
IT SEEMS THAT THE TOURNAMENT CHAIRMAN MR. RAME COMMITTED SUICIDE!!
W-WHY WOULD HE DO THAT?!
WELL, I STILL DON'T KNOW THE DETAILS...
...BUT THEY SAID THE KING OF MONACO WILL TAKE DIRECT COMMAND OF THE TOURNAMENT FROM NOW ON...
?!

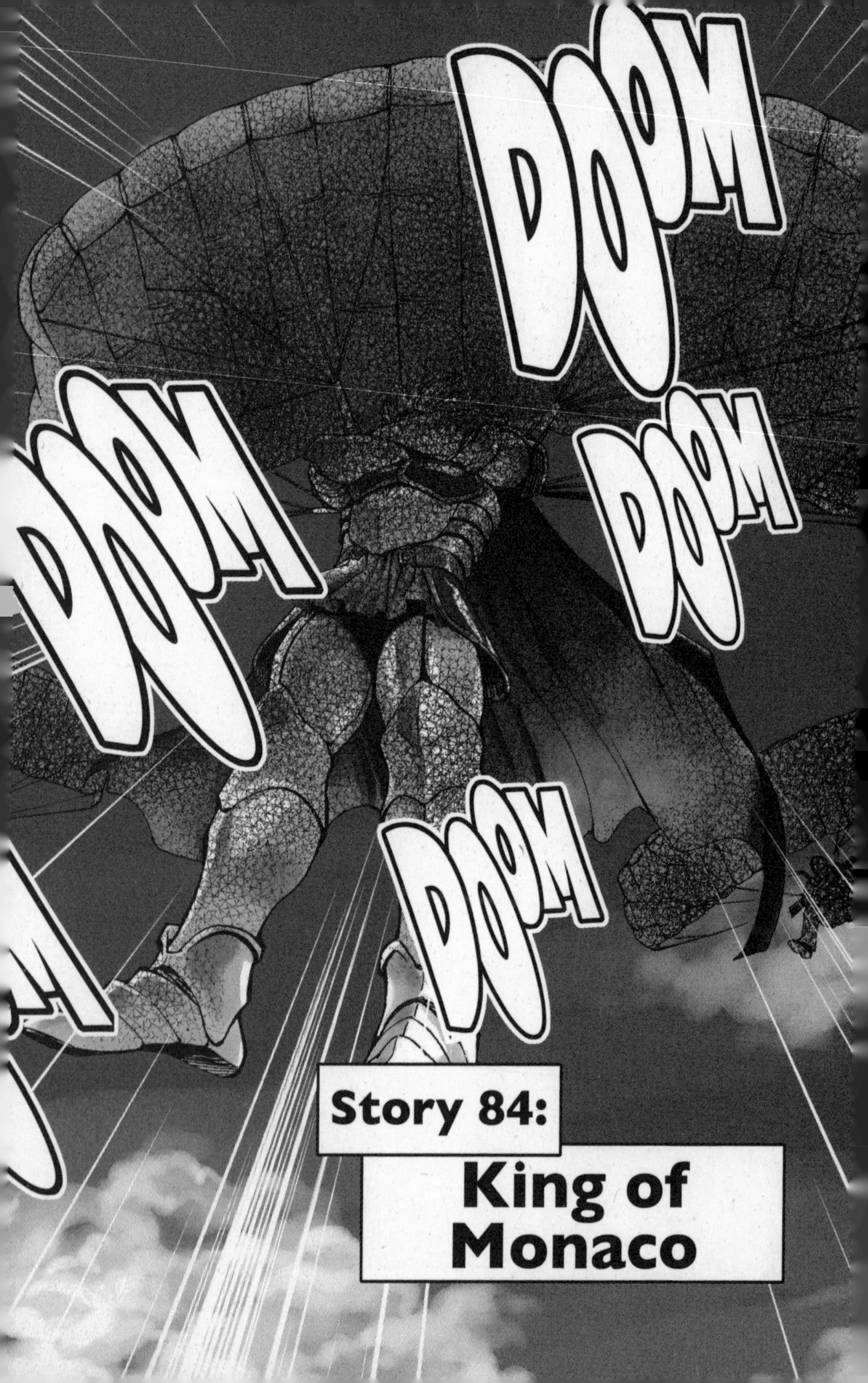
DOOM
DOOM
DOOM
DOOM
Story 84:
King of Monaco

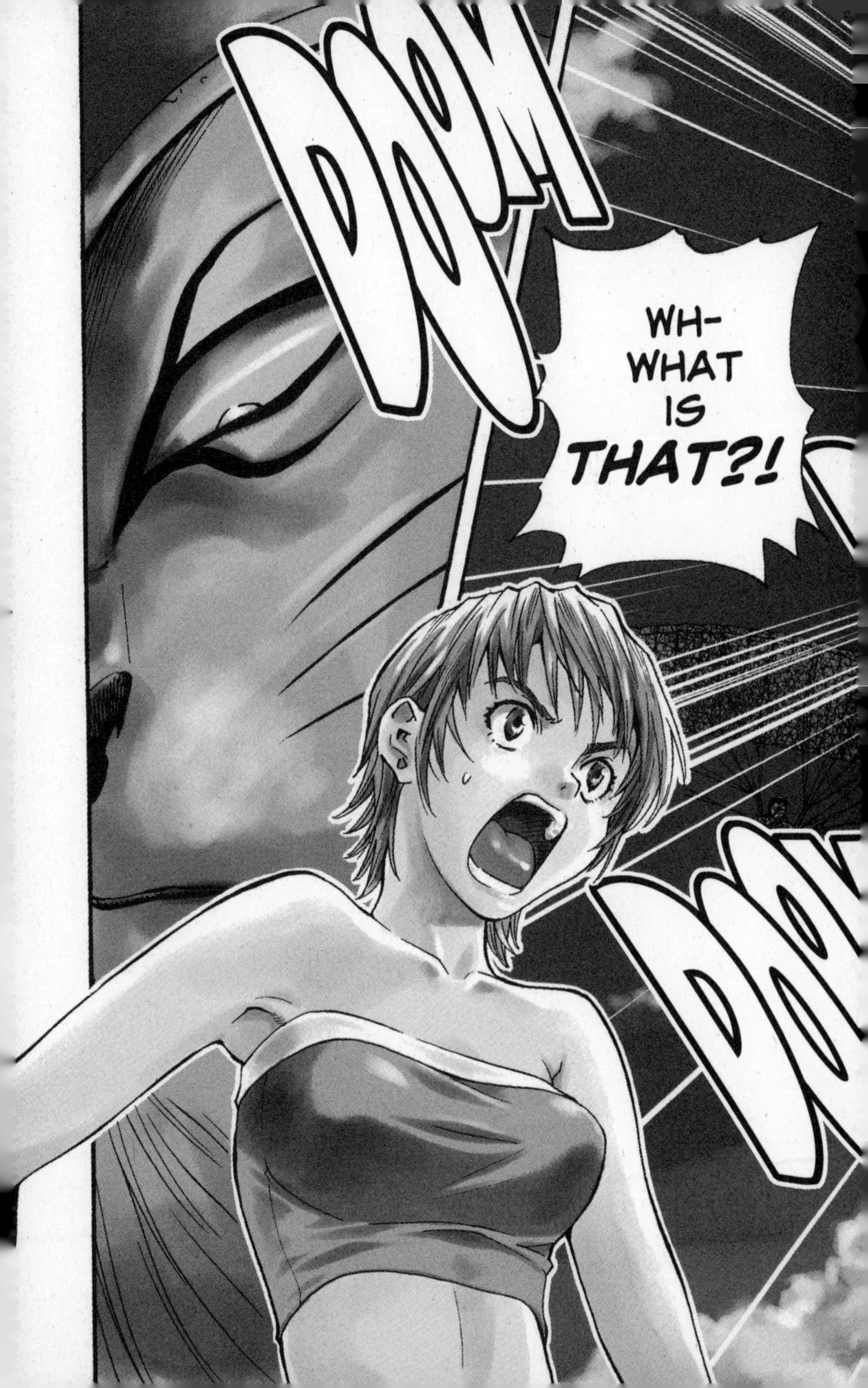
DOOM
WH-
WHAT
IS
THAT?!

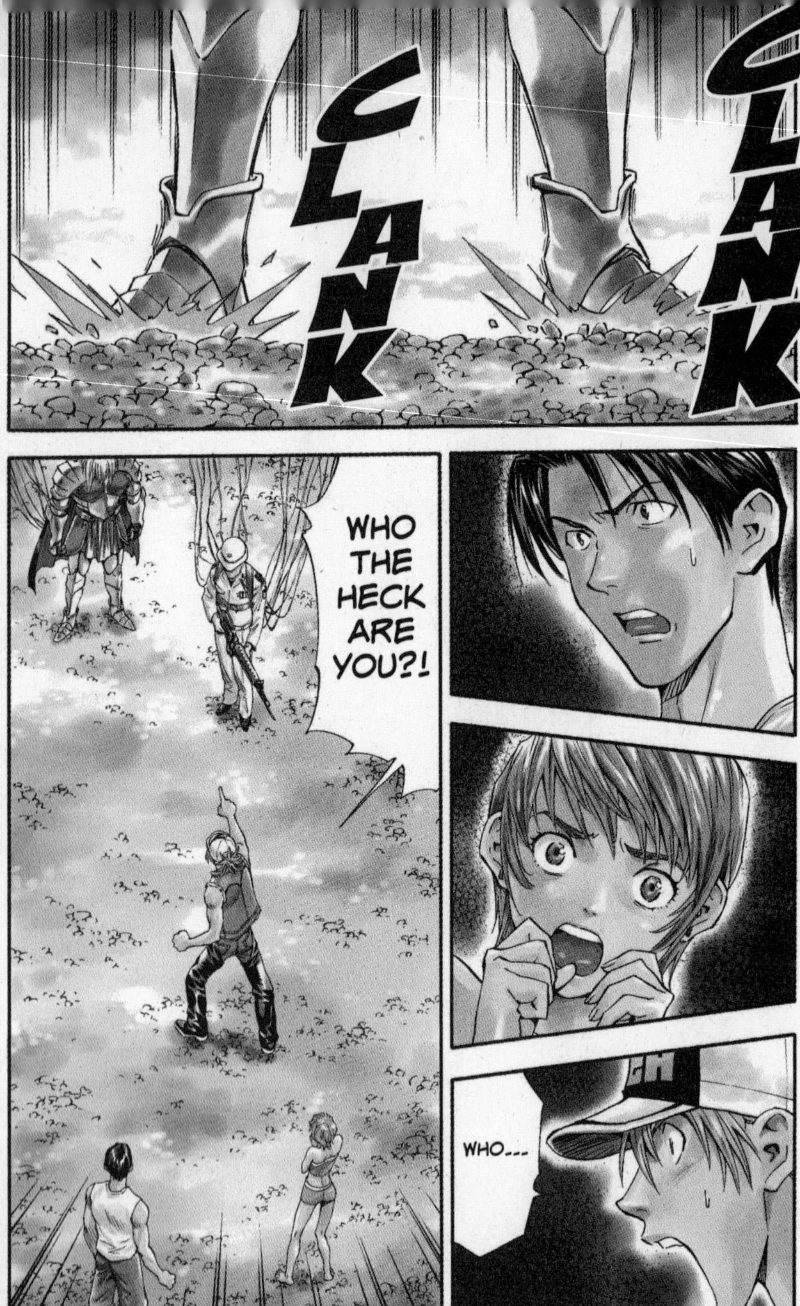
CLANK
CLANK
WHO...
WHO THE HECK ARE YOU?!

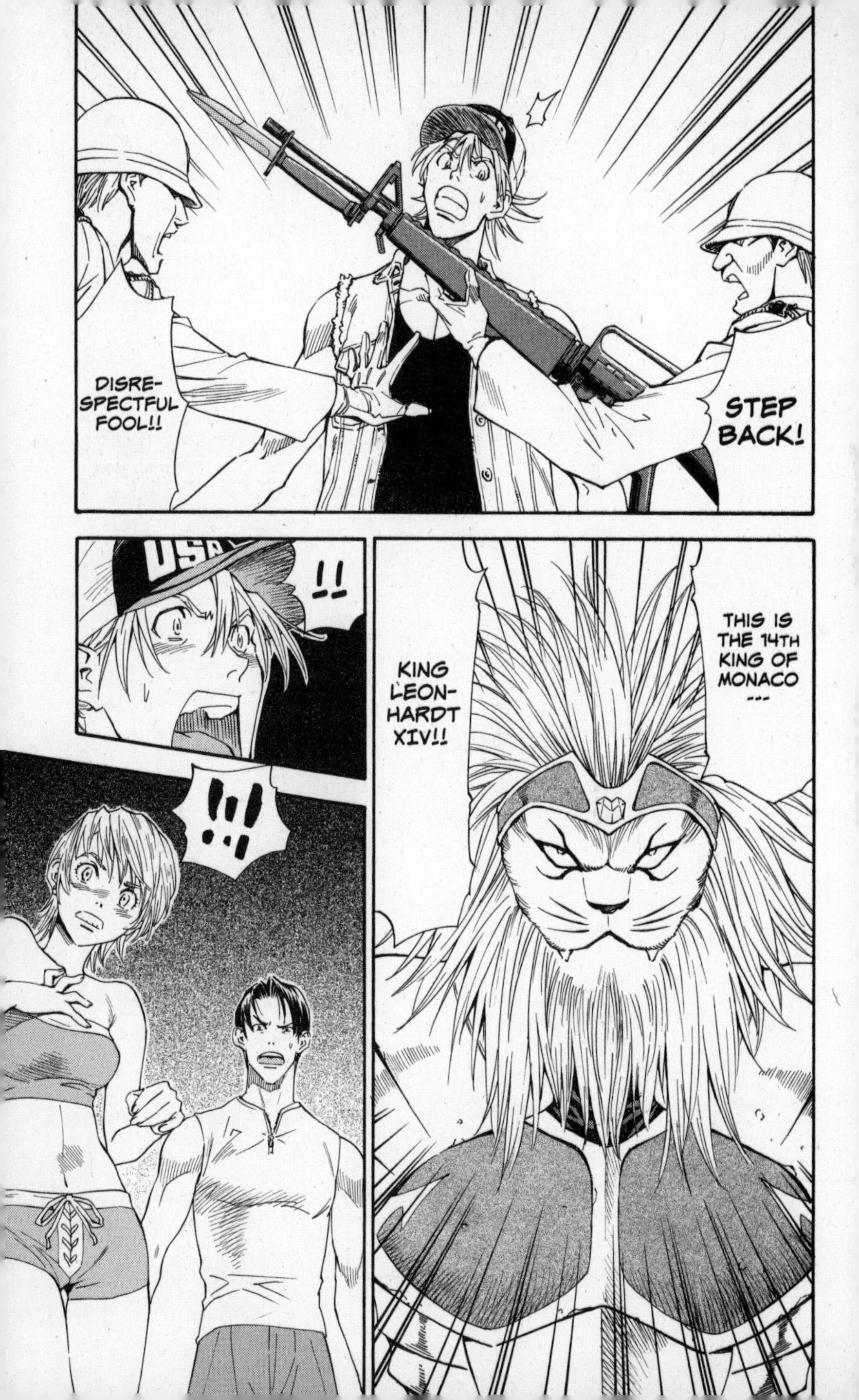
STEP BACK!
DISRE-SPECTFUL FOOL!!
THIS IS THE 14TH KING OF MONACO ---
KING LEON-HARDT XIV!!
!!
!!!

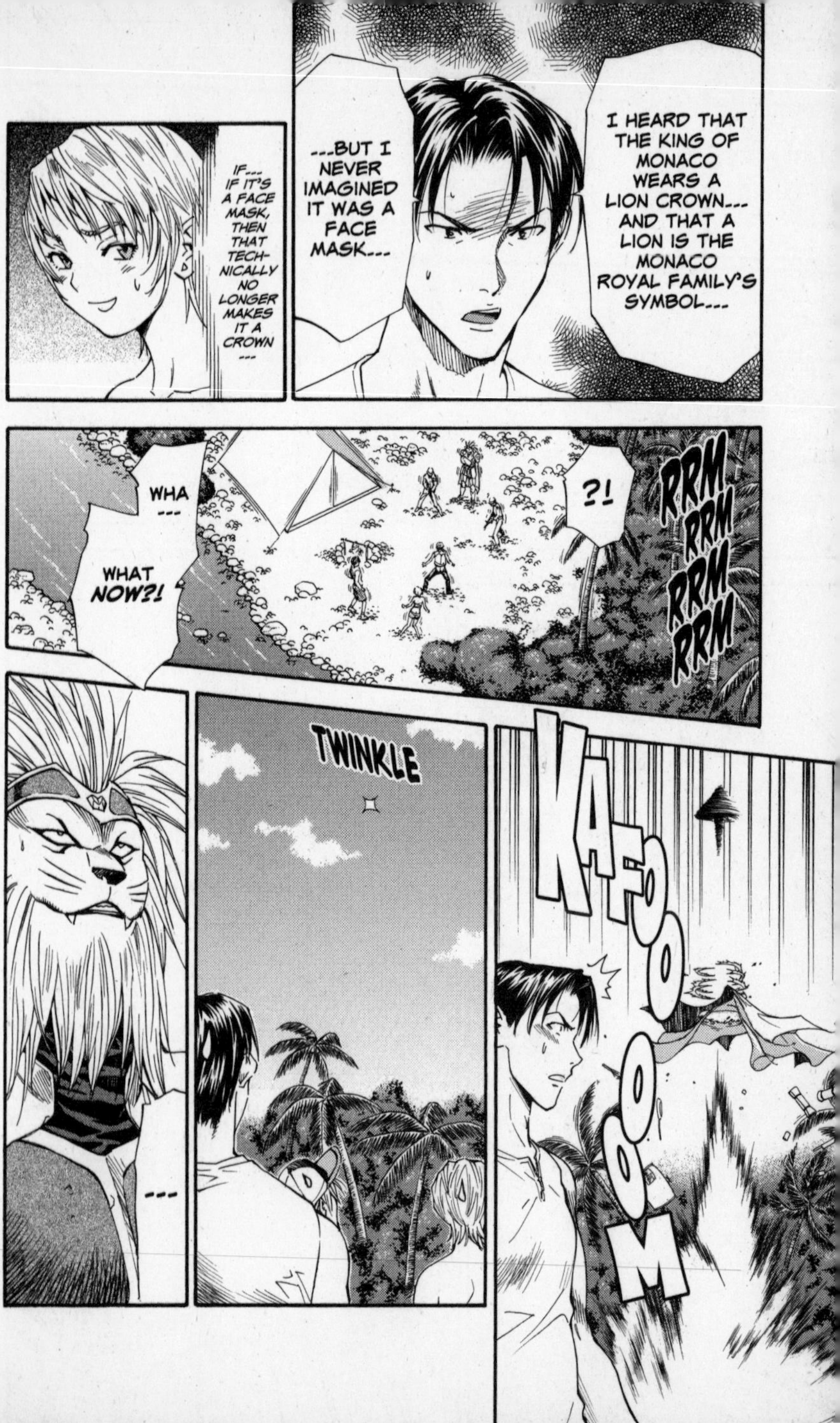
I HEARD THAT THE KING OF MONACO WEARS A LION CROWN--- AND THAT A LION IS THE MONACO ROYAL FAMILY'S SYMBOL---
---BUT I NEVER IMAGINED IT WAS A FACE MASK---
IF--- IF IT'S A FACE MASK, THEN THAT TECHNICALLY NO LONGER MAKES IT A CROWN ---
RRM RRM RRM RRM
?!
WHA ---
WHAT NOW?!
KA-FOOOOOOM
TWINKLE

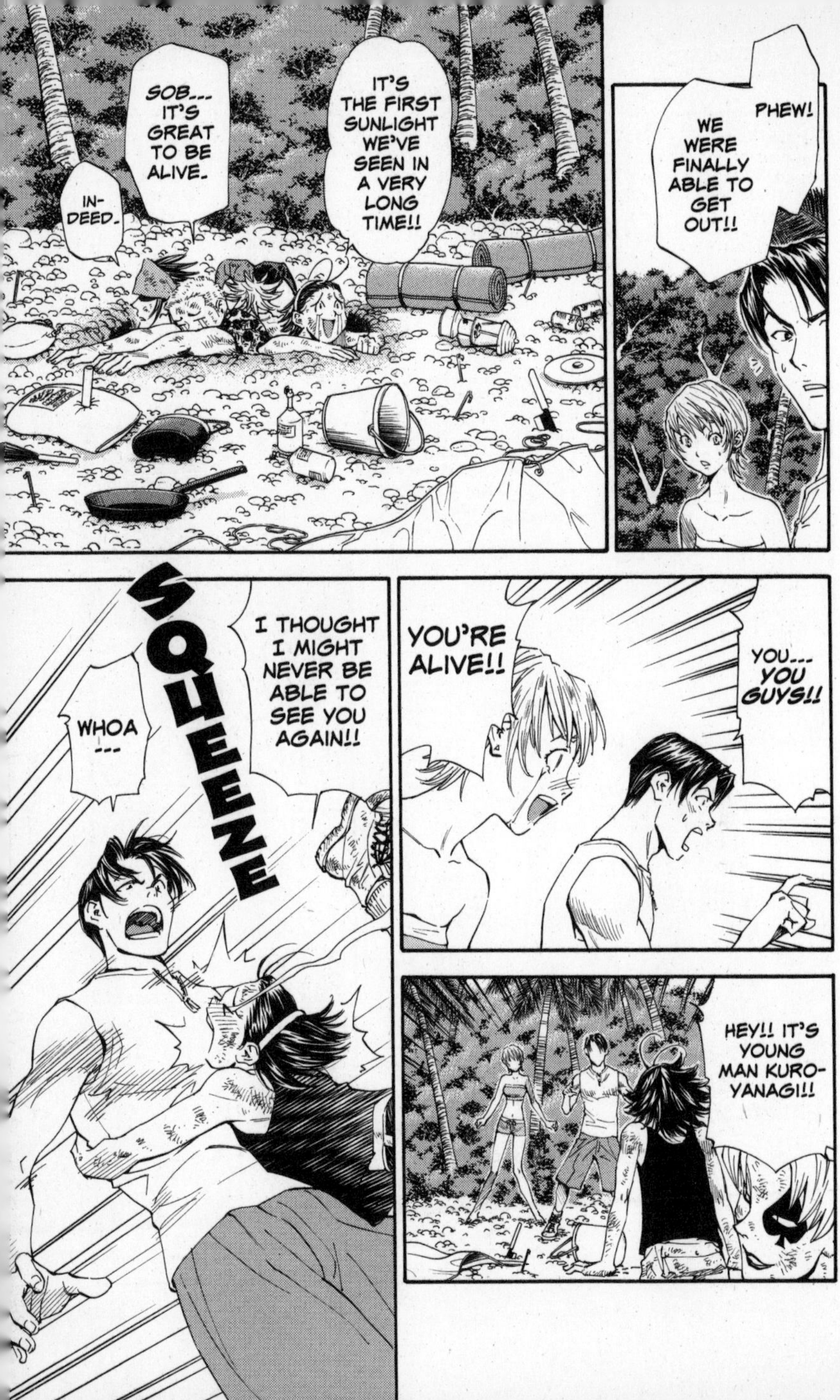
PHEW!
WE WERE FINALLY ABLE TO GET OUT!!
IT'S THE FIRST SUNLIGHT WE'VE SEEN IN A VERY LONG TIME!!
SOB... IT'S GREAT TO BE ALIVE.
IN-DEED.
YOU... YOU GUYS!!
YOU'RE ALIVE!!
HEY!! IT'S YOUNG MAN KURO-YANAGI!!
I THOUGHT I MIGHT NEVER BE ABLE TO SEE YOU AGAIN!!
SQUEEZE
WHOA...

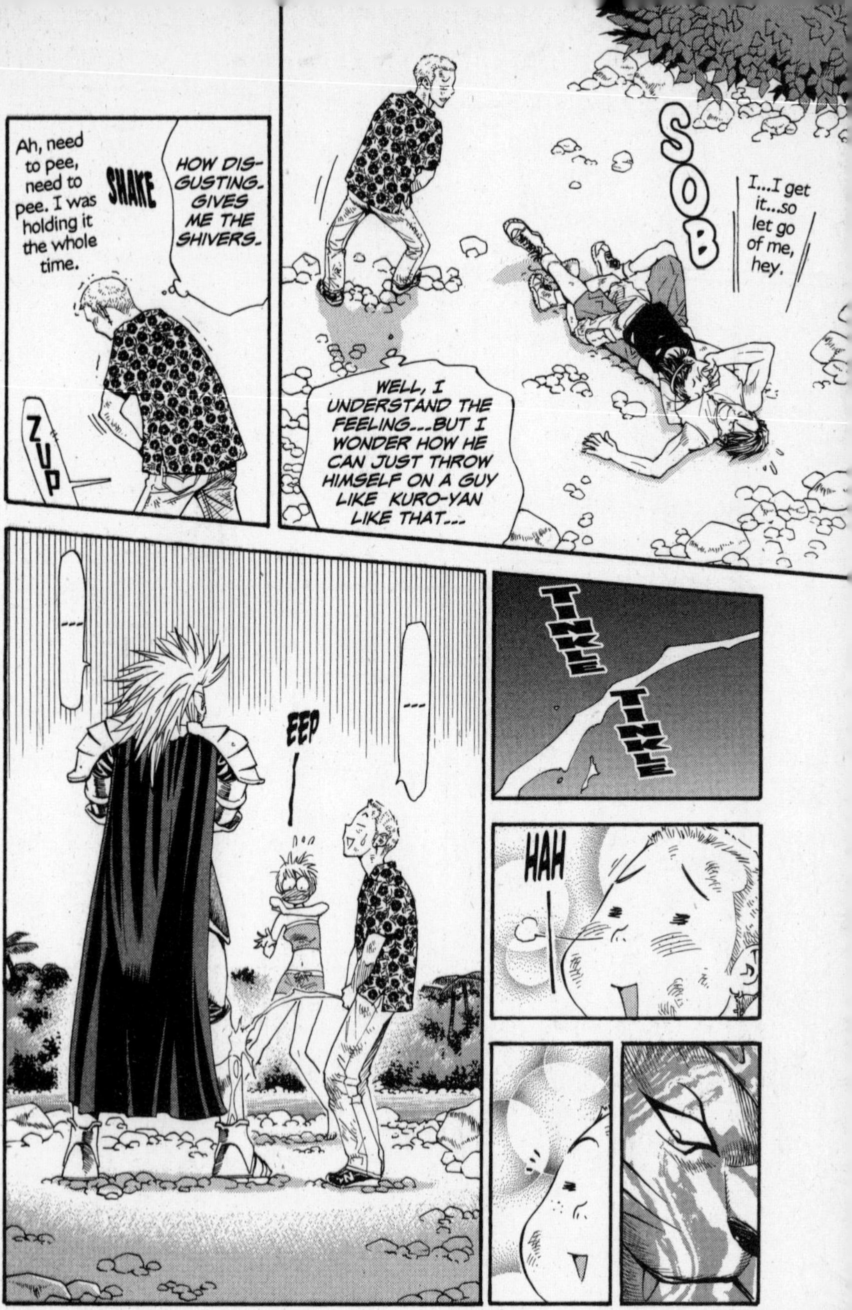
SOB
I...I get it...so let go of me, hey.
WELL, I UNDERSTAND THE FEELING...BUT I WONDER HOW HE CAN JUST THROW HIMSELF ON A GUY LIKE KURO-YAN LIKE THAT...
HOW DIS-GUSTING... GIVES ME THE SHIVERS...
SHAKE
Ah, need to pee, need to pee. I was holding it the whole time.
ZUP
TINKLE
TINKLE
HAH
...
EEP
...

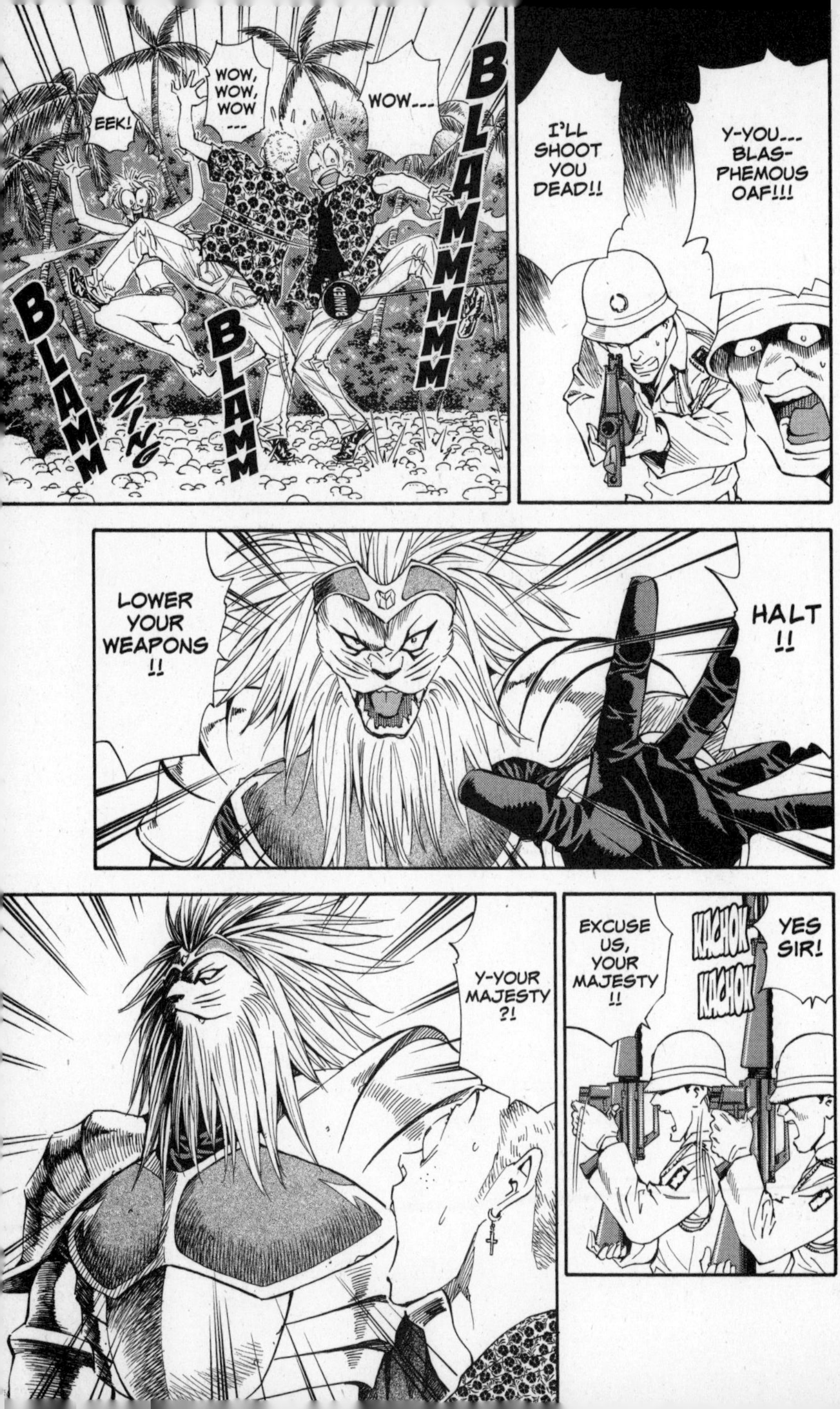
Y-YOU... BLAS-PHEMOUS OAF!!!
I'LL SHOOT YOU DEAD!!
BLAMMMMMM
WOW...
WOW, WOW, WOW ...
EEK!
BLAMM
ZING
BLAMM
HALT !!
LOWER YOUR WEAPONS !!
YES SIR!
KACHOK
KACHOK
EXCUSE US, YOUR MAJESTY !!
Y-YOUR MAJESTY ?!

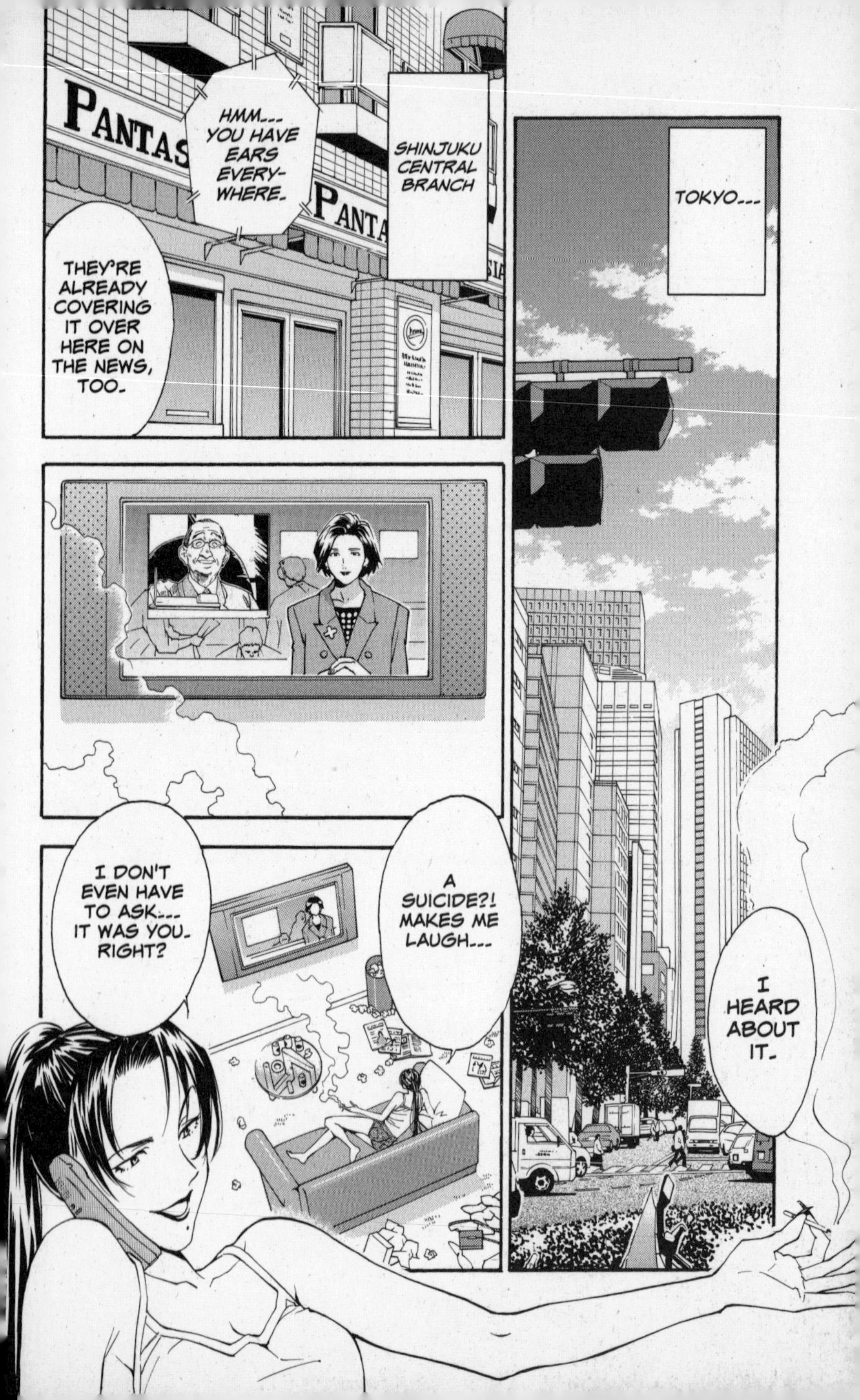
TOKYO...
I HEARD ABOUT IT.
SHINJUKU CENTRAL BRANCH
HMM... YOU HAVE EARS EVERY-WHERE.
PANTAS
THEY'RE ALREADY COVERING IT OVER HERE ON THE NEWS, TOO.
A SUICIDE?! MAKES ME LAUGH...
I DON'T EVEN HAVE TO ASK... IT WAS YOU. RIGHT?

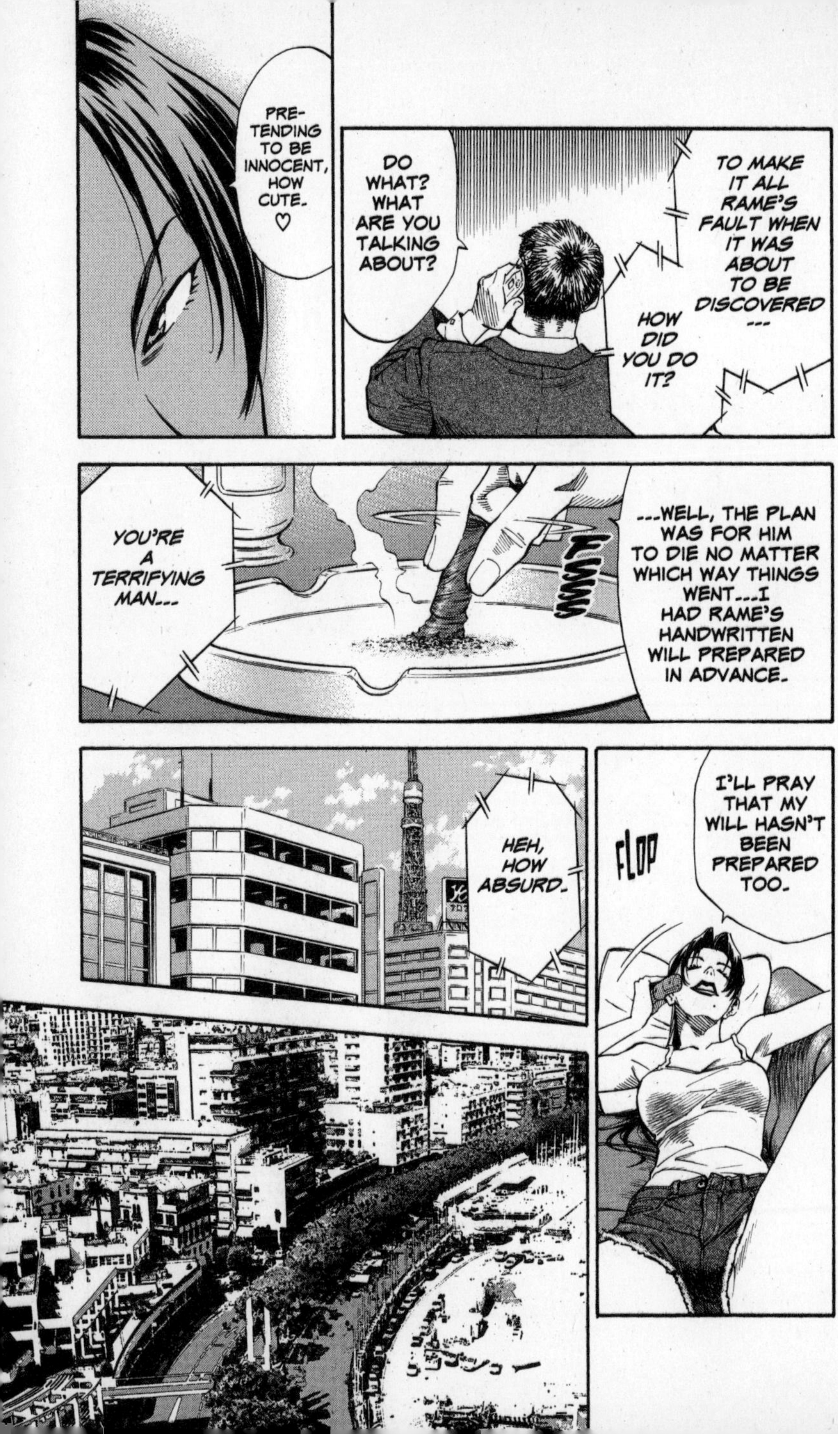
TO MAKE IT ALL RAME'S FAULT WHEN IT WAS ABOUT TO BE DISCOVERED---
HOW DID YOU DO IT?
DO WHAT? WHAT ARE YOU TALKING ABOUT?
PRE-TENDING TO BE INNOCENT, HOW CUTE. ♡
---WELL, THE PLAN WAS FOR HIM TO DIE NO MATTER WHICH WAY THINGS WENT---I HAD RAME'S HANDWRITTEN WILL PREPARED IN ADVANCE.
FSSS
YOU'RE A TERRIFYING MAN---
I'LL PRAY THAT MY WILL HASN'T BEEN PREPARED TOO.
FLOP
HEH, HOW ABSURD.

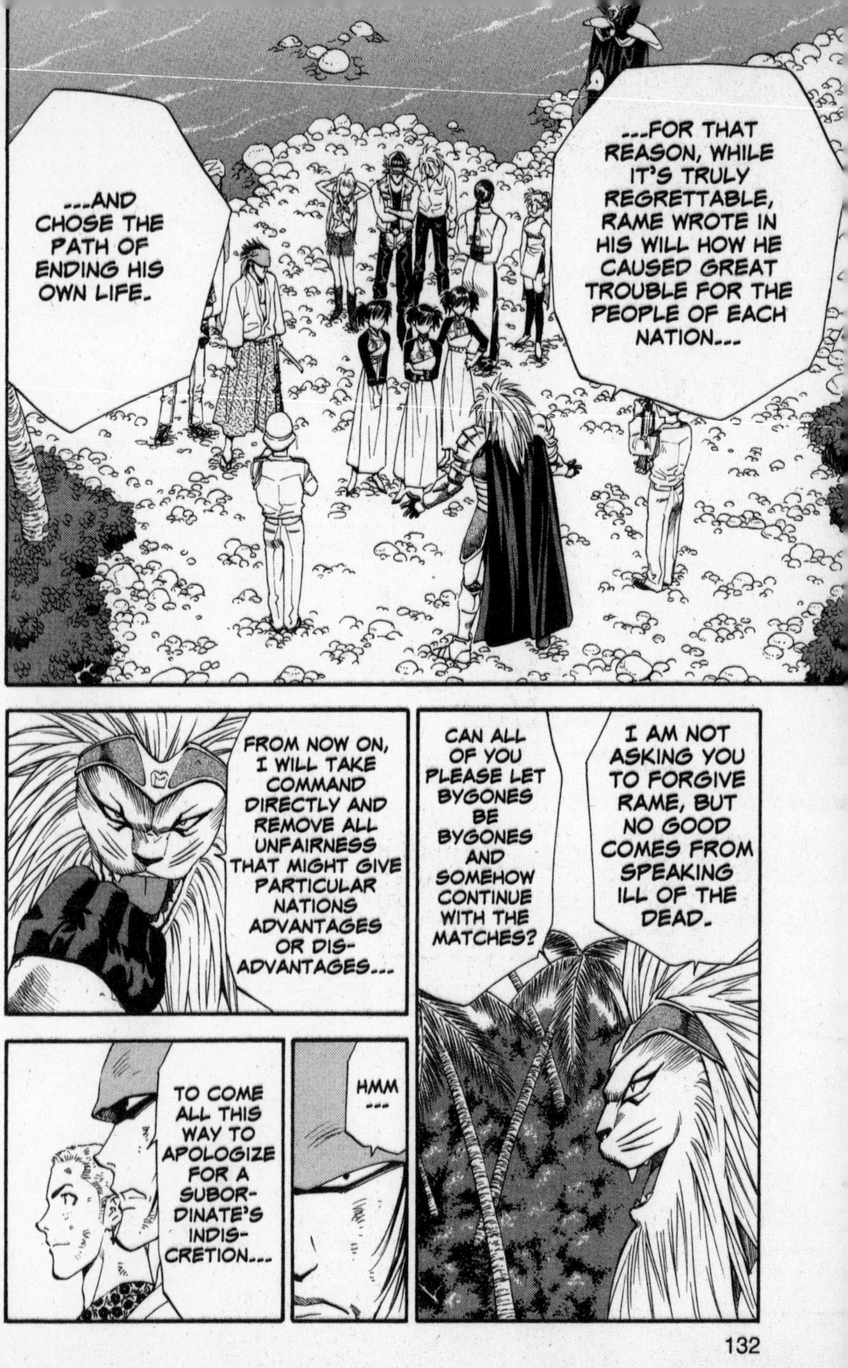
...FOR THAT REASON, WHILE IT'S TRULY REGRETTABLE, RAME WROTE IN HIS WILL HOW HE CAUSED GREAT TROUBLE FOR THE PEOPLE OF EACH NATION...
...AND CHOSE THE PATH OF ENDING HIS OWN LIFE.
I AM NOT ASKING YOU TO FORGIVE RAME, BUT NO GOOD COMES FROM SPEAKING ILL OF THE DEAD.
CAN ALL OF YOU PLEASE LET BYGONES BE BYGONES AND SOMEHOW CONTINUE WITH THE MATCHES?
FROM NOW ON, I WILL TAKE COMMAND DIRECTLY AND REMOVE ALL UNFAIRNESS THAT MIGHT GIVE PARTICULAR NATIONS ADVANTAGES OR DIS-ADVANTAGES...
HMM...
TO COME ALL THIS WAY TO APOLOGIZE FOR A SUBOR-DINATE'S INDIS-CRETION...

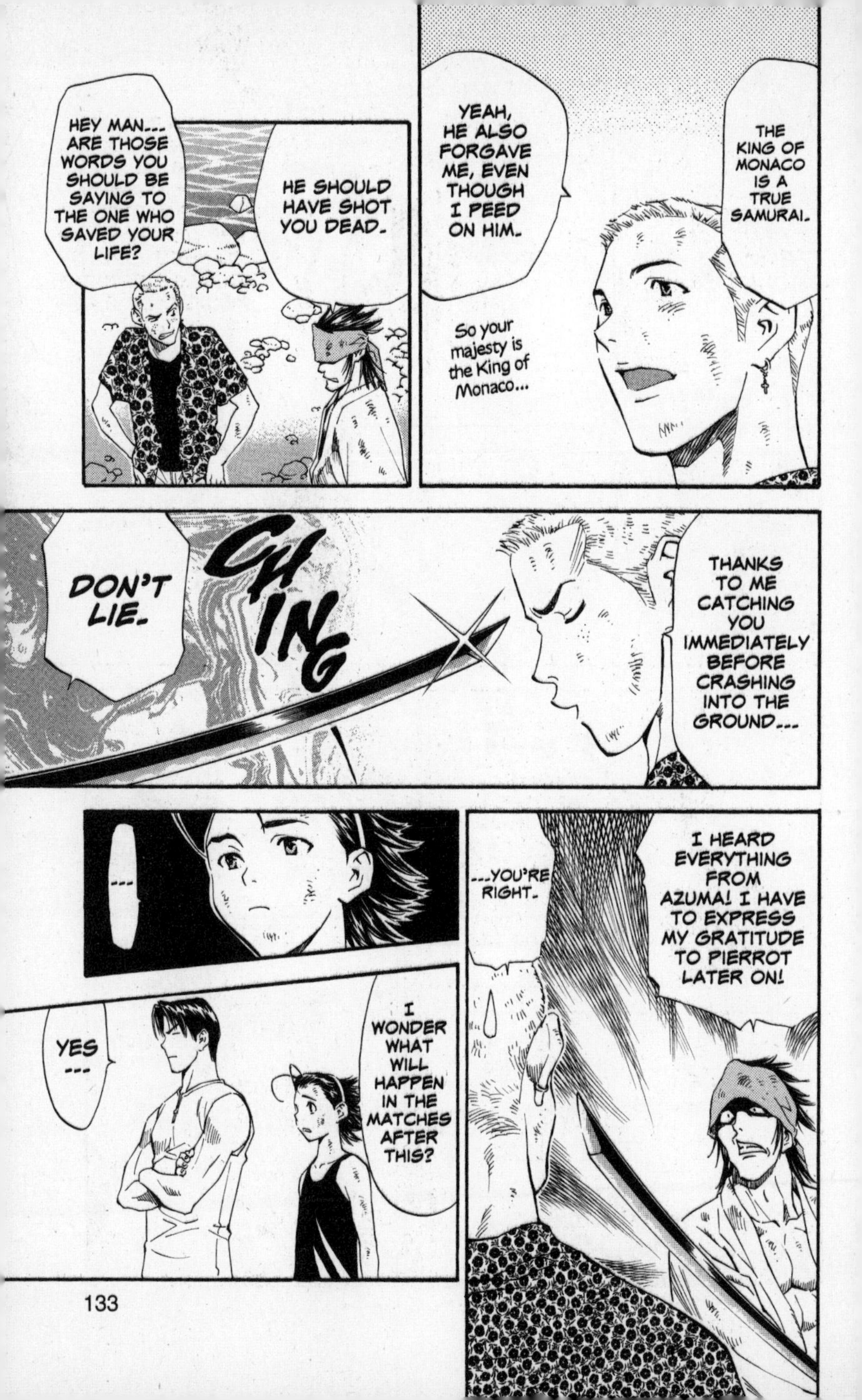
THE KING OF MONACO IS A TRUE SAMURAI.
YEAH, HE ALSO FORGAVE ME, EVEN THOUGH I PEED ON HIM.
So your majesty is the King of Monaco...
HE SHOULD HAVE SHOT YOU DEAD.
HEY MAN... ARE THOSE WORDS YOU SHOULD BE SAYING TO THE ONE WHO SAVED YOUR LIFE?
THANKS TO ME CATCHING YOU IMMEDIATELY BEFORE CRASHING INTO THE GROUND...
CHING
DON'T LIE.
I HEARD EVERYTHING FROM AZUMA! I HAVE TO EXPRESS MY GRATITUDE TO PIERROT LATER ON!
...YOU'RE RIGHT.
...
I WONDER WHAT WILL HAPPEN IN THE MATCHES AFTER THIS?
YES...

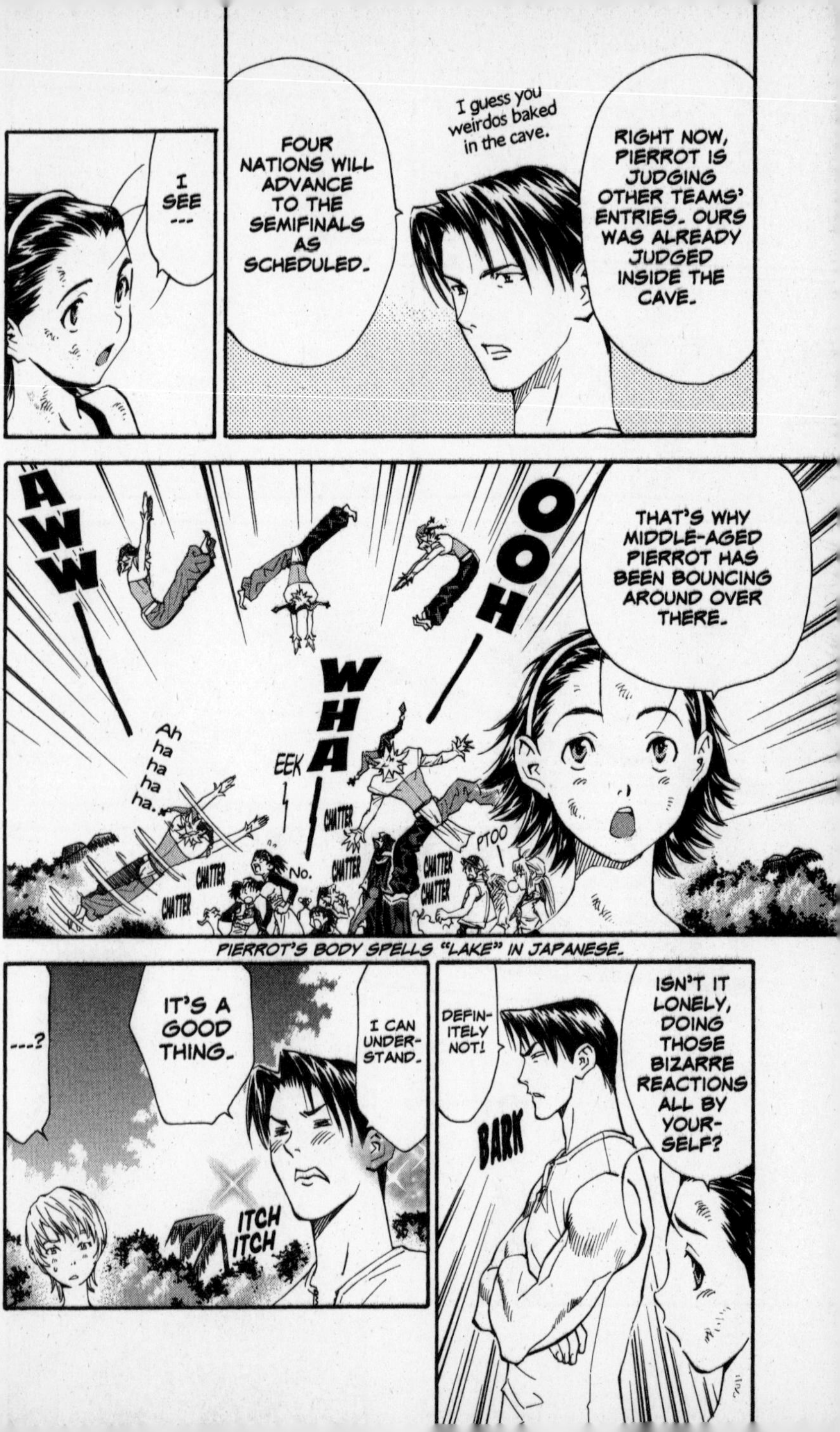
RIGHT NOW, PIERROT IS JUDGING OTHER TEAMS' ENTRIES. OURS WAS ALREADY JUDGED INSIDE THE CAVE.
I guess you weirdos baked in the cave.
FOUR NATIONS WILL ADVANCE TO THE SEMIFINALS AS SCHEDULED.
I SEE ---
THAT'S WHY MIDDLE-AGED PIERROT HAS BEEN BOUNCING AROUND OVER THERE.
OOH
WHA
AWW
PTOO
CHATTER CHATTER
CHATTER
EEK
CHATTER
No.
Ah ha ha ha ha.
CHATTER
CHATTER
PIERROT'S BODY SPELLS "LAKE" IN JAPANESE.
ISN'T IT LONELY, DOING THOSE BIZARRE REACTIONS ALL BY YOURSELF?
DEFINITELY NOT!
BARK
I CAN UNDERSTAND.
IT'S A GOOD THING.
---?
ITCH ITCH

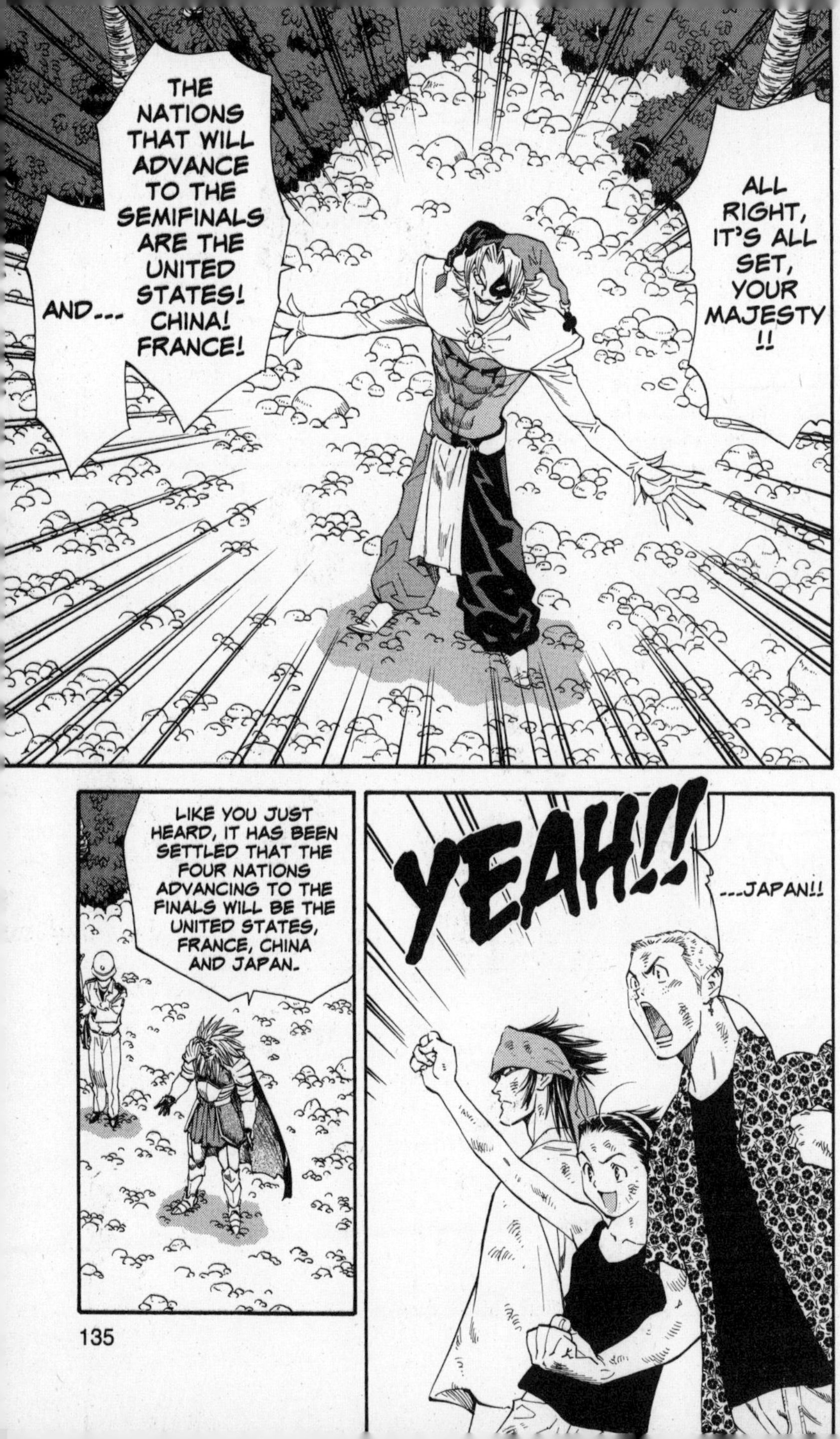
ALL RIGHT, IT'S ALL SET, YOUR MAJESTY!!
THE NATIONS THAT WILL ADVANCE TO THE SEMIFINALS ARE THE UNITED STATES! CHINA! FRANCE!
AND...
...JAPAN!!
YEAH!!
LIKE YOU JUST HEARD, IT HAS BEEN SETTLED THAT THE FOUR NATIONS ADVANCING TO THE FINALS WILL BE THE UNITED STATES, FRANCE, CHINA AND JAPAN.

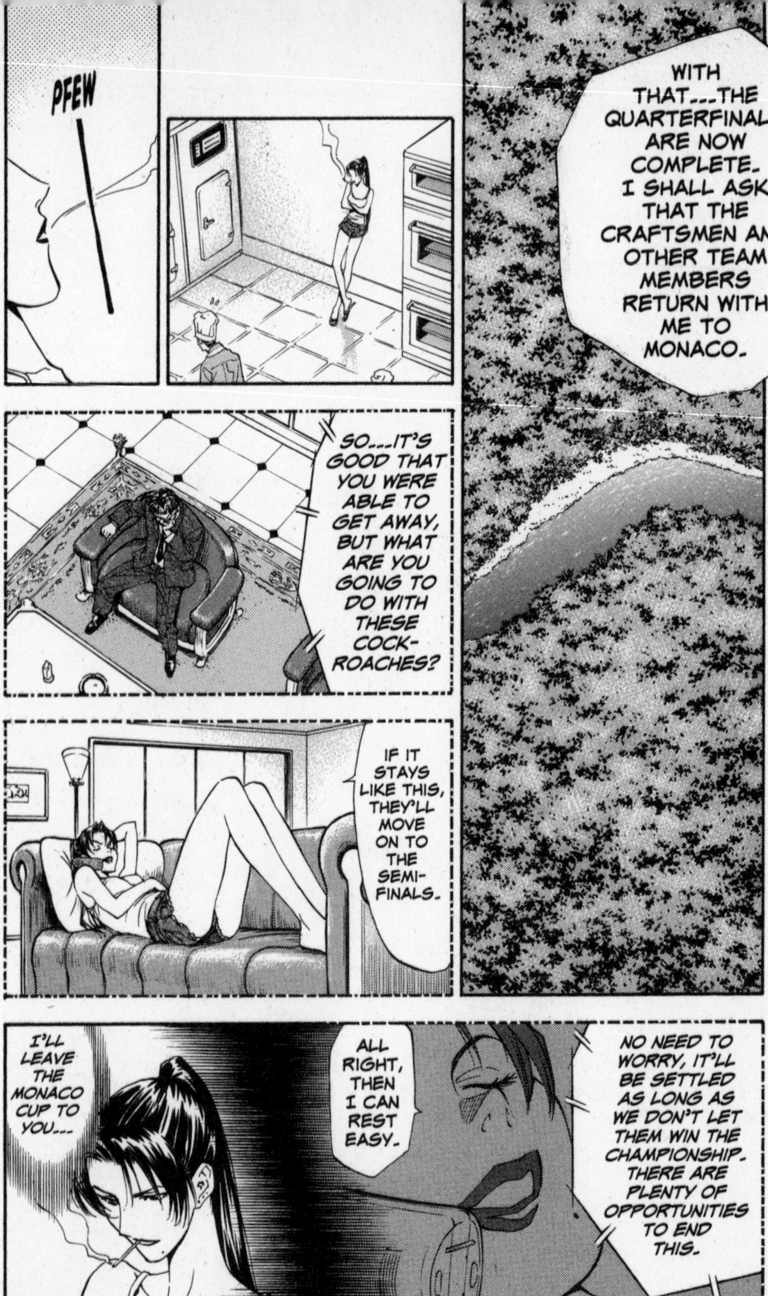

WITH THAT...THE QUARTERFINALS ARE NOW COMPLETE. I SHALL ASK THAT THE CRAFTSMEN AND OTHER TEAM MEMBERS RETURN WITH ME TO MONACO.
PFEW
SO...IT'S GOOD THAT YOU WERE ABLE TO GET AWAY, BUT WHAT ARE YOU GOING TO DO WITH THESE COCK-ROACHES?
IF IT STAYS LIKE THIS, THEY'LL MOVE ON TO THE SEMI-FINALS.
NO NEED TO WORRY, IT'LL BE SETTLED AS LONG AS WE DON'T LET THEM WIN THE CHAMPIONSHIP. THERE ARE PLENTY OF OPPORTUNITIES TO END THIS.
ALL RIGHT, THEN I CAN REST EASY.
I'LL LEAVE THE MONACO CUP TO YOU...

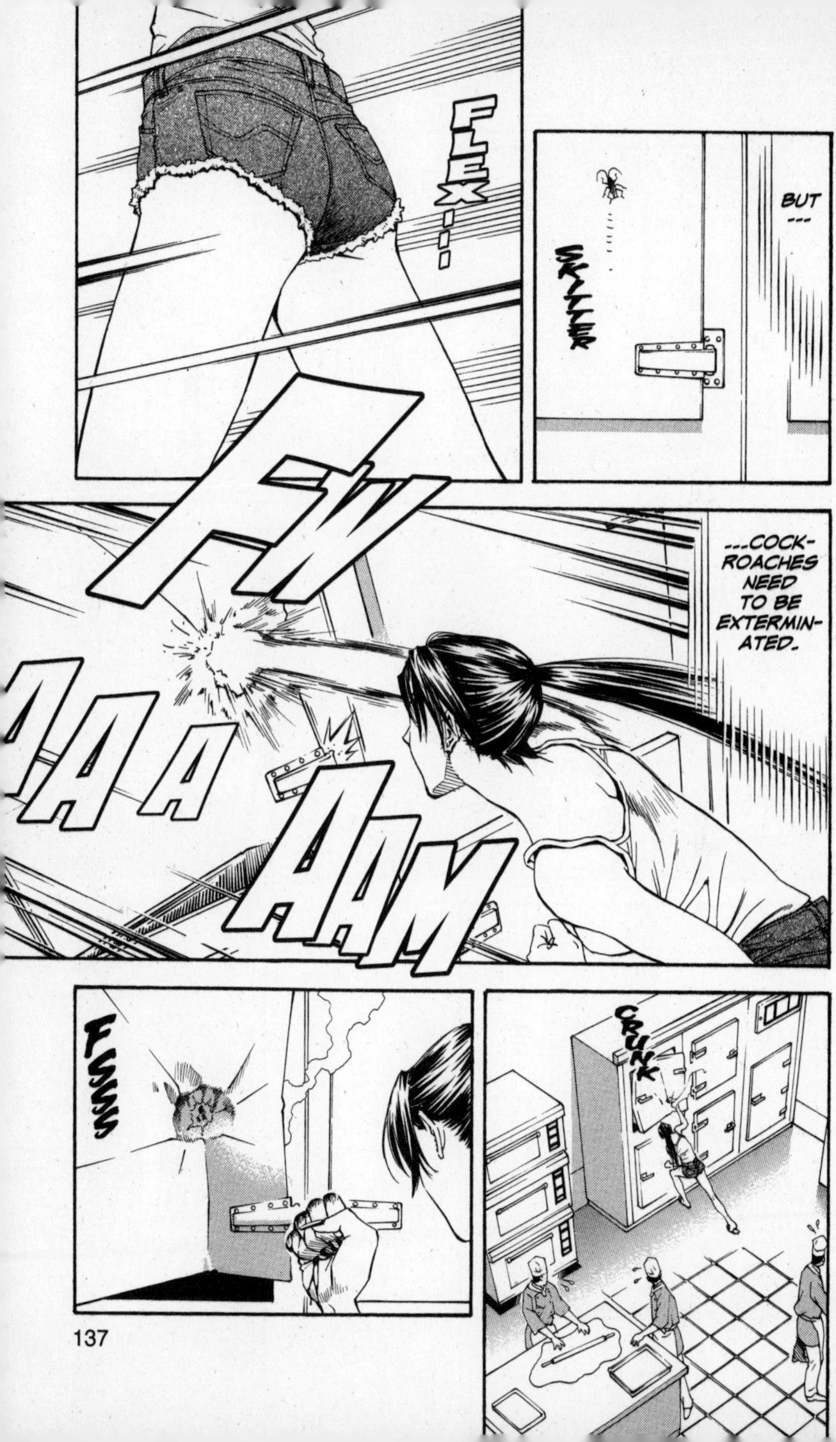
BUT---
SKITTER
FLEX!!!
---COCK-
ROACHES
NEED
TO BE
EXTERMIN-
ATED.
FWK
AAAAAAM
CRUNK
FSSSS

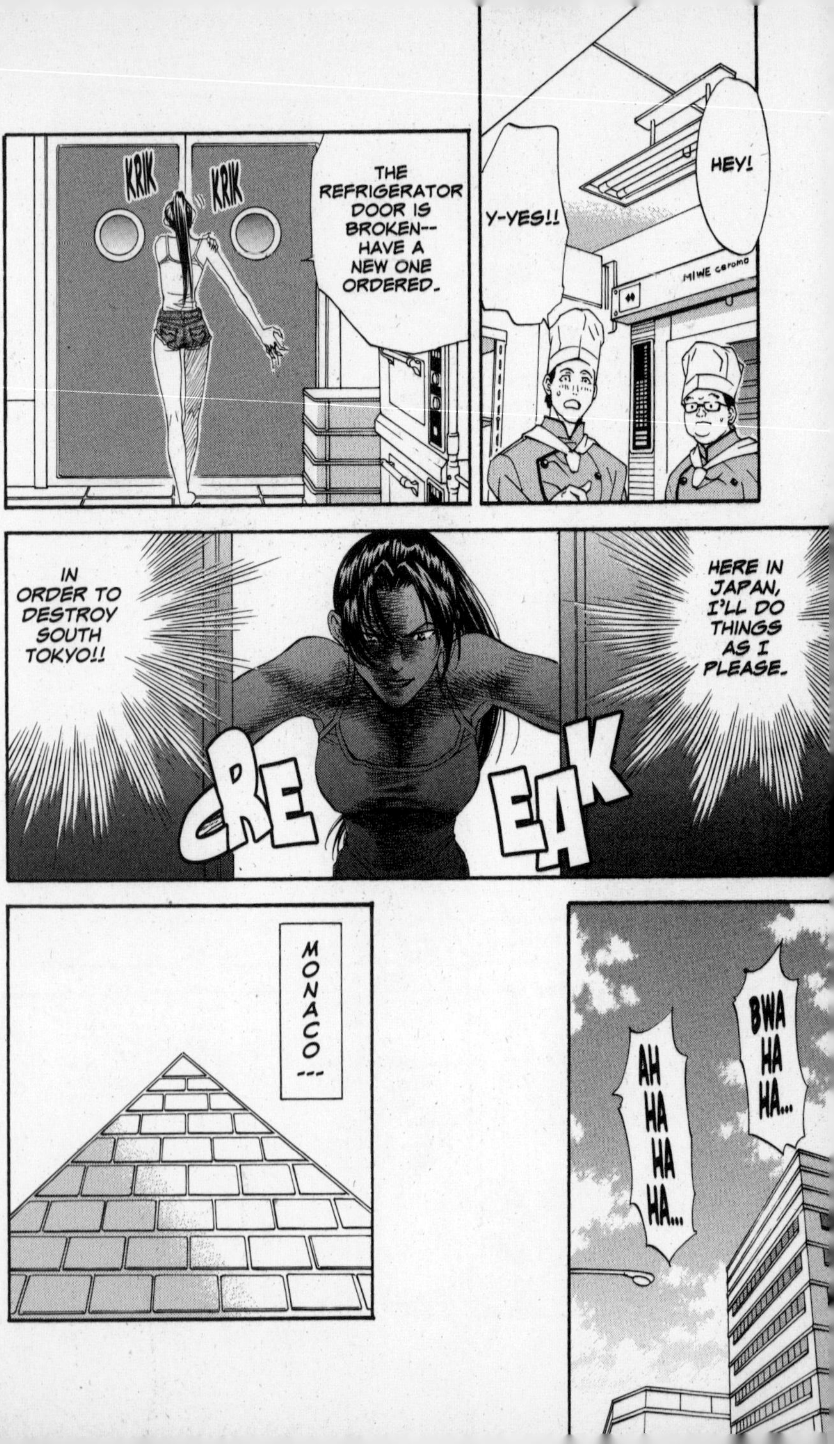
HEY!
Y-YES!!
MIWE ceramo
THE REFRIGERATOR DOOR IS BROKEN-- HAVE A NEW ONE ORDERED.
KRIK
KRIK
HERE IN JAPAN, I'LL DO THINGS AS I PLEASE.
CREEAK
IN ORDER TO DESTROY SOUTH TOKYO!!
BWA HA HA...
AH HA HA HA HA...
MONACO---

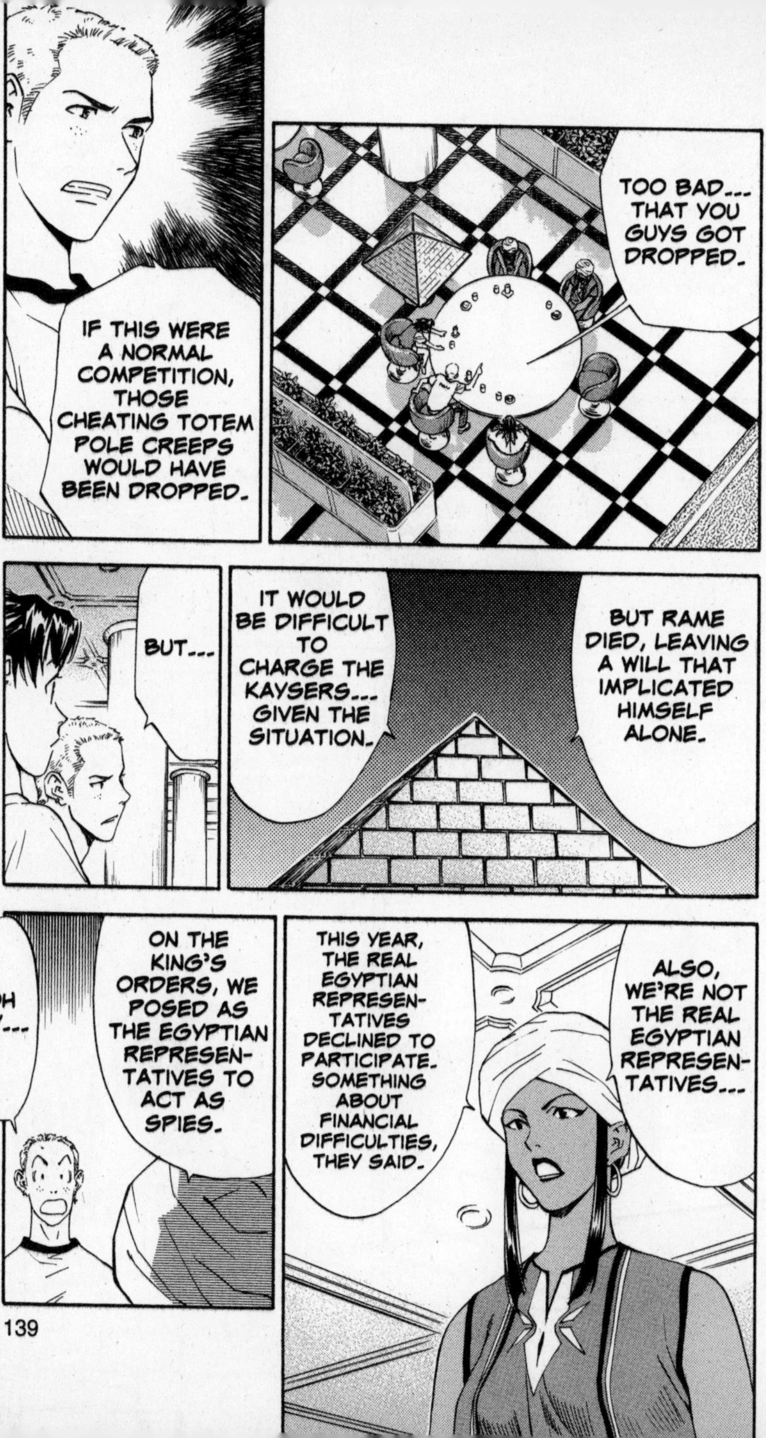
TOO BAD... THAT YOU GUYS GOT DROPPED.
IF THIS WERE A NORMAL COMPETITION, THOSE CHEATING TOTEM POLE CREEPS WOULD HAVE BEEN DROPPED.
BUT RAME DIED, LEAVING A WILL THAT IMPLICATED HIMSELF ALONE.
IT WOULD BE DIFFICULT TO CHARGE THE KAYSERS... GIVEN THE SITUATION.
BUT...
ALSO, WE'RE NOT THE REAL EGYPTIAN REPRESEN-TATIVES...
THIS YEAR, THE REAL EGYPTIAN REPRESEN-TATIVES DECLINED TO PARTICIPATE. SOMETHING ABOUT FINANCIAL DIFFICULTIES, THEY SAID.
ON THE KING'S ORDERS, WE POSED AS THE EGYPTIAN REPRESEN-TATIVES TO ACT AS SPIES.
OH MY...

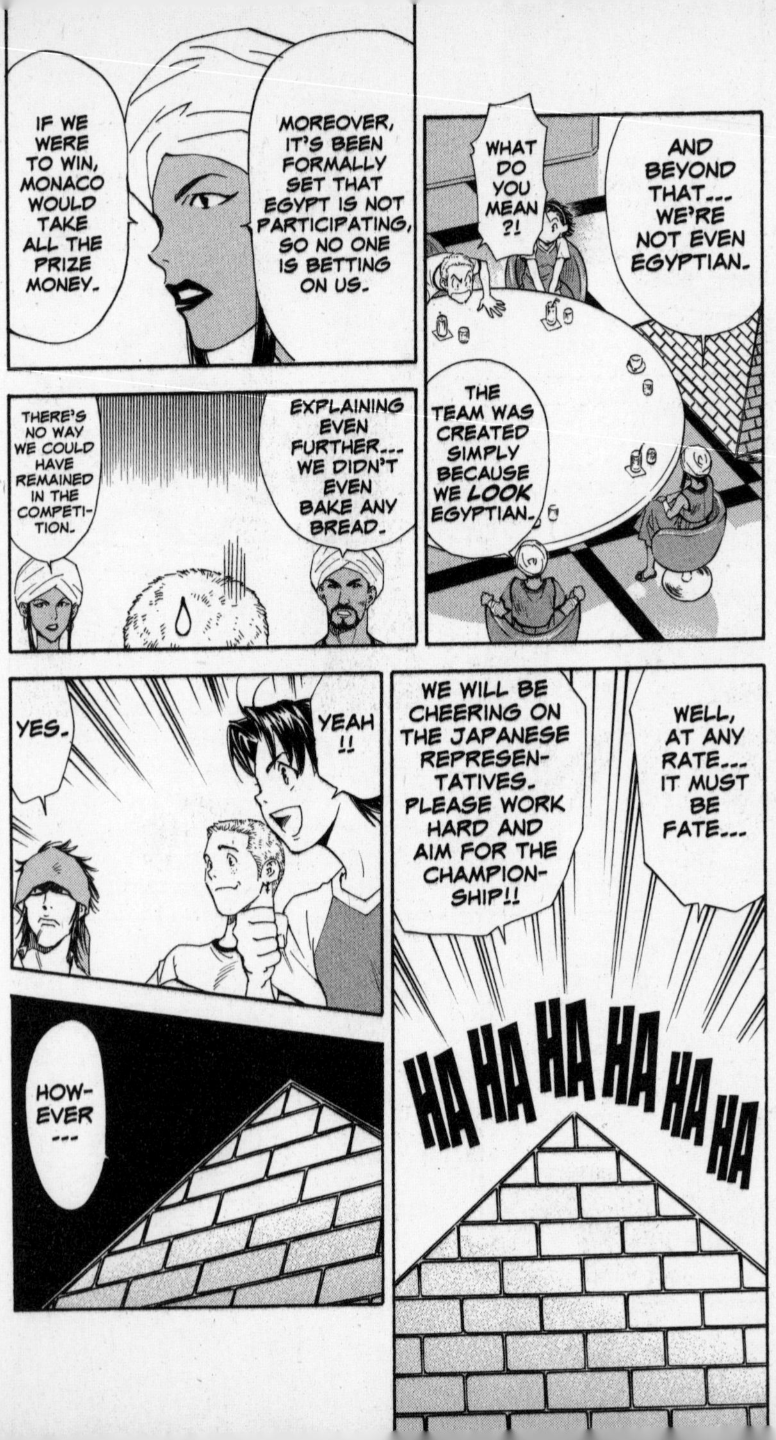

IF WE WERE TO WIN, MONACO WOULD TAKE ALL THE PRIZE MONEY.
MOREOVER, IT'S BEEN FORMALLY SET THAT EGYPT IS NOT PARTICIPATING, SO NO ONE IS BETTING ON US.
AND BEYOND THAT... WE'RE NOT EVEN EGYPTIAN.
WHAT DO YOU MEAN?!
THE TEAM WAS CREATED SIMPLY BECAUSE WE *LOOK* EGYPTIAN.
EXPLAINING EVEN FURTHER... WE DIDN'T EVEN BAKE ANY BREAD.
THERE'S NO WAY WE COULD HAVE REMAINED IN THE COMPETITION.
WELL, AT ANY RATE... IT MUST BE FATE...
WE WILL BE CHEERING ON THE JAPANESE REPRESENTATIVES. PLEASE WORK HARD AND AIM FOR THE CHAMPIONSHIP!!
HA HA HA HA HA HA HA HA
YEAH!!
YES.
HOW-EVER...

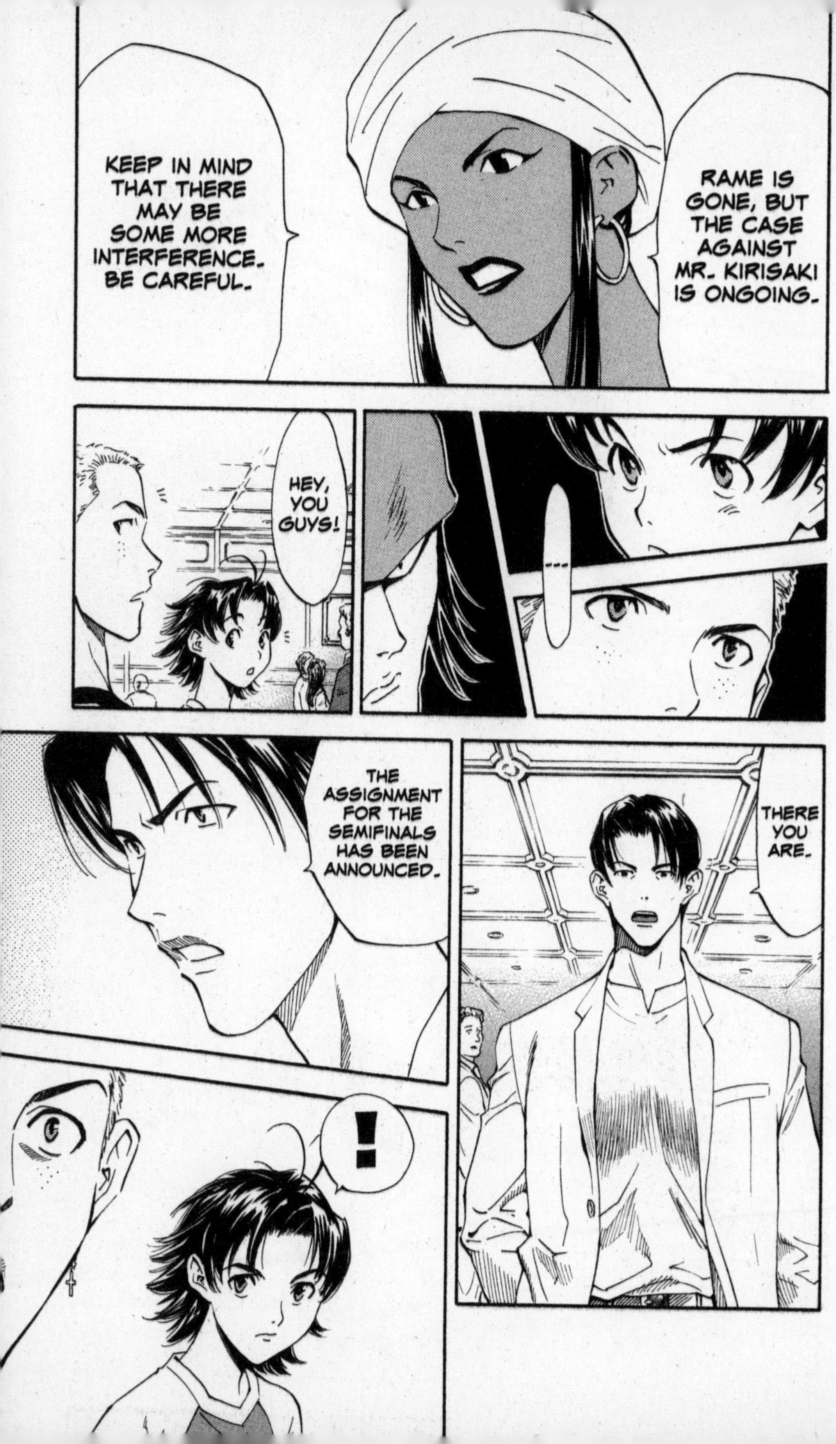
RAME IS GONE, BUT THE CASE AGAINST MR. KIRISAKI IS ONGOING.
KEEP IN MIND THAT THERE MAY BE SOME MORE INTERFERENCE. BE CAREFUL.
...
HEY, YOU GUYS!
THERE YOU ARE.
THE ASSIGNMENT FOR THE SEMIFINALS HAS BEEN ANNOUNCED.
!

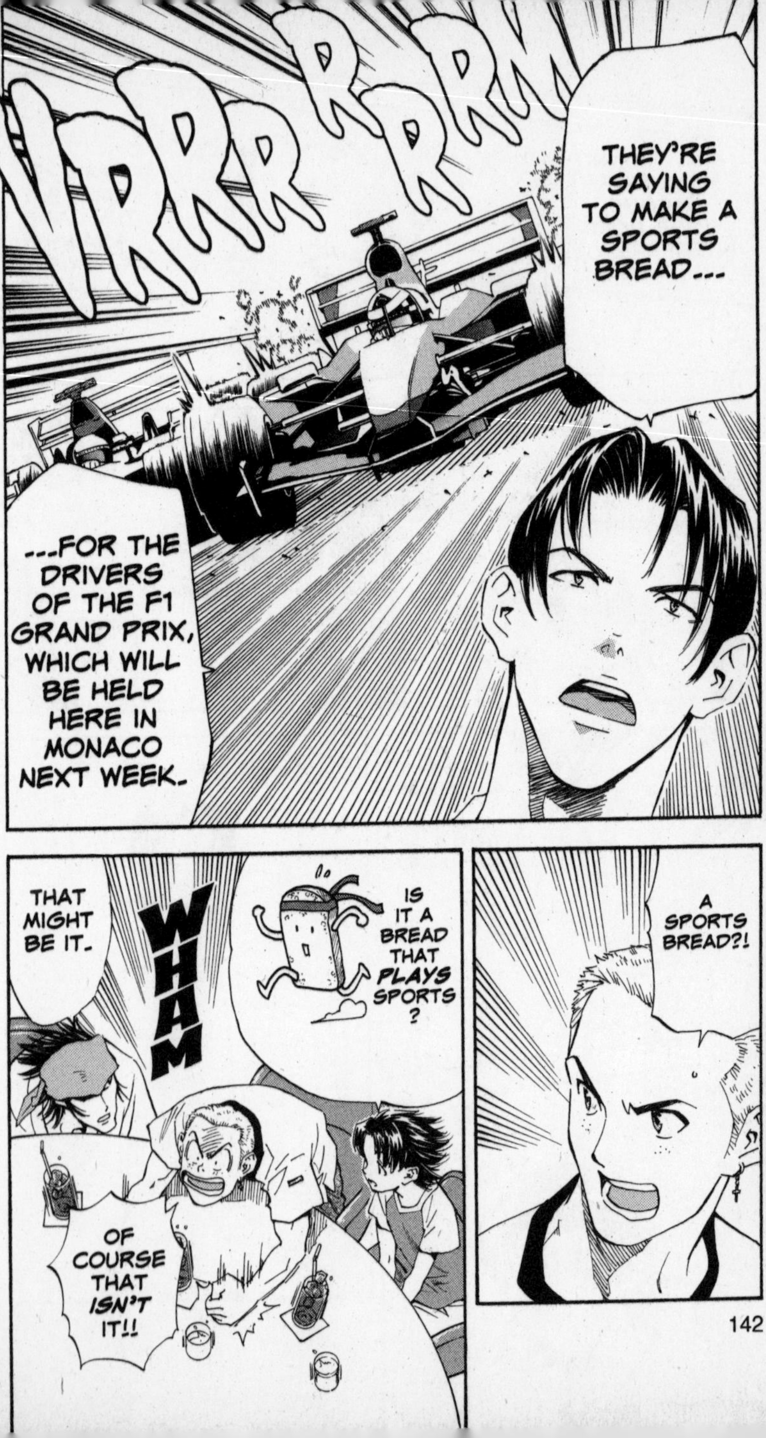
VRRRRRRM
THEY'RE SAYING TO MAKE A SPORTS BREAD...
...FOR THE DRIVERS OF THE F1 GRAND PRIX, WHICH WILL BE HELD HERE IN MONACO NEXT WEEK.
A SPORTS BREAD?!
IS IT A BREAD THAT *PLAYS* SPORTS?
WHAM
THAT MIGHT BE IT.
OF COURSE THAT *ISN'T* IT!!

TO BE CONTINUED!

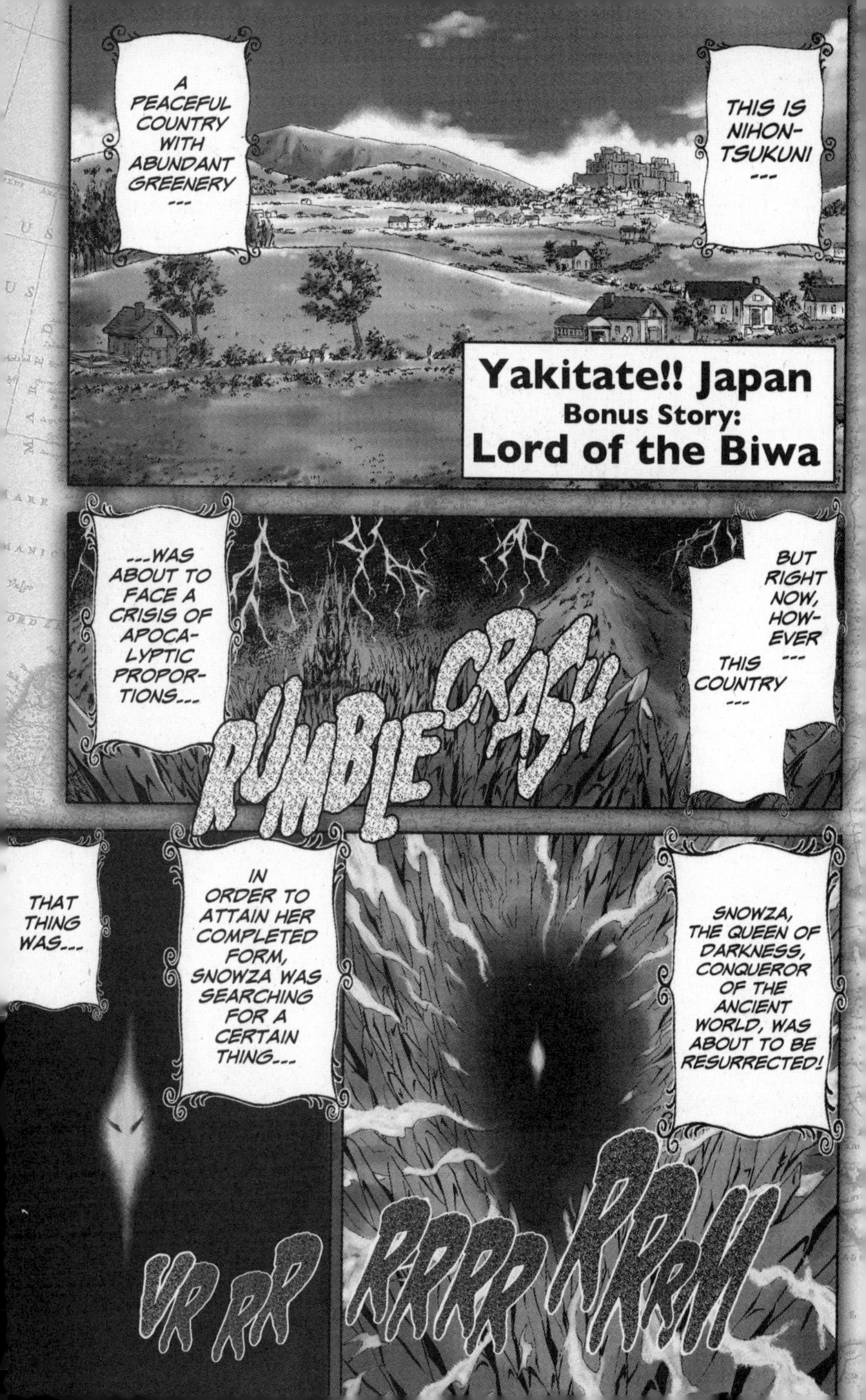

THIS IS NIHON-TSUKUNI---
A PEACEFUL COUNTRY WITH ABUNDANT GREENERY---
Yakitate!! Japan
Bonus Story:
Lord of the Biwa
BUT RIGHT NOW, HOWEVER--- THIS COUNTRY---
---WAS ABOUT TO FACE A CRISIS OF APOCALYPTIC PROPORTIONS---
RUMBLE CRASH
SNOWZA, THE QUEEN OF DARKNESS, CONQUEROR OF THE ANCIENT WORLD, WAS ABOUT TO BE RESURRECTED!
RRRRR RRRRR
IN ORDER TO ATTAIN HER COMPLETED FORM, SNOWZA WAS SEARCHING FOR A CERTAIN THING---
THAT THING WAS---
VR RR

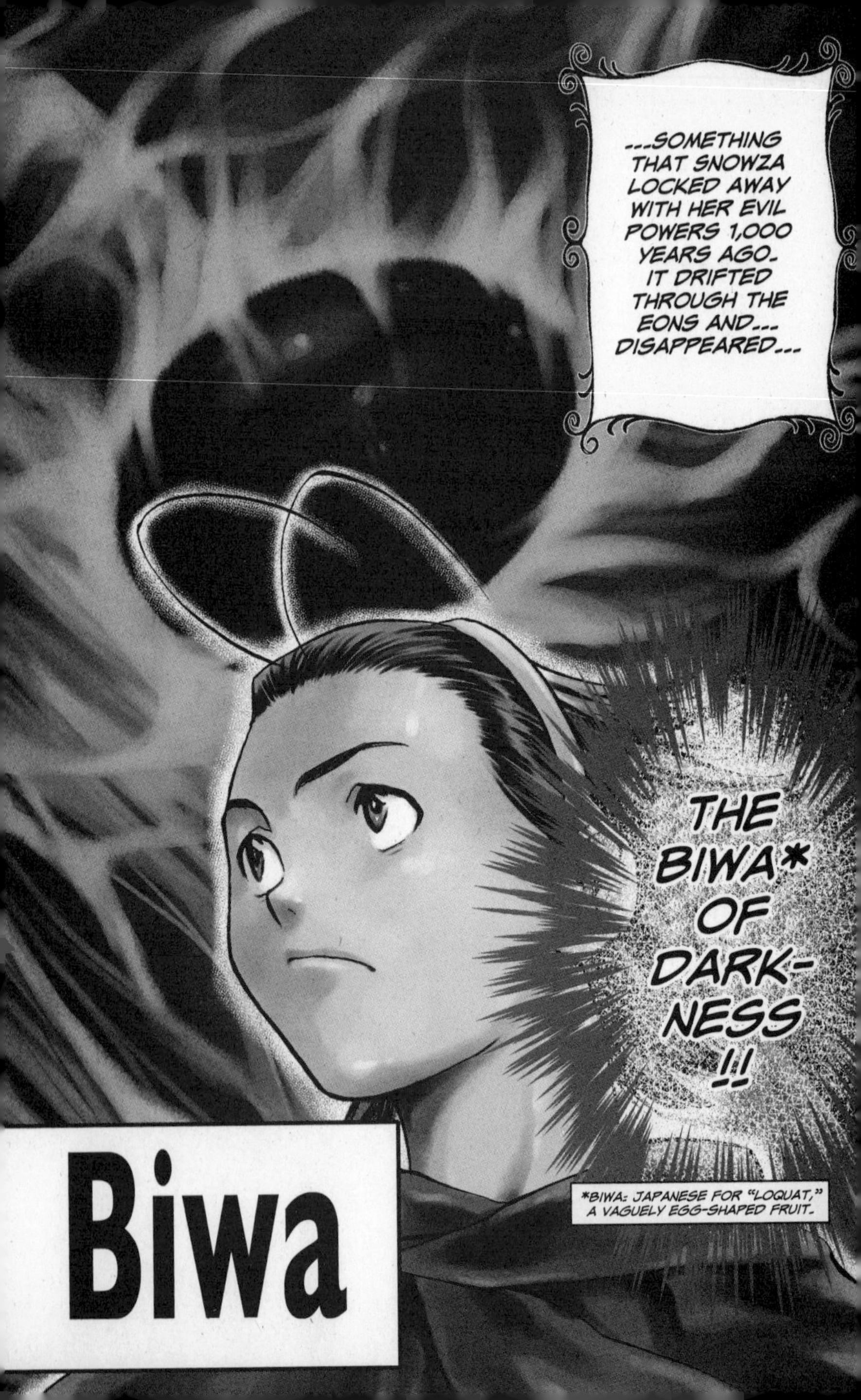
...SOMETHING THAT SNOWZA LOCKED AWAY WITH HER EVIL POWERS 1,000 YEARS AGO. IT DRIFTED THROUGH THE EONS AND... DISAPPEARED...
THE BIWA* OF DARK-NESS !!
Biwa
*BIWA: JAPANESE FOR "LOQUAT," A VAGUELY EGG-SHAPED FRUIT.

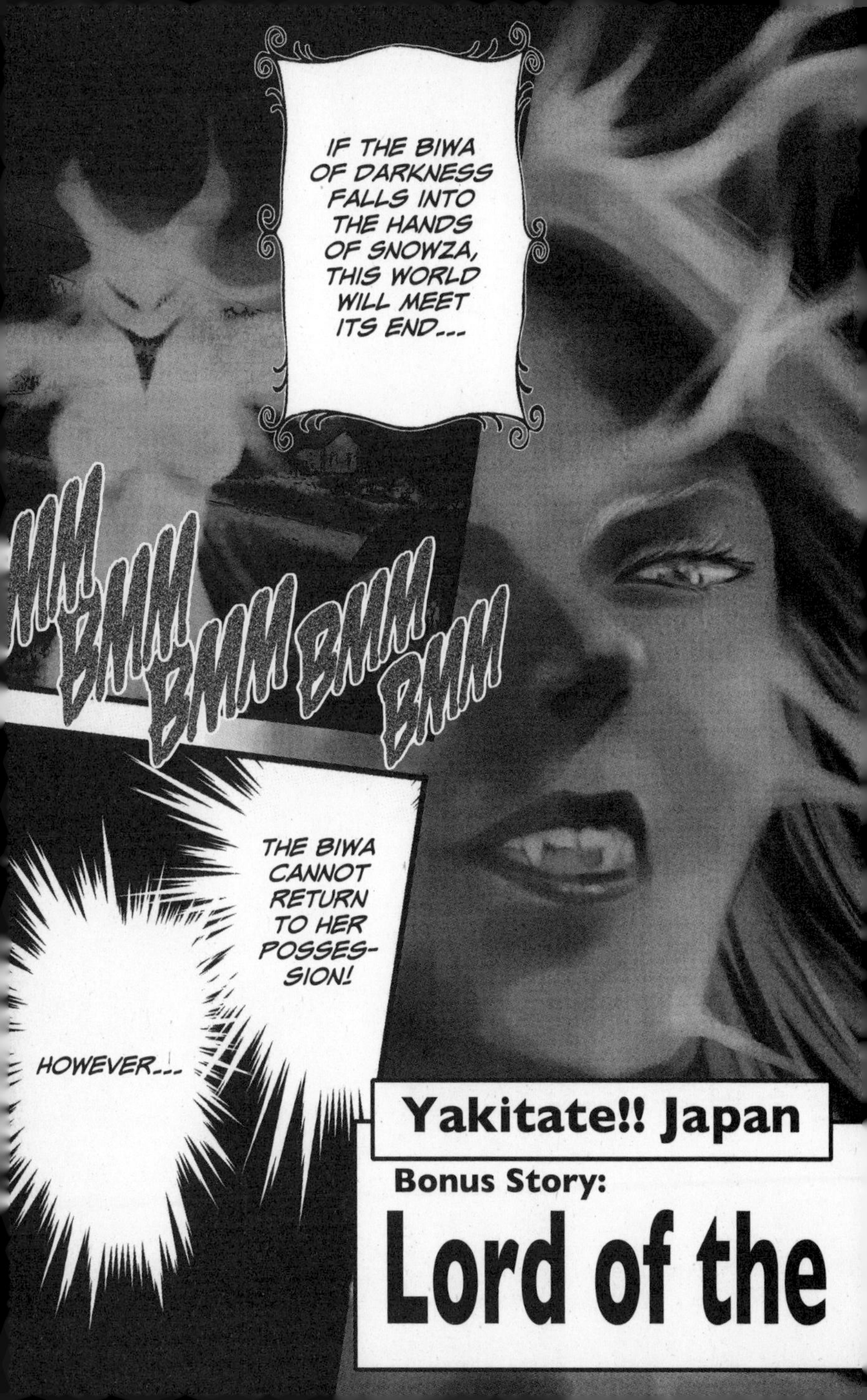
IF THE BIWA OF DARKNESS FALLS INTO THE HANDS OF SNOWZA, THIS WORLD WILL MEET ITS END...
BMM BMM BMM BMM BMM
THE BIWA CANNOT RETURN TO HER POSSESSION!
HOWEVER...
Yakitate!! Japan
Bonus Story:
Lord of the

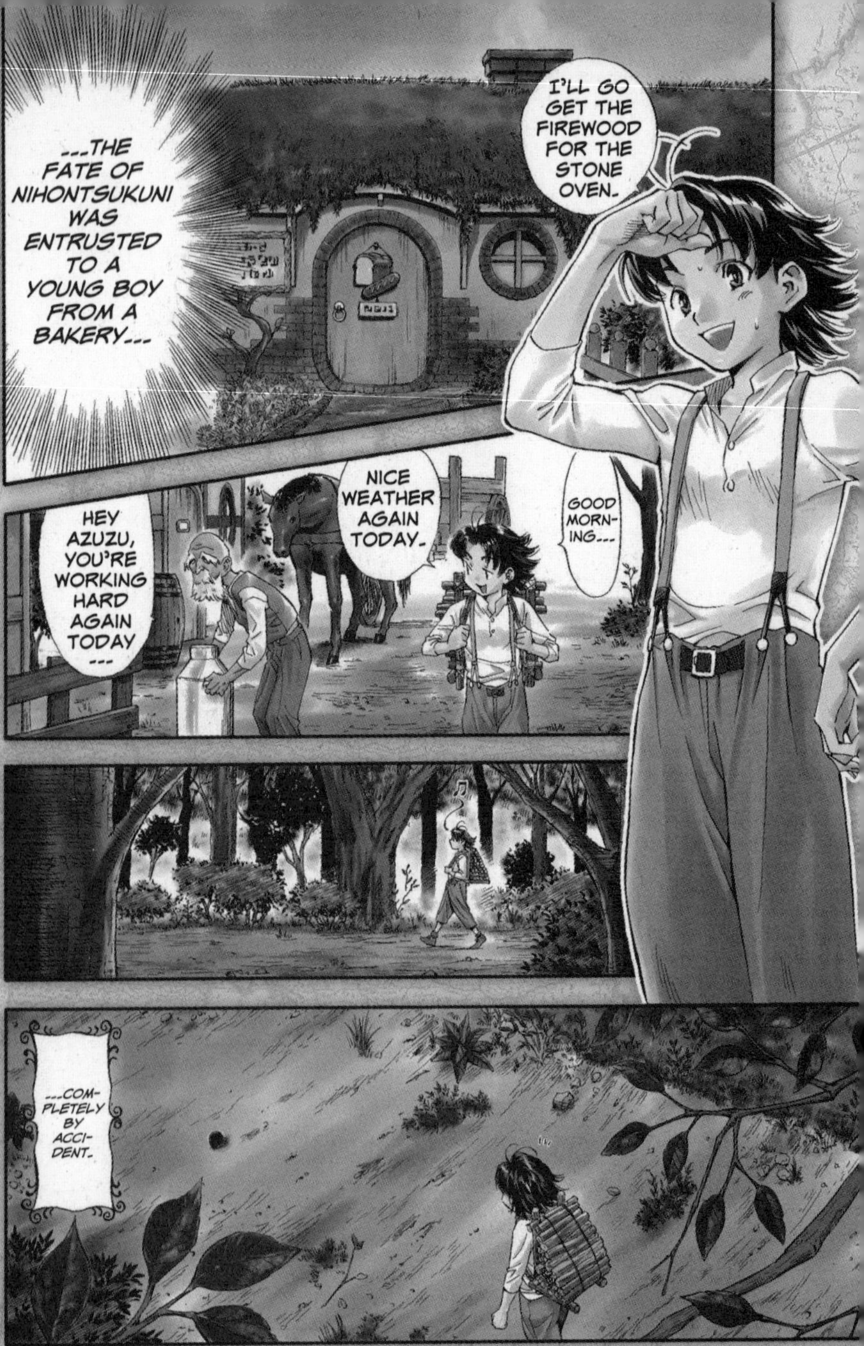
I'LL GO GET THE FIREWOOD FOR THE STONE OVEN.
...THE FATE OF NIHONTSUKUNI WAS ENTRUSTED TO A YOUNG BOY FROM A BAKERY...
GOOD MORNING...
NICE WEATHER AGAIN TODAY.
HEY AZUZU, YOU'RE WORKING HARD AGAIN TODAY...
...COMPLETELY BY ACCIDENT.

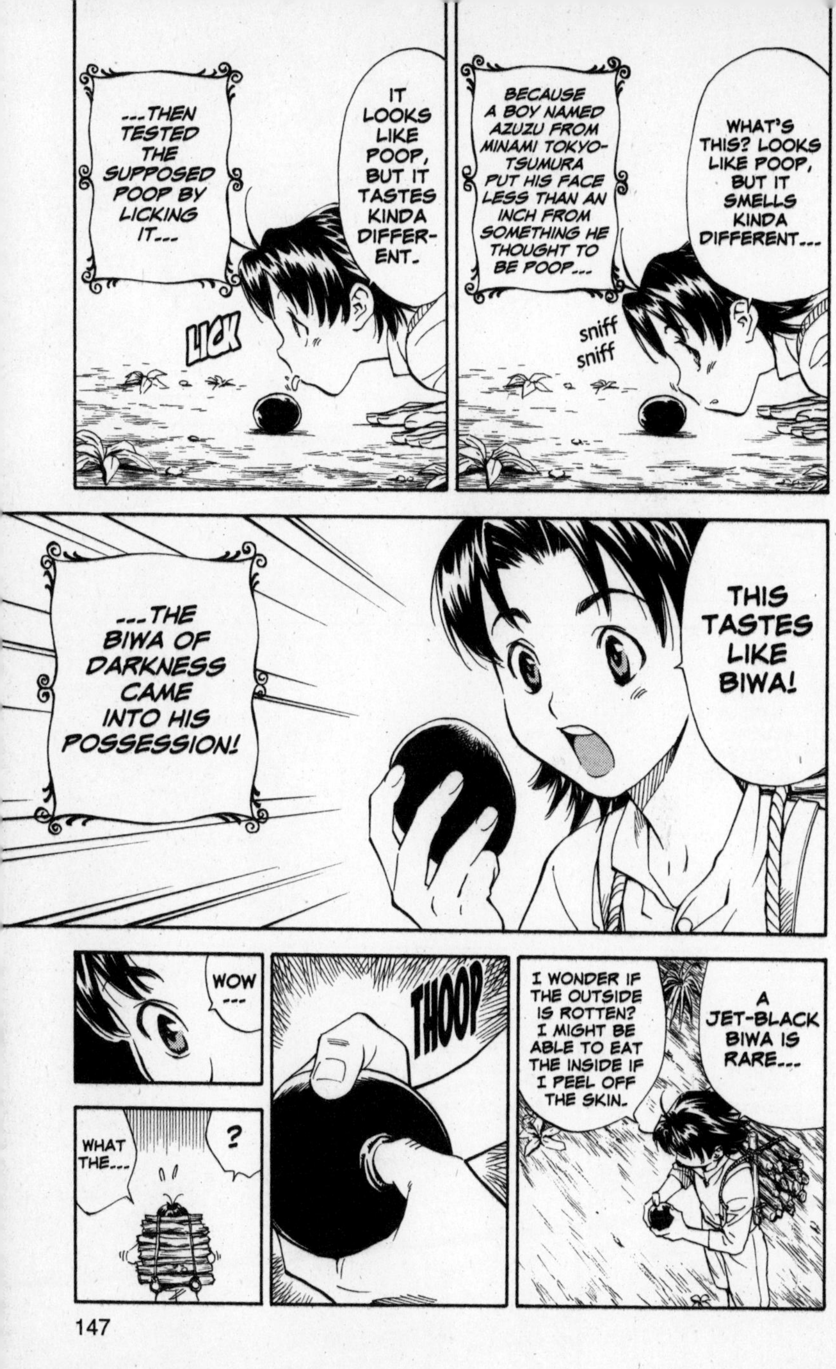
WHAT'S THIS? LOOKS LIKE POOP, BUT IT SMELLS KINDA DIFFERENT...
BECAUSE A BOY NAMED AZUZU FROM MINAMI TOKYO-TSUMURA PUT HIS FACE LESS THAN AN INCH FROM SOMETHING HE THOUGHT TO BE POOP...
sniff sniff
IT LOOKS LIKE POOP, BUT IT TASTES KINDA DIFFER-ENT.
...THEN TESTED THE SUPPOSED POOP BY LICKING IT...
LICK
THIS TASTES LIKE BIWA!
...THE BIWA OF DARKNESS CAME INTO HIS POSSESSION!
A JET-BLACK BIWA IS RARE...
I WONDER IF THE OUTSIDE IS ROTTEN? I MIGHT BE ABLE TO EAT THE INSIDE IF I PEEL OFF THE SKIN.
THOOP
WOW...
?
WHAT THE...

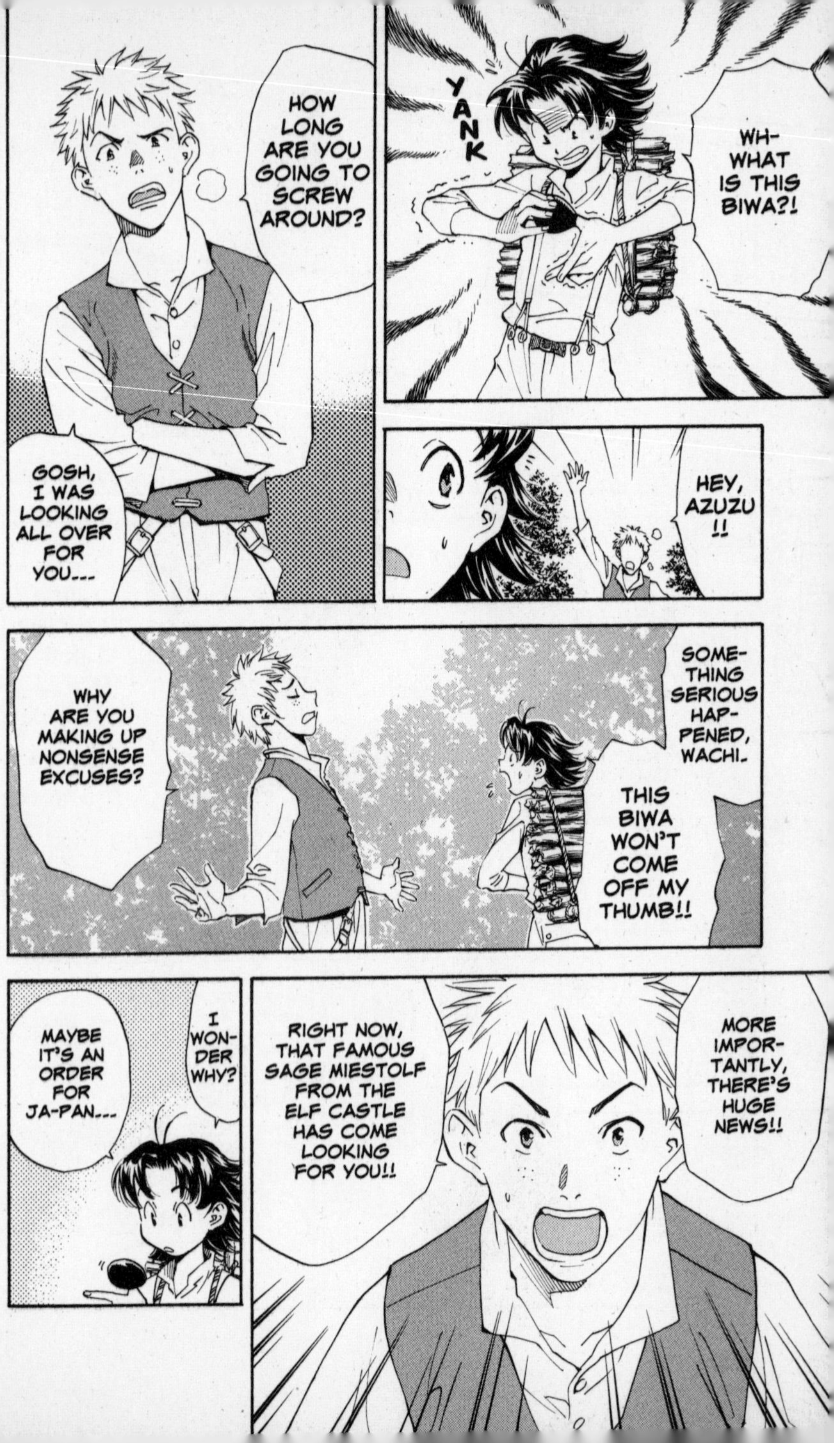
YANK
WH- WHAT IS THIS BIWA?!
HEY, AZUZU!!
HOW LONG ARE YOU GOING TO SCREW AROUND?
GOSH, I WAS LOOKING ALL OVER FOR YOU...
SOMETHING SERIOUS HAPPENED, WACHI.
THIS BIWA WON'T COME OFF MY THUMB!!
WHY ARE YOU MAKING UP NONSENSE EXCUSES?
MORE IMPORTANTLY, THERE'S HUGE NEWS!!
RIGHT NOW, THAT FAMOUS SAGE MIESTOLF FROM THE ELF CASTLE HAS COME LOOKING FOR YOU!!
I WONDER WHY?
MAYBE IT'S AN ORDER FOR JA-PAN...

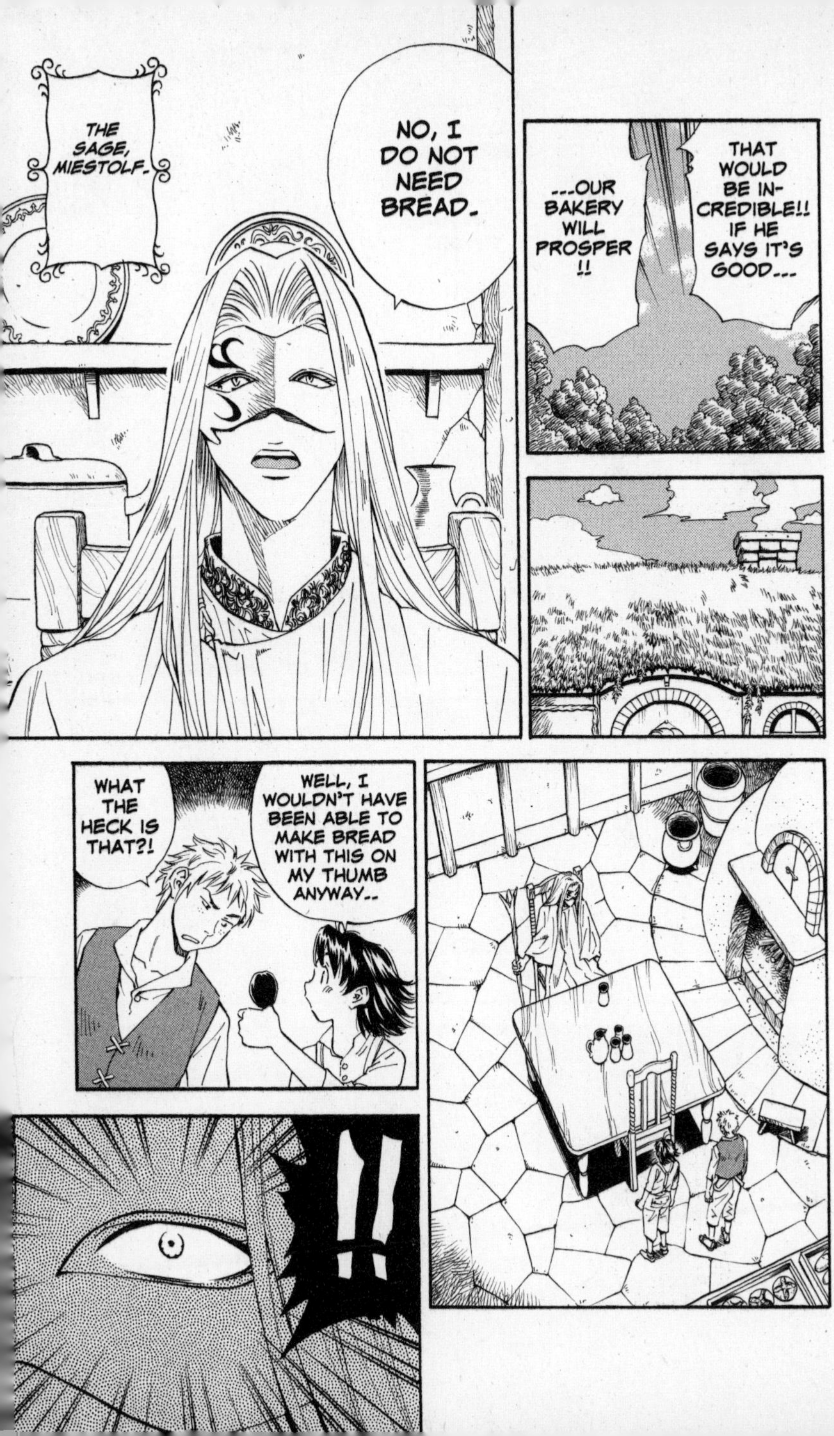
THAT WOULD BE IN-CREDIBLE!! IF HE SAYS IT'S GOOD...
...OUR BAKERY WILL PROSPER!!
NO, I DO NOT NEED BREAD.
THE SAGE, MIESTOLF.
WELL, I WOULDN'T HAVE BEEN ABLE TO MAKE BREAD WITH THIS ON MY THUMB ANYWAY..
WHAT THE HECK IS THAT?!
!!

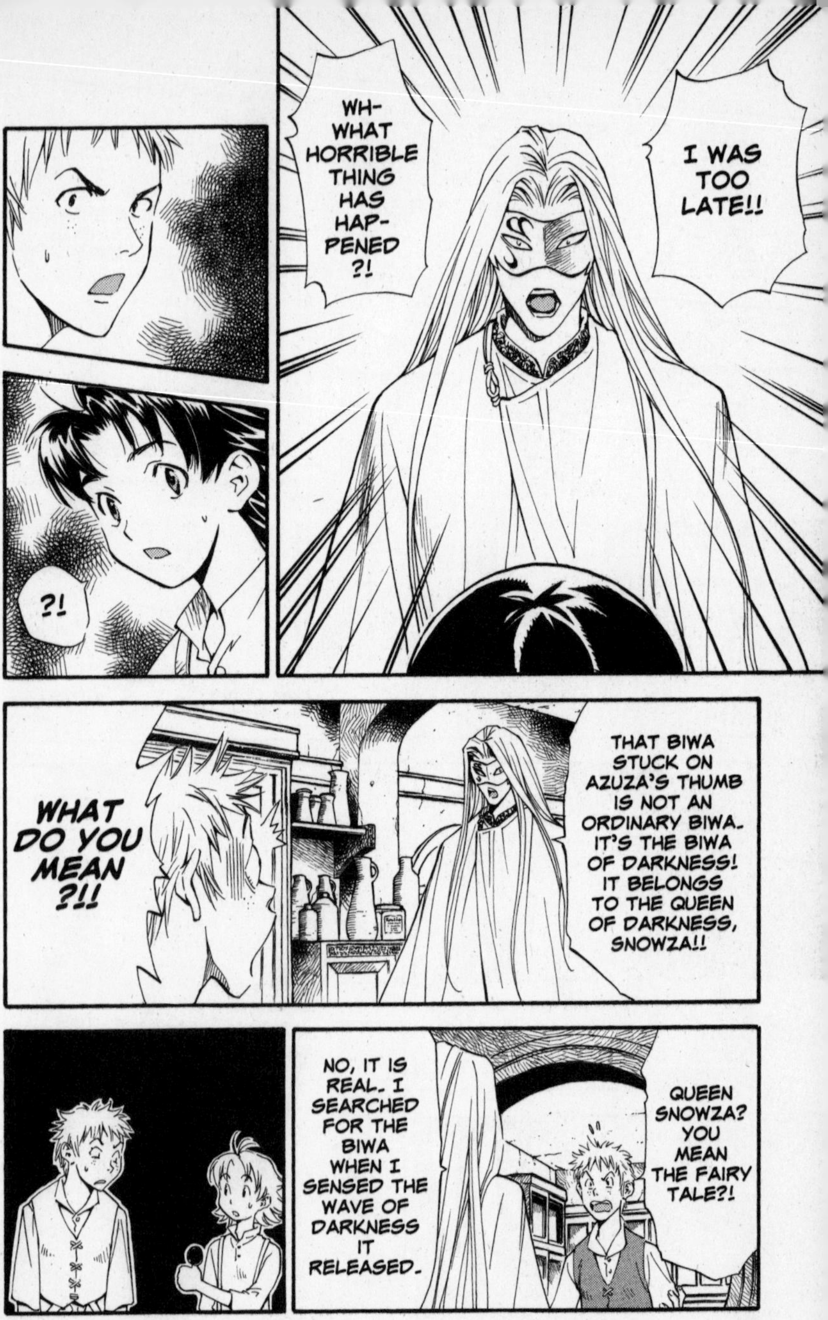
I WAS TOO LATE!!
WH-WHAT HORRIBLE THING HAS HAP-PENED?!
?!
THAT BIWA STUCK ON AZUZA'S THUMB IS NOT AN ORDINARY BIWA. IT'S THE BIWA OF DARKNESS! IT BELONGS TO THE QUEEN OF DARKNESS, SNOWZA!!
WHAT DO YOU MEAN?!!
QUEEN SNOWZA? YOU MEAN THE FAIRY TALE?!
NO, IT IS REAL. I SEARCHED FOR THE BIWA WHEN I SENSED THE WAVE OF DARKNESS IT RELEASED.

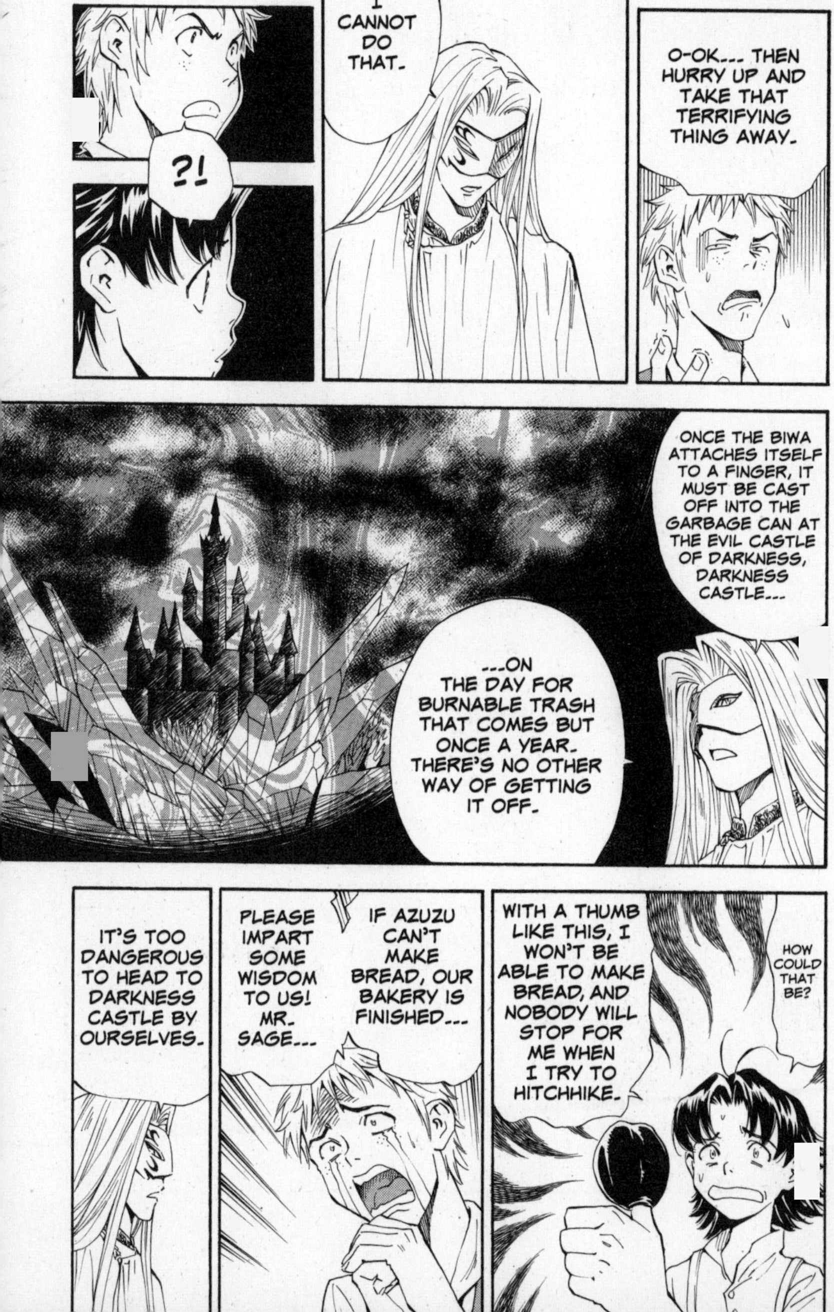
O-OK... THEN HURRY UP AND TAKE THAT TERRIFYING THING AWAY.
I CANNOT DO THAT.
?!
ONCE THE BIWA ATTACHES ITSELF TO A FINGER, IT MUST BE CAST OFF INTO THE GARBAGE CAN AT THE EVIL CASTLE OF DARKNESS, DARKNESS CASTLE...
...ON THE DAY FOR BURNABLE TRASH THAT COMES BUT ONCE A YEAR. THERE'S NO OTHER WAY OF GETTING IT OFF.
HOW COULD THAT BE?
WITH A THUMB LIKE THIS, I WON'T BE ABLE TO MAKE BREAD, AND NOBODY WILL STOP FOR ME WHEN I TRY TO HITCHHIKE.
IF AZUZU CAN'T MAKE BREAD, OUR BAKERY IS FINISHED...
PLEASE IMPART SOME WISDOM TO US! MR. SAGE...
IT'S TOO DANGEROUS TO HEAD TO DARKNESS CASTLE BY OURSELVES.

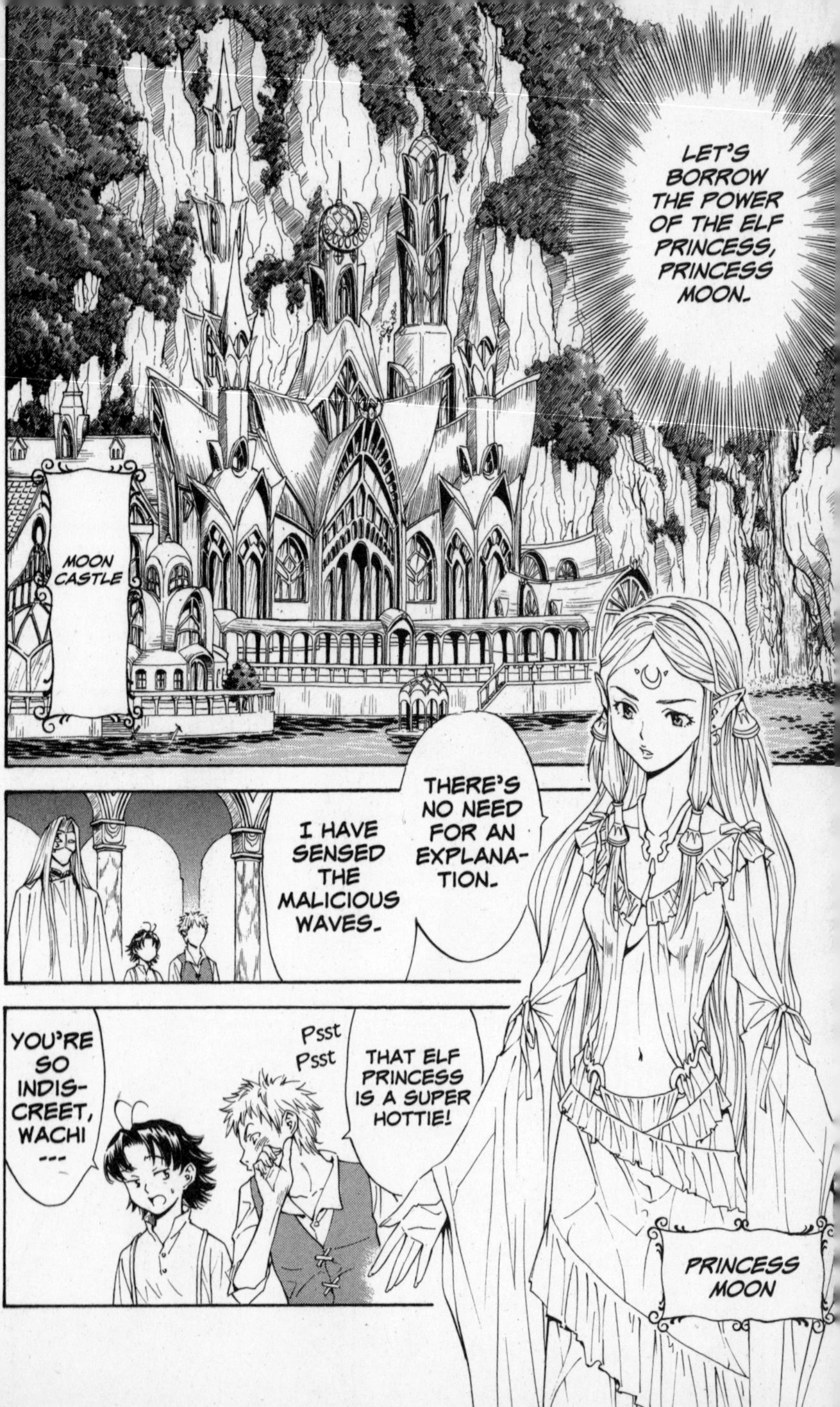
LET'S BORROW THE POWER OF THE ELF PRINCESS, PRINCESS MOON.
MOON CASTLE
PRINCESS MOON
THERE'S NO NEED FOR AN EXPLANA-TION.
I HAVE SENSED THE MALICIOUS WAVES.
Psst Psst
THAT ELF PRINCESS IS A SUPER HOTTIE!
YOU'RE SO INDIS-CREET, WACHI...

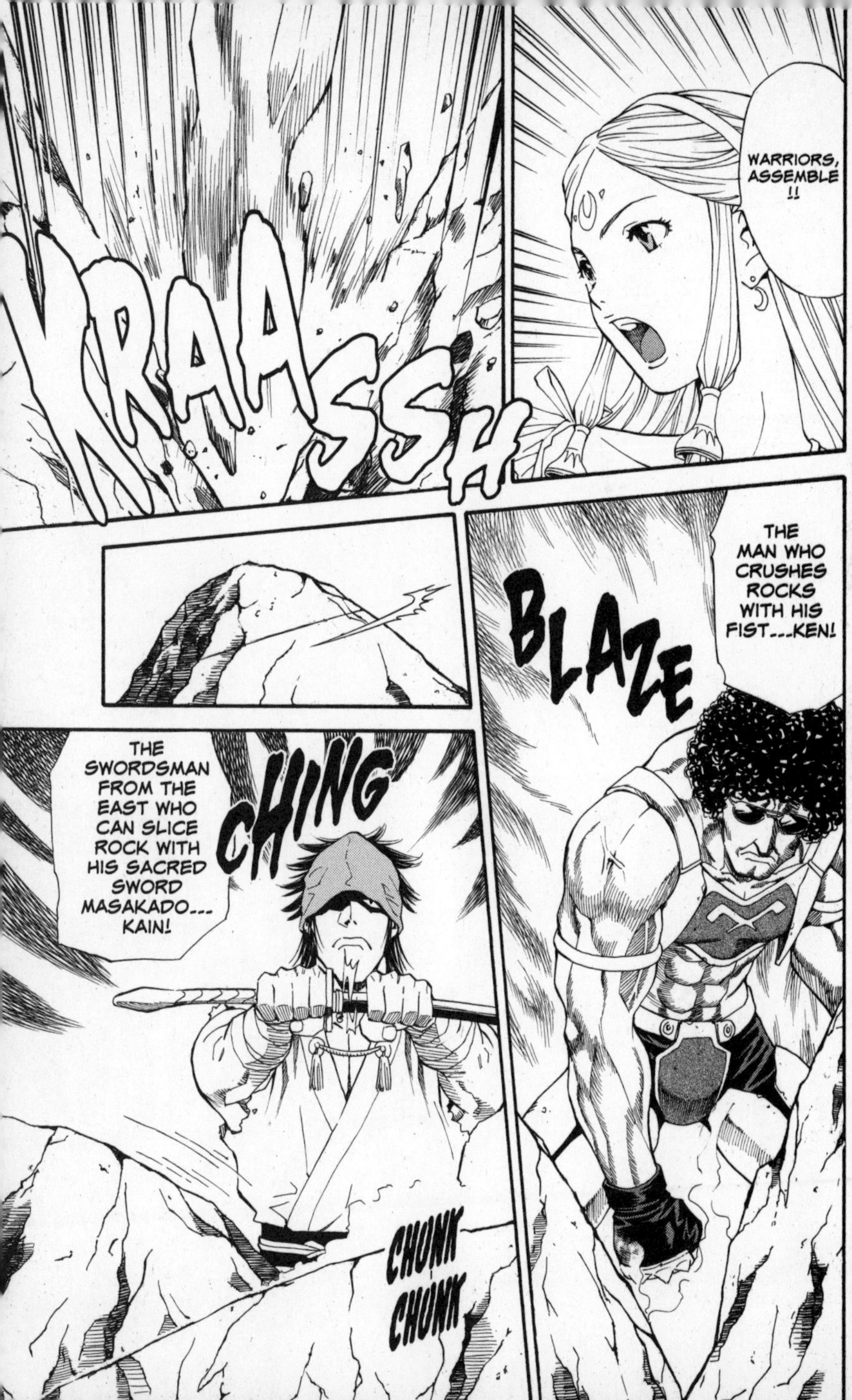
WARRIORS, ASSEMBLE!!
KRAASSH
THE MAN WHO CRUSHES ROCKS WITH HIS FIST...KEN!
BLAZE
CHING
THE SWORDSMAN FROM THE EAST WHO CAN SLICE ROCK WITH HIS SACRED SWORD MASAKADO... KAIN!
CHUNK CHUNK

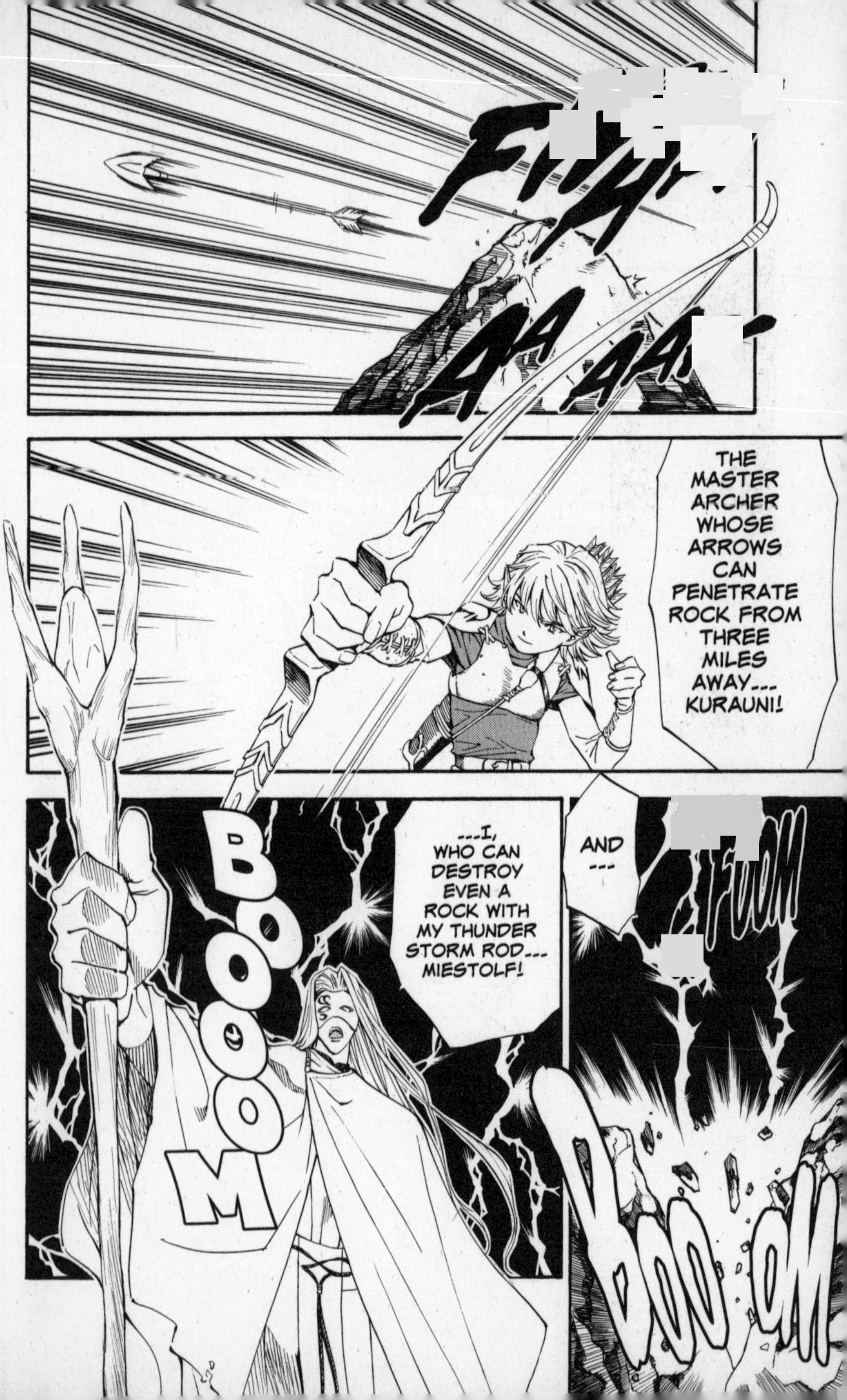
THE MASTER ARCHER WHOSE ARROWS CAN PENETRATE ROCK FROM THREE MILES AWAY... KURAUNI!
AND ---
FOOM
BOOOOM
---I, WHO CAN DESTROY EVEN A ROCK WITH MY THUNDER STORM ROD... MIESTOLF!
BOOOOM

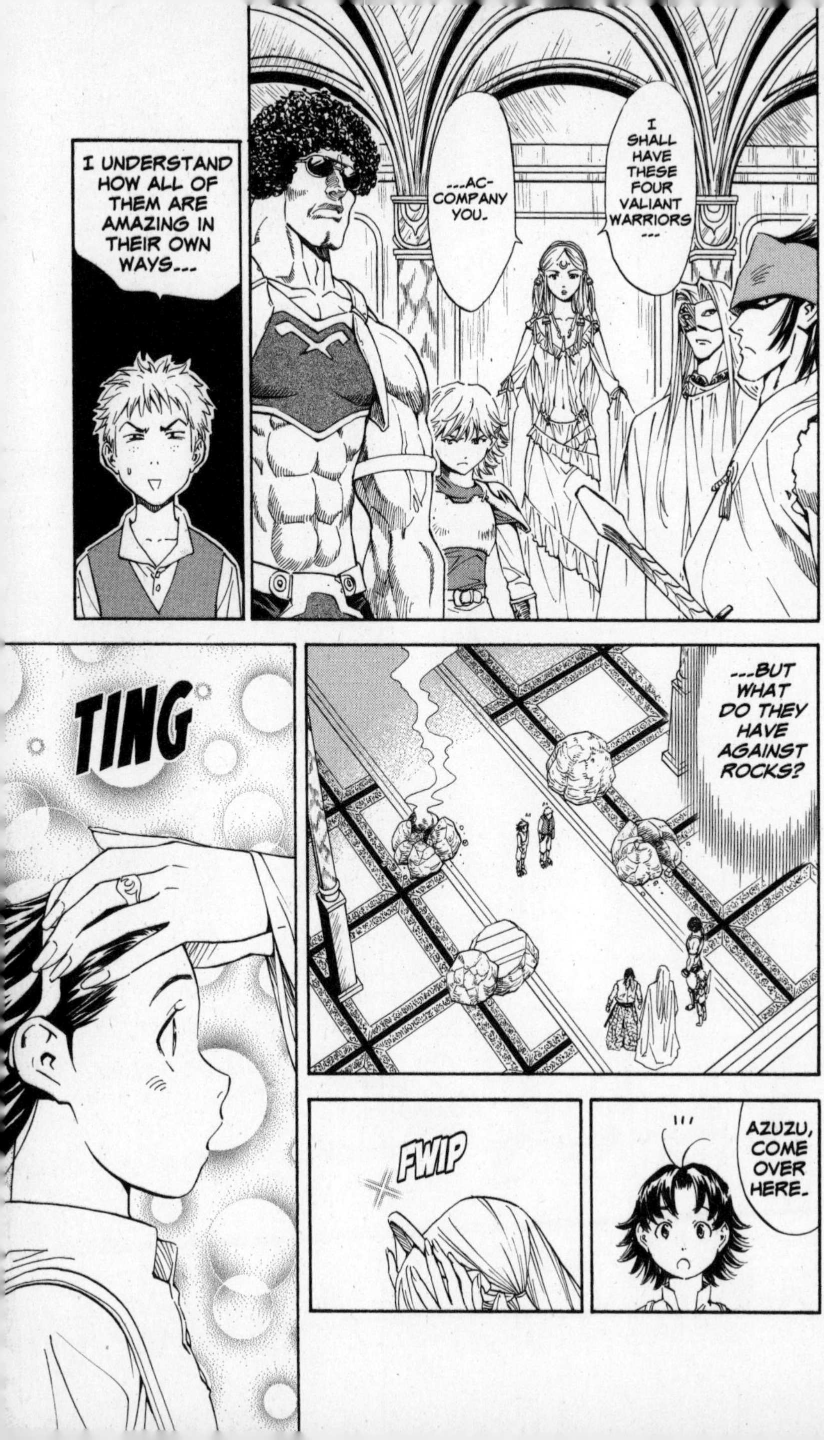
I SHALL HAVE THESE FOUR VALIANT WARRIORS...
...AC-COMPANY YOU.
I UNDERSTAND HOW ALL OF THEM ARE AMAZING IN THEIR OWN WAYS...
...BUT WHAT DO THEY HAVE AGAINST ROCKS?
AZUZU, COME OVER HERE.
FWIP
TING

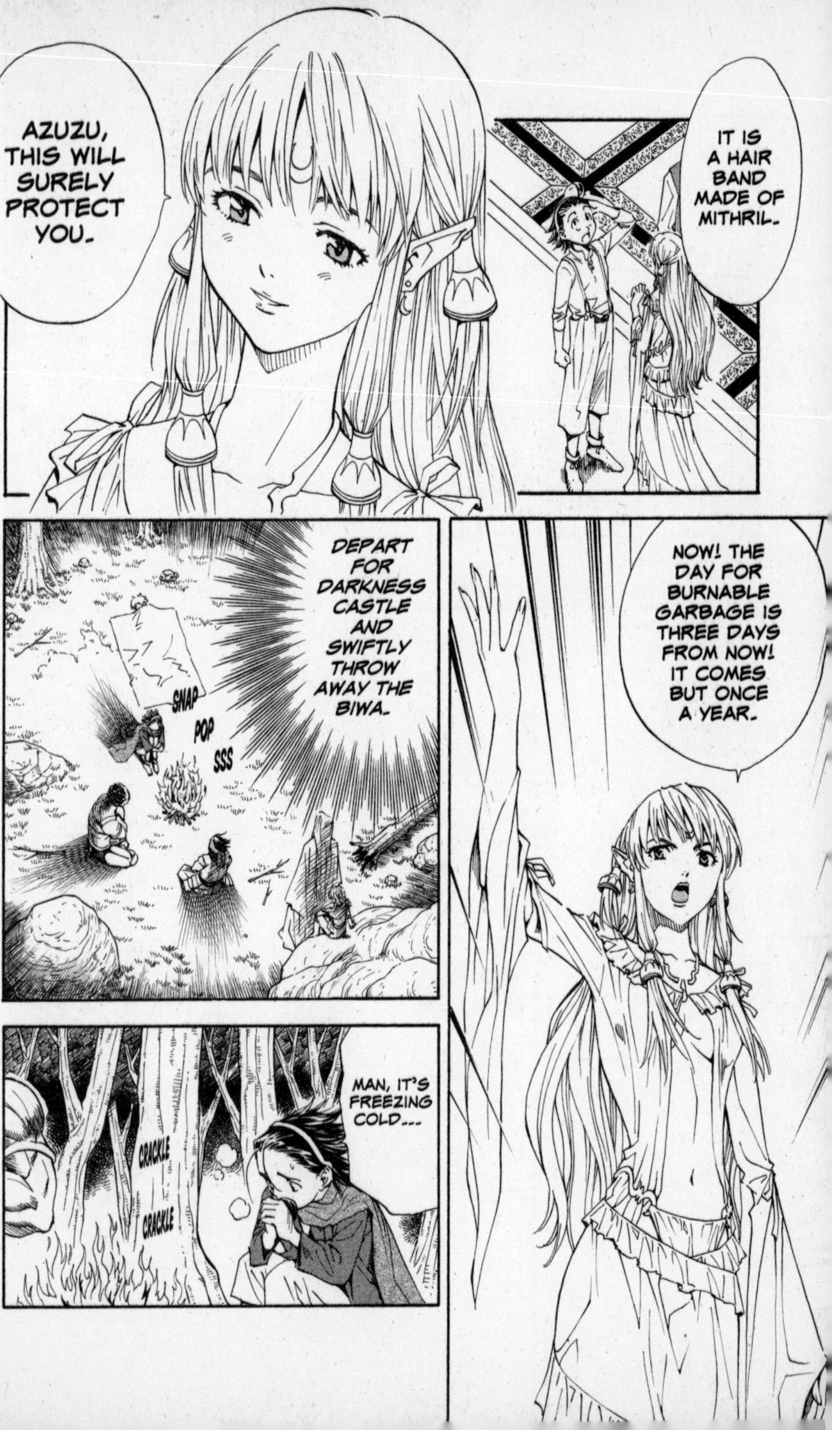
IT IS A HAIR BAND MADE OF MITHRIL.
AZUZU, THIS WILL SURELY PROTECT YOU.
NOW! THE DAY FOR BURNABLE GARBAGE IS THREE DAYS FROM NOW! IT COMES BUT ONCE A YEAR.
DEPART FOR DARKNESS CASTLE AND SWIFTLY THROW AWAY THE BIWA.
SNAP
POP
SSS
MAN, IT'S FREEZING COLD...
CRACKLE
CRACKLE

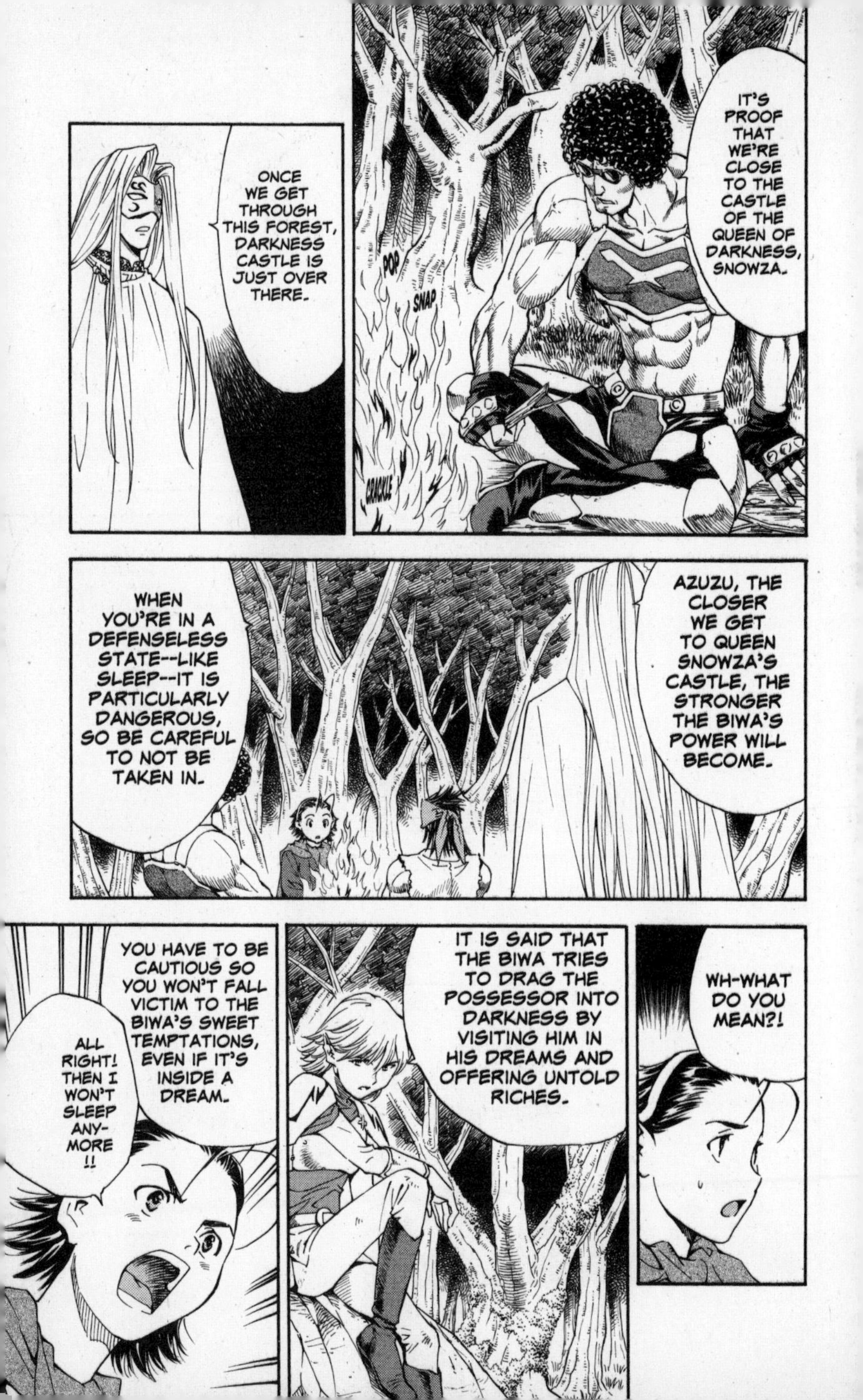
IT'S PROOF THAT WE'RE CLOSE TO THE CASTLE OF THE QUEEN OF DARKNESS, SNOWZA.
POP
SNAP
CRACKLE
ONCE WE GET THROUGH THIS FOREST, DARKNESS CASTLE IS JUST OVER THERE.
AZUZU, THE CLOSER WE GET TO QUEEN SNOWZA'S CASTLE, THE STRONGER THE BIWA'S POWER WILL BECOME.
WHEN YOU'RE IN A DEFENSELESS STATE--LIKE SLEEP--IT IS PARTICULARLY DANGEROUS, SO BE CAREFUL TO NOT BE TAKEN IN.
WH-WHAT DO YOU MEAN?!
IT IS SAID THAT THE BIWA TRIES TO DRAG THE POSSESSOR INTO DARKNESS BY VISITING HIM IN HIS DREAMS AND OFFERING UNTOLD RICHES.
YOU HAVE TO BE CAUTIOUS SO YOU WON'T FALL VICTIM TO THE BIWA'S SWEET TEMPTATIONS, EVEN IF IT'S INSIDE A DREAM.
ALL RIGHT! THEN I WON'T SLEEP ANY-MORE!!

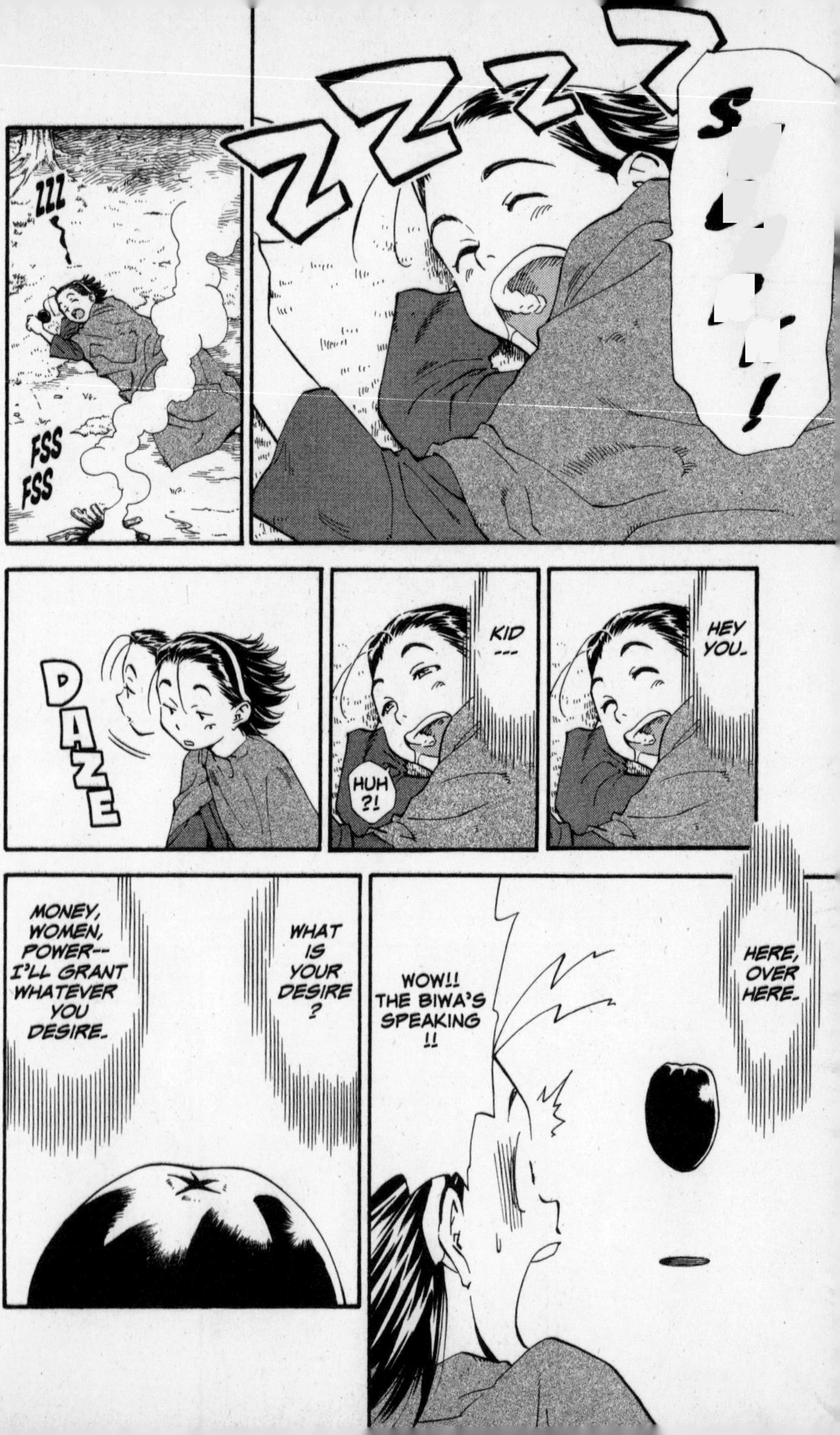
ZZZZ
ZZZ
FSS FSS
HEY YOU...
KID ---
HUH ?!
DAZE
HERE, OVER HERE...
WOW!! THE BIWA'S SPEAKING !!
WHAT IS YOUR DESIRE ?
MONEY, WOMEN, POWER-- I'LL GRANT WHATEVER YOU DESIRE...

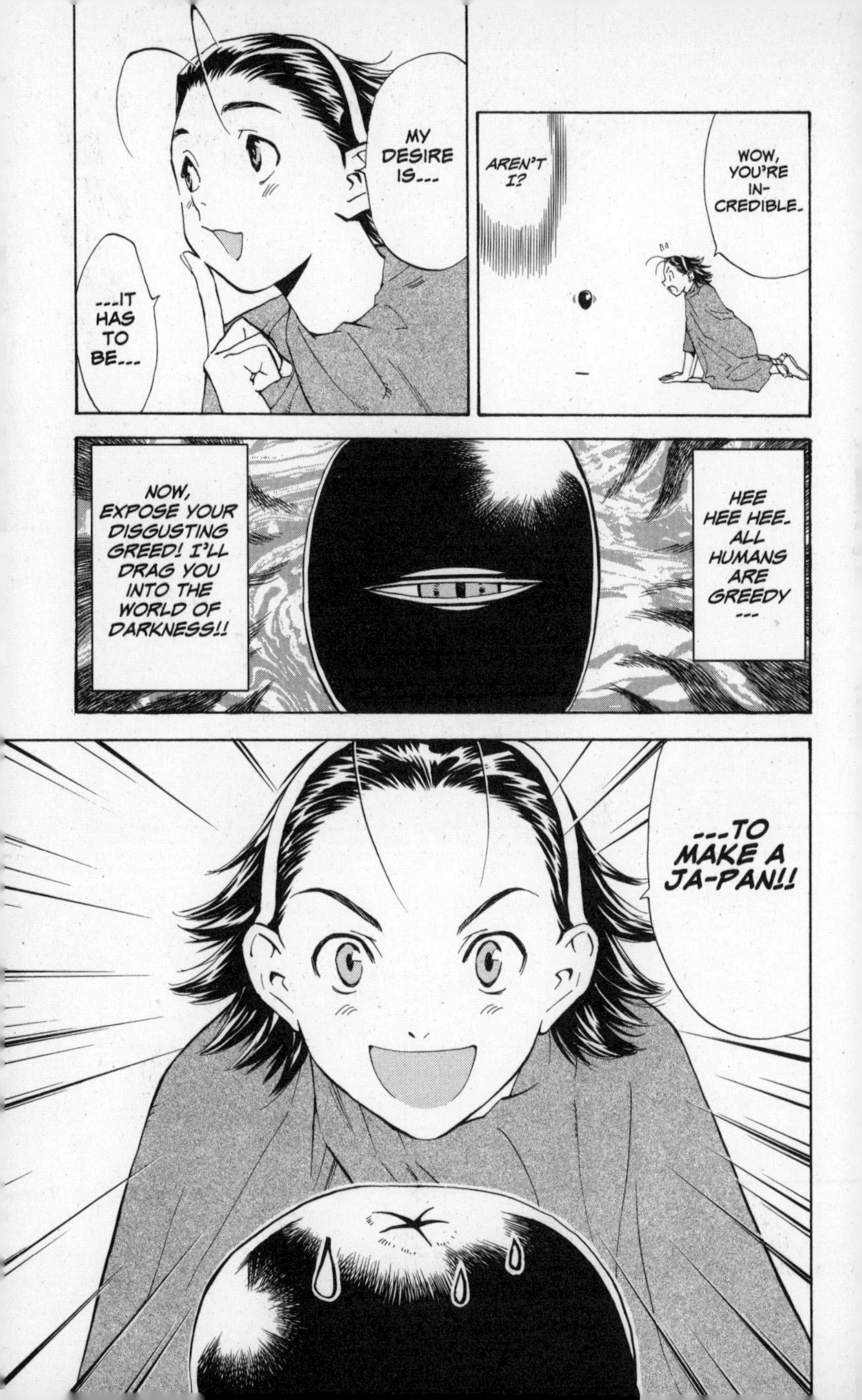

WOW, YOU'RE IN-CREDIBLE.
AREN'T I?
MY DESIRE IS...
...IT HAS TO BE...
HEE HEE HEE. ALL HUMANS ARE GREEDY...
NOW, EXPOSE YOUR DISGUSTING GREED! I'LL DRAG YOU INTO THE WORLD OF DARKNESS!!
...TO MAKE A JA-PAN!!

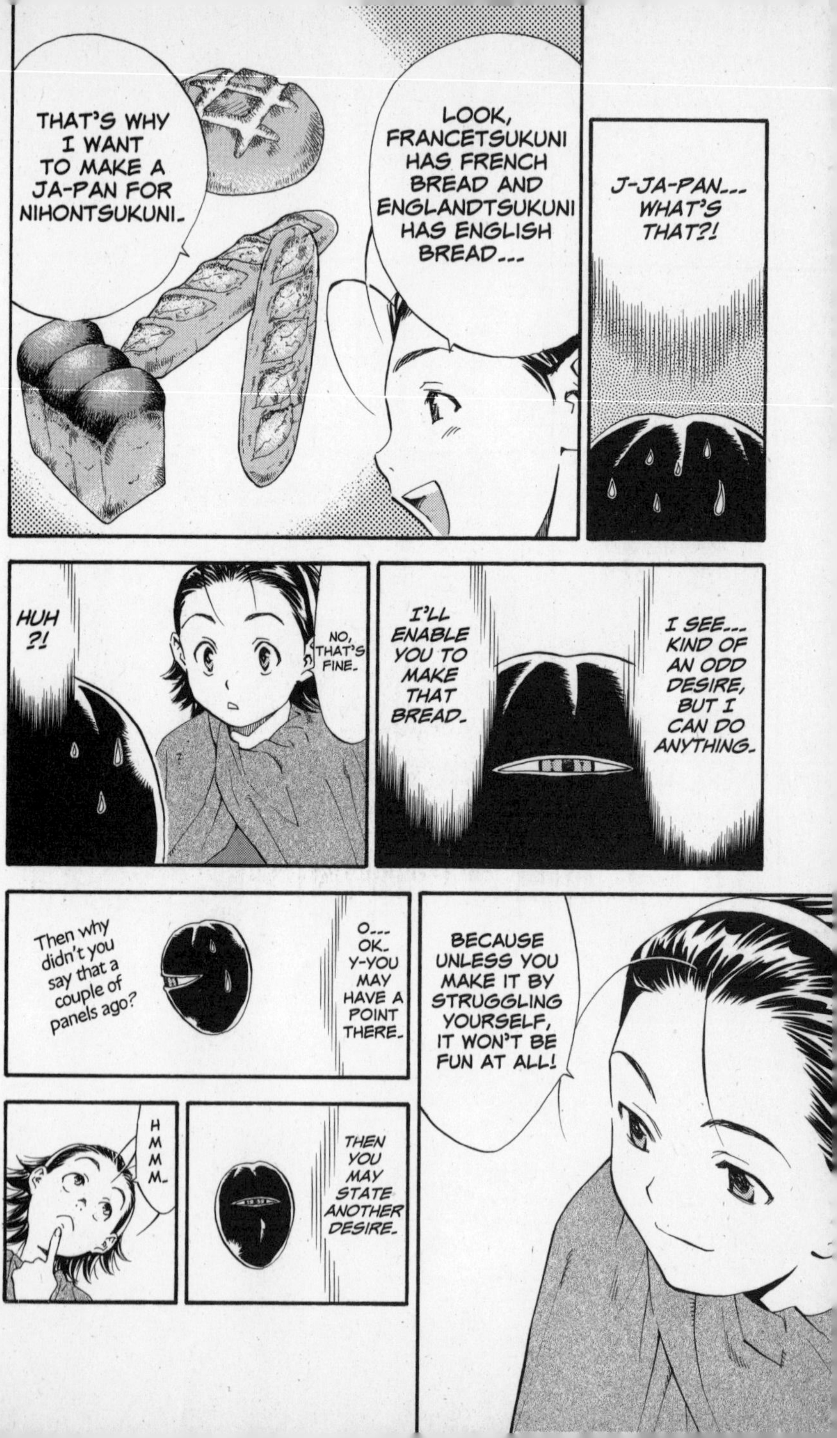
J-JA-PAN... WHAT'S THAT?!
LOOK, FRANCETSUKUNI HAS FRENCH BREAD AND ENGLANDTSUKUNI HAS ENGLISH BREAD...
THAT'S WHY I WANT TO MAKE A JA-PAN FOR NIHONTSUKUNI.
I SEE... KIND OF AN ODD DESIRE, BUT I CAN DO ANYTHING.
I'LL ENABLE YOU TO MAKE THAT BREAD.
NO, THAT'S FINE.
HUH ?!
BECAUSE UNLESS YOU MAKE IT BY STRUGGLING YOURSELF, IT WON'T BE FUN AT ALL!
O... OK. Y-YOU MAY HAVE A POINT THERE.
Then why didn't you say that a couple of panels ago?
THEN YOU MAY STATE ANOTHER DESIRE.
HMMM.

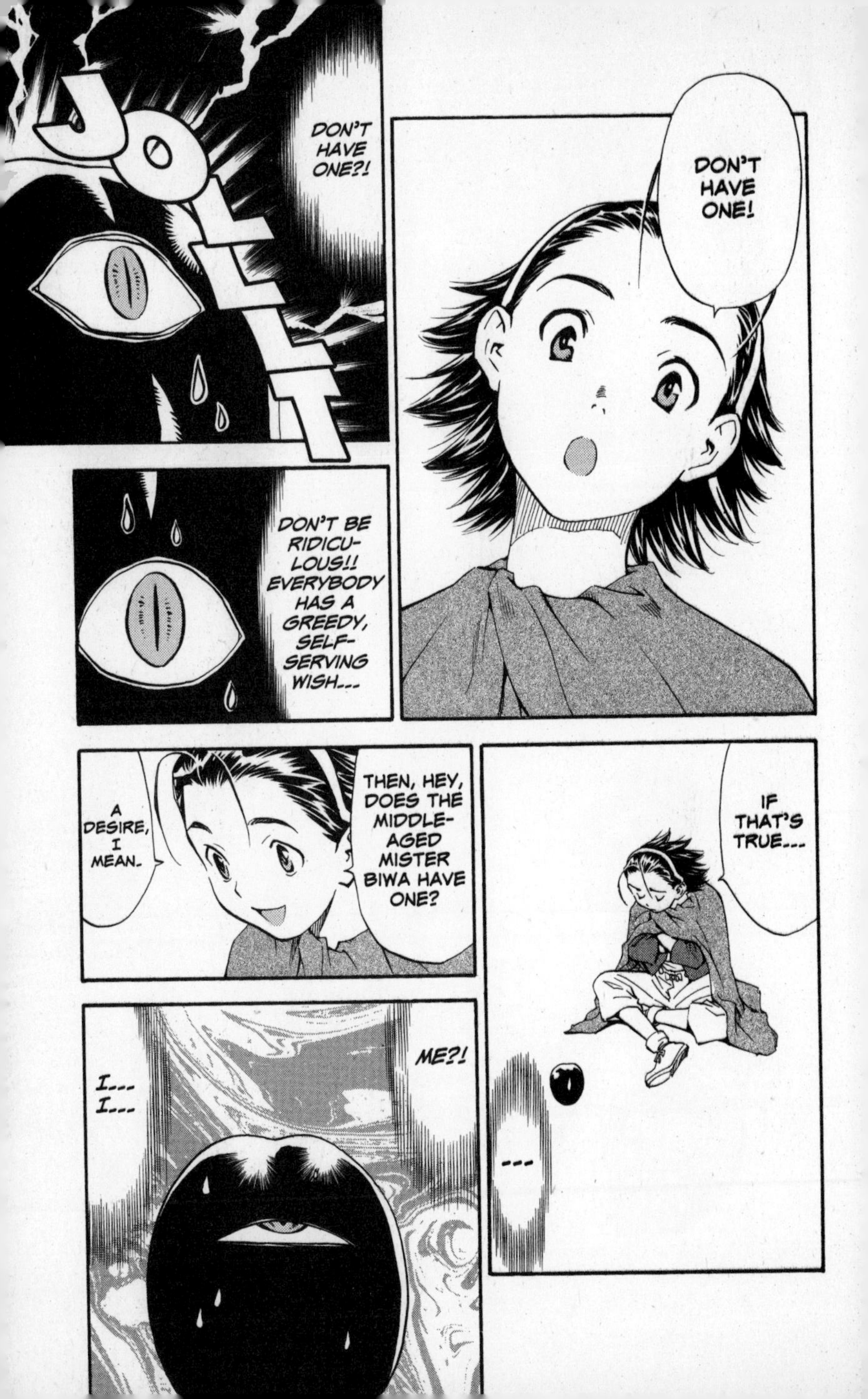
DON'T HAVE ONE!
JOLT
DON'T HAVE ONE?!
DON'T BE RIDICULOUS!! EVERYBODY HAS A GREEDY, SELF-SERVING WISH...
IF THAT'S TRUE...
...
THEN, HEY, DOES THE MIDDLE-AGED MISTER BIWA HAVE ONE?
A DESIRE, I MEAN.
ME?!
I... I...

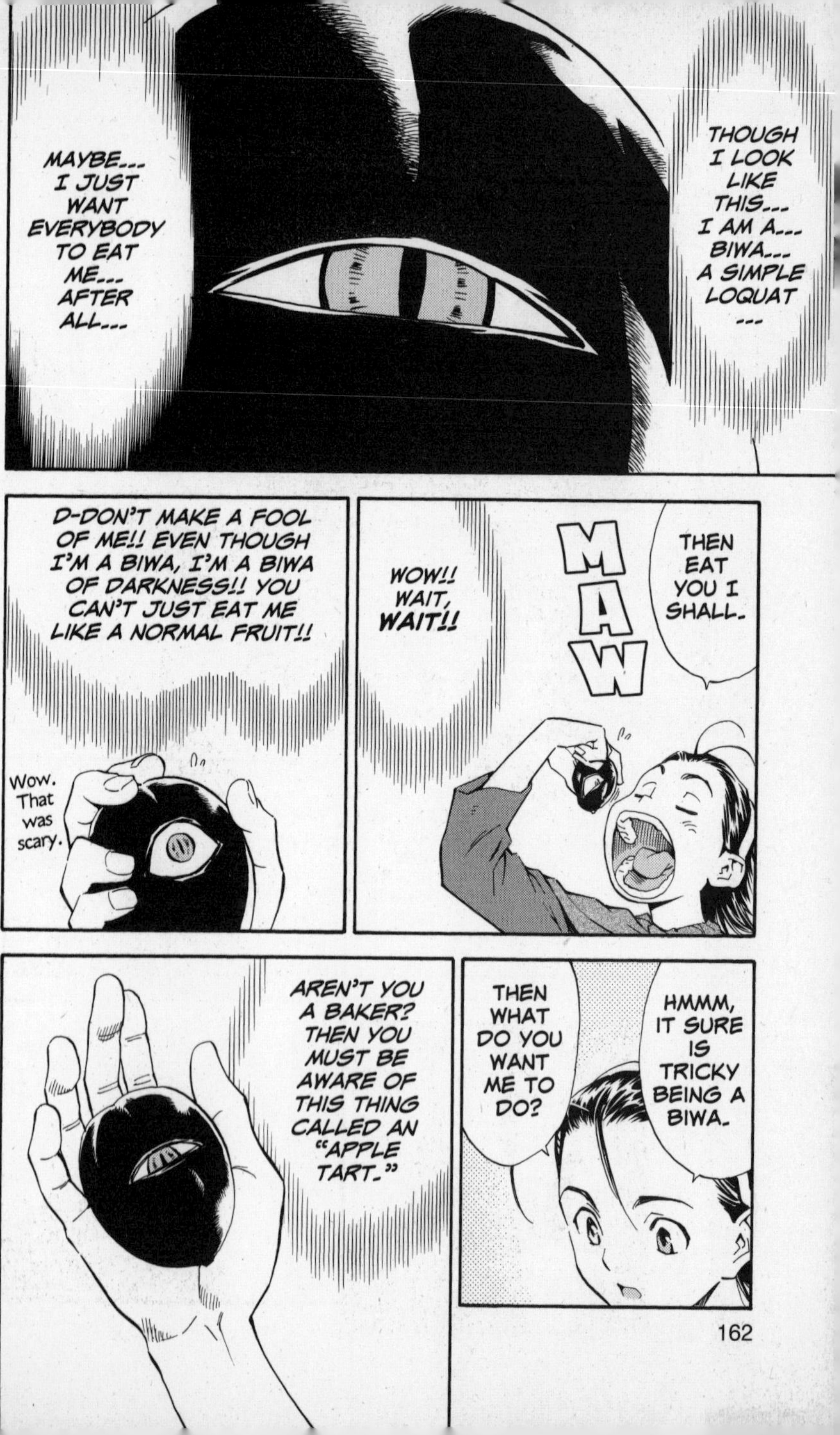
THOUGH I LOOK LIKE THIS... I AM A... BIWA... A SIMPLE LOQUAT ...
MAYBE... I JUST WANT EVERYBODY TO EAT ME... AFTER ALL...
THEN EAT YOU I SHALL.
MAW
WOW!! WAIT, **WAIT!!**
D-DON'T MAKE A FOOL OF ME!! EVEN THOUGH I'M A BIWA, I'M A BIWA OF DARKNESS!! YOU CAN'T JUST EAT ME LIKE A NORMAL FRUIT!!
Wow. That was scary.
HMMM, IT SURE IS TRICKY BEING A BIWA.
THEN WHAT DO YOU WANT ME TO DO?
AREN'T YOU A BAKER? THEN YOU MUST BE AWARE OF THIS THING CALLED AN "APPLE TART."

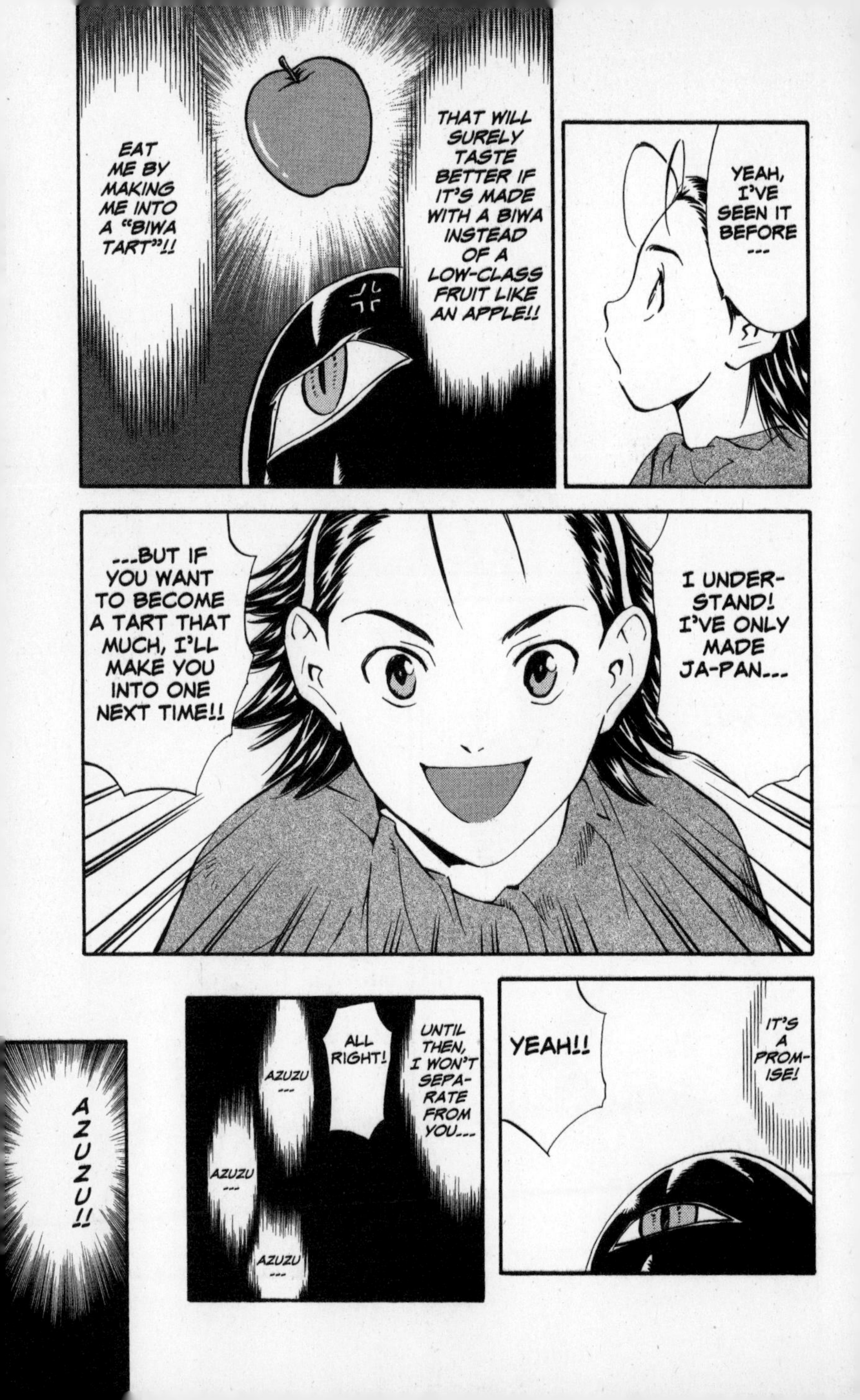
YEAH, I'VE SEEN IT BEFORE---
THAT WILL SURELY TASTE BETTER IF IT'S MADE WITH A BIWA INSTEAD OF A LOW-CLASS FRUIT LIKE AN APPLE!!
EAT ME BY MAKING ME INTO A "BIWA TART"!!
I UNDER-STAND! I'VE ONLY MADE JA-PAN---
---BUT IF YOU WANT TO BECOME A TART THAT MUCH, I'LL MAKE YOU INTO ONE NEXT TIME!!
IT'S A PROM-ISE!
YEAH!!
UNTIL THEN, I WON'T SEPA-RATE FROM YOU---
ALL RIGHT!
AZUZU---
AZUZU---
AZUZU---
AZUZU!!

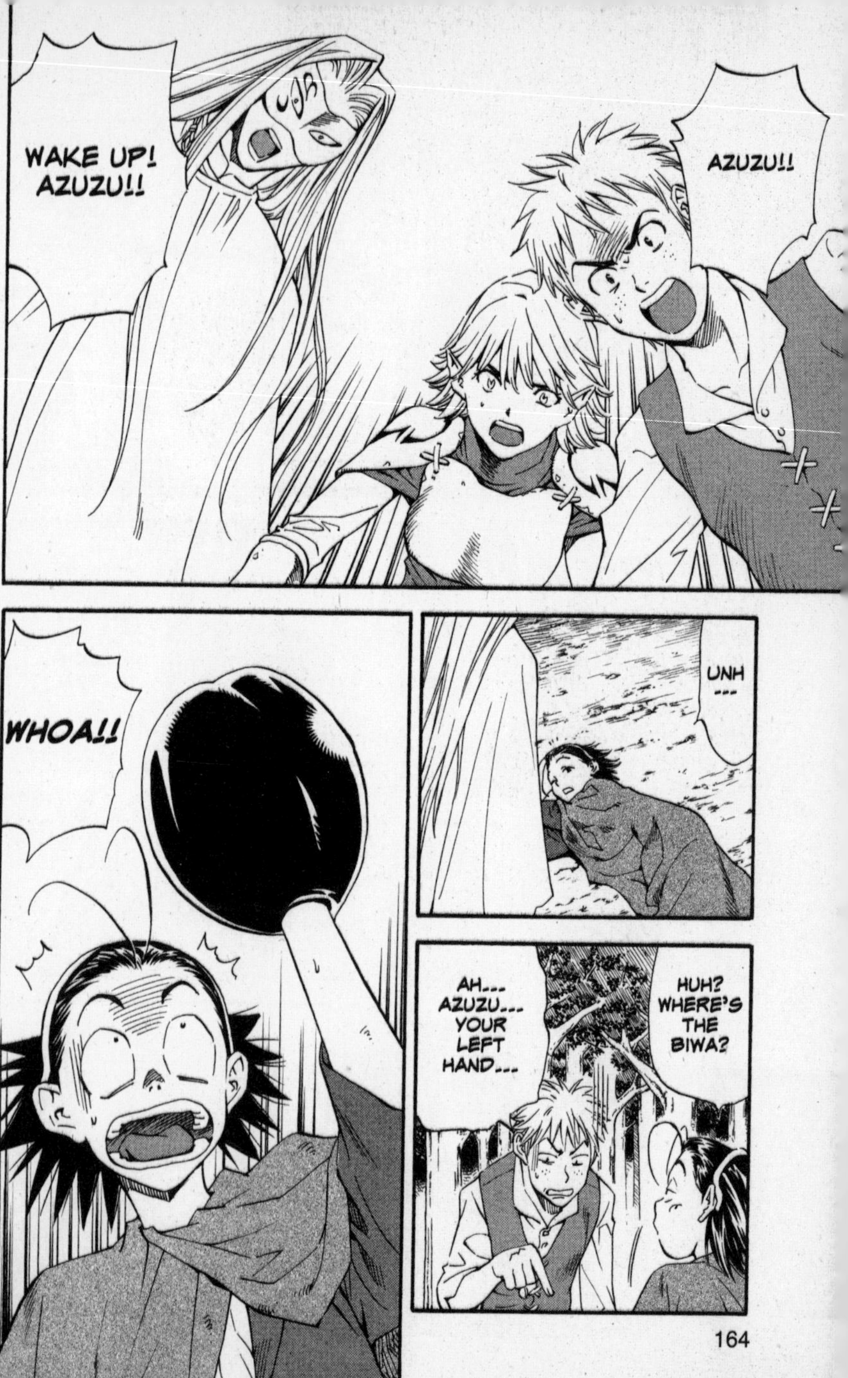
AZUZU!!
WAKE UP! AZUZU!!
UNH ...
HUH? WHERE'S THE BIWA?
AH... AZUZU... YOUR LEFT HAND...
WHOA!!

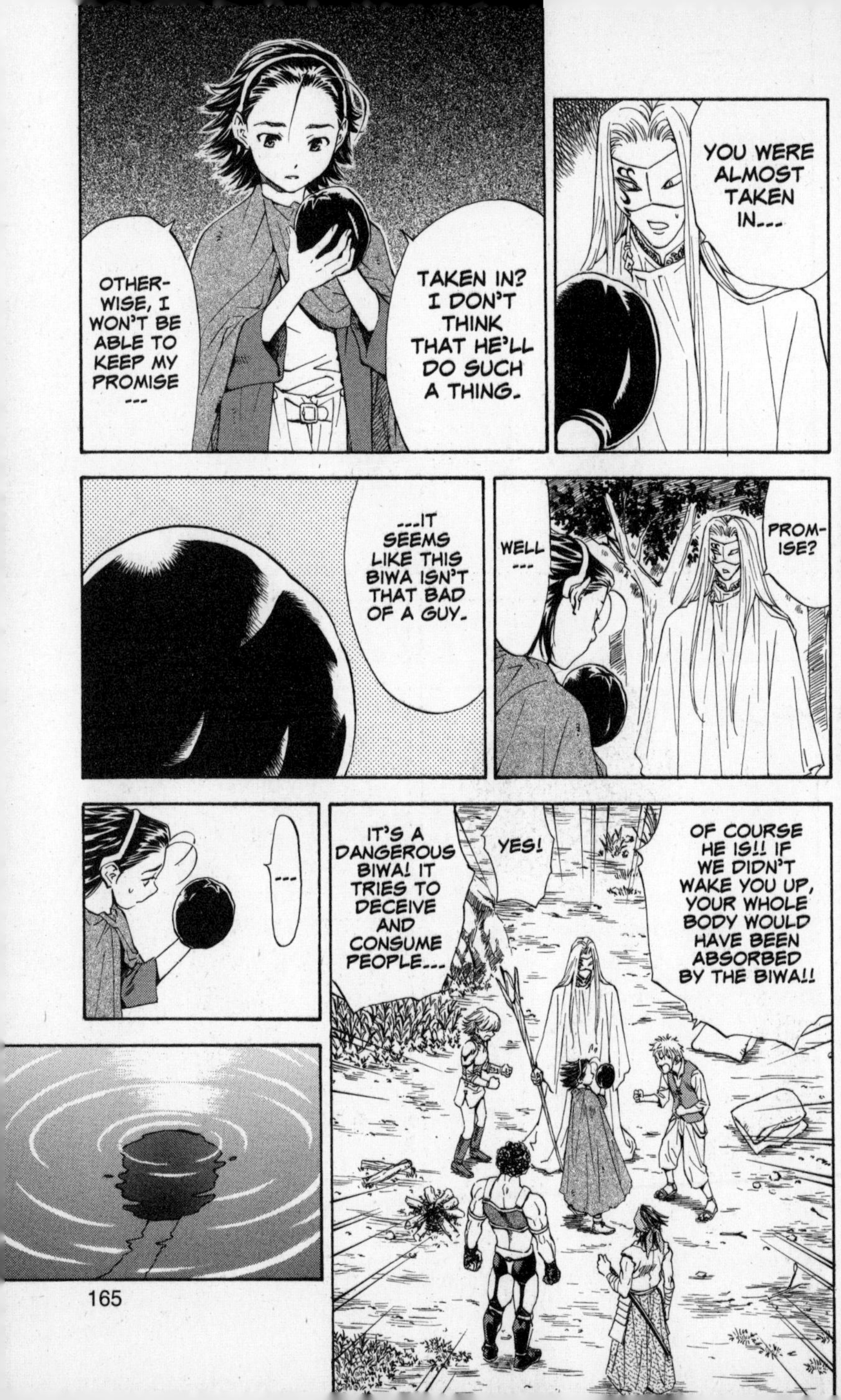
YOU WERE ALMOST TAKEN IN...
TAKEN IN? I DON'T THINK THAT HE'LL DO SUCH A THING.
OTHER-WISE, I WON'T BE ABLE TO KEEP MY PROMISE...
PROM-ISE?
WELL...
...IT SEEMS LIKE THIS BIWA ISN'T THAT BAD OF A GUY.
OF COURSE HE IS!! IF WE DIDN'T WAKE YOU UP, YOUR WHOLE BODY WOULD HAVE BEEN ABSORBED BY THE BIWA!!
YES!
IT'S A DANGEROUS BIWA! IT TRIES TO DECEIVE AND CONSUME PEOPLE...
...

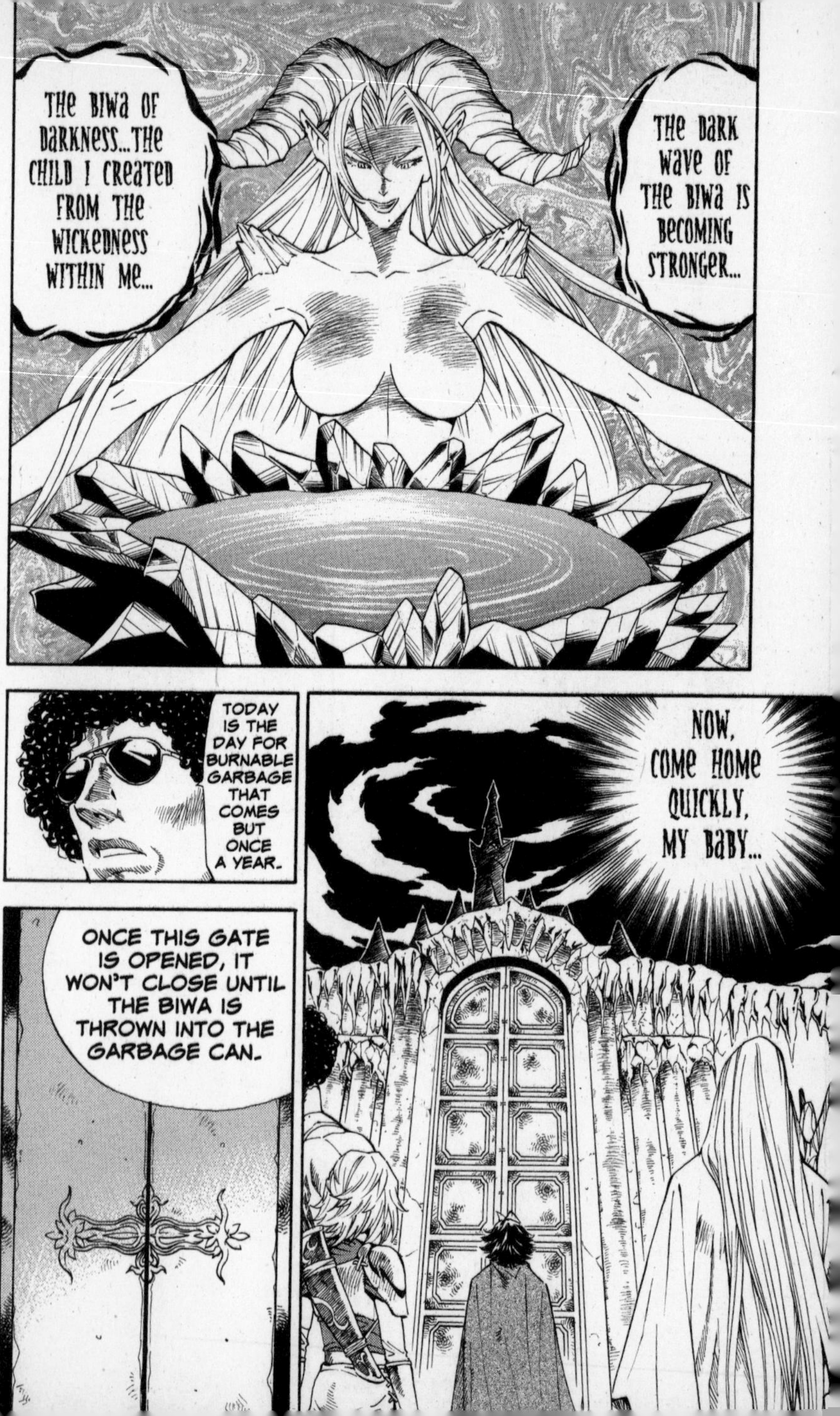
THE DARK WAVE OF THE BIWA IS BECOMING STRONGER...
THE BIWA OF DARKNESS...THE CHILD I CREATED FROM THE WICKEDNESS WITHIN ME...
NOW, COME HOME QUICKLY, MY BABY...
TODAY IS THE DAY FOR BURNABLE GARBAGE THAT COMES BUT ONCE A YEAR.
ONCE THIS GATE IS OPENED, IT WON'T CLOSE UNTIL THE BIWA IS THROWN INTO THE GARBAGE CAN.

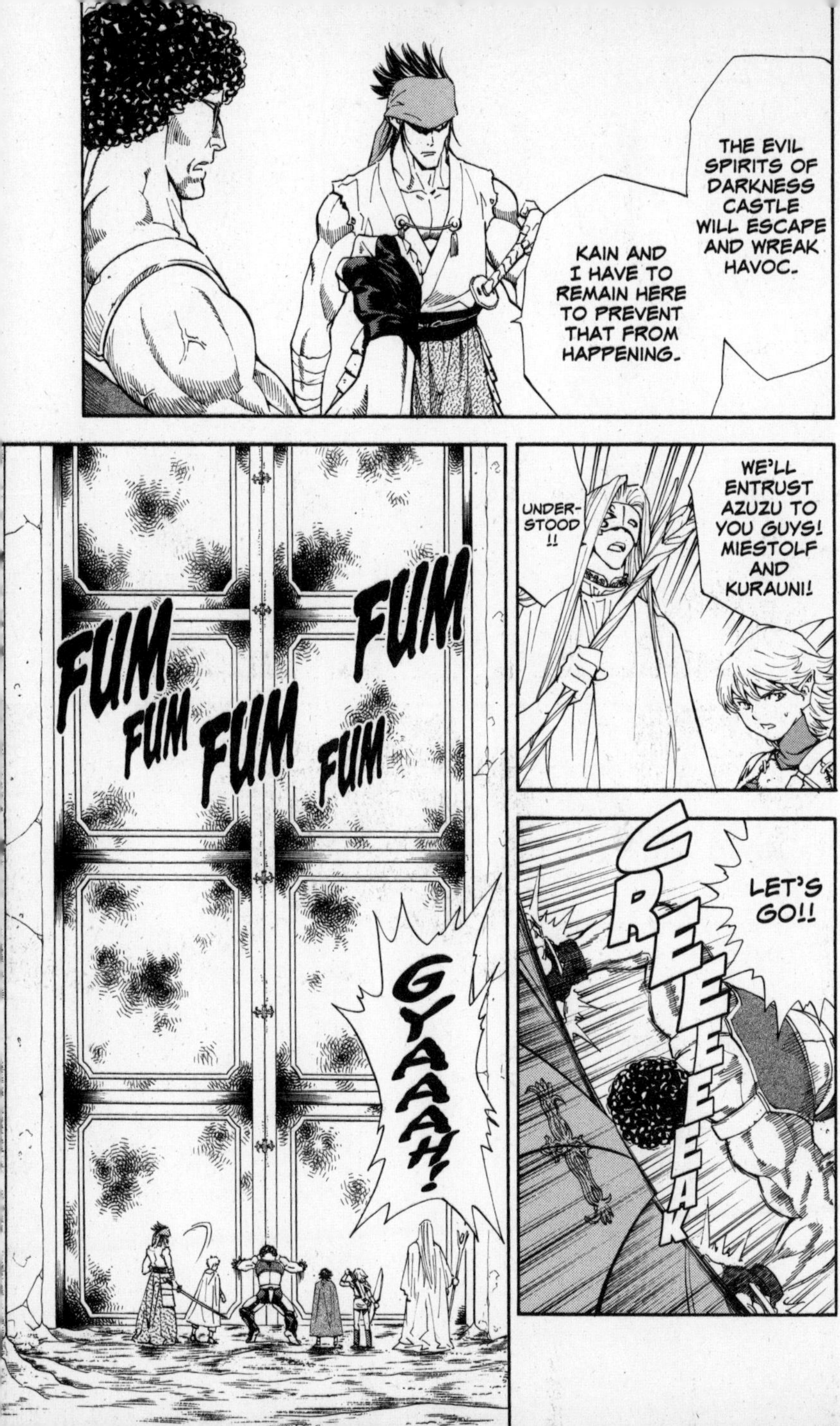
THE EVIL SPIRITS OF DARKNESS CASTLE WILL ESCAPE AND WREAK HAVOC.
KAIN AND I HAVE TO REMAIN HERE TO PREVENT THAT FROM HAPPENING.
WE'LL ENTRUST AZUZU TO YOU GUYS! MIESTOLF AND KURAUNI!
UNDER-STOOD!!
LET'S GO!!
CREEEEEAK
FUM FUM FUM FUM FUM
GYAAAH!

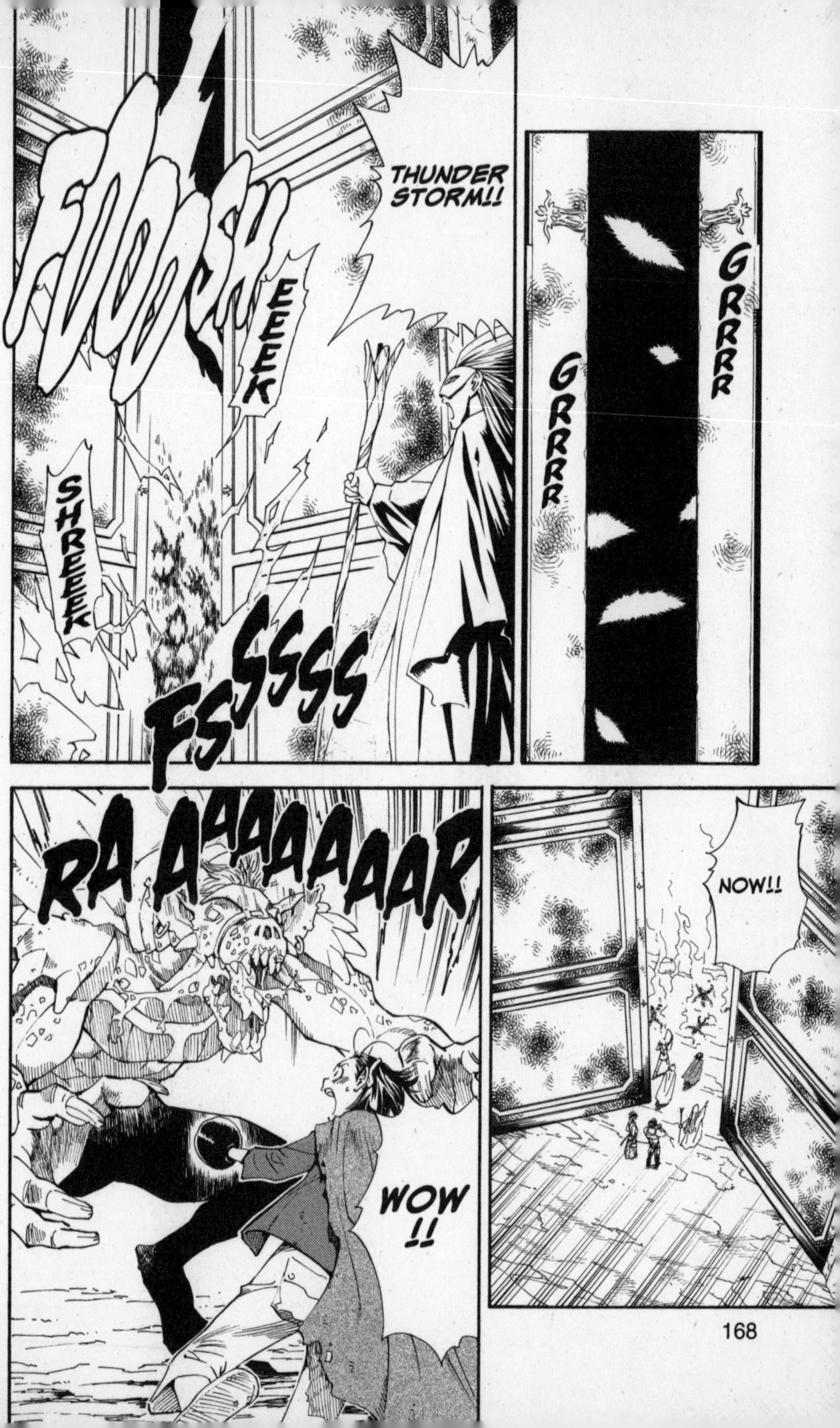
GRRRR
GRRRR
THUNDER STORM!!
FWOOSH
EEEEK
SHREEEEK
FSSSSS
NOW!!
RAAAAAAAR
WOW!!

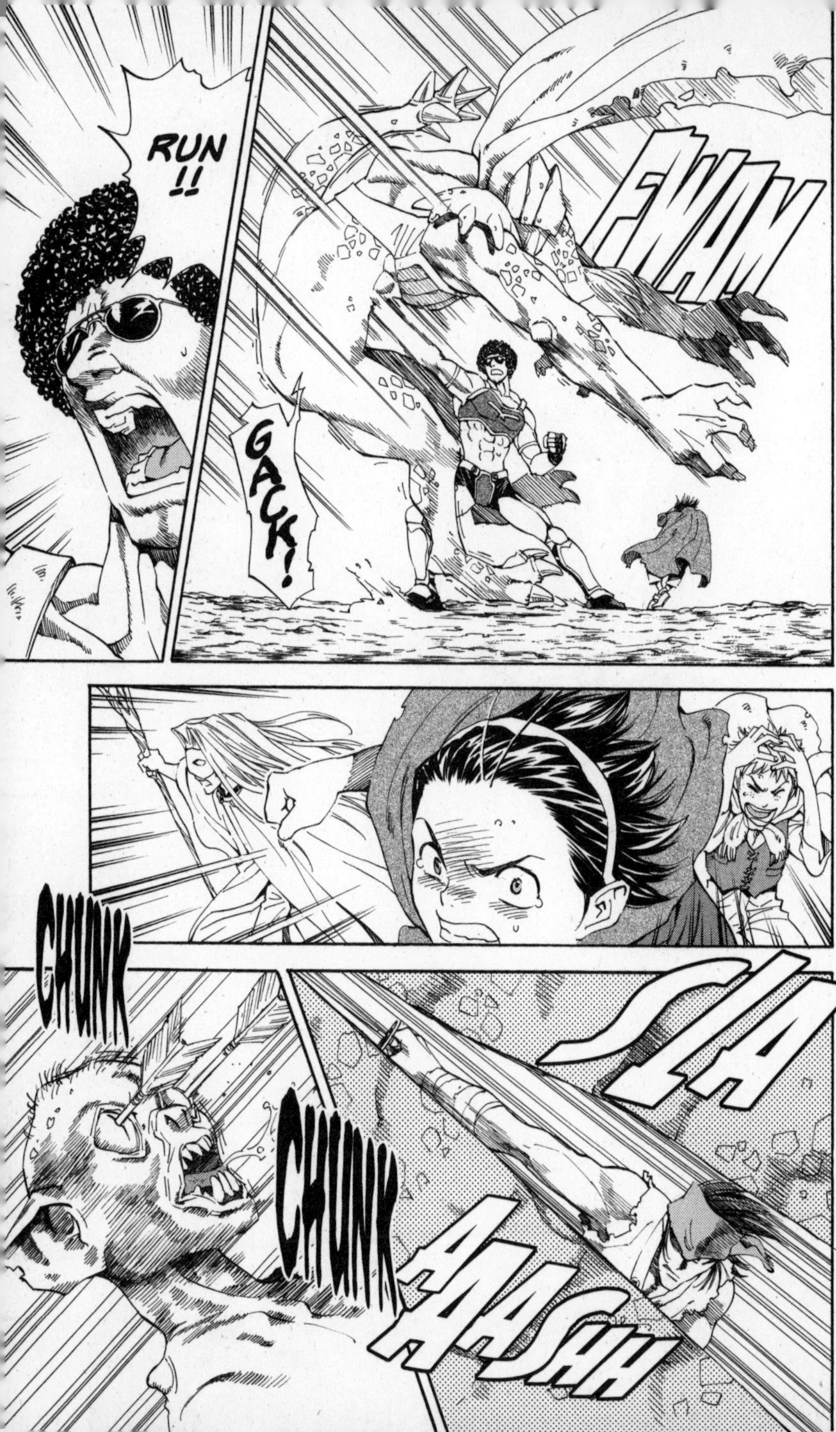
FWAM
GACK!
RUN !!
SLA
AASHH
CHUNK
CHUNK

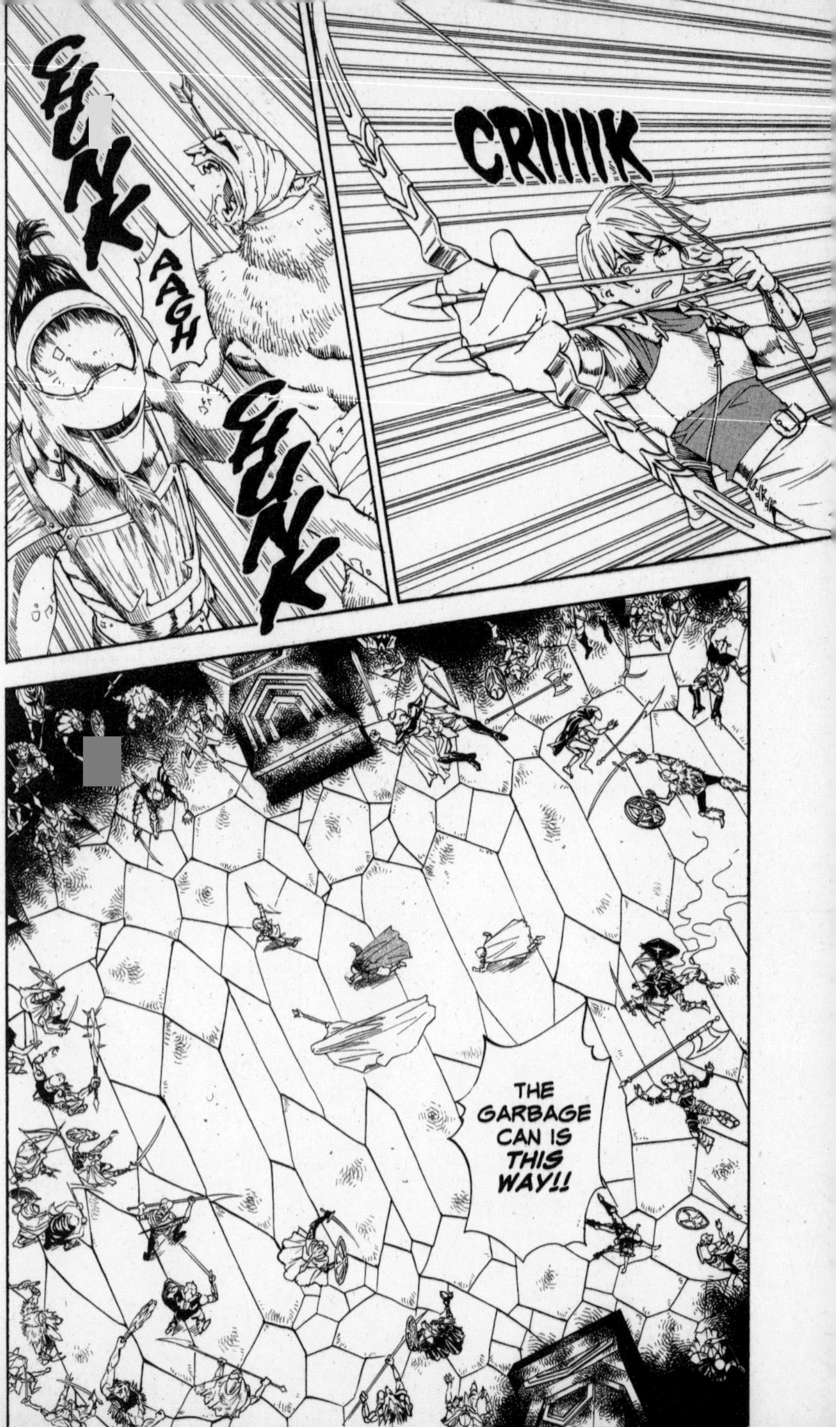
CRIIIK
CHUNK
AAGH
CHUNK
THE GARBAGE CAN IS THIS WAY!!

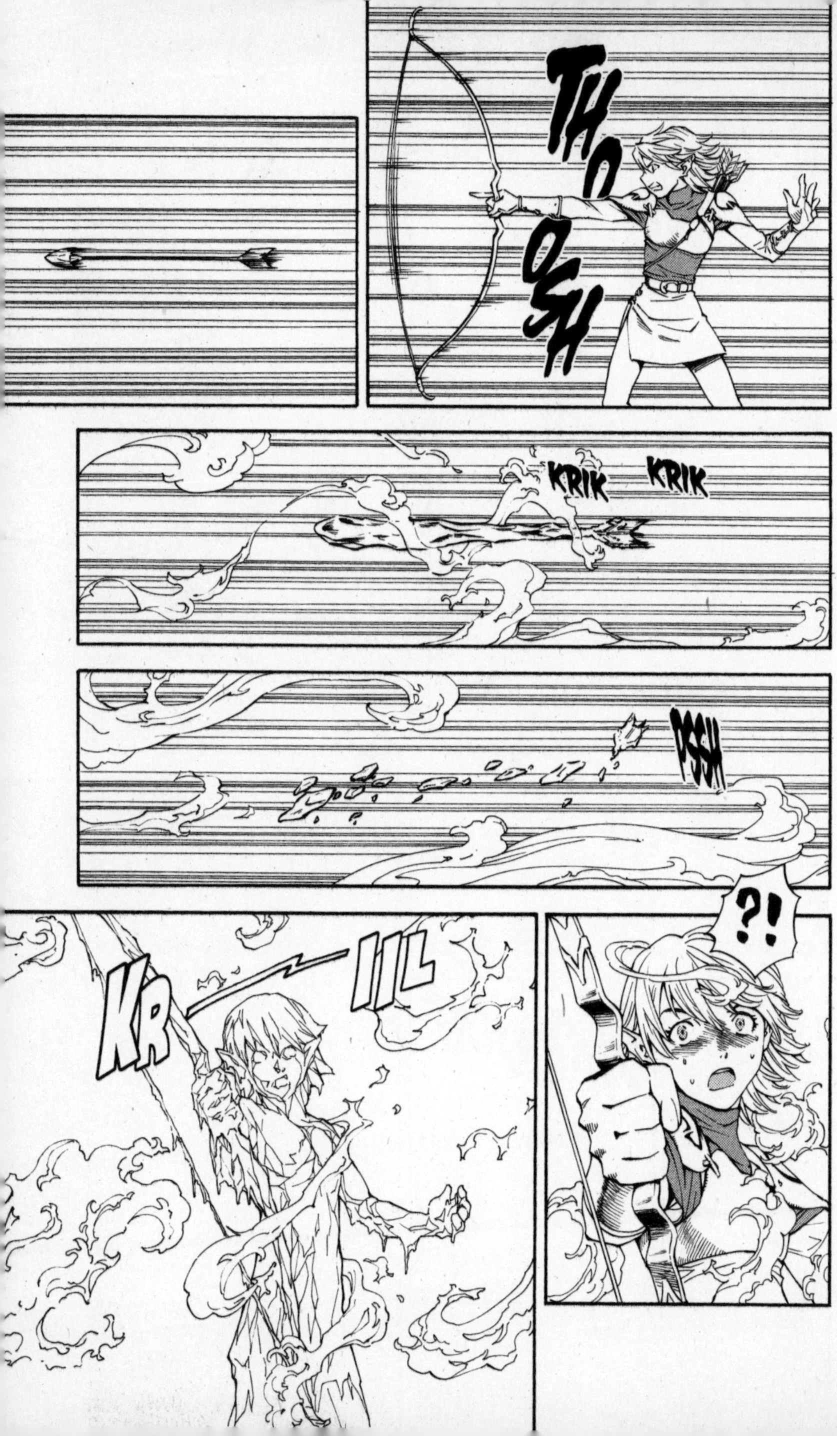
THOOSH
KRIK KRIK
DSSH
?!
KRIIL

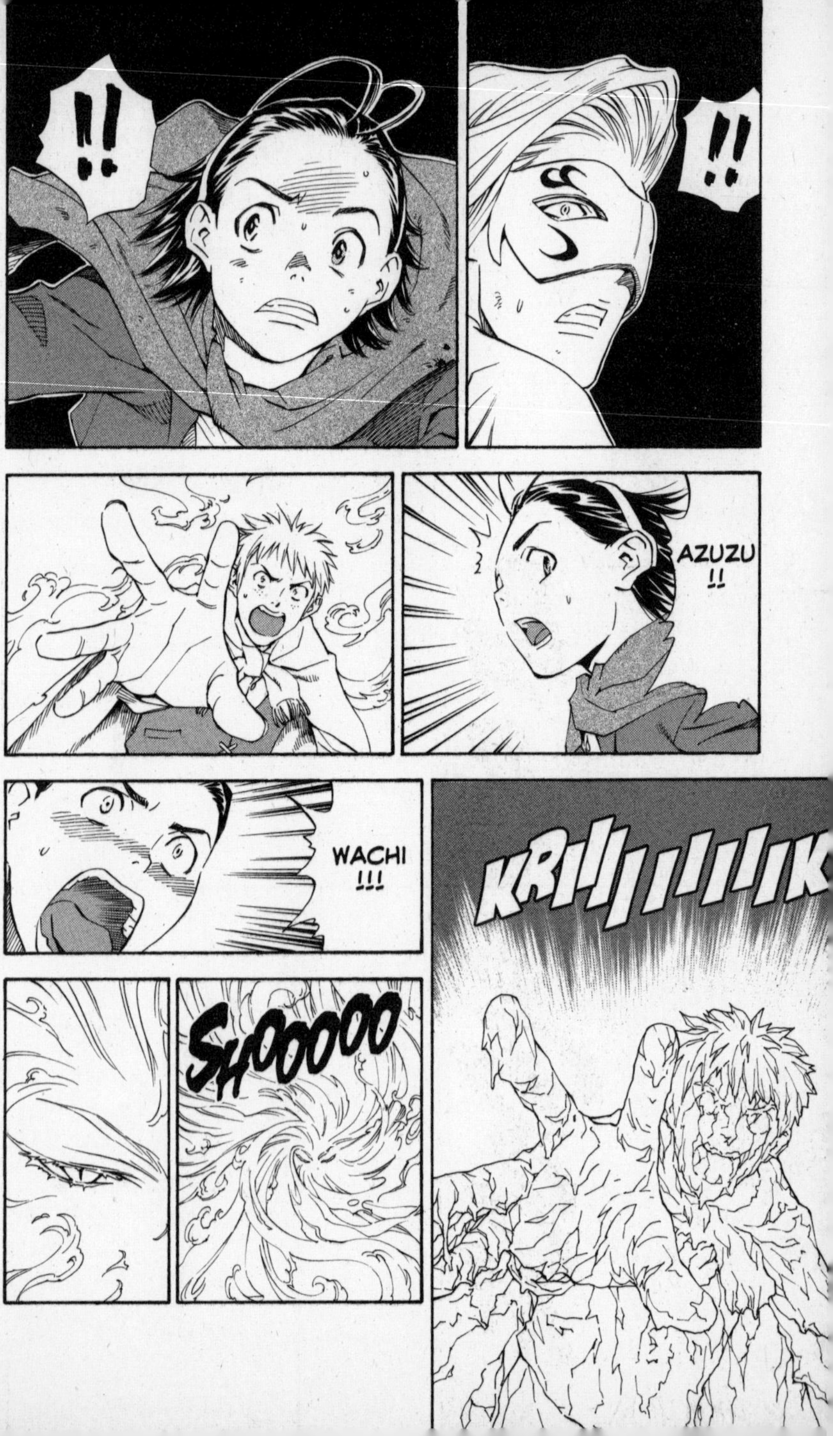
!!
!!
AZUZU !!
KRIIIIIIIIK
WACHI !!!
SHOOOOO

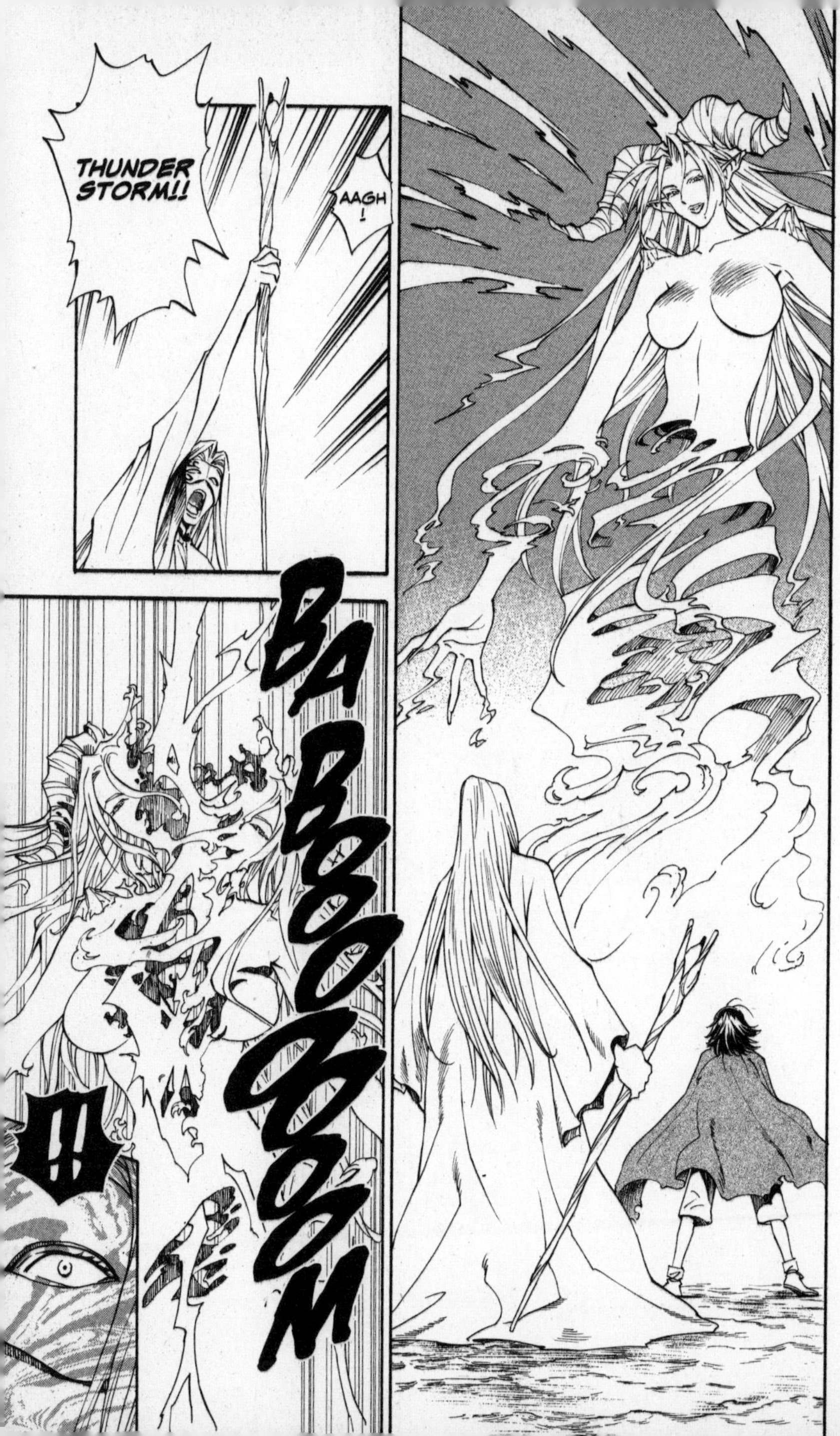
THUNDER STORM!!
AAGH!
BABOOOOOOM
!!

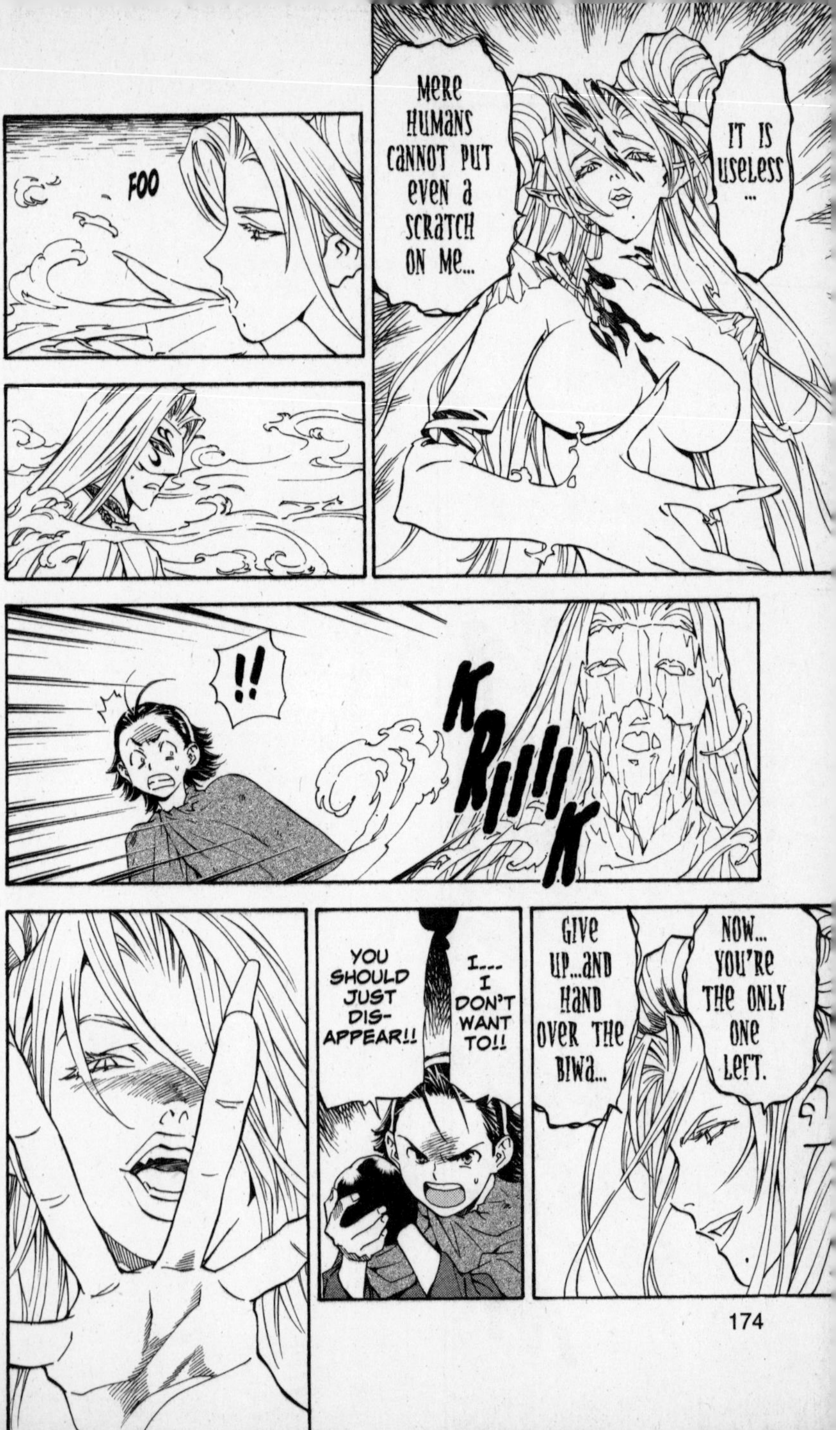
IT IS USELESS ...
MERE HUMANS CANNOT PUT EVEN A SCRATCH ON ME...
FOO
KRIIIIK
!!
NOW... YOU'RE THE ONLY ONE LEFT.
GIVE UP...AND HAND OVER THE BIWA...
I... I DON'T WANT TO!!
YOU SHOULD JUST DIS-APPEAR!!

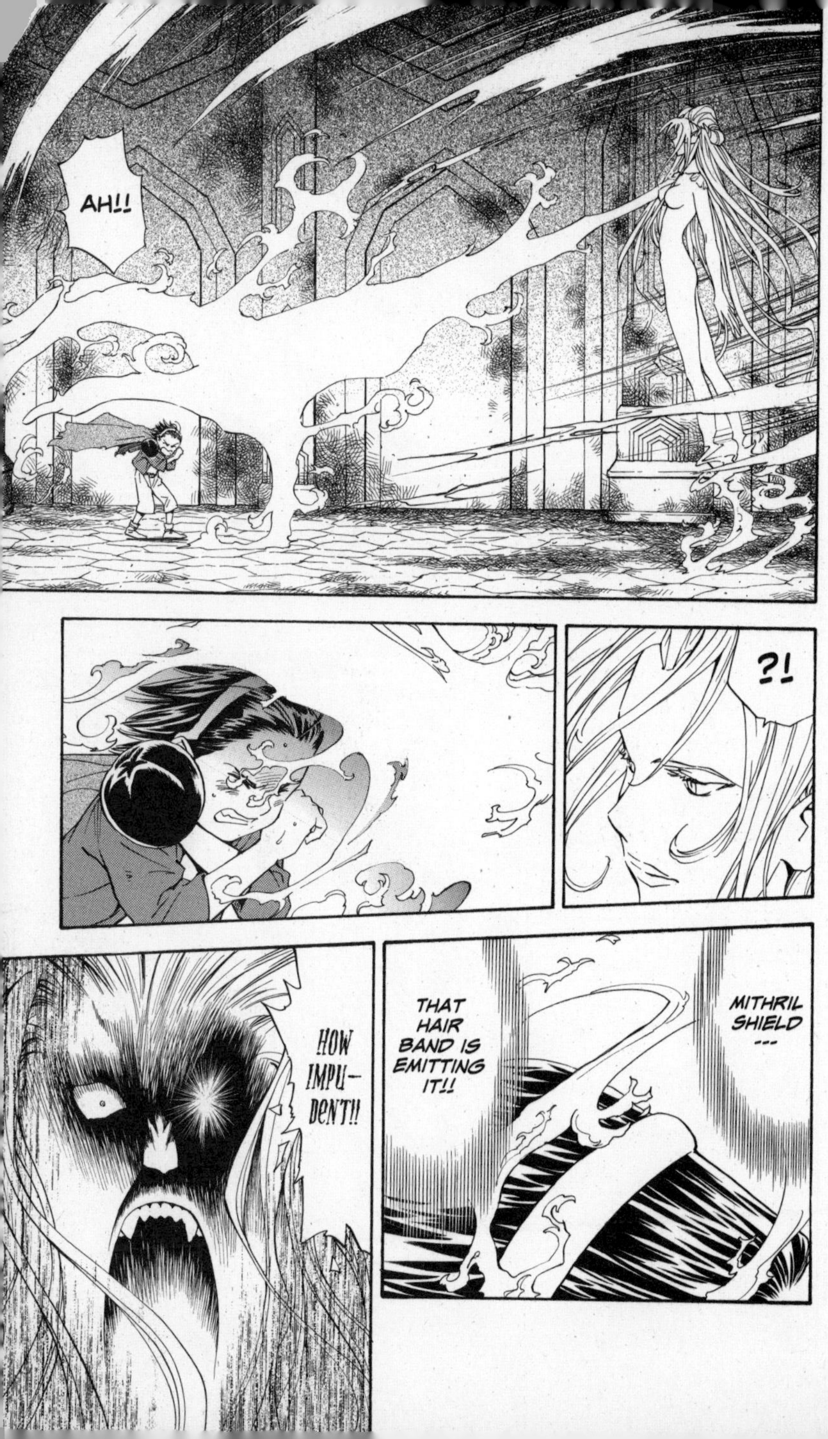
AH!!
?!
MITHRIL SHIELD---
THAT HAIR BAND IS EMITTING IT!!
HOW IMPU-DENT!!

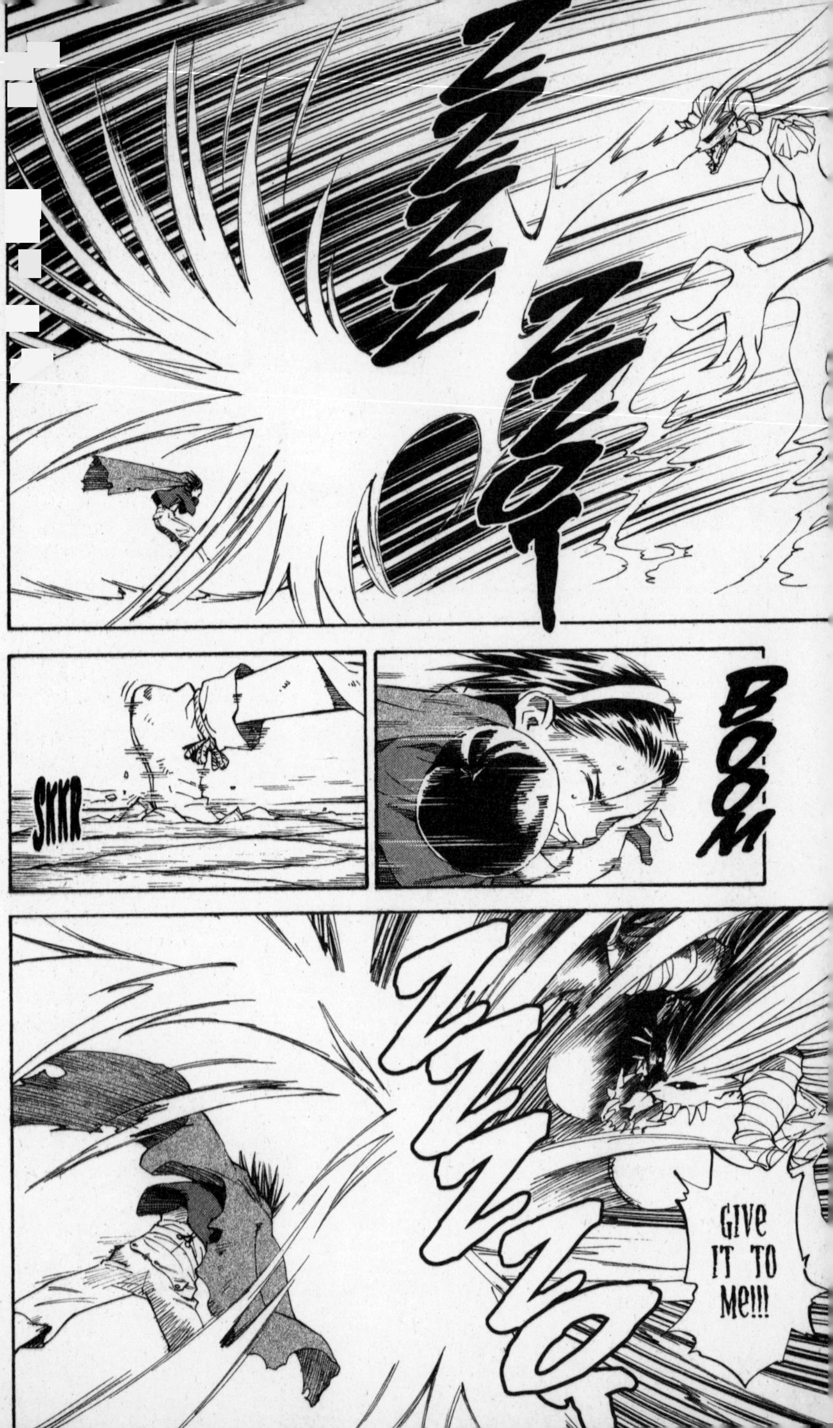
BOOM
SKKR
GIVE IT TO ME!!!

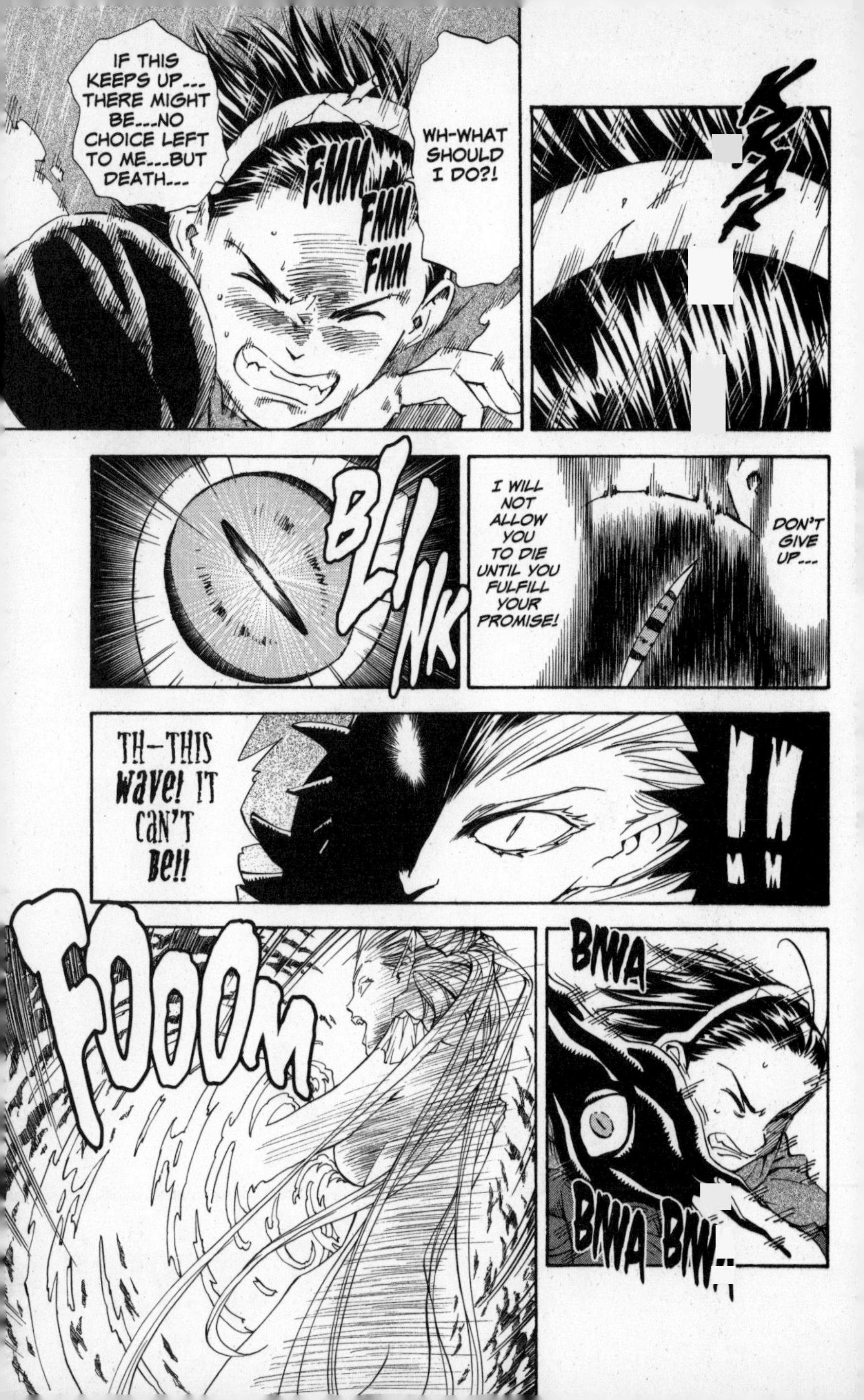
WH-WHAT SHOULD I DO?!
IF THIS KEEPS UP... THERE MIGHT BE...NO CHOICE LEFT TO ME...BUT DEATH...
FMM FMM FMM
DON'T GIVE UP...
I WILL NOT ALLOW YOU TO DIE UNTIL YOU FULFILL YOUR PROMISE!
BLINK
!!
TH-THIS wave! IT CAN'T BE!!
BIWA
BIWA BIW
FOOOM

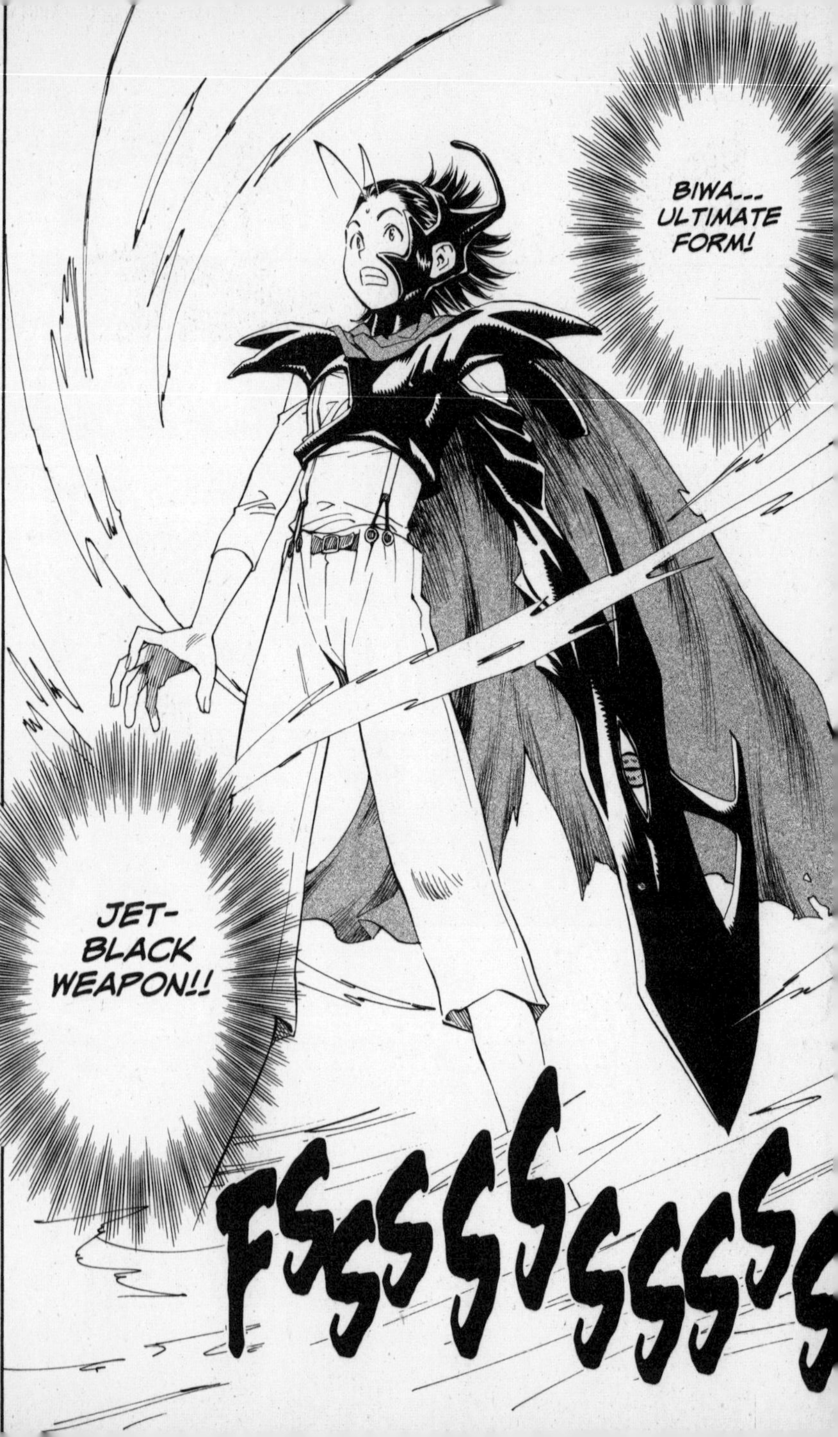
BIWA...
ULTIMATE
FORM!
JET-
BLACK
WEAPON!!
FSSSSSSSSSS

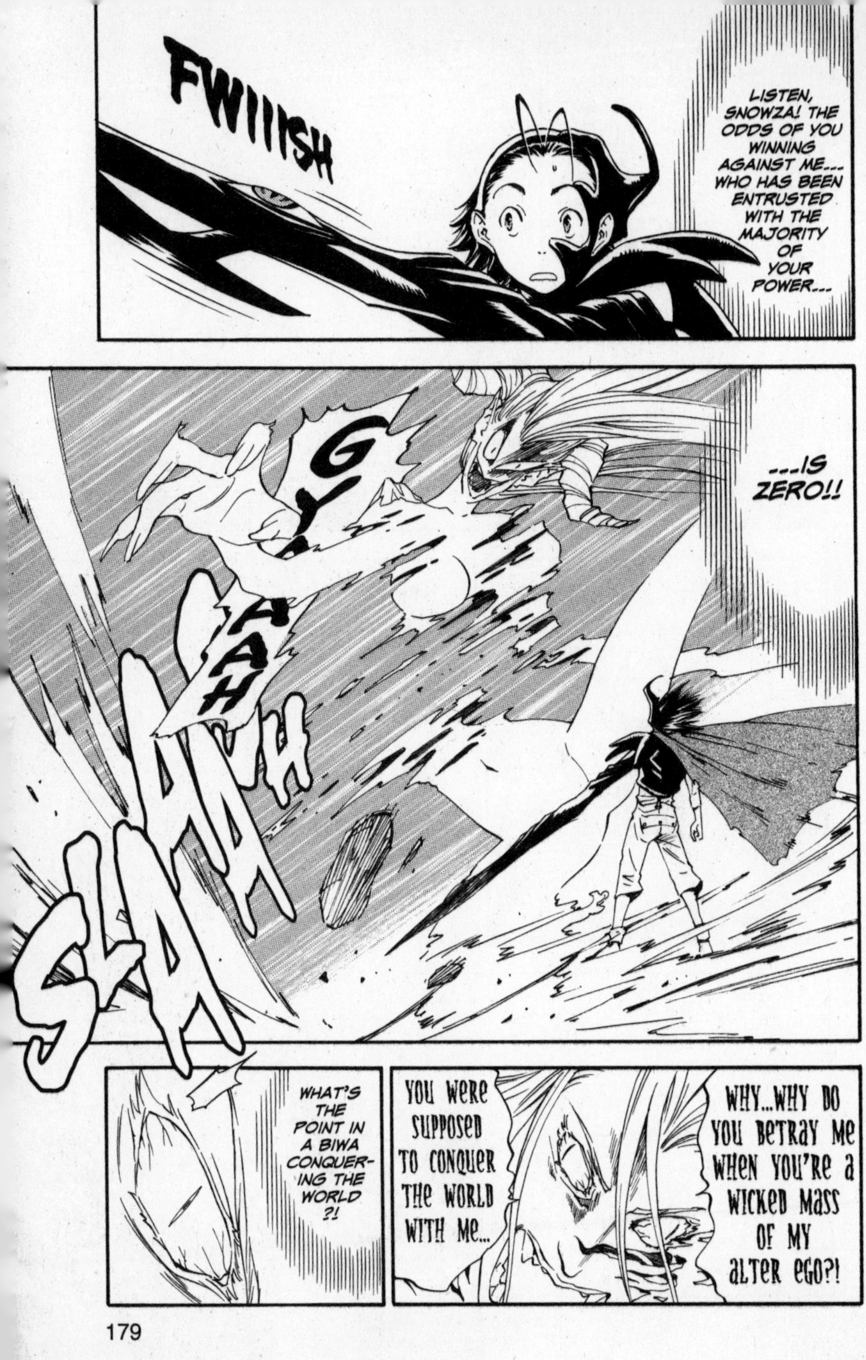
FWIIISH
LISTEN, SNOWZA! THE ODDS OF YOU WINNING AGAINST ME... WHO HAS BEEN ENTRUSTED WITH THE MAJORITY OF YOUR POWER...
...IS ZERO!!
GYAAAHH
WHY...WHY DO YOU BETRAY ME WHEN YOU'RE A WICKED MASS OF MY ALTER EGO?!
YOU WERE SUPPOSED TO CONQUER THE WORLD WITH ME...
WHAT'S THE POINT IN A BIWA CONQUERING THE WORLD?!

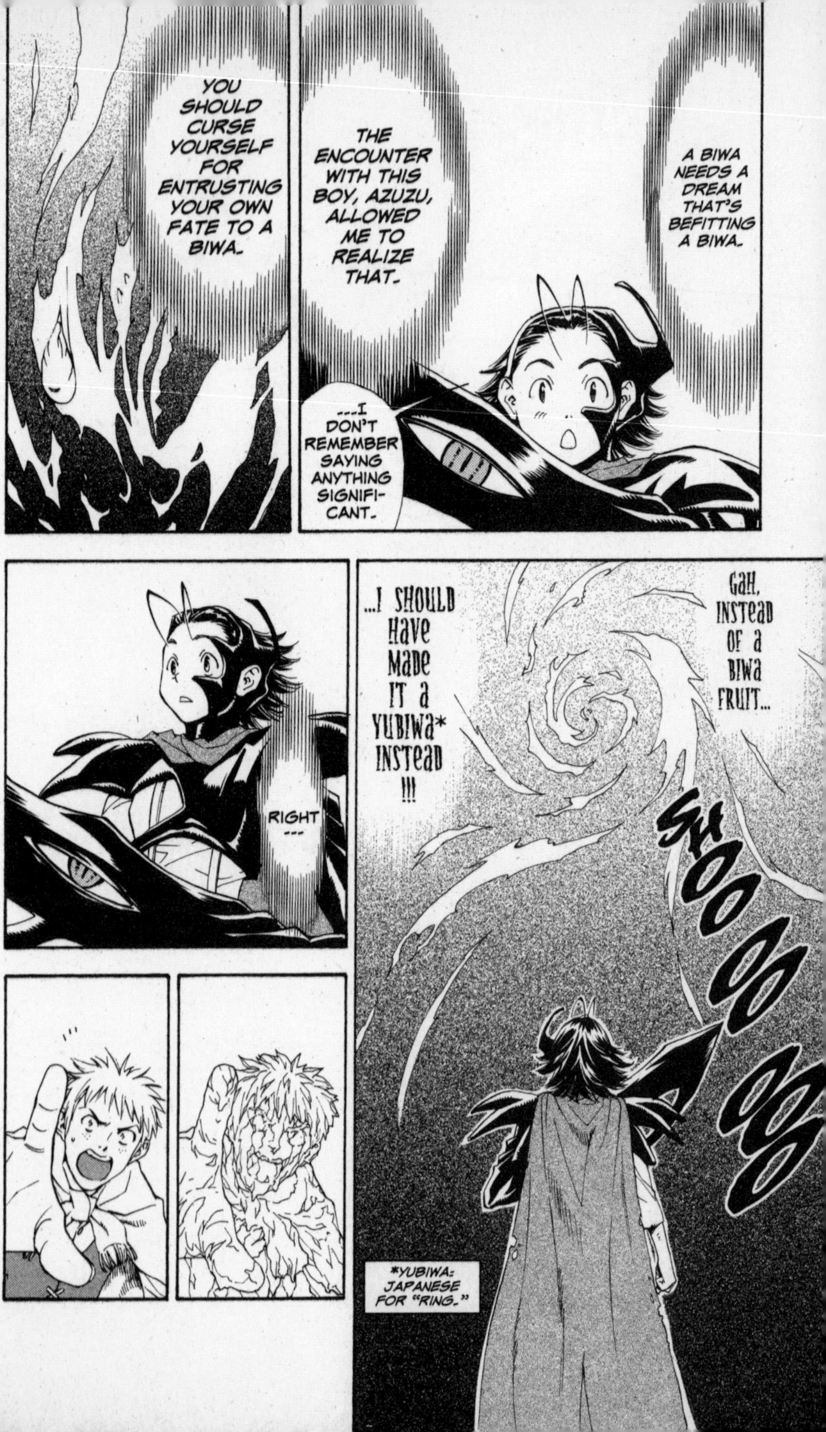
A BIWA NEEDS A DREAM THAT'S BEFITTING A BIWA.
THE ENCOUNTER WITH THIS BOY, AZUZU, ALLOWED ME TO REALIZE THAT.
...I DON'T REMEMBER SAYING ANYTHING SIGNIFICANT.
YOU SHOULD CURSE YOURSELF FOR ENTRUSTING YOUR OWN FATE TO A BIWA.
GAH, INSTEAD OF A BIWA FRUIT...
...I SHOULD HAVE MADE IT A YUBIWA* INSTEAD!!!
SHOOOOOOO
*YUBIWA: JAPANESE FOR "RING."
RIGHT...

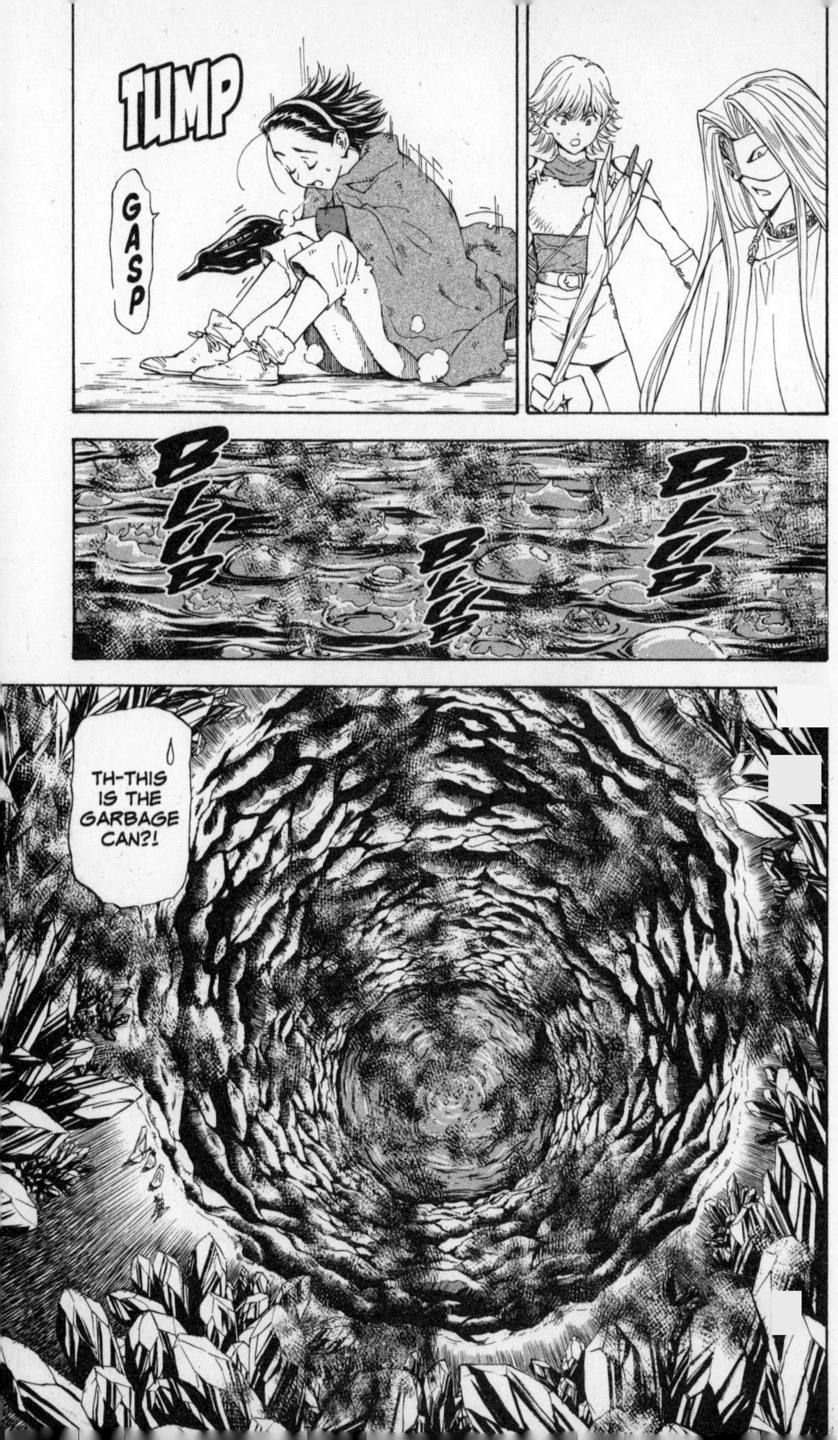
TUMP
GASP
BLUB
BLUB
BLUB
TH-THIS IS THE GARBAGE CAN?!

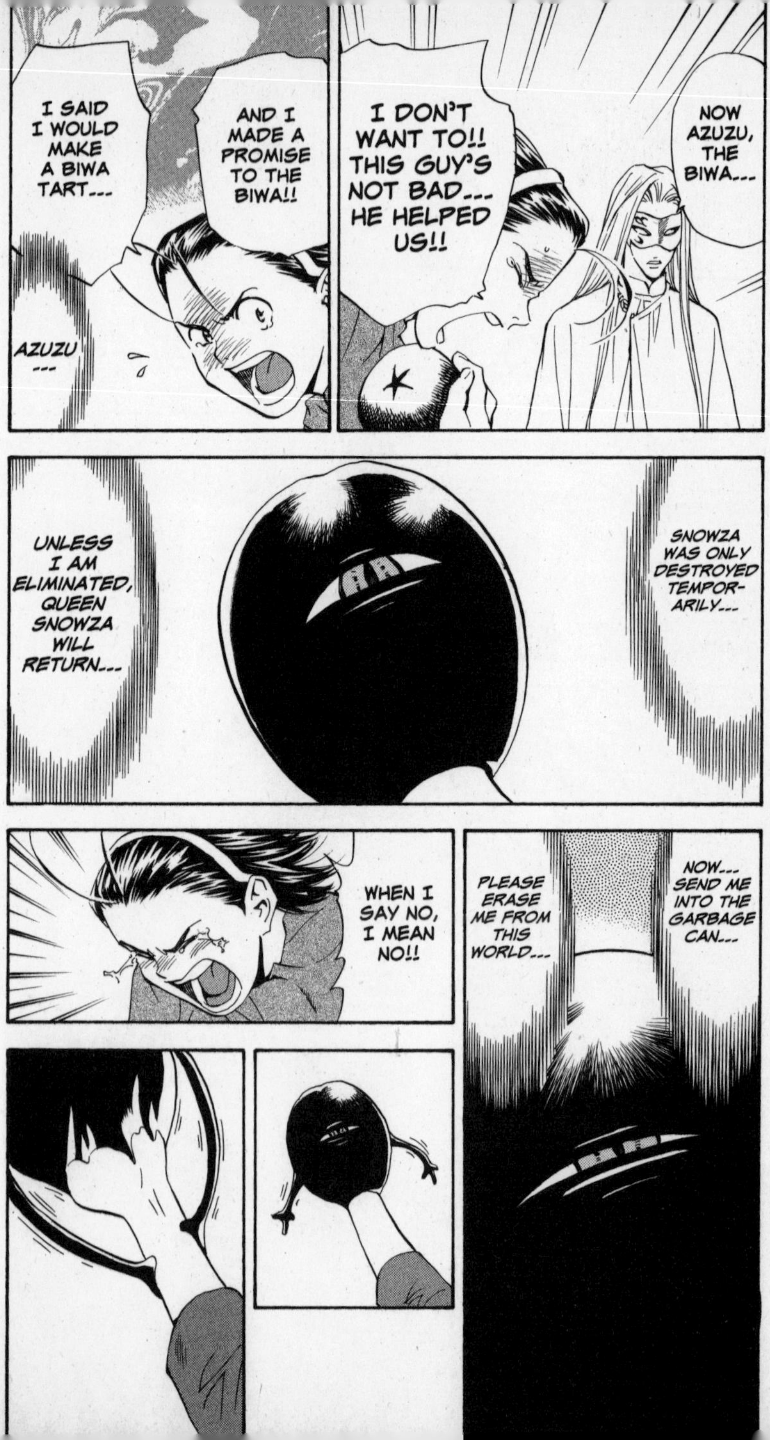
NOW AZUZU, THE BIWA...
I DON'T WANT TO!! THIS GUY'S NOT BAD... HE HELPED US!!
I SAID I WOULD MAKE A BIWA TART...
AND I MADE A PROMISE TO THE BIWA!!
AZUZU...
SNOWZA WAS ONLY DESTROYED TEMPOR-ARILY...
UNLESS I AM ELIMINATED, QUEEN SNOWZA WILL RETURN...
NOW... SEND ME INTO THE GARBAGE CAN...
PLEASE ERASE ME FROM THIS WORLD...
WHEN I SAY NO, I MEAN NO!!

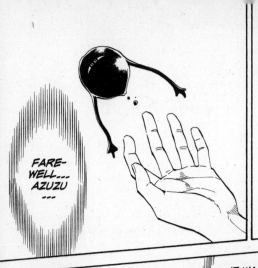

FARE-WELL... AZUZU ---
BIWA!!
IT WAS ONLY FOR A SHORT TIME, BUT IT WAS FUN, AZUZU...
WE'LL PART WAYS HERE ---
...BUT I SHALL NOT FORGET THE WARMTH OF YOUR HAND AND YOUR GENTLE HEART.
LIVE ON AND PURSUE YOUR DREAM OF "JA-PAN" ---

AND ---

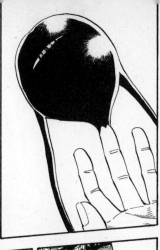

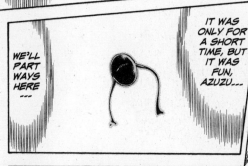

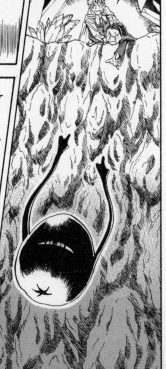

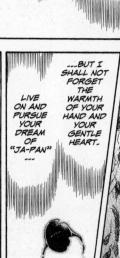

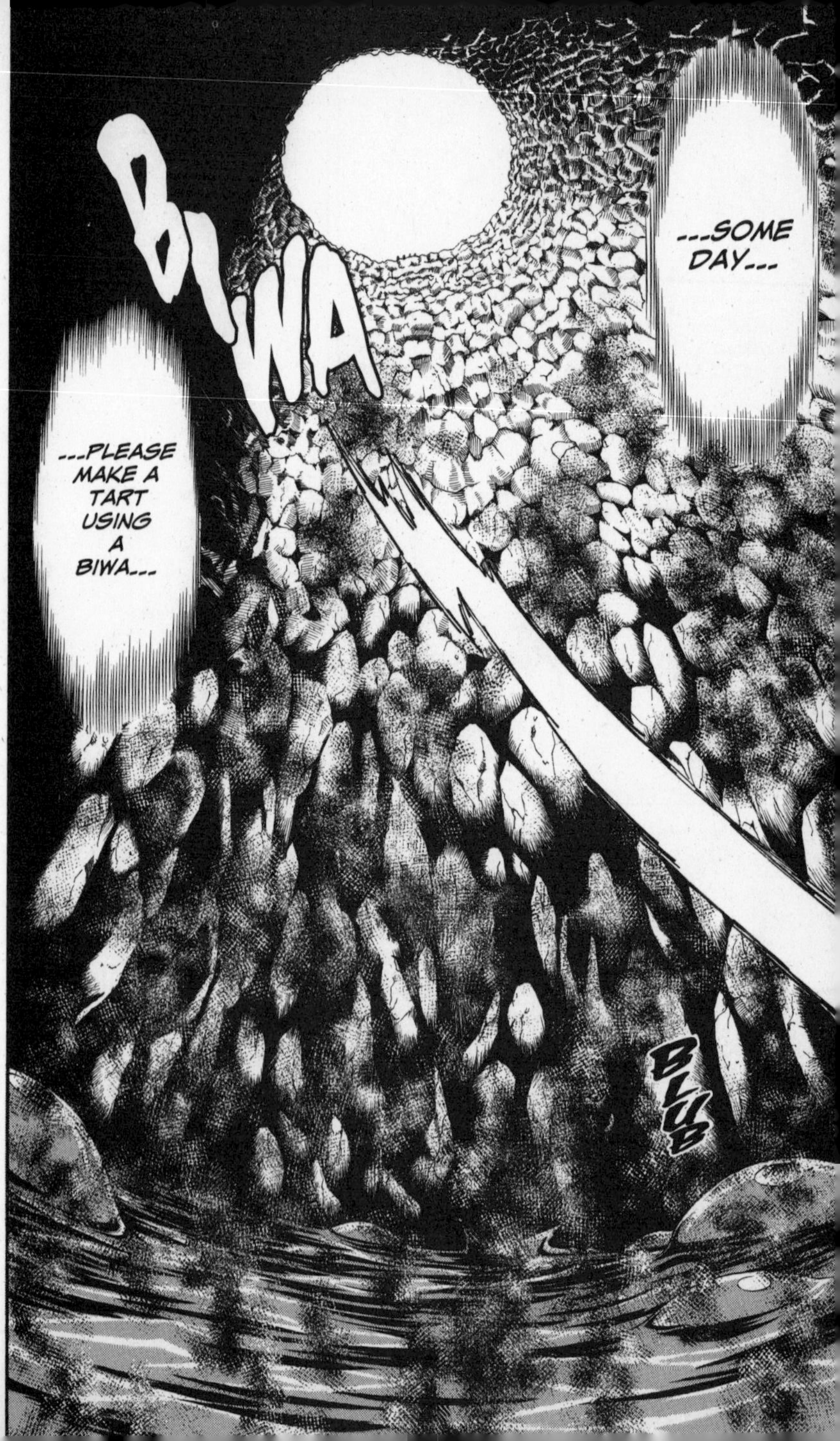
---SOME DAY---
BIWA
---PLEASE MAKE A TART USING A BIWA---
BLUB

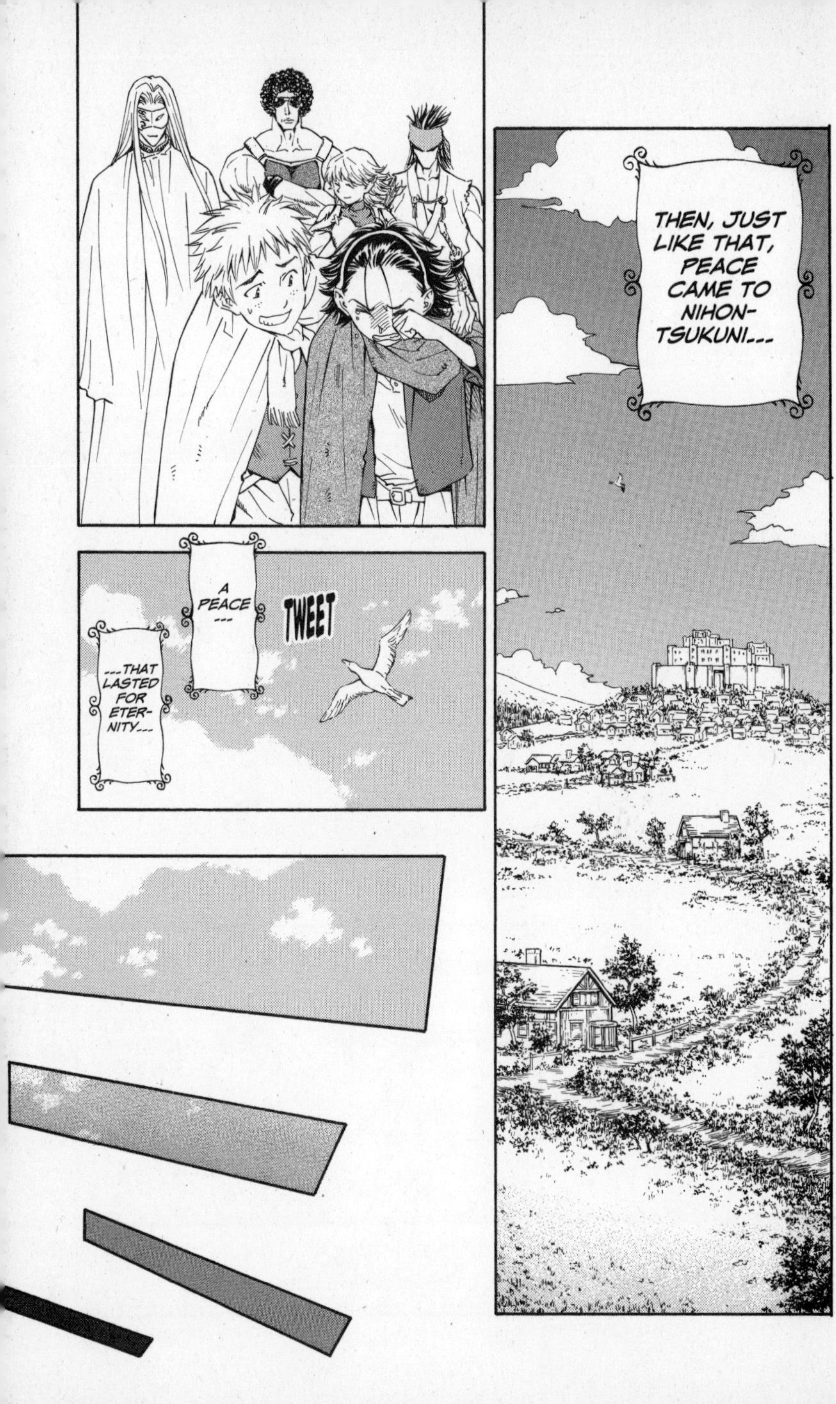
THEN, JUST LIKE THAT, PEACE CAME TO NIHON-TSUKUNI...
A PEACE---
TWEET
---THAT LASTED FOR ETERNITY---

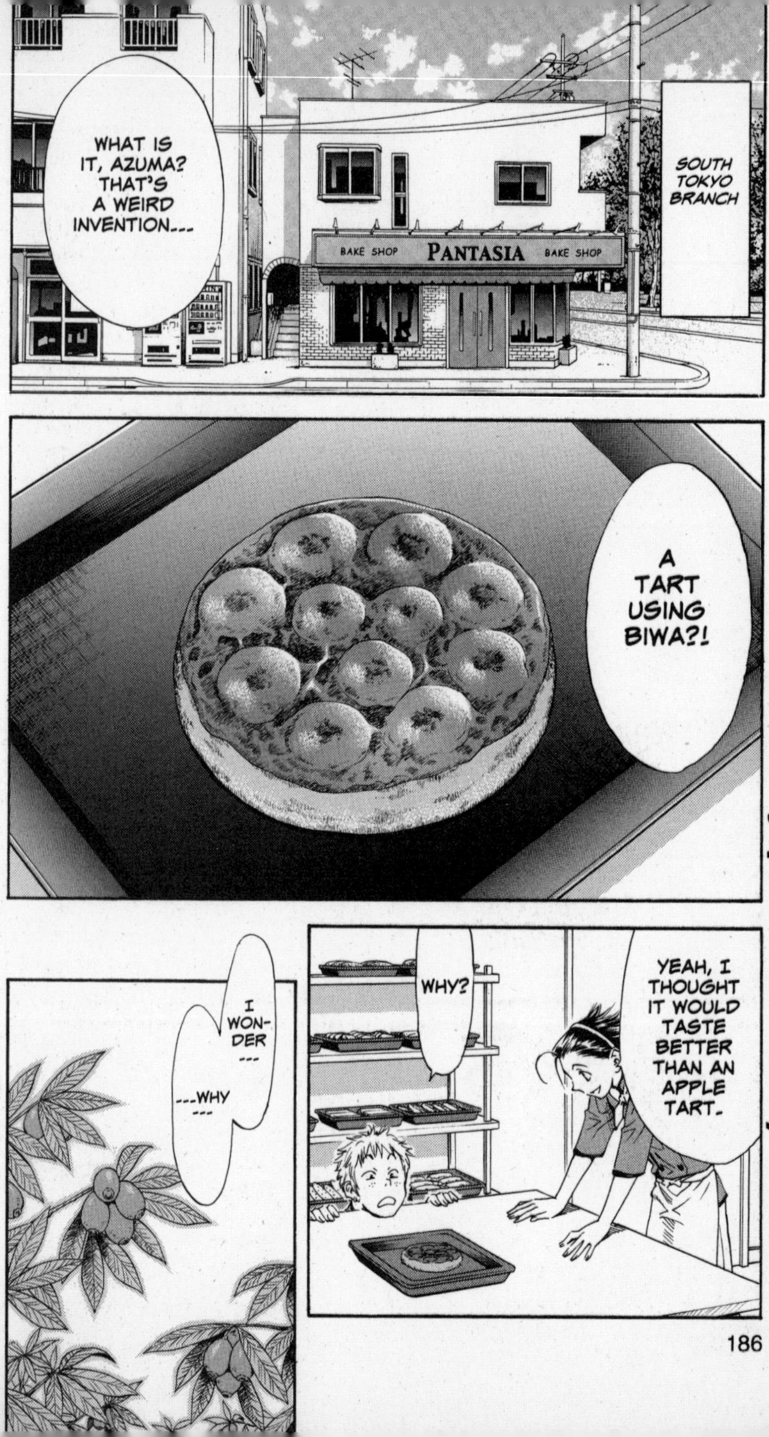
SOUTH TOKYO BRANCH
WHAT IS IT, AZUMA? THAT'S A WEIRD INVENTION...
BAKE SHOP PANTASIA BAKE SHOP
A TART USING BIWA?!
YEAH, I THOUGHT IT WOULD TASTE BETTER THAN AN APPLE TART.
WHY?
I WONDER...
...WHY...

Yakitate!! Japan Bonus Story: The End

Bonus ♡

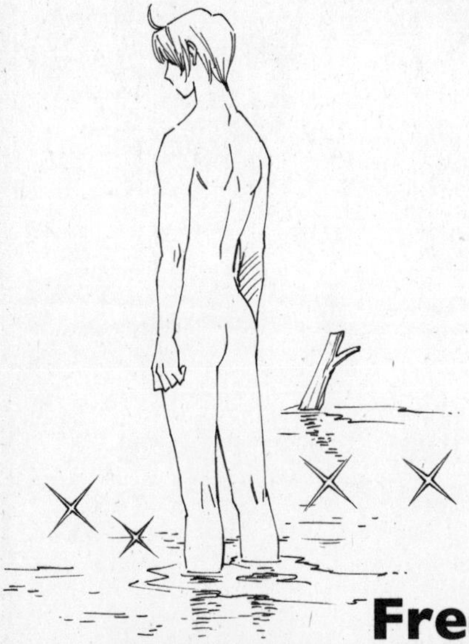

“Me in the middle”

The middle period: from newcomer to the present day...Hashiguchi sensei in his mid 20s.

Free

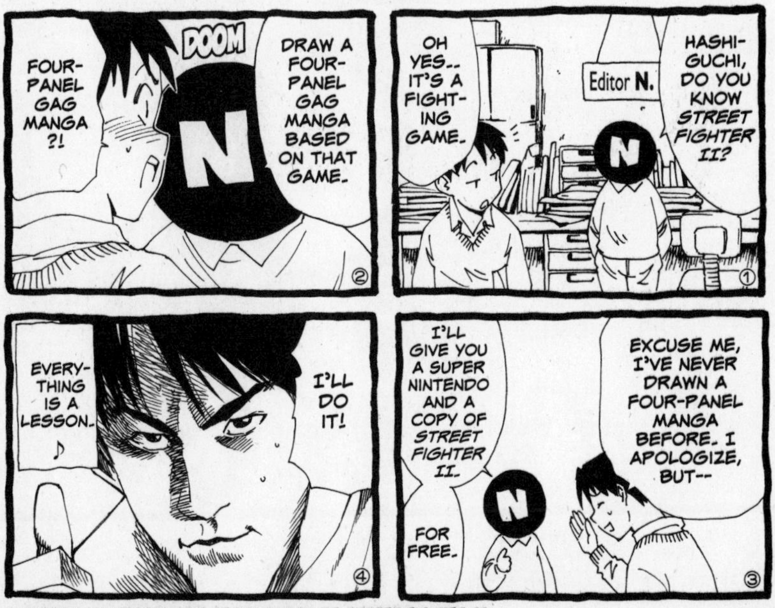

Editor N.
HASHIGUCHI, DO YOU KNOW *STREET FIGHTER II*?
OH YES... IT'S A FIGHTING GAME.
DOOM
DRAW A FOUR-PANEL GAG MANGA BASED ON THAT GAME.
FOUR-PANEL GAG MANGA?!
EXCUSE ME, I'VE NEVER DRAWN A FOUR-PANEL MANGA BEFORE. I APOLOGIZE, BUT--
I'LL GIVE YOU A SUPER NINTENDO AND A COPY OF *STREET FIGHTER II*.
FOR FREE.
I'LL DO IT!
EVERYTHING IS A LESSON... ♪

AND FOR THAT REASON, THE SERIALIZATION OF *STREET FIGHTER II LAUGH OUT LOUD FOUR-PANEL GAG MANGA SUPPLEMENTARY STORY* BEGAN IN *CORO CORO COMICS* SHORTLY THEREAFTER...

Ran Pub

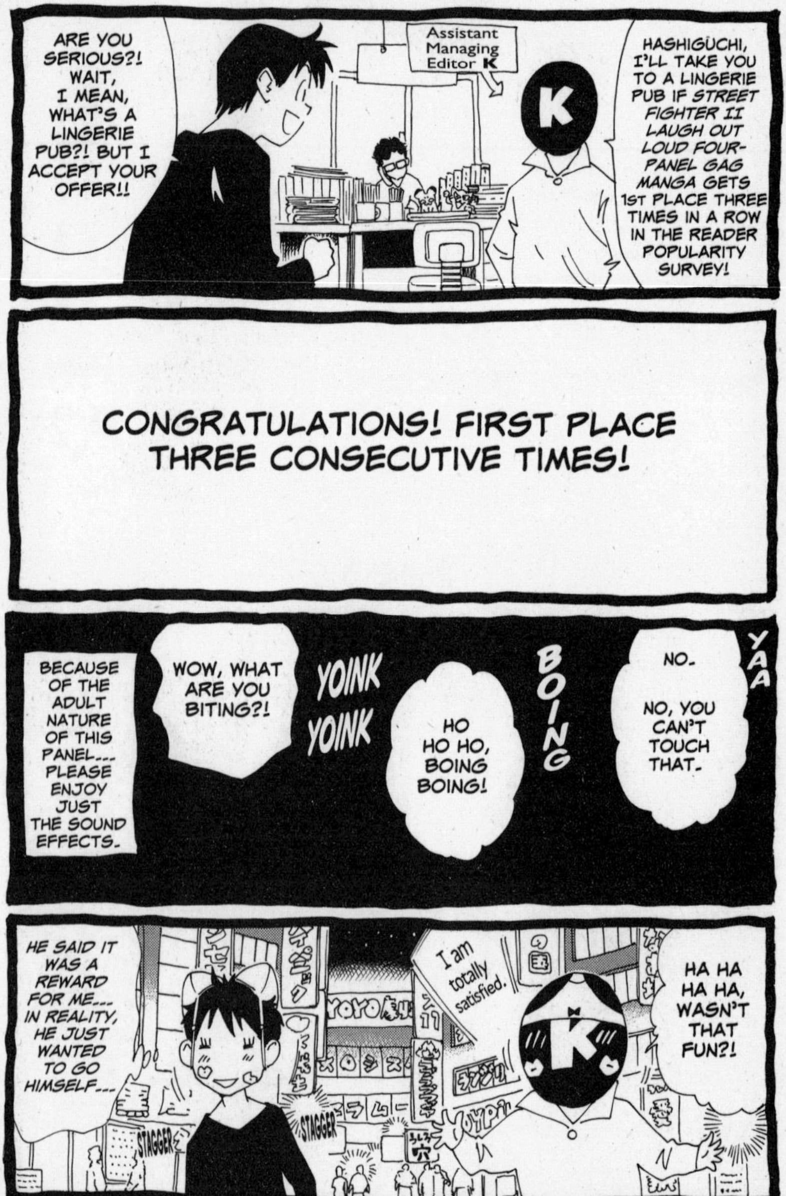
HASHIGUCHI, I'LL TAKE YOU TO A LINGERIE PUB IF STREET FIGHTER II LAUGH OUT LOUD FOUR-PANEL GAG MANGA GETS 1ST PLACE THREE TIMES IN A ROW IN THE READER POPULARITY SURVEY!
Assistant Managing Editor K
ARE YOU SERIOUS?! WAIT, I MEAN, WHAT'S A LINGERIE PUB?! BUT I ACCEPT YOUR OFFER!!
CONGRATULATIONS! FIRST PLACE THREE CONSECUTIVE TIMES!
YAA
NO.
NO, YOU CAN'T TOUCH THAT.
BOING
HO HO HO, BOING BOING!
YOINK
YOINK
WOW, WHAT ARE YOU BITING?!
BECAUSE OF THE ADULT NATURE OF THIS PANEL... PLEASE ENJOY JUST THE SOUND EFFECTS.
HA HA HA HA, WASN'T THAT FUN?!
I am totally satisfied.
STAGGER
STAGGER
HE SAID IT WAS A REWARD FOR ME... IN REALITY, HE JUST WANTED TO GO HIMSELF...